T0235173

Lecture Notes in Computer Science   10353

Commenced Publication in 1973
Founding and Former Series Editors:
Gerhard Goos, Juris Hartmanis, and Jan van Leeuwen

More information about this series at http://www.springer.com/series/7407

Narayan Desai · Walfredo Cirne (Eds.)

Job Scheduling Strategies for Parallel Processing

19th and 20th International Workshops, JSSPP 2015
Hyderabad, India, May 26, 2015
and JSSPP 2016, Chicago, IL, USA, May 27, 2016
Revised Selected Papers

 Springer

Editors
Narayan Desai
Google
Seattle
USA

Walfredo Cirne
Google
Mountain View
USA

ISSN 0302-9743   ISSN 1611-3349   (electronic)
Lecture Notes in Computer Science
ISBN 978-3-319-61755-8   ISBN 978-3-319-61756-5   (eBook)
DOI 10.1007/978-3-319-61756-5

Library of Congress Control Number: 2017945740

LNCS Sublibrary: SL1 – Theoretical Computer Science and General Issues

Printed on acid-free paper

This Springer imprint is published by Springer Nature
The registered company is Springer International Publishing AG
The registered company address is: Gewerbestrasse 11, 6330 Cham, Switzerland

Preface

This volume contains the papers presented at the 19th and 20th Workshops on Job Scheduling Strategies for Parallel Processing (JSSPP'2015 and JSSPP'2016). The JSSPP Workshops take place in conjunction with the IEEE International Parallel Processing Symposia.

The proceedings of previous workshops are also available from Springer as LNCS volumes 949, 1162, 1291, 1459, 1659, 1911, 2221, 2537, 2862, 3277, 3834, 4376, 4942, 5798, 6253, 7698, 8429, and 8828. These volumes are available as printed books and online.

In 2015, the workshop was help in Hyderabad, India, on May 26. In 2016, it took place in Chicago, USA, on May 27. For each year, 4 papers were submitted, of which we accepted seven. All submitted papers went through a complete review process, with the full version being read and evaluated by an average of four reviewers. We would like to especially thank the Program Committee members and additional reviewers for their willingness to participate in this effort and their detailed, constructive reviews. The Program Committee for 2015 and 2016 comprised:

- Henri Casanova, University of Hawaii at Manoa
- Julita Corbalan, Technical University of Catalonia
- Dick Epema, Delft University of Technology
- Hyeonsang Eom, Seoul National University
- Dror Feitelson, The Hebrew University
- Liana Fong, IBM T.J. Watson Research Center
- Eitan Frachtenberg, Facebook
- Alfredo Goldman, University of São Paulo
- Allan Gottlieb, New York University
- Alexandru Iosup, Delft University of Technology
- Morris Jette, SchedMD LLC (2015 only)
- Srikanth Kandula, Microsoft
- Rajkumar Kettimuthu, Argonne National Laboratory
- Dalibor Klusáček, Masaryk University
- Madhukar Korupolu, Google
- Zhiling Lan, Illinois Institute of Technology
- Bill Nitzberg, Altair Engineering
- P.-O. Östberg, Umeå University
- Larry Rudolph, MIT
- Uwe Schwiegelshohn, Technical University of Dortmund
- Leonel Sousa, Universidade Técnica de Lisboa
- Mark Squillante, IBM T.J. Watson Research Center
- Wei Tang, Google
- Ramin Yahyapour, GWDG, University of Göttingen

As a primary venue of the parallel scheduling community, the Job Scheduling Strategies for Parallel Processors Workshop offers a good vantage point to witness its evolution. During these two decades, we have seen parallel scheduling grow in scope and importance, following the popularization of parallel systems. Fundamental issues in the area remain relevant today (e.g., scheduling goal and evaluation, workload modeling, performance prediction). Meanwhile, a new set of issues have emerged, owing to the new workloads, increased scale, and differing priorities of cloud systems. Together, the traditional and new issues make for a lively and discussion-rich workshop, where academic researchers and participants from industry meet and exchange ideas and experiences.

The JSSPP Workshops traditionally start with a keynote talk. In 2015, Benjamin Hindman from Mesosphere explored how to leverage multilevel schedulers to separate concerns and better accommodate competing perspectives (e.g., scheduling goals for the resource provider can differ substantially from those of the user) in parallel scheduling. In 2016, we surveyed big challenges and open problems in modern parallel scheduling. This volume includes a summary of the 2016 keynote.

Following the trend of previous years, we see parallel scheduling challenges arising at multiple levels of abstractions. The days of shared-memory vs. message-passing parallelism are definitely over. Parallelism today happens at all levels, including combining different clusters or clouds at the user-level to support a target application.

For node-level parallelism, the driving forces are the simultaneous increase in capacity and heterogeneity of a single node. As the number of cores sharing the same memory increases (often introducing non-trivial communication topologies) and special purpose parallel processors (like GPUs) become prevalent, new approaches and research remain relevant.

Kang et al. show how to minimize energy consumption in task migration within a many-core chip. Many-core chips are also the environment targeted by Chu et al., who focus on how to space-share these chips among competing applications. Singh and Auluck explore the judicious use of task replication in the real-time scheduling context. Tsujita and Endo investigate a data-driven approach to schedule GPU load, using Cholesky decomposition as a concrete, relevant use case. Negele et al. evaluate the use of lock-free data structures in the OS scheduler. While requiring a complete reworking of the operating system, their results show a promising payoff.

Cluster-level parallelisms are also driven by increases in scale and heterogeneity. But their scale seems to expose more systemic effects on how people interact with them, giving rise to the need for sophisticated user and workload modeling. Along these lines, Schlagkamp investigates the relationship between user behavior (think time, more precisely) and parallel scheduling. Emeras et al. describe Evalix, a predictor for job resource consumption that makes novel use of user information. In such an environment, sophisticated and realistic simulation is another clear need. Dutot et al. present BatSim, a language-independent simulator that allows for different levels of realism in the simulation (at different computational costs).

On distributed scheduling itself, Pascual et al. explore how space-filling curves can lead to better scheduling of large-scale supercomputers. Li et al. also targeted large-scale supercomputers, particularly on how to better leverage the multidimensional torus topology of machines like Blue waters. Klusáček and Chlumsky rely on the multilevel scheduler support of Torque to introduce a job scheduler based on planning and metaheuristics, in opposition to simple queueing. Breitbart et al. explore which jobs can be co-scheduled such that memory bandwidth does not become a bottleneck, therefore negating the benefits of co-scheduling. Zhuang et al. focus on how to improve the selection of a disruption time for a cluster, so as to reduce the impact on its users.

Another key part of the JSSPP experience is the discussion of real-life production experiences, providing useful feedback to researchers, as well as refining best practices. Klusáček et al. describe the reconfiguration of MetaCentrum, covering motivation, process, and evaluation. Particularly interesting is the fact that such work "was supported by a significant body of research, which included the proposal of new scheduling approaches as well as detailed simulations based on real-life complex workload traces", showcasing the productive synergy between top-notch research and production practice that takes place at JSSPP.

Enjoy the reading!

We hope you can join us in the next JSSPP workshop, this time in Orlando, Florida, USA, on June 2, 2017.

May 2017   Walfredo Cirne
                                                                     Narayan Desai

Contents

JSSPP 2015

Controlled Duplication Scheduling of Real-Time Precedence Tasks on Heterogeneous Multiprocessors

Jagpreet Singh[1]($\boxtimes$) and Nitin Auluck[2]

[1] Indian Institute of Information Technology Allahabad,
Allahabad, Uttar Pradesh, India
jagpreets@iiita.ac.in, jagpreets@iitrpr.ac.in
[2] Indian Institute of Technology Ropar, Rupnagar, Punjab, India
nitin@iitrpr.ac.in

Abstract. Duplication based heuristics have been widely utilized for scheduling communication intensive, precedence constrained tasks on multiple processors. Duplicating the predecessor of a task on the processor to which the task is assigned can result in the minimization of the communication cost. This helps in reducing the schedule length. However, this reduction comes at the cost of extra computing power required to duplicate the tasks. We have tried to address this trade-off in this paper. We propose "controlled" duplication algorithms for scheduling real-time periodic tasks with end-to-end deadlines on heterogeneous multiprocessors. We observe that whether to duplicate tasks or not is decided by the task deadlines. In the case that the deadline can be met without duplication, more schedule holes are created. These holes can be used to schedule other tasks. Simulations show that the proposed algorithms efficiently utilize the holes and improve the success ratio by 15%–50% versus comparable algorithms.

1 Introduction

The requirement of scientific and industrial applications to generate logical as well as time bound results have posed various challenges, namely: exploiting the parallelism offered by the current hardware and completing applications under strict timing constraints. Due to these requirements, heterogeneous systems have gained widespread popularity. These systems allow for the combination of high performance, low cost and different capability hardware with the help of heterogeneous interconnections such as: Network on a chip (NoC) and Network of Workstations (NoWs). The timing constraints are fulfilled by employing an efficient real-time scheduler. The scheduling algorithm allocates and schedules jobs to ensure that all the task instances in the task set meet their deadlines. If a task set meets its deadlines, then it is said to be schedulable.

Definition 1 *(Task Set). A task set (Fig. 1) models multiple real-time applications where each application (known as a task) is represented as a directed*

© Springer International Publishing AG 2017
N. Desai and W. Cirne (Eds.): JSSPP 2015/2016, LNCS 10353, pp. 3–21, 2017.
DOI: 10.1007/978-3-319-61756-5_1

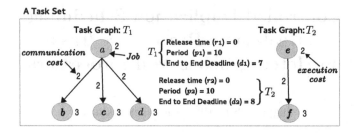

Fig. 1. A task set

acyclic graph (DAG) with release time, period and hard end-to-end deadline. The nodes of each DAG represent subtasks[1] and the edges represent the precedence constraints, as well as the communication cost between the subtasks.

In real-time systems, scheduling algorithms can be broadly classified into two categories: static and dynamic. In static algorithms, information about the tasks is known in advance, which is not the case in dynamic algorithms. Heuristics for real-time scheduling on heterogeneous multiprocessors have been proposed for both the static [3,8,16] as well as the dynamic [15,23] environments. This paper falls into the domain of static algorithms.

Scheduling a DAG on multiprocessors in real-time and non real-time systems is a challenging problem [12,13]. It has become harder with the introduction of heterogeneous processing and networking components. Basically, the problem on these two systems differs because of the properties of the task graph and the objective. The majority of the algorithms in non real-time systems consider a single task graph with an objective of minimizing the maximum schedule length, also known as the *makespan* [12]. On the other hand, in real-time systems, the input to the algorithm is a task set (periodic or non-periodic) consisting of a number of independent or dependent tasks with deadlines. The main objective is to meet the hard deadlines and decrease the tardiness of the soft deadlines, where tardiness is the subtraction of the deadline from the schedule length.

More often than not, the real-time algorithms are inspired from or are an extension of a non-real time scheduling approach [3,4,15]. On the basis of the design, these algorithms for scheduling a DAG on multiprocessors (homogeneous & heterogeneous) are broadly classified into: list-based and clustering based, with or without duplication. List-based scheduling [15] assigns priorities to all the ready jobs, stores them in a list and later assigns to processors according to the priorities to minimize a particular cost function. In clustering, the jobs are combined to form clusters on the basis of communication delays, data dependencies etc. After that, the clusters are allocated to processors [3,9].

Duplication has been widely used to achieve reliability and fault tolerance in real-time and non real-time scheduling [15,21]. It has also proved to be a vital heuristic for minimizing the makespan [1]. By duplicating the heavily commu-

---

[1] (The terms node, job and subtask have been used interchangeably).

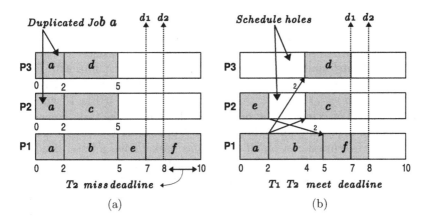

Fig. 2. For task set in Fig. 1, (a) schedule with duplication that misses the deadline (b) schedule without duplication that meets the deadlines

nicating jobs on a single processor, the interprocessor communication cost can be minimized. The jobs are made to start earlier and hence, finish earlier, which reduces the overall makespan of the task graph. Duplication is a well researched heuristic for non real-time scheduling of a single task graph on heterogeneous multiprocessors [4–6,18].

However, duplication in the context of meeting deadlines is still relatively unexplored. We observe that, duplicating a job utilizes the extra computing power (or a schedule hole) on a processing element (PE). This extra computing power may be used to schedule jobs of other task instances. Therefore, although using duplication can help a task graph instance to meet its deadline, it may cause the other tasks to miss their deadlines because of the unavailability of the appropriate schedule holes. Hence, an interesting tradeoff exists between the number of duplicated jobs and the number of schedule holes available. This article identifies this tradeoff and proposes controlled duplication based heuristics. Simulations have shown that the proposed algorithms improve the success ratio by 15% to 50% vs. the other known non-duplication and duplication based algorithms, even under higher processor utilizations and communication costs.

2   Motivation-W^2H^2

The design of a duplication heuristic has two steps: "*where* to duplicate jobs" and "*how* to perform duplication". Mainly, there are two strategies that are used for the first step: duplicating subtasks in schedule holes [5] or allocating extra space other than the holes [4]. The first approach, also known as an insertion based approach, adds more to the computational complexity of the algorithm to find an appropriate schedule hole for duplication, but is more effective than the second non-insertion based approach. A number of approaches have been used for the second step: (1) duplicate a single immediate predecessor (SIP) [5],

(2) duplicate a chain of predecessors till the root node (COP) [4], (3) duplicate the immediate predecessors, and then the ancestors (IPFA) [6].

Duplication in real-time systems adds two more challenges to the above: "*when* to duplicate" and "*how much* duplication" is to be performed. Figure 2 demonstrates these challenges. It shows schedules of two task instances: $T1$ ($r = 0, p = 10, d = 7$) and $T2$ ($r = 0, p = 10, d = 8$) of Fig. 1, where r, p and d are defined as release time, period and deadline of the tasks respectively. Both tasks are required to be scheduled on 3 processing elements $P1$-$P3$ and have the same execution cost on all PEs. Since task $T1$ has a lesser deadline, it is given the higher priority and is scheduled first. If $T1$ is scheduled with duplication, it finishes before its deadline at 7. However, task $T2$ is unschedulable now (Fig. 2(a)). In the other case, scheduling $T1$ without duplication leaves enough schedule holes on $P2$ and $P3$ which are then used by $T2$ to meet its deadline (Fig. 2(b)).

The first challenge: "*when* to duplicate" exists because of our objective of meeting deadlines. In case, the deadline of a task is higher (as for $T1$), there are enough chances to meet it without duplicating any job, which can create more schedule holes for other tasks to use, hence, increasing the schedulability. Interestingly, finding whether a task graph can be scheduled under a certain deadline is an NP-Complete problem [11]. Here, we make use of *tentative scheduling* which refers to temporarily scheduling the jobs of the task graph without duplication on processors, to evaluate the upper bound on the makespan. If the upper bound meets the deadline, then the temporary schedule for that task becomes the final schedule, otherwise it is removed. This upper bound approach has been proposed in RTCDA-W^2H heuristic to implement the "when to duplicate" challenge. To further enhance the performance, if we decide to perform duplication in the first step, our motive is to control the amount of duplication according to the deadline, which is the next challenge of finding *how much* duplication is required. The proposed RTCDA-W^2H^2 extends RTCDA-W^2H with steps to control the amount of duplication to propose a controlled duplication algorithm. Hence, RTCDA-W^2H^2 addresses all the four proposed challenges with respect to duplication: <u>w</u>here, <u>h</u>ow, <u>w</u>hen and <u>h</u>ow much ($\mathbf{W^2H^2}$).

Next, we discuss the related work (Sect. 3) followed by the assumptions and the system model in Sect. 4. Algorithms RTCDA-W^2H and RTCDA-W^2H^2 are described in Sects. 5 and 6 respectively. Time complexities of the algorithms are described in Sect. 7. Simulation results with a discussion are presented in Sect. 8. Finally, Sect. 9 concludes the paper with possible future directions.

3   Related Work

Researchers have focused on developing heuristics driven by specific Quality of Service (QoS) parameters such as Reliability [21], Fault-Tolerance [15] and Security [22, 24]. Qin et al. [15] have presented two dynamic list scheduling algorithms: DASAP (Dynamic AS early As Possible) and DALAP (Dynamic As Late As Possible) for scheduling task graphs. Stavrinides et al. [19] demonstrate a dynamic, list-based scheduling algorithm with a bin-packing heuristic. It has been reported that exploiting schedule holes with bin-packing (First Fit, Best Fit and Worst Fit) significantly improves the success ratio. Dave et al. [9] have used a cluster-based algorithm named COSYN (CO-SYNthesis of Hardware-Software) which is not only able to schedule the tasks, but also find an optimal hardware-software architecture which involves the selection of processors, FPGAs, ASICs and communication links.

S. Ranaweera et al. in [16] used duplication for enhancing the schedulability of periodic time critical applications for pipelined execution on heterogeneous systems. Auluck et al. in [2,3] proposed algorithms which are an extension of the original duplication strategy proposed in [4]. The algorithm in [3], named RT-DBA (real-time duplication based algorithm), is the closest to our work. RT-DBA is a low complexity algorithm with a few shortcomings. This has motivated the research in this paper. Firstly, it performs duplication for all the tasks in the task set, which may not be always required, as our motive is not to minimize the makespan, but to meet deadlines. A late deadline can be met without duplication. The over use of duplication can reduce possible schedule holes (created due to precedence delays). These holes can be utilized by the other tasks in the task set to meet their deadlines. Secondly, RT-DBA uses a very static approach for scheduling and does not consider the current processor scheduling load. Lastly, it does not utilize schedule holes for scheduling or duplication. Doing so can help in achieving a better utilization of the computing power. We introduced the idea of controlled duplication in [17]. The initial results of RTCDA were presented with the upper bound evaluated using sequential scheduling of jobs of a task on a single processor. This work enhances RTCDA [17] with an improved upper bound using tentative scheduling and proposes an enhanced version of the EDF algorithm to propose RTCDA-W^2H. In addition, we present one more enhancement, RTCDA-W^2H^2 that addresses the "how much" challenge.

4 System Model

The system consists of a set P of m heterogeneous processors and a task set T of n precedence-constrained task graphs. All the processors $p \in P$ are connected with a fully connected, contention free network. It is assumed that the local memory of a processor is used for data exchange between assigned subtasks. A vector of the form $<G(V_i, E_i, \mu_i, c_i), rt(i), pe(i), dl(i)>$ represents a task $t_i \in T$. The first element of the vector is the directed acyclic graph G. The node set V_i represents the jobs s_{ijk} (k is the instance, V_i remains the same during instances) of t_i and the edges in E_i represent the communication between the jobs. An edge $e_{ij} \in E$ represents the communication from node s_{ijk} to node s_{ilk}. A positive weight $\mu_i(j, p_q)$ is associated with node s_{ijk}. This represents its computation cost on processor $p_q \in P$ and the non-negative weight $c_i(j, l)$ associated with edge $e_{ij} \in E$ represents the communication cost from s_{ijk} to s_{ilk}. The elements μ_i and c_i are matrices of the order $v_i \times m$ and $v_i \times v_i$ (v_i is the number of subtasks in task t_i). We further assume that the DAG has single *entry* and *exit* nodes.

Table 1. Mathematical notations used for task parameters

Notation	Task parameter
T	Task set of independent periodic task graphs (DAGs)
P	Set of available processors
n	Number of tasks in the task set
m	Number of processors
SQ_t & SQ_{st}	Task and subtask schedule queues respectively
i, j, k	Ids used for task, subtask and task instance respectively
q	Processor id
t_i	i^{th} task of T
V_i & v_i	Set & number of subtasks of task t_i
p_q & p_{ub}	q^{th} processor & the processor which gives the upper bound
s_{ijk}	j^{th} subtask of kth instance of task t_i
$s_{i(entry)k}$ and $s_{i(exit)k}$	Entry and exit subtasks of kth instance of task t_i
rt_i, pe_i, dl_i	Release time, period and deadline of task t_i
$c_i(j, l)$	Communication cost from s_{ijk} to s_{ilk} for all k
$\mu_i(j, q)$	Execution cost of s_{ijk} on p_q for all k
$\overline{\mu_i(j)}$	Average execution cost of s_{ijk} for all k
$bl(s_{ijk})$ & $sl(s_{ijk})$	b-level and s-level of s_{ijk}
$aft(s_{ijk})$	Actual minimum finish time of s_{ijk} after it is scheduled
$pred(s_{ijk})$ & $succ(s_{ijk})$	Predecessors and successors of s_{ijk}
$P_z(s_{ijk})$	Set of processors on which s_{ijk} is scheduled
$H_h^S(p_q)$ & $H_h^F(p_q)$	H_h^S & H_h^F are the start and finish times of a hole between s_h & s_{h+1}, where $s_1, s_2, \cdots, s_h$ are the subtasks already scheduled on p_q

If a DAG has multiple entry (exit) nodes, then they are connected to zero-cost pseudo entry (exit) nodes with zero-cost edges. Performing this operation does not affect the final schedule. Next, $rt(i)$ is the release time of the task t_i and $pe(i)$ represents its period. Hence, each task graph has an instance after every pe time units. The release time, $rt(ik)$ of the kth task instance of t_i is evaluated as $rt(i) + (k - 1) * pe(i)$. The deadline $dl(i)$ is the relative end-to-end deadline of the task t_i, i.e., the exit node $s_{i(exit)k}$ of the kth invocation of task t_i should finish by the absolute time $dl(ik) = rt(ik) + dl(i)$, where $dl(ik)$ is the deadline of the kth invocation of the task t_i.

5   RTCDA-W²H: "when to Duplicate"

5.1   RTCDA-W²H Concept

RTCDA-W^2H (Algorithm 1) proposes a solution to the challenge of "when to duplicate". Notations and mathematical equations used in RTCDA-W^2H are described in Tables 1 and 2 respectively. The central idea of the algorithm is to evaluate a "without duplication" upper bound (UB) (step 5, Algorithm 1) on

Table 2. Mathematical equations for RTCDA and subtask parameters

(1)	**Release time of kth instance of t_i** $rt(ik) = rt(i) + (k-1) \times pe(i)$
(2)	**b-level and s-level of s_{ijk}** $bl(s_{i(exit)k}) = \overline{\mu_i(exit)}$ $sl(s_{i(entry)k}) = zero$ $bl(s_{ijk}) = \overline{\mu_i(j)} + \max\limits_{s_{ilk} \in succ(s_{ijk})} \left(c_i(j,l) + bl_i(s_{ilk}) \right)$ $sl(s_{ijk}) = \max\limits_{s_{ilk} \in pred(s_{ijk})} \left(c_i(l,j) + sl_i(s_{ilk}) + \overline{\mu_i(l)} \right)$
(3)	**Data Arrival Time (DAT) of $s_{i(entry)k}$ and s_{ijk} (from its predecessors) on p_q** $DAT(s_{ijk}, p_q) = \max\limits_{s_{ilk} \in pred(s_{ijk})} \left(\min\limits_{p \in P_z(s_{ilk})} \left(\underset{if\ p=p_q}{EFT}(s_{ilk},p) \| \underset{if\ p \neq p_q}{EFT}(s_{ilk},p) + c_i(l,j) \right) \right)$ $DAT(s_{i(entry)k}, p_q) = rt(ik)$
(4)	**Schedule hole (SH) on p_q, where s_{ijk} can be scheduled** $SH(s_{ijk}, p_q) = H_h^S$ if $\left[H_h^F - max(DAT(s_{ijk}, p_q), H_h^S) \right] > \mu_i(j,q)$
(5)	**Earliest Finish Time (EFT) of s_{ijk} on p_q** $EFT(s_{ijk}, p_q) = max(DAT(s_{ijk}, p_q), H_h^S) + \mu_i(j,q)$, where $H_h^S = SH(s_{ijk}, p_q)$
(6)	**Earliest Finish Time (EFT) of s_{ijk}** $EFT(s_{ijk}) = \min\limits_{p_q \in P} EFT(s_{ijk}, p_q)$
(7)	**Earliest Tentative Start Time (ETST) of s_{ijk} on p_{ub}** $ETST(s_{ijk}, p_{ub}) = max \bigcap (DAT(s_{ijk}, p_{ub}), H_h^S)$, where $H_h^S = SH(s_{ijk}, p_{ub})$ and $P_z(s_{ijk}) = p_{ub}$ for all $s_{ijk} \in V_i$

Algorithm 1. RTCDA-W^2H pseudocode

Data: Task Set T
Result: Return $true$ if task set meets deadlines otherwise return $false$.
       Schedule of Tasks on processors

1   Evaluate *hyperperiod* (hp);
2   Maintain task schedule queue (SQ_t) of all instances of tasks upto hp in T;
3   **while** SQ_t *is non empty* **do**
4   Fetch the higher priority ready task instance (t_{ik});
5   Evaluate *Upper_Bound* (UB^{ik}) by calling
        RTCDA-W^2H-Sched$(t_{ik}, false, UB^{ik})$;
6   **if** $dl(ik) \leq UB^{ik}$ **then**
7   Make tentative schedule from step 5 as the final schedule;
8   **else**
9   Schedule task graph with duplication, call
           RTCDA-W^2H-Sched$(t_{ik}, true, UB^{ik})$;
10   **if** $dl(ik) > UB^{ik}$ **then** Scheduling task set failed, return $false$;
11 return $true$;

---

the makespan of every task instance using tentative scheduling. If the deadline of that instance is greater than or equal to the UB (step 6), then the tentative schedule obtained while evaluating the upper bound in step 5 becomes the final schedule (step 7), otherwise the task instance is scheduled with duplication (step 8). RTCDA-W^2H is a combination of list-based and duplication scheduling heuristics. It begins by calculating the hyper period (hp) of the task set T. The hp is evaluated as the least common multiple of all tasks periods. The schedule is generated from time unit *zero* till hp (steps 1–2). The same schedule is repeated after hp. Each task t_i has $hp/pe(i)$ number of instances in the generated schedule. The separate priority schemes for tasks $t_i \in T$ and subtasks $s_{ijk} \in V_i$ are used to generate schedule queues (step 2). These priority schemes direct RTCDA-W^2H to select a task instance among all tasks and a further ordering of subtasks for allocation to the processing elements (Sect. 5.2). A task t_{ik}, is fetched from the head of SQ_t for processing. The next step is to evaluate the UB using tentative scheduling (step 5) and scheduling with duplication if the UB does not meet the deadline (Sect. 5.3). Algorithm 2 is used for both "without duplication" and "duplication" scheduling by setting the *dupl* parameter to *false* and *true* respectively.

5.2   Assigning Priorities

The tasks in the task set are considered for scheduling, one at a time and are prioritized according to a modified version of the *earliest deadline first* (EDF) algorithm [14]. Since the information of all the tasks is available in advance, the task schedule queue SQ_t is generated before the actual scheduling. The kth task instance of a task i is given higher priority than the lth instance of task j if the deadline of the former task $dl(ik)$ is lesser than the latter i.e., $dl(jl)$, irrespective of their release times, which is not the case in the original EDF. In EDF, a task starts its execution after it is released (if a processor is available) and is preempted if another task with a lesser deadline arrives. However, as our algorithm is non-preemptive, we assign a higher priority to a task which is released later but has a lesser deadline. If two task instances have the same deadline, then the ties are broken by assigning a higher priority to the instance with the earlier release time $rt(ik)$ (Eq. 1, Table 2).

After the selection of a task instance t_{ik} for scheduling, all the subtasks s_{ijk} of t_{ik} are inserted in the subtask schedule queue (SQ_{st}) according to a non-increasing order of their *b-level* ($bl(s_{ijk})$) values. The ties are broken using s-level ($sl(s_{ijk})$) values. The b-level (s-level) stands for the bottom (start) level, which is evaluated recursively in a bottom-up (top-down) fashion, traversing the task graph starting from the exit (entry) node as shown in Eq. 2 in Table 2 (step 1, Algorithm 2).

In the equations above, $bl(s_{i(exit)k}) = \overline{\mu_i(exit)}$ and $sl(s_{i(entry)k}) = zero$, whereas $succ(s_{ijk})$ and $pred(s_{ijk})$ is the list of immediate successors and predecessors of s_{ijk} and $\overline{\mu_i(j)}$ represents the average execution cost of subtask s_{ijk}. The $bl(s_{ijk})$ value is the critical path from the subtask s_{ijk} to $s_{i(exit)k}$. We have used $b - level$ as the primary priority parameter because the critical path based algorithms are known to generate better schedules. Secondly, sl is the distance of a subtask s_{ijk} from $s_{i(entry)k}$. The subtask with lower *s-level* is given higher priority, as it is present at a higher level in the task graph. It is worth noting that sorting the nodes according to *b-level* also performs a topological sort on all the $s_{ijk} \in V_i$, which satisfies the precedence constraints.

5.3 Scheduling a Task Instance with an Upper Bound

We define an *upper bound* (UB^{ik}) for every k^{th} invocation of task t_i. The UB^{ik} is the time up to which the task instance t_{ik} can be scheduled without duplicating any of its jobs. This bound is computed at run time considering the release time $rt(ik)$ of t_{ik}. One straightforward way to evaluate the upper bound is to use an already proposed "without duplication" heuristic to schedule a DAG on heterogeneous multiprocessors. The heuristic will tentatively schedule all the jobs of the task graph instance t_{ik} by considering the current load on all the processors. Here, the upper bound is the actual finish time, $aft(s_{i(exit)k})$, of the exit job $s_{i(exit)k}$. A well known "without duplication" low complexity insertion based heuristic is Heterogeneous Earliest Finish Time (HEFT) [20]. HEFT greedily allocates jobs to processors that give the earliest finish time. HEFT is very effective for scheduling applications with low communication costs. However, in our experiments, we observed that as the communication cost among jobs increases, the greedy approach of HEFT tends to generate schedule lengths even greater than the sequential schedules or the trivial upper bound $(TUB(ik))$. The $TUB(ik)$ for a task instance t_{ik} is defined as the minimum schedule length when all the jobs of t_{ik} are scheduled on a single processor. Again, we use tentative scheduling to find $TUB(ik)$. The processor which gives the $TUB(ik)$ is called the upper bound processor p_{ub}. RTCDA-W^2H uses a modified version of HEFT (Algorithm 2) that generates schedules with a worst case length of $TUB(ik)$ i.e., $UB^{ik} \leq TUB(ik)$.

The subtasks $s_{ijk} \in V_i$ are inserted into SQ_{st} (step 2) for processing according to their b-level $(bl(s_{ijk}))$ and s-level (sl) values (step 1). Before scheduling, RTCDA-W^2H calculates the $TUB(ik)$ and tentative earliest start time of all $s_{ijk} \in V_i$ (Eq. 7, Table 2) on processor p_{ub} if they execute according to their order in SQ_{st} on processor p_{ub} (step 3). The p_{ub} represents the processor on which the current task instance t_{ik} has the UB^{ik}. A subtask s_{ijk} is fetched from the head of SQ_{st} till all the jobs are processed (steps 4 and 5). Next, the algorithm finds the earliest finish time of s_{ijk} with or without duplication, as decided by the input parameter *dupl* using algorithm 3 (step 6 of Algorithm 2). Algorithm 3 is called to evaluate EFT of s_{ijk}, where boolean parameter *dupl* decides whether to duplicate jobs while calculating EFT or not. The parameter p_z in a call to Algorithm 3 stores the processor that gives the $EFT(s_{ijk})$.

Job s_{ijk} is tentatively scheduled on all the processors and p_z is set to the processor which gives that minimum finish time (steps 2 and 6, Algorithm 3). Equation 5 in Table 2 describes the evaluation of $EFT(s_{ijk}, p_q)$ on a particular processor p_q. Since RTCDA-W^2H is an insertion based algorithm, we look for an earliest available schedule hole of minimum size equal to the execution cost of

---

Algorithm 2. RTCDA-W^2H-Sched(t_{ik},$dupl$,UB^{ik})

Data: *Task instance* : t_{ik}, *bool dupl, UB,Processor* p_{ub}
Result: *Schedule of task* t_{ik}

1 *Evaluate* $sl(s_{i(exit)k})$ *and* $bl(s_{i(entry)k})$ *of* t_{ik};
2 *Insert the subtasks* $s_{ijk} \in V_i$ *in* SQ_{st} *in non-increasing values of* $bl(s_{ijk})$,
   breaking ties in non-decreasing values of $sl(s_{ijk})$;
3 *Evaluate* $TUB(ik)(t_{ik}, p_{ub})$ *and* $ETST(s_{ijk}, p_{ub})$ *for all* $s_{ijk} \in V_i$ *following their*
   order in SQ_{st};
4 **while** *there are unscheduled subtasks in* SQ_{st} **do**
5 | *fetch the subtask* s_{ijk} *from the head of* SQ_{st};
6 | *Find* $EFT_{s_{ijk}} \leftarrow EFT(s_{ijk}, dupl, p_z)$;   // processor p_z gives EFT;
7 | **if** $p_z \neq p_{ub}$ **then**
8 | | $shift = true$;
9 | | **foreach** $s_{ilk} \in succ(s_{ijk})$ **do**
10 | | | **if** $EFT_{s_{ijk}} + c_i(j,l) > ETST(s_{ijk}, p_{ub})$ **then** $shift \leftarrow false$;
11 | **if** $shift$ **then**
12 | | $Schedule(s_{ijk}, p_z, dupl)$;
13 | **else** $Schedule(s_{ijk}, p_{ub}, dupl)$;
14 $UB^{ik} = aft(s_{i(exit)k})$;

Algorithm 3. EFT(s_{ijk},$dupl$,p_z)

Data: *Subtask* : s_{ijk}, *duplication (true/false)*: $dupl$, *Processor*: p_z
Result: *Returns Earliest Finish Time of* s_{ijk}, p_z *store the processor on which*
          s_{ijk} *has EFT*

1 $EFT \leftarrow INFTY$;
2 **foreach** $p_q \in P$ **do**
3 | $Temp \leftarrow EFT(s_{ijk}, p_q)$;
4 | **if** $dupl$ **then**
5 | | *Perform duplication (in schedule holes) of immediate predecessors in the*
   | | *order that they delay* s_{ilk} *the most, if it improves* $Temp$;
6 | **if** $Temp < EFT$ **then** $p_z \leftarrow p_q$; $EFT \leftarrow Temp$;
7 *return* EFT;

---

s_{ijk} on p_q i.e., $\mu_i(j,q)$ which can accommodate s_{ijk}. The start time of this hole H_h^S should be greater than the data arrival time of s_{ijk} from its predecessors on p_q (Eqs. 3–5 in Table 2).

During the evaluation of $EFT(s_{ijk})$ (Algorithm 3), we look for the possibility of duplicating predecessors of s_{ijk} if it improves the $EFT(s_{ijk})$ on p_z (steps 4–6). RTCDA-W^2H is flexible in performing duplication. Here, we allow duplication of immediate predecessors only and the predecessors are selected for duplication according to a non-increasing order of the time that they delay s_{ijk}. Duplication of a job is only performed if it improves the $EFT(s_{ijk})$.

In case the processor on which s_{ijk} has the earliest finish time is the same as that of p_{ub}, s_{ijk} is scheduled on p_{ub} (step 13, Algorithm 2). In the other scenario, RTCDA-W^2H makes sure that scheduling s_{ijk} on any processor p_z other than p_{ub} does not increase the worst case schedule length i.e., $TUB(ik)$ by satisfying the following condition for all $s_{ilk} \in succ(s_{ijk})$ (steps 8–13, Algorithm 2).

$$Condition - 1 : EFT_{s_{ijk}} + c_i(j, l) \leq ETST(s_{ilk}, p_{ub})$$

If a subtask s_{ijk} satisfies the above equation, then it is scheduled on p_z, other wise on p_{ub}. Subroutine *Schedule* (steps 12 and 13, Algorithm 2) has a similar pseudo code as Algorithm 2, except that it schedules the subtask after finding the EFT. Condition-1 is the primary difference with the original HEFT algorithm. Removing this condition will convert RTCDA-W^2H into HEFT. We call this condition "selective duplication", since it does not allow schedule lengths to be greater than the trivial upper bound, $TUB(ik)$. The results show that selective duplication improves the performance of RTCDA-W^2H over the original HEFT algorithm.

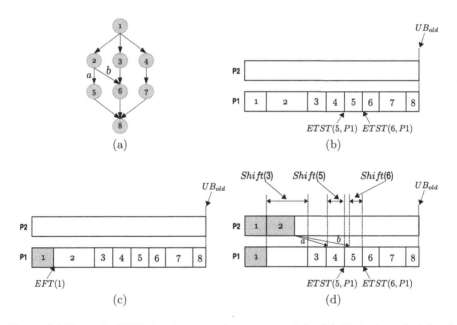

Fig. 3. (a) Example DAG showing precedence among jobs (b) Tentative schedule of example DAG on upper bound processor P1 (c) Job 1 scheduled on P1 (d) Job 2 has EFT on P2. Duplication of Job 1 leads to updation in the tentative schedule of remaining jobs and hence of UB_{old}

6 RTCDA-W^2H^2: How Much to Duplicate

RTCDA-W^2H^2 proposes an extension to RTCDA-W^2H (when duplicating) by inculcating an approach to dynamically improve the upper bound UB^{ik} after a subtask is scheduled on a processor other than the upper bound processor p_{ub}. After every update in UB^{ik}, we again determine if $dl_{ik} \geq UB^{ik}$, if it's true, then the remaining subtasks are scheduled without duplication. Thus, even after deciding that a task instance will be scheduled with duplication, RTCDA-W^2H^2 controls the amount of duplication and hence solves the "how much to duplicate" problem.

The concept of RTCDA-W^2H^2 is elaborated with the scheduling of jobs with precedence relations on two processing elements as depicted in an example DAG shown in Fig. 3(a). All eight jobs of the task graph are assumed to be processed in the order of their values from 1–8. Let's say processor $P1$ gives the trivial upper bound (UB_{old}) of the task instance as shown in Fig. 3(b). The actual scheduling starts with job 1 and $EFT(job1)$ is evaluated. Let's say Job 1 has an EFT on the upper bound processor $P1$ and is scheduled on $P1$ (refer to 3(c)). The unfilled boxes on P1 represent the tentative schedule where as the grey filled boxes refer to the actual scheduling of jobs. The next job in the schedule queue is job 2. Figure 3(d) shows a state when job 2 has an EFT on processor $P2$ with the help of a replicated copy of job 1. Job 2 can be scheduled on $P2$, which is not an upper bound processor, only if both of it's successor jobs 5 and 6 satisfy the selective duplication Condition-1, i.e.,

$$EFT(2) + c(2,5) \leq ETST(5, P1)$$
$$EFT(2) + c(2,6) \leq ETST(6, P1)$$

If the above conditions are satisfied, job 2 is scheduled on $P2$. According to the above procedure, RTCDA-W^2H continues with the scheduling of the remaining jobs. However, in RTCDA-W^2H^2, an additional step is performed to update the value of the upper bound. It is observed that with the actual scheduling of job 2 on $P2$, which is not the upper bound processor, three of the unscheduled jobs have been affected in the tentative trivial upper bound schedule on $P1$. Two of these jobs are the successors of job 2 i.e., job 5 and job 6 and the third is the next job in the schedule queue, job 3. We define a set AF of all these affected jobs as follows:

Definition 2. Set of Shift Affected Jobs (AF). *If a job s_{ijk} is scheduled on a processor other than the upper bound processor, then the set of $succ(s_{ijk})$ and the next job in the schedule queue is defined as the set AF.*

For all the jobs $s_{ilk} \in AF$, we evaluate a parameter $shift(s_{ilk})$ as shown in Eq. 1.

$$shift(s_{ilk}) = ETST(s_{ilk}, p_{ub}) - DAT(s_{ilk}, p_{ub}) \tag{1}$$

The parameter $shift$ describes the maximum improvement in the $ETST$ of the affected jobs on p_{ub} in the tentative upper bound schedule considering available schedule holes. The overall improvement in the upper bound is evaluated as:

$$min\_shift = \min_{s_{ilk} \in AF} \left(shift(s_{ilk})\right) \tag{2}$$

$$UB_{new}^{ik} = UB_{old}^{ik} - min\_shift \tag{3}$$

RTCDA-W^2H^2 keeps improving the UB^{ik} whenever a job is scheduled on a processor other than p_{ub}. As soon as $dl_{ik} \leq UB_{new}^{ik}$, the remaining jobs are scheduled without duplication, hence, controlling the amount of duplication. The above discussed steps to update UB^{ik} should be added to the if-condition at step 11 of Algorithm 2 to implement the required functionality of RTCDA-W^2H^2. Hence, RTCDA-W^2H^2 includes schemes to handle all W^2H^2 challenges.

7   Time Complexity

The time complexity of RTCDA-W^2H^2 and RTCDA-W^2H has been found to be $O(n^2 I_{max}^2 v_{max}^2 m d_{max})$, where I_{max}, v_{max} and d_{max} are defined as the maximum number of instances of a task in a task set, maximum subtasks in a task and maximum in-degree of a task in a task set respectively. This time complexity is higher than that of RTDBA [3] $O(n I_{max} v_{max}^2)$ because both the proposed algorithms are insertion based and take $O(n I_{max} v_{max})$ time in finding a particular hole for scheduling jobs. However, the increase in the time complexity is reflected in the performance of RTCDA-W^2H^2 as described by better results. Since this is a static variation of the scheduling problem, the increase in complexity has been compensated with increasing performance of the heuristics.

For an instance of a task t_{ik}, the algorithm evaluates $bl(s_{ijk})$, $sl(s_{ijk})$ for all the jobs. These two parameters can be found by a breadth-first search on the DAG. It visits every vertex exactly once, so the time taken is $O(v_i)$. RTCDA-W^2H^2 spends a significant amount of time in searching for a valid schedule hole for a subtask on a processor. Therefore, the time required to find a valid hole is proportional to the number of holes present on a processor, which is further equal to the number of jobs already scheduled on it. In the worst case, before scheduling t_n, all of the other tasks and their instances may have finished. Hence, the total number of the scheduled jobs are as given by the equation:

$$nholes \leq \left(\frac{hp}{p_1} \times v_1 + \frac{hp}{p_2} \times v_2 + \cdots + \frac{hp}{p_{n-1}} \times v_{n-1}\right)$$
$$\leq v_{max}\left(\frac{hp}{p_1} + \frac{hp}{p_2} + \cdots + \frac{hp}{p_{n-1}}\right)$$
$$\leq v_{max}\left(I_1 + I_2 + \cdots + I_{n-1}\right)$$
$$\leq n I_{max} v_{max} \tag{4}$$

In evaluating the upper bound UB of a task, we schedule all jobs on all the processors with schedule holes, which gives $O(n I_{max} v_{max}^2 m)$. While scheduling

Table 3. Simulation parameters

Parameter	Range	Parameter	Range
Number of tasks in a task set	2–100	Number of subtasks in a task	10–2000
Subtask execution cost	1–100	Communication to Computation Ratio (CCR)	0.5, 1, 5, 10
Utilization (UT)	0.3–1.0	Heterogeneity Factor (HF)	5–40

a job, we find the EFT of the job on all the processors. Therefore, scheduling all the jobs takes $O(nI_{max}v_{max}^2 m)$ time. Each task duplication also considers the schedule holes between all previously scheduled tasks for the processor. Therefore, each task duplication has a time complexity of $O(nI_{max}v_{max})$. The maximum number of duplications would be d_{max} which gives the complexity $O(nI_{max}v_{max}^2 md_{max})$. The controlled duplication step can be done on $O(v_i)$ time. Therefore, the total time becomes $O(n^2 I_{max}^2 v_{max}^2 md_{max})$ for scheduling a maximum of nI_{max} instances.

8 Simulation Results

The proposed algorithms RTCDA-W^2H and RTCDA-W^2H^2 have been compared with RTDBA [3] and three real-time variants of the HEFT scheduling algorithm viz. RTHEFT, RTHEFTD and RTHEFTUB. RTHEFT is the real-time version of HEFT proposed in [20]. This algorithm schedules jobs of every task instance with the earliest finish time heuristic without duplicating any job. RTHEFTD, a "duplication" version of HEFT has been proposed by [5]. This algorithm always uses duplication for scheduling task instances. RTHEFTUB is essentially our RTCDA-W^2H, without doing the selective duplication step proposed in Condition-1 i.e., RTHEFTUB can generate schedules more than the trivial upper bound. The parameters used for the simulation are summarized in Table 3. The number of processors are varied by keeping the ratio $\left(\frac{average\_subtasks\_in\_taskset}{number\_of\_processors}\right)$ as constant [7].

Total utilization UT of a task set is the summation of the utilization of all the tasks in the task set. For a single task, UT is defined as $UT = \frac{average\_computation}{m*period}$, whereas *average_computation* is the summation of the averages of jobs execution costs in the task. Parameters CCR, HF are averaged over all the tasks in the task set. CCR of a task is defined as $\frac{total\_communication}{average\_computation}$. HF of a task corresponds to the average standard deviation of the job execution costs. For a job s_{ijk} of a task t_i, it is evaluated as $\sqrt{\sum_{p_q \in P} (\overline{\mu_i(j)} - \mu_i(j, p_q))^2}$. For every combination of CCR and UT, 1000 task sets were generated by uniformly selecting the remaining parameters using a well known real-time benchmark, Task Graphs For Free (TGFF) [10]. The task deadlines have been set equal to their periods. All the algorithms have been implemented in C++. Schedulability or Success Ratio (SR) is used as the primary performance metric.

Definition 3 *(Success Ratio). It is defined as the ratio of the number of task sets that meet their deadlines to the total number of task sets considered [3] i.e.* $SR = \frac{number\_of\_tasksets\_meeting\_deadlines}{total\_number\_of\_tasksets}.$

8.1   Effects of CCR and UT

Figures 4 and 5 show the effect of varying CCR and UT on the algorithms. The results show that RTCDA-W^2H^2 and RTCDA-W^2H improve the SR more than the others in every combination of CCR and UT. Among all algorithms, RTHEFTD and RTDBA achieved the lowest SR values, even lesser than those of RTHEFT, which is a "without duplication" algorithm. The primary reason for this is that they "always" perform duplication of the jobs. Also, RTDBA is not an insertion based algorithm. This reflects in its SR being lower than RTHEFTD. All three proposed upper bound algorithms managed to improve the SR by >15% for UT >= 0.7 across all CCR values (Figs. 4 and 5). Hence, these algorithms make an efficient use of schedule holes by switching between "without duplication" and "duplication" scheduling algorithms at run time. In Fig. 4(a), for a low CCR of 0.5, "without duplication" RTHEFT scheduled all task sets with UT $\leq$ 0.5. However, for higher utilizations and higher CCR values, upper bound

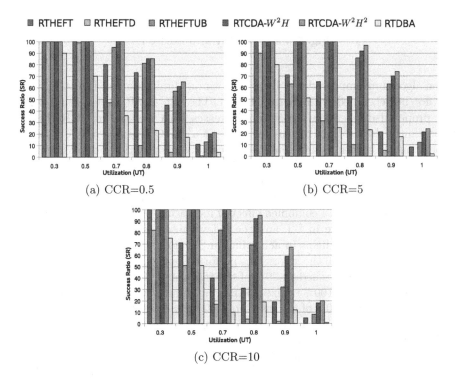

Fig. 4. Effect of UT with fixed CCR

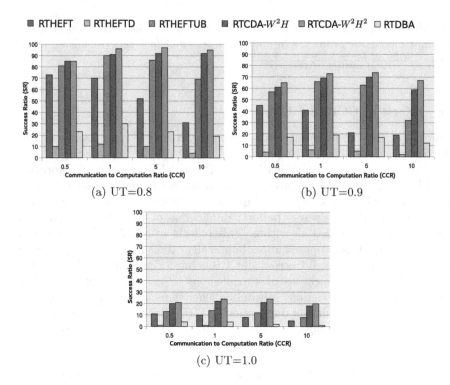

Fig. 5. Effect of CCR with fixed UT

based algorithms improved the SR by performing duplication for the tasks which can not be scheduled without duplication. The gap in SR values of RTHEFT and proposed duplication algorithms increases with increase in CCR (Fig. 5). Importantly, duplications are less effective at a low CCR value = 0.5, however, upper bound algorithms first tentatively schedule tasks without duplication and then try duplication, only when the "without duplication" approach fails. This helps in increasing the SR by 10–20%.

Generally, the SR for all the algorithms decreases with an increase in UT at all CCRs. This scenario is a combined effect of increasing the demand of computing power with an increase in UT and the delay caused by communication costs. However, duplications helps in achieving an SR close to 70% for UT = 0.9. At maximum UT = 1.0, all the algorithms perform poorly. However, RTCDA based algorithms are able to schedule 20% of the task sets. The UT = 1.0 describes a case when the CPU is 100% utilized. However, heterogeneity in the computation costs help scheduling 20% of the task sets (refer to Sect. 8.2 for details). RTCDA-W^2H and RTCDA-W^2H^2 have performed slightly better than RTHEFTUB by making use of selective duplication that bounds their schedule lengths to the trivial upper bound at higher CCR values. The major difference in their SR can be seen at CCR value = 10 across different utilizations (Fig. 5), due to RTHEFTUB generating schedules larger than the trivial upper bound. RTCDA-

W^2H^2 is able to schedule 5–10% more task sets than RTCDA-W^2H due to a control in the amount of duplication while scheduling.

8.2   Effects of Heterogeneity

To study the effect of heterogeneity, task sets are generated by keeping CCR and UT fixed to 1.0 and 0.8 respectively and by varying the execution costs in a range of 1–50. The parameter HF is varied from 1 to 20 as shown in Fig. 6. A low value of HF = 1, depicts less variation in the execution costs of jobs on multiprocessors. Hence, for a UT = 0.8, a task set will require approximately 80% of the total CPU computing power to meet all deadlines, because each job will execute almost for its average execution cost. The remaining 20% of the computing power is only utilized by duplicated copies of jobs to reduce the delay caused by the higher communication cost. Hence, more jobs are delayed. This reduces the success ratio. With the increase in HF, the SR has been found to increase, because more variation in execution costs causes jobs to schedule on processors with execution cost less than their averages hence, providing more computing power for duplication.

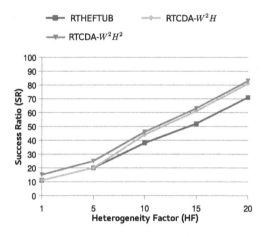

Fig. 6. Effect of heterogeneity

9   Conclusion

We have observed that duplication is not always required for the scheduling of real-time static tasks. Whether to duplicate or not depends on the task deadlines. In addition, the controlled duplication strategy has addressed the W^2H^2 duplication challenges. Increasing the simulation time using RTMIP and local search techniques further improves the success ratio by >20% for a maximum utilization of 1.0. In the future work, we will look to decrease the time complexity of the algorithms. Also, energy consumption of computation and communication resources can be optimized for the cases where 100% SR is achieved.

References

1. Ahmad, I., Kwok, Y.K.: On exploiting task duplication in parallel program scheduling. IEEE Trans. Parallel Distrib. Syst. **9**, 872–892 (1998)
2. Auluck, N., Agrawal, D.P.: An integrated scheduling algorithm for precedence constrained hard and soft real-time tasks on heterogeneous multiprocessors. In: Yang, L.T., Guo, M., Gao, G.R., Jha, N.K. (eds.) EUC 2004. LNCS, vol. 3207, pp. 196–206. Springer, Heidelberg (2004). doi:10.1007/978-3-540-30121-9_19
3. Auluck, N., Agrawal, D.: Enhancing the schedulability of Real-Time heterogeneous networks of workstations (NOWs). IEEE Trans. Parallel Distrib. Syst. **20**(11), 1586–1599 (2009)
4. Bajaj, R., Agrawal, D.P.: Improving scheduling of tasks in a heterogeneous environment. IEEE Trans. Parallel Distrib. Syst. **15**, 107–118 (2004)
5. Bansal, S., Kumar, P., Singh, K.: Dealing with heterogeneity through limited duplication for scheduling precedence constrained task graphs. J. Parallel Distrib. Comput. **65**, 479–491 (2005)
6. Baskiyar, S., Dickinson, C.: Scheduling directed a-cyclic task graphs on a bounded set of heterogeneous processors using task duplication. J. Parallel Distrib. Comput. **65**, 911–921 (2005)
7. Davare, A., Chong, J., Zhu, Q., Densmore, D.M., Sangiovanni-Vincentelli, A.L.: Classification, customization, and characterization: using MILP for task allocation and scheduling. Technical report UCB/EECS-2006-166, EECS Department, University of California, Berkeley, December 2006
8. Dave, B., Jha, N.: COFTA: hardware-software co-synthesis of heterogeneous distributed embedded systems for low overhead fault tolerance. IEEE Trans. Comput. **48**(4), 417–441 (1999)
9. Dave, B., Lakshminarayana, G., Jha, N.: COSYN: hardware-software co-synthesis of heterogeneous distributed embedded systems. IEEE Trans. Very Large Scale Integr. VLSI Syst. **7**(1), 92–104 (1999)
10. Dick, R.P., Rhodes, D.L., Wolf, W.: TGFF: task graphs for free (1998)
11. Garey, M.R., Johnson, D.S.: Computers and Intractability: A Guide to the Theory of NP-Completeness. Series of Books in the Mathematical Sciences (1979). W.H. Freeman, first edn
12. Kwok, Y.K., Ahmad, I.: Static scheduling algorithms for allocating directed task graphs to multiprocessors. ACM Comput. Surv. **31**, 406–471 (1999)
13. Liu, C., Anderson, J.: Supporting graph-based real-time applications in distributed systems. In: Proceedings - 17th IEEE International Conference on Embedded and Real-Time Computing Systems and Applications, RTCSA 2011, vol. 1, pp. 143–152 (2011)
14. Liu, C.L., Layland, J.W.: Scheduling algorithms for multiprogramming in a hard-real-time environment. J. ACM (JACM) **20**(1), 46–61 (1973)
15. Qin, X., Jiang, H.: A dynamic and reliability-driven scheduling algorithm for parallel real-time jobs executing on heterogeneous clusters. J. Parallel Distrib. Comput. **65**(8), 885–900 (2005)
16. Ranaweera, S., Agrawal, D.P.: Scheduling of periodic time critical applications for pipelined execution on heterogeneous systems. In: International Conference on Parallel Processing, p. 0131, Los Alamitos, CA, USA (2001)
17. Singh, J., Auluck, N.: Controlled duplication for scheduling real-time precedence tasks on heterogeneous multiprocessors. In: Student Research Symposium High Performance Computing (HiPC11), Bangalore, India, December 2011

18. Singh, J., Betha, S., Mangipudi, B., Auluck, N.: Contention aware energy efficient scheduling on heterogeneous multiprocessors. IEEE Trans. Parallel Distrib. Syst. **26**(5), 1251–1264 (2015)
19. Stavrinides, G.L., Karatza, H.D.: Scheduling multiple task graphs in heterogeneous distributed real-time systems by exploiting schedule holes with bin packing techniques. Simul. Model. Pract. Theory **19**(1), 540–552 (2011)
20. Topcuouglu, H., Hariri, S., Wu, M.Y.: Performance-effective and low-complexity task scheduling for heterogeneous computing. IEEE Trans. Parallel Distrib. Syst. **13**, 260–274 (2002)
21. Tosun, S.: Energy and reliability-aware task scheduling onto heterogeneous MPSoC architectures. J. Supercomputing **62**(1), 1–25 (2011)
22. Xie, T., Qin, X.: Security-aware resource allocation for real-time parallel jobs on homogeneous and heterogeneous clusters. IEEE Trans. Parallel Distrib. Syst. **19**(5), 682–697 (2008)
23. YuHai, Y., Shengsheng, Y., XueLian, B.: A new dynamic scheduling algorithm for real-time heterogeneous multiprocessor systems. In: Workshop on Intelligent Information Technology Application (IITA 2007), Zhang Jiajie, China, pp. 112–115 (2007)
24. Zhu, X., Lu, P.: Multi-Dimensional scheduling for real-time tasks on heterogeneous clusters. J. Comput. Sci. Technol. **24**(3), 434–446 (2009)

On the Design and Implementation
of an Efficient Lock-Free Scheduler

Florian Negele[1], Felix Friedrich[1], Suwon Oh[2], and Bernhard Egger[2(✉)]

[1] Department of Computer Science, ETH Zürich, Zürich, Switzerland
{negelef,felix.friedrich}@inf.ethz.ch
[2] Department of Computer Science and Engineering,
Seoul National University, Seoul, Korea
{suwon,bernhard}@csap.snu.ac.kr

Abstract. Schedulers for symmetric multiprocessing (SMP) machines use sophisticated algorithms to schedule processes onto the available processor cores. Hardware-dependent code and the use of locks to protect shared data structures from simultaneous access lead to poor portability, the difficulty to prove correctness, and a myriad of problems associated with locking such as limiting the available parallelism, deadlocks, starvation, interrupt handling, and so on. In this work we explore what can be achieved in terms of portability and simplicity in an SMP scheduler that achieves similar performance to state-of-the-art schedulers. By strictly limiting ourselves to only lock-free data structures in the scheduler, the problems associated with locking vanish altogether. We show that by employing implicit cooperative scheduling, additional guarantees can be made that allow novel and very efficient implementations of memory-efficient unbounded lock-free queues. Cooperative multitasking has the additional benefit that it provides an extensive hardware independence. It even allows the scheduler to be used as a runtime library for applications running on top of standard operating systems. In a comparison against Windows Server and Linux running on up to 64 cores we analyze the performance of the lock-free scheduler and show that it matches or even outperforms the performance of these two state-of-the-art schedulers in a variety of benchmarks.

Keywords: Lock-free scheduling · Cooperative multitasking · Run-time environments · Multicore architectures

1 Introduction

For several decades now, operating systems have provided native support for symmetric multiprocessing (SMP). One of their key functions is to schedule active processes (or *tasks*) onto available logical cores. State-of-the-art schedulers of modern operating systems such as the completely fair scheduler (CFS) [24] in the Linux kernel implement complex algorithms and - together with the scheduler framework - comprise many thousand lines of code.

© Springer International Publishing AG 2017
N. Desai and W. Cirne (Eds.): JSSPP 2015/2016, LNCS 10353, pp. 22–45, 2017.
DOI: 10.1007/978-3-319-61756-5_2

A significant part of the complexity of state-of-the-art schedulers stems from guaranteeing mutual exclusion in parts of the code that access shared data structures. This form of blocking synchronization is typically implemented with *locks* in one of the different variants such as *spinlocks*, *mutexes*, *semaphores*, or *monitors* [11]. Despite its conceptual simplicity, mutual exclusion has many well documented and understood drawbacks. For instance, mutual exclusion limits the progress of all contending tasks to a single one, effectively preventing any parallelism amongst the contenders for as long as the lock is held. In addition, synchronization primitives that ensure mutual exclusion traditionally suffer from well-known problems such as deadlocks, livelocks, starvation or the failure to release resources.

Yet another issue is the design decision of what amount of shared data is to be protected by the same lock. Coarse-grained locking reduces the overhead of acquiring the lock but greatly decreases the available parallelism. The common practice of fine-grained locking, on the other hand, enables more parallelism but leads to more complicated implementations and a bigger overhead of acquiring and releasing the locks. To make matters worse, great care has to be taken that locks acquired during interrupt service routines do not lead to deadlocks. This can be a problem especially for operating system schedulers that are typically invoked as a result of either blocking system calls or timer interrupts. As a result, it is often difficult if not impossible to prove the correctness of algorithms that use locks to achieve mutual exclusion, but whose correct operation is essential to the reliability of an operating system.

The prevalent form of multitasking, preemptive multitasking, is based on timer interrupts. Since interrupts can occur at any point in a user program, it is necessary to save and restore the entire volatile state of the processor core while handling the interrupt. This not only introduces an overhead but also ties an implementation of the operating system kernel to a certain hardware platform. As a result, operating systems supporting a wide range of hardware platforms contain different implementations of hardware-dependent functionality for each platform.

Our experience in porting our own kernel to different platforms has resulted in the quest for developing a runtime kernel that is as simple yet parallel and hardware-independent as possible. In this paper, we describe one part of this experiment, the design and implementation of the task scheduler.

In order to avoid the difficulties associated with blocking synchronization and interrupt-based preemptive multitasking, we have made the following two guiding principles

- exclusively employ non-blocking algorithms and
- use implicit cooperative multitasking.

Several kernels exist that employ either one of the above principles [5,12,19,29], but only the combination of non-blocking algorithms with cooperative multitasking allows for certain optimizations and guarantees that render the implementation of a lock-free runtime and scheduler viable.

In cooperative multitasking tasks relinquish control of the core voluntarily by issuing a call to the scheduler. Some of the most obvious advantages are that task switches only occur at well-known points in the program and are thus extremely light-weight. In addition, a runtime based on cooperative multitasking can run on hardware without any interrupt support which is an important property for certain embedded systems. On top of all that, it improves portability of the code. The main problem with cooperative multitasking is where to place the calls to the scheduler. In order to keep the application code as portable as possible, we have opted for implicit cooperative multitasking, that is, the calls to the scheduler are inserted automatically by the compiler.

Non-blocking algorithms have been researched as an alternative to blocking synchronization since the early 1990s [14,19,21,28]. The general principle of accessing shared data is not based on waiting for exclusive access but rather relies on atomic test-and-set or fetch-and-add operations. It has been shown [6] that compare-and-swap (CAS) is the most versatile and only necessary atomic operation that needs to be provided by the underlying hardware. Lock-free programming by itself is usually difficult to get right because it comes with its very own set of shortcomings. Probably the most prominent problem is the so-called *ABA problem* [15], a hidden update of a variable by one task that goes undetected by a second task. The standard solutions, like hazard-pointers [22] or the Repeat Offender Problem [9], suffers from a linear increase in execution time in the number of threads accessing the data structure. This is obviously a serious drawback for a lock-free scheduler. We show how the guarantees of cooperative scheduling can be used to implement an unbounded and lock-free queue that accesses hazard pointers in constant time.

Kernels of today's operating systems such as Windows or Linux are heavily optimized with respect to performance, which comes at the price of a high complexity. But admittedly such systems also implement many more features. For example, our runtime system does not support protection features such as process isolation. These arguments make a comparison of our system with today's standard operating systems unfair in both directions. In order to still be able to assess its performance, the cooperative scheduler based on lock-free programming has been implemented and tested against schedulers of Windows Server 2008R2 and Linux operating systems. A wide range of microbenchmarks and real-world application shows that the lock-free cooperative scheduler matches or even outperforms the performance of these two state-of-the-art schedulers.

The remainder of this paper is organized as follows: Sect. 2 gives some background information and discusses related work. Section 3 describes our implementation of cooperative multitasking, and in Sect. 4 the design of our efficient unbounded and lock-free queue and its application to the scheduler are discussed. Sections 5 and 6 describe the experimental setup and discuss the results. Section 7 concludes the paper.

2   Background and Related Work

Lock-free programming has been an active research topic since the early 1990s. The prerequisite for lock-free programming is the availability of an atomic update operation such as compare-and-swap (CAS). The CAS operation was introduced with the IBM System 370 hardware architecture [15]. It atomically reads a shared memory location, compares its contents with an expected value and replaces it with another value if there was a match. Its return value is the original contents of the shared memory location. This operation has been proved by Herlihy to be universal, which implies that it can actually implement all other atomic operations such as test-and-set or fetch-and-add [7]. Hwang and Briggs belong to the earliest researchers who have presented non-blocking queues based on the compare-and-swap operation [14]. Further examples include the works by Mellor-Crummey [21], Herlihy [6,10], Massalin and Pu [19], and Valois [28]. Michael and Scott also provide an algorithm and give a good overview and comparison with existing implementations [23]. Their implementation draws ideas from the work by Valois, is simple and one of the fastest to date. In contrast to others, their lock-free queue is also practical because it explicitly allows empty queues and concurrent dequeue and enqueue operations. In addition, it does not require a double compare-and-swap instruction operating on two, potentially discontiguous memory locations instead of a single one. This particular lock-free queue is therefore very popular and adopted widely in the literature.

Lock-free queue implementations typically allocate memory during enqueue operations. We find it surprising that memory allocations have always been considered necessary in order to implement non-blocking synchronization [5,8,9,23,28]. But the fact that memory has to be allocated for each synchronization operation has never been considered an issue in itself. Applied to the task scheduler, a memory allocation is clearly not desirable. Even more so, when it triggers a full garbage collection run. While the Michael and Scott queue [23] supports explicit memory deallocation, it employs modification counters in order to deal with the ABA or hidden-update problem [15]. The ABA problem describes situations when a thread modifying a queue fails to recognize that its contents has been changed temporarily. This often results in a corrupted linked list and occurs with a high probability when nodes are reused heavily. In addition to the ABA problem, there is also an issue when concurrent dequeue operations deallocate memory that is still referenced and about to be used by other operations. Without any further precaution, any memory deallocation must be considered to render memory references of contending processes invalid. These references are generally known as *hazard pointers*, a term coined by Michael [22]. He invented the methodology of hazard pointers in order to deal with the safe memory reclamation of lock-free objects in general. His idea was to provide for every participating thread a list of those pointers which are about to be dereferenced in non-blocking algorithms. The set of all hazard pointers is made accessible to other threads in order to recognize if the reclamation of memory has to be deferred because it is potentially still in use. We improve on Michel's solution by combining the guarantees provided by cooperative multitasking with lock-free queues. This enables us to store the hazard pointers with constant space- and time-overhead in processor-local storage, thus rendering the task switch time constant.

Using non-blocking algorithms and data structures for implementing multi-processor operating systems has been investigated for over twenty years now. Massalin and Pu were amongst the earliest to deliver a non-blocking implementation of an operating system kernel [19]. The kernel of their multiprocessor operating system called Synthesis included support for threads and virtual memory as well as a file system. They showed that operating system kernels using non-blocking synchronization are practical and achieve at least the same performance as conventional systems. Similar conclusions have later been confirmed many times, for example by Greenwald and Cheriton [5]. However, the implementations of the resulting non-blocking operating system kernels relied on an atomic double compare-and-swap operation called DCAS. This operation is an extended version of the more common single compare-and-swap operation known as CAS that allows to atomically compare and exchange the values of two dis-contiguous memory locations instead of one. Based on their results, the authors argue that this operation in contrast to its simpler variant is sufficient for practical non-blocking operating systems. Unfortunately, the hardware support for this particular operation is still very limited and most modern hardware architectures do not provide it at all. For portability reasons, in this work we rely only on the single compare-and-swap operation in order to achieve the broadest hardware support available.

There are several other implementations of non-blocking operating systems that followed the very same approach. Hohmuth and Härtig for example focused on non-blocking real-time systems by utilizing only the single compare-and-swap operation in order to improve portability [12]. None of these approaches, however, combine lock-free programming with the prevention of task switches during the execution of a lock-free algorithm; only the combination of which allows the implementation of constant time- and space-overhead scheduling queues.

3   Implicit Cooperative Multitasking

When it comes to multitasking, the designer of a scheduler has to decide how tasks are preempted or have to relinquish their execution control respectively. The available possibilities basically narrow down to choosing preemptive or cooperative multitasking. Our decision was against preemptive multitasking because its implementation requires special hardware support in order to transfer the control of execution from a task back to the scheduler. Usually, this form of preemption is implemented using hardware interrupt handlers and is therefore completely transparent to the preempted task. Generally speaking, interrupts and external devices that trigger them, demand a deep understanding of the underlying hardware architecture and are inherently not portable at all. When cooperative multitasking is applied, the transfer of execution control is completely software driven and requires no special hardware support. Using this approach, we were able to write the scheduler in a high-level programming language rendering its implementation completely portable across various hardware architectures. Threads resemble user-level threads, or 'Green threads' known from other runtime systems and can therefore run on top of other operating systems.

Cooperative multitasking used to be prevalent in the design of most operating systems but has now been superseded to quite some extent. One reason is that the integrity of the whole system depends on user-level tasks to actually behave cooperatively. In practice, this requires programmers of applications to periodically perform a call to the scheduler in order to give it a chance to pass the execution control on to another task. Wrongly uncooperative or even malicious code compromises the correctness of the whole system and has to be validated carefully. It is hard to prove that arbitrary programs are indeed cooperative in this respect even if their source code is available for inspection. In our case, we only demand programmers to compile their code using our scheduler-aware compiler such that we can employ what we call *implicit cooperative multitasking*.

3.1   Implicit Task Switches

Instead of requiring programmers to scatter several calls to the scheduler all over their code, we use a modified compiler that generates these calls automatically behind the scenes. This approach guarantees the cooperativeness of arbitrary programs by instrumentalizing their binary code with automatically inserted task switches into the translated machine code. Our approach is therefore highly suitable for embedded systems because their whole code base including operating system and application code is often built using a cross compiler anyway. Using compiler-generated calls to the scheduler, the user code does not have to call the scheduler explicitly and looks exactly the same as with preemptive multitasking. All functions are therefore turned automatically into coroutines according to Conway and Knuth [3].

Software instrumented instruction counters have been shown to provide a bearable overhead [20]. So, in order to implement implicit task switches efficiently, we modified our compiler to reserve a dedicated general-purpose register which stores a pointer to the descriptor of the currently running task. This descriptor contains a counter called the *quantum*, which specifies how long the current task is allowed to run until the next task switch is necessary. In order to stay portable and keep the check for a necessary task switch as small as possible, the compiler does not measure the time between two consecutive checks but rather the amount of generated instructions. The actual duration of hardware operations usually varies amongst different instructions and is obviously machine-dependent. Counting the number of instructions has the advantage that the result is always constant and statically known while translating the code. This could provide a certain time-inaccuracy. But the counter granularity can be specified to provide even very low scheduling latencies for a practical realtime system. The quantum is therefore not related to actual execution time but rather stores the number of instructions an activity is allowed to execute until the next cooperative task switch. Since the task switches are always synchronous, the quantum can be chosen to be rather small and does not need to be time specific.

The compiler generates a special sequence of instructions at various places in the machine code in order to update the quantum and call the scheduler whenever this number reaches zero. The policy used to identify optimal places for the insertion of these instructions is quite simple. For each procedure in the code, the compiler keeps track of the number of instructions it generated so far. Whenever this number exceeds an upper limit or there is a potential branch backwards in the instruction sequence, the compiler decrements the quantum by the number of instructions generated since the last implicit task switch. This strategy is portable and can be applied to virtually any programming language. It effectively handles all kinds of loops and even indirect recursions, if the task switch is also inserted in the beginning of the procedure. However, the purpose of the quantum is not to satisfy strict deadlines but rather to ensure that each thread will eventually switch to another one.

An example of an implicitly generated instruction sequence of a task switch check in-between ten instructions targeting the AMD64 hardware architecture [1] looks as follows. Here, the dedicated general-purpose register is called rcx and the check requires only three simple instructions.

```
sub    [rcx + 88], 10   ; decrement quantum by 10
jge    skip             ; check if it is negative
call   Switch           ; perform task switch
skip:
```

If the decremented quantum is zero or below, the code notifies the scheduler using a call to SWITCH. With the exception of the immediate value for the subtraction instruction, each instruction sequence looks the same and its impact on performance and space overhead is in general marginal. In addition, the memory access in the first instruction almost always results in a cache hit because this sequence is performed quite regularly.

The idea of implicitly inserting calls to the task scheduler has been implemented by many programming languages in the form of coroutines or variations thereof [2, 25]. Since these calls are always inserted in-between programming language statements, they are in general as efficient as explicit synchronous task switches. One advantage of this approach is that tasks or coroutines respectively can be represented in a very light-weight fashion. Since the compiler is in charge of when the control of execution is yielded, the amount of processor state that has to be associated with the current task during a task switch can be minimized. Most often, the processor state that must be restored after a task switch is already covered by the underlying calling convention implemented by the compiler. In the simplest case, the compiler temporarily stores the required registers on the stack when calling a function and the remaining context information consists only of the program counter and the stack pointers. In comparison, preemptive multitasking can seldom determine the part of the processor state that is actually in use, because the preemption can happen anytime during the execution of the code. A preemptive scheduler has therefore to be prepared for

procedure SWITCHTO(*activity*, *finalizer*)
   uncooperative
      current ← GETACTIVITY()   ▷ Store context
      current→*frame* ← GETFRAMEPOINTER()

      activity→*quantum* ← *Default*   ▷ Prepare activity
      activity→*index* ← *current*→*index*
      activity→*finalizer* ← *finalizer*
      activity→*previous* ← *current*

      SETACTIVITY(*activity*)   ▷ Restore context
      SETFRAMEPOINTER(*activity*→*frame*)
   return

Fig. 1. Algorithm for task switches

the worst case and consequently stores and restores the complete processor state. In comparison to cooperative task switches, the cost for hardware preemption might therefore be quite expensive.

The actual cost for a single task switch is shown in Fig. 1. The real code of the scheduler is as compact as the pseudo-code given in this paper. It is encompassed by an uncooperative statement block in order to ensure that the compiler does not generate implicit task switches therein in order to prevent unwanted recursion. This is similar to the "do not preempt" flag employed by other schedulers such as in Sun Solaris [27].

In the beginning, the procedure makes use of two compiler-intrinsic functions called GETACTIVITY and GETFRAMEPOINTER which allow to query the current activity and the address of the current stack frame in a portable manner. In a second step, it prepares the given activity for the task switch by resetting its quantum to a default value and forwarding the index of the currently executing processor and the procedure arguments. Dynamic scheduling adaptation features like quantum stretching for example could be easily adopted by varying the default value for each task. The actual task switch is performed in the last step, where the context of the new activity is restored using the corresponding intrinsic procedures SETACTIVITY and SETFRAMEPOINTER. The only context information that is necessary to be restored in our case is the frame pointer, since every other piece of information is already stored on the stack. As the actual stack pointer and the program counter of the function caller are already pushed on the stack by the compiler upon entering the function, it suffices to store the address of the current stack activation frame. The stack pointer and the program counter are finally restored by returning from the procedure which pops the corresponding values from the stack automatically. Context switching is therefore as cheap as a standard function call.

3.2 Task Switch Finalizers

Figure 2 shows the procedure SWITCH which is implicitly called by the compiler. The scheduler currently supports a limited number of priorities and maintains

```
procedure SWITCH
   uncooperative
      current ← GETACTIVITY()
      activity ← SELECT(current→priority)
      if activity ≠ null then
         SWITCHTO(activity, ENQUEUESWITCH)
         FINALIZESWITCH()
      else
         current→quantum ← Default


procedure ENQUEUESWITCH(previous)
   uncooperative
      priority ← previous→priority
      ENQUEUE(previous, readyQueue[priority])
      if priority ≠ Idle then
         if INCREMENT(working) < Processors then
            RESUMEANYPROCESSOR()
```

Fig. 2. Algorithm for basic task scheduling

a global ready queue for each priority. Starting with the highest priority, the scheduler tries to select a task from the corresponding ready queue. If there is a task, the scheduler performs the actual switch to that task.

This simple scheduling mechanism is potentially executed on all processors at the same time. As discussed in Sect. 4, our queue implementation is lock-free and because of that, there is no need to protect this code from concurrent access. However, there is a subtle problem whenever an actual task switch happens. While a next task has already been selected and removed from a ready queue, the currently executing task still has to be put on the corresponding queue in order to be available for the subsequent task switch. If this is done prior to the actual task switch, there might be a race condition concerning the task descriptor. Another processor concurrently performing a task switch could remove the task from the queue and switch to it. The first processor that is still in the progress of task switching and the second one both operate in the context of the same task with disastrous consequences.

The solution to this problem are *task switch finalizers*, which are function pointers passed as argument to the SWITCH function. Task switch finalizers are always executed by the resumed task by calling the FINALIZESWITCH shown in Fig. 3 after returning from the task switch but before continuing its interrupted work. In this particular case, the task switch finalizer passed to the SWITCHTO function is called ENQUEUESWITCH as shown in Fig. 2. It basically just enqueues the suspended task into the corresponding ready queue and resumes any idling processor if necessary. Since this code is executed by the resumed task, it is now safe to enqueue the suspended task into the ready queue.

This technique can be extended in order to allow arbitrary operations to be executed on behalf of the previously executed task. The possibility of executing code after a task switch happened provides a certain entanglement of processes

procedure FINALIZESWITCH
  uncooperative
    current ← GETACTIVITY()
    current→finalizer(*current→previous, current→value*)

Fig. 3. Algorithm of a the task switch finalizer

and is extremely useful in this context and probably unique to cooperative multitasking. In addition, task switch finalizers are very important for implementing synchronization primitives like mutexes and monitors. In these cases, a task is not enqueued in a ready queue but rather in a queue associated with the primitive in order to dequeue it again whenever the primitive gets signaled. However, due to the non-blocking nature of their implementation, the condition why a task got enqueued might already have changed in-between checking the condition and enqueueing the task. Task switch finalizers allow to reevaluate this condition a second time after inserting the task into the queue in order to prevent lost wakeup calls. Task switch finalizers are represented as function pointers in order to provide a generic framework for implementing arbitrary synchronization primitives on top of our lock-free scheduler. They are not intended to be used by the application programmer.

3.3 Protection and Usability

The discussed system does not support protection mechanisms such as process isolation. We see and understand the point of protecting processes for general purpose operating systems. But apart from the fact that our work was primarily motivated by researcher's curiosity, we have also evidence of the commercial need for simple systems where process protection does not play the primary role. If we had to implement process protection for our system, we would try to support software isolated processes [13].

Porting our runtime system from one architecture to the next is very simple by design. Moreover, the process model of the scheduler can be supported on top of other operating systems where the offered threads play the role of virtual processors for a native machine implementation. Therefore the restriction to use the special compiler is, for such cases, only given on a per-application basis.

4   Unbounded Lock-Free Scheduler Queues

The several known implementations of unbounded lock-free FIFO queues, for example [23, 28], which have in common that they use separately allocated node data structures to store the actually enqueued elements in a singly linked list. A sentinel node at the beginning of the list eases the handling of empty queues.

Unbounded queues inevitably need to allocate new nodes to accommodate newly enqueued elements. It is this handling of the nodes of newly enqueued or dequeued elements that poses one of the major obstacles with unbounded lock-free queues. In a first approach, a new node is allocated every time a node is enqueued and deallocated as soon as the element is removed from the queue. The frequent allocations and deallocations constitute a significant overhead compared to the relatively simple ENQUEUE and DEQUEUE operations. To reduce the number of these clearly undesirable dynamic memory operations we have investigated some form of node reuse. The reuse of nodes, however, triggers the ABA problem.

4.1 The ABA Problem

The ABA problem describes a situation in lock-free algorithms where an update of a value goes unnoticed by a thread which as a consequence corrupts the lock-free data structure. Due to the explicit use of atomic operations for synchronization it is impossible to protect an update of the data structure involving several operations from concurrent access. Lock-free algorithms therefore first query and store a value of the global data structure, for example the tail node of a queue, and later compare the locally stored value with the global one to detect modifications by another thread. If values are reused, the same value may appear due to an operation on the data structure by another thread but go unnoticed by the original contender. It is important to note that the ABA problem also occurs when nodes are not explicitly reused because in a series of memory allocations and deallocations with a bounded amount of memory it is impossible to guarantee that all allocations return different starting addresses.

The ABA problem can be solved by using a double-word compare-and-swap (DCAS) operation which can atomically access and modify to separate values. The DCAS operation can be used to pair values with a version counter that is incremented with every modification of the value [18]. The limited support of DCAS on contemporary hardware limits the applicability of this solution. We would like to mention that employing pointer tagging is of limited value, particularly in a scheduler with a high traffic on queues. Even a significant number of bits for tagging does not solve the problem, not in theory and even not in practice as experiments revealed to us. We employ a different approach known as *hazard pointers*.

4.2 Hazard Pointers

Without any further precaution, any memory deallocation must be considered to render memory references of contending processes invalid. These references are generally known as *hazard pointers* [22]. If deallocated memory is reclaimed too early, any subsequent dereferencing of pointers to this memory region is unsafe and therefore called hazardous. Hazard pointers store the references of nodes that are about to be accessed by a thread; per thread up to two hazard pointers are required for the implementation of our queue. Hazard pointers solve the ABA problem but suffer from two problems: first, hazard pointers are associated with the thread accessing the lock-free queue and typically allocated in thread-local storage. Before deallocating a node, each thread must thus access and search the hazard pointers stored in the thread-local storage of other threads which is against all principles of distributed and parallel programming. Second, the space- and time-overhead of comparing all hazard pointers is linear in the number of participating threads. In the context of a task scheduler this is clearly not ideal: the more threads are active the longer the ENQUEUE and DEQUEUE operations during a task switch will take. Our contribution here is to make use of the guarantees provided by cooperative multitasking. By not releasing control of the processor core during context switches, the maximum number of active threads executing a task switch is bounded by the number of cores. We can thus associate the hazard pointers with the *cores* instead of the threads, thereby achieving a constant space- and time-overhead to search through the hazard pointers, independent of the number of currently active threads. In addition, this also allows us to store the hazard pointers in processor-local storage, thus eliminating the need for threads to access other threads' local storage.

4.3   Implementation

The basic data structure of a concurrent and unbounded lock-free queue is pre- sented in Fig. 4. The queue is implemented using a linked list of nodes. The very first node is called the HEAD and is always a dummy element whose sole purpose is to unify the operations on empty and non-empty lists. TAIL always references the last node in the list or one of its predecessors. This reference is intentionally allowed to lag behind because queue operations potentially modify head and tail nodes at the same time which cannot be done simultaneously using independent CAS operations.

The actual data of an element is represented by extensions of a separate data structure called ITEM. Users can enqueue elements of arbitrary values by extending this base type and using instantiations thereof as arguments for the corresponding procedure. An item is assumed to be either owned by the user or the queue and may not be enqueued twice.

The global data structure PROCESSORS stores the hazard pointers and two pooled nodes that are used to hold references to nodes that are not an element of any queue at the moment and may be reused by any processor. The guarantees of the cooperative scheduler (no context switches within an uncooperative block) limits the number of threads accessing the queue concurrently to N, the number of processors. The index of the processor core the contending thread is running on is used as the index into the PROCESSORS array. This constant-size global data structure simplifies the process of searching for hazard pointers and also yields constant-time complexity when searching for hazardous references.

Figure 5 shows the operations ACQUIRE and RELEASE which query the set of all hazard pointers in order to safely reuse pooled nodes from the global PROCESSORS array. As for all subsequent operations, the assumption is that the corresponding code is executed without any intervening task switches as indicated by the uncooperative statement block in lines 2 and 16 for example. The ACQUIRE operation checks if a node associated with an item is hazardous by comparing it against the complete set of hazard pointers. This operation returns

```
structure ITEM
    node: pointer to Node

structure NODE
    next: pointer to Node
    item: pointer to Item

structure QUEUE
    head: pointer to Node
    tail: pointer to Node

structure PROCESSOR
    hp₁: pointer to Node
    hp₂: pointer to Node
    pool₁: pointer to Node
    pool₂: pointer to Node

variable
    processors: array N of Processor
```

Fig. 4. Data structures and global variables of a lock-free queue for a system with N processors

either the same node if it is safe to be reused or it returns a pooled node if the latter is still potentially used by another processor. A return value of null indicates that there is no node available for reuse. Because the resulting node could be referenced by another processor, the reference has to be rechecked for all remaining processors. ACQUIRE must only be called for items that are owned by the calling process; the item and its associated node are therefore not part of any other queue. A potentially hazardous node is atomically exchanged against the value of the pooled node that corresponds to the hazard pointer of the processor in question. The set of pooled nodes always contains pairwise different entries, and because the node in question is also different from all pool entries there is at least one more node than nodes referenced by hazard pointers. As a consequence at most N exchanges are required until a node is found that is not referenced by any hazard pointer, that is, the loop always terminates in constant time and renders the whole operation wait-free. The RELEASE operation is called by users of the queue to deallocate an item. This operation simply reclaims either the node associated with the item or a previously pooled one if the former is hazardous. RELEASE calls Acquire and contains no loops; it is therefore also wait-free.

The lock-free ENQUEUE and DEQUEUE operations are shown in Fig. 6. The code is similar to the implementations of Valois [28] and Michael and Scott [22,23]. Lines 3–5 enable node reuse, and the handling of hazard pointers as described by Michael [22] are implemented by lines 9–12, 18, 23–30, 32–33, and 38–39. As stated above, in the absence of context switches during execution of these operations the ID of the currently executing processor core can be used

```
 1: procedure ACQUIRE(item)
 2:     uncooperative
 3:         node ← item→node
 4:         repeat
 5:             for all p ∈ processors do
 6:                 if node = NULL then
 7:                     break
 8:                 else if node = p.hp₁ then
 9:                     swap(node, p.pool₁)
10:                 else if node = p.hp₂ then
11:                     swap(node, p.pool₂)
12:             end for
13:         until no more swaps
14:         return node

15: procedure RELEASE(item)
16:     uncooperative
17:         node ← Acquire(item)
18:         if node ≠ NULL then
19:             deallocate(node)
```

Fig. 5. Wait-free acquire and release procedures for safe node reuse

as an index into the global PROCESSORS array. In addition, since each processor core accesses only its own elements in the global array, the hazard pointers do not have to be modified using atomic operations.

Another contribution regarding these algorithms is the improved handling of retired nodes at the end of the Dequeue operation. Michael adds all retired nodes into a thread-local list which is scanned for candidates to be reclaimed every once in a while. We associate the retired node with the item that is returned by the Dequeue operation. In case this item is appended to the same or another queue, the ENQUEUE operation will first try to reuse the node by calling the ACQUIRE operation on the item. The node is therefore guaranteed to be *reused* and the algorithm does not need to acquire more nodes than items in the queues. As a consequence, the sum of all allocated nodes is bounded by the number of all elements in all used queues plus $2N$ nodes which are potentially pooled.

4.4   Use in the Scheduler

The unbounded lock-free queue as shown in this section is used by the cooperative scheduler. A thread is implemented as an extension of a queue ITEM. When a new thread is created, a queue NODE is allocated along with the task control structure. During a task switch, the currently executing thread is enqueued in a queue and another one is dequeued. Our approach ensures that this operation is fast and only in exceptional cases needs to allocate a new node, namely in the unlikely event that all pooled nodes are currently hazardous. As shown above, the number of additionally allocated nodes is limited to $2N$. These additional

```
 1: procedure ENQUEUE(item, queue)
 2:     uncooperative
 3:         node ← Acquire(item)
 4:         if node = NULL then
 5:             node ← allocate()
 6:         node→item ← item
 7:         node→next ← NULL
 8:         repeat
 9:             repeat
10:                 tail ← queue→tail
11:                 processors[current].hp₁ ← tail
12:             until tail = queue→tail
13:             next ← tail→next
14:             if next ≠ NULL then
15:                 CAS(queue→tail, tail, next)
16:                 continue
17:         until CAS(tail→next, NULL, node) = NULL
18:         processors[current].hp₁ ← NULL
19:         CAS(queue→tail, tail, node)

20: procedure DEQUEUE(queue)
21:     uncooperative
22:         repeat
23:             repeat
24:                 head ← queue→head
25:                 processors[current].hp₁ ← head
26:             until head = queue→head
27:             repeat
28:                 next ← head→next
29:                 processors[current].hp₂ ← next
30:             until next = head→next
31:             if next = NULL then
32:                 processors[current].hp₁ ← NULL
33:                 processors[current].hp₂ ← NULL
34:                 return NULL
35:             CAS(queue→tail, head, next)
36:             item ← next→item
37:         until CAS(queue→head, head, next) = head
38:         processors[current].hp₁ ← NULL
39:         processors[current].hp₂ ← NULL
40:         item→node ← first
41:         return item
```

Fig. 6. Lock-free enqueue and dequeue operations with hazard pointers and node reuse

nodes are accumulated over the course of the whole runtime of the scheduler and their allocation overhead is therefore compensated.

The total number of allocated nodes is thus at least T and at most $T + 2N$ where T and N denote the number of active threads and the number of available processor cores, respectively. In other words, the presented scheduler ensures that the number of allocations does not depend on the number of task switches.

In the current implementation, no private run queues with load-balancing is used. All threads are stored in a number of global scheduler queues to provide several levels of priority. Scheduling of ready-to-run threads of identical priority is performed in a round robin fashion.

5   Performance Metrics and Experimental Setup

The unbounded lock-free scheduler only constitutes one part of a lock-free runtime that also features a lock-free garbage collector. Our main motivation for the lock-free runtime is to avoid the difficulties associated with blocking synchronization and interrupt-based preemptive multitasking. We therefore compare the scheduler and its supporting routines in terms of simplicity and portability. Simplicity and portability are not exact measures, and at the end of the day, raw performance still matters.

Although our work is designed to be portable across several hardware architectures, we do not intend to contrast its performance on different architectures. There are several mechanisms like caching, branch prediction, and out-of-order execution that increase the performance but are typically implemented directly in hardware and are therefore completely transparent to the programmer [4]. Even though they do speed up the execution of code in general, they often render the performance of processors as well as code non-deterministic at the same time. In order to be able to minimize their effect and to concentrate on the performance of the actual code, we conducted all of our experiments on identical hardware. However, this approach makes it difficult to reason about the absolute execution time of our algorithms in general and to compare it to performance numbers presented in other work. Instead, our focus is on relating our work to existing solutions when executed under high contention.

All our experiments to measure performance have been conducted on an x86 machine running with 128 GB main memory and four AMD Opteron 6380 G34 processors each featuring 16 cores and running in 64-bit mode at 2.5 GHz. This setup provides a total of 64 logical processors and allows us to evaluate and compare the performance of our system under high contention. Time is provided by a built-in high precision hardware timer which has an accuracy of at least 10 MHz.

The experiments consist of several concurrent programs designed to let us compare the performance of the schedulers and synchronization primitives under heavy load. We conducted each experiment on three different 64-bit platforms, namely Windows Server 2008 R2, a Linux based system with kernel version 2.6.32, and our native runtime that employs our lock-free scheduler. All programs have been compiled using the same compiler in order to execute the same machine code on each platform. If not stated otherwise, the only difference of the generated machine code lies within the libraries used to create and synchronize threads. On Windows we use the API functions for creating threads and critical sections whereas on Linux we call the PThreads library with the corresponding functions. On our native kernel we use the corresponding synchronization primitives provided by our lock-free scheduler.

The benchmarks comprise of micro-benchmarks and real-world programs. The micro-benchmarks are crafted after other benchmarks used in related work [16,17,26]. The micro-benchmarks measure the time to create a certain number of threads, the overhead of a context switch, and local and global locking performance.

The real-world applications were taken from an existing test suite for concurrent programs [2]. The benchmarks include of the following full-blown programs: [16,17,26].

City. A simulation of a city that has N houses. Each house has its own thread that continuously consumes K units of electricity from a power plant and K units of water from a river. The power plant is a concurrent thread which can store up to C units of energy produced from water.

Eratosthenes. This programs employs the Sieve of Eratosthenes in order to computes all prime numbers within the range $1..N$. Each sieve is a concurrent thread that removes the multiples of one prime number.

Mandelbrot. This program computes Mandelbrot fractal in parallel by partitioning a plane of C points into N parts. The number of iterations per point is limited by K.

Matrix. This program distributes the multiplication of a matrix with size N to a set of M threads which all run in parallel and are not dependent on each other.

News. A simulation of a broadcasting agency having N customers and M reporters. Each reporter publishes K different news messages which are read concurrently by all customers.

ProducerConsumer. A simulation of N pairs of producers and consumers which all use a single global buffer of size C in order to exchange K messages in total.

TokenRing. This program simulates a game with N players designed as concurrent thread which pass a token K times around.

6   Experimental Results

We compare our cooperative scheduler against two state-of-the-art contenders on shared-memory multiprocessors, namely the Linux and Windows Server operating systems. In all graphs and tables, `Native` refers to our cooperative runtime, and `Linux` and `Windows` refer to the respective server operating systems.

Microbenchmarks. The first microbenchmark measures the time required to create, schedule, and destroy a thread for the three platforms. The benchmark creates between one and 10'000'000 threads consisting of an empty thread body. The effect is that the threads are created, enqueued in the scheduler queue, terminated when scheduled for the first time, and then destructed. The benchmark

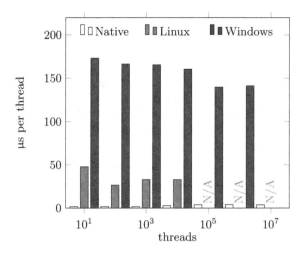

Fig. 7. Thread creation times.

ends when the last thread has been stopped. Figure 7 shows the average time per thread for the three systems. Thanks to the extremely light-weight implementation of threads, the lock-free runtime clearly outperforms the other two operating systems. The figure also reveals that our runtime manages to create up to 10 million threads without a significant performance degradation, while the benchmark fails for Linux (at 100'000) and Windows (at 1'000'000 threads). The fact that our runtime can manage much more threads than Linux and Windows is due to the usage of micro stacks with a granularity finer than a page size.

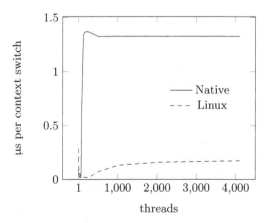

Fig. 8. Context switch time.

Figure 8 shows the average time required to complete a context switch for Native and Linux. In this benchmark, the compiler generates no implicit calls to the scheduler. Instead, the threads contain a loop that consists only of an explicit call to the scheduler. We observe that Native preforms much worse than Linux. Since the lock-free scheduler contains only global ready queues for the threads, the contention on the queue caused by the atomic CAS operations of the lock-free algorithm is severe. Note, however, that the context switching time quickly stabilizes and then remains constant.

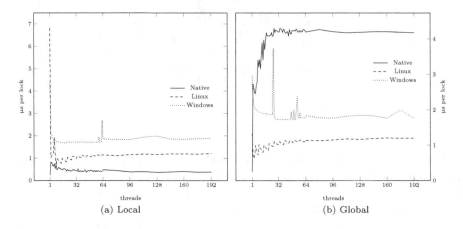

Fig. 9. Locking.

In Fig. 9, the performance of local and global locks is shown. In the former case, each thread repeatedly locks and unlocks a dedicated lock. In the latter case, all threads compete to lock and unlock the same lock. The local lock benchmark reveals that – while the differences are minimal – our runtime implements the most efficient locks; this may be thanks to less sophisticated book-keeping and statistics. In the global lock benchmark on the other hand, the relative cost per lock in our runtime system increases which we attribute to the high memory contention surrounding the shared lock.

Real-world applications. A matrix multiplication benchmark is used to measure speedup in dependence of the number of threads (Fig. 10(a)). The matrix multiplication is not optimized for good cache performance; the individual threads each compute one or several, but separate rows of the result matrix. In this benchmark, we compare Linux and Windows against our runtime system. All platforms show the typical close-to-linear speedup until all logical cores are fully utilized. For slightly more threads than available cores, we observe that the relative speedup drops. This is caused by the comparatively long scheduling epochs or, in other words, uneven progress of the threads. As soon as more threads are available, the amount of work per thread is reduced and the speedup recovers. The absolute total run-time of

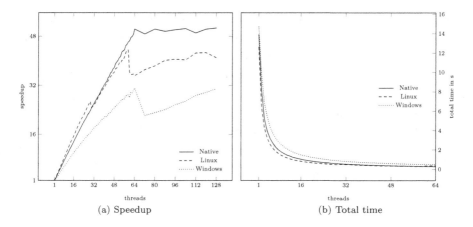

(a) Speedup   (b) Total time

Fig. 10. Matrix multiplication.

the matrix multiplication for the different platforms is shown in Fig. 10(b). We observe that at one thread the differences between the platforms are the most significant, ranging from 12.5 s (Linux) to 14.7 s (Native). This is caused by the different initialization of the memory system. Our native runtime does not enable any special performance enhancing measures; Linux seems most mature in this respect. The overall difference between our system and the best performing system, Linux in this case, is caused by the overhead of the check of the quantum and call to the scheduler inserted by our compiler. The compiler does not (yet) contain any optimizations; we expect that gap to vanish almost completely with an optimizing compiler. With more threads, this overhead becomes less of an issue since the limiting factor is not the raw computational power but the memory system.

Table 1. Runtime comparison between the cooperative lock-free scheduler, denoted Native, and the Linux and Windows kernels.

Benchmark	Native	Linux	Windows
City ($N = 1000, K = 10, C = 100$)	61 ms	63 ms	138 ms
Eratosthenes ($N = 10000$)	3'629 ms	4'750 ms	6'347 ms
Mandelbrot ($N = 100, C = 2000, K = 5000$)	4'066 ms	5'287 ms	5'040 ms
News ($N = 1000, M = 10, K = 10$)	1'260 ms	374 ms	280 ms
Producer ($N = 1, C = 10, K = 10000$)	1'382 ms	269 ms	225 ms
Producer ($N = 64, C = 10, K = 10000$)	54'495 ms	105'086 ms	31'032 ms
Token Ring ($N = 1000, K = 1000$)	4'506 ms	15'672 ms	8'759 ms

Table 1, finally, compares the runtime of various real-world benchmarks on the different platforms. City perform comparably on Linux and our system but runs twice as long on Windows. `Eratosthenes` and `Mandelbrot` show a similar result in favor of our runtime system. `News` contains a tight innermost loop and suffers from the overhead of the implicit calls to the cooperative scheduler. Also here we expect the performance gap to be reduced with an optimizing compiler. In the case of `Producer` with N = 1, only one thread locks the shared resource. Linux and Windows seem to detect and optimize for this case whereas our runtime is not optimized. `Producer` (N = 64), and `Token Ring` are very lock-intensive; the fast locks and light-weight thread implementation provides a significant advantage in comparison to `Linux`.

Overall, the results from microbenchmarks and real-world applications show that the lock-free cooperative scheduler and its runtime perform surprisingly well over a wide range of performance measures compared to Linux and Windows; and this despite (or thanks to) its simple design.

7   Conclusion and Future Work

In this paper we demonstrated that implicit, compiler-supported cooperative multitasking can be ideally combined with lock-free programming in order to implement a lightweight, efficient lock-free scheduler. Our key contributions are

1. The observation that the number of processes executing in uncooperative blocks is limited by the number of cores. This implies that thread-local storage conventionally used for storing hazard-pointers can be replaced by processor-local storage, making a highly efficient solution of the ABA problem feasible.
2. A very efficient implementation of a lock-free queue with node-reuse.
3. The newly introduced task switch finalizers: task switch finalizers are an elegant way to deal in a scheduler with the omnipresent challenge of lock-free programming, namely the fact that in principle at any point in time one process can invalidate the data of another.
4. The design and implementation of a simple, lightweight, reliable and portable scheduler.

We compared our implementation of the runtime kernel with that of two contemporary general purpose operating systems. A qualitative comparison, code complexity measured in lines of code, indicates the extreme simplicity of the discussed scheduler in comparison to other approaches.

Runtime comparisons of real-world programs and Micro-benchmarks showed overall comparable performance for the three systems. The lock-free scheduler outperforms partially where expected, namely for thread creation time and locking. The relatively poor result with regards to context switch times can be explained with the very frequent use of locking instructions.

Of course our approach has not only advantages. Cooperative scheduling comes with the price that a special compiler has to be used or a compiler has to be adapted in order to support the implicit scheduling. Moreover, there is computing time wasted for something that can in principle be done in hardware. However, we could not really observe a considerable overhead by the quantum checking code. In any case this could be improved by compiler optimizations and a proper register allocator. All significant overheads that we observed could basically explained with heavy use of locking instructions. Ideally, dedicated hardware would support cooperative multitasking with a managed instruction counter and a procedure that would be called when the counter reaches zero. Quite similar to timer interrupts but only at defined points in the code in order to support synchronous behavior.

Beyond the scope of this paper are our lock-free implementation of remaining features of a complete runtime kernel including process synchronization features such as mutexes, semaphores and monitors and a garbage collector.

The compiler used for this work was written from scratch and does not yet contain an optimizing phase. The compiler could be equipped with optimizations that remove a considerable portion of the quantum checks, making the scheduler coarser grained overall. At the moment tiny loops imply a huge number of quantum checks that could so be avoided.

The biggest obstacle for an efficient implementation of lock-free data structures is the CAS instruction that has to be executed at each access to a shared data structure. Such locked operations are known for their slowness due to the cross-core synchronization, already with a limited number of cores. Usage of such operations is thus particularly prohibitive in a scheduler when extremely short context switching times are pursued. Therefore it would be interesting to adopt processor-local ready queues for the scheduler and perform – lock-free – load balancing between cores only now and then. A dramatic speed increase in particular for context switches is expected.

Acknowledgments. This work was supported, in part, by grant IZKSZ2_162084 from the Swiss National Science Foundation, by BK21 Plus for Pioneers in Innovative Computing (Dept. of Computer Science and Engineering, SNU) funded by the National Research Foundation (NRF) of Korea (Grant 21A20151113068), the Basic Science Research Program through NRF funded by the Ministry of Science, ICT & Future Planning (Grant NRF-2015K1A3A1A14021288), and by the Promising-Pioneering Researcher Program through Seoul National University in 2015. ICT at Seoul National University provided research facilities for this study.

References

1. Advanced Micro Devices, Inc. AMD64 Architecture Programmer's Manual Volume 2: System Programming, May 2013. Revision 3.23
2. Bläser, L.: A component language for pointer-free concurrent programming and its application to simulation. PhD thesis, ETH Zrich (2007)
3. Conway, M.E.: Design of a separable transition-diagram compiler. Commun. ACM **6**(7), 396–408 (1963)
4. Fog, A.: The Microarchitecture of Intel. Technical University of Denmark, AMD and VIA CPUs (2014)
5. Greenwald, M., Cheriton, D.: The synergy between non-blocking synchronization and operating system structure. In: Second Symposium on Operating Systems Design and Implementation, OSDI 1996 (1996)

6. Herlihy, M.: A methodology for implementing highly concurrent data structures. In: Proceedings of the Second ACM SIGPLAN Symposium on Principles & Practice of Parallel Programming, PPOPP 1990 (1990)
7. Herlihy, M.: Wait-free synchronization. ACM Trans. Program. Lang. Syst. **13**(1), 124–149 (1991)
8. Herlihy, M., Luchangco, V., Martin, P., Moir, M.: Dynamic sized lockfree, data structures. Technical report (2002)
9. Herlihy, M., Luchangco, V., Moir, M.: The repeat offender problem: a mechanism for supporting dynamic-sized, lock-free data structures. In: Malkhi, D. (ed.) DISC 2002. LNCS, vol. 2508, pp. 339–353. Springer, Heidelberg (2002). doi:10.1007/3-540-36108-1_23
10. Herlihy, M., Luchangco, V., Moir, M.: Obstruction-free synchronization: double-ended queues as an example. In: Proceedings of the 23rd International Conference on Distributed Computing Systems, ICDCS 2003 (2003)
11. Herlihy, M., Shavit, N.: The Art of Multiprocessor Programming. Morgan Kaufmann Elsevier Science (2008)
12. Hohmuth, M., Härtig, H.: Pragmatic nonblocking synchronization for realtime systems. In: Proceedings of the 2001 USENIX Annual Technical Conference, USENIX 2001 (2001)
13. Hunt, G.C., Larus, J.R.: Singularity: rethinking the software stack. SIGOPS Oper. Syst. Rev. **41**(2), 37–49 (2007)
14. Hwang, K., Briggs, F.A.: Computer Architecture and Parallel Processing. McGraw-Hill, New York (1984)
15. IBM Corporation. IBM System/370 Extended Architecture Principles of Operation. Publication Number SA22-7085-0 (1983)
16. Joukov, N., Iyer, R., Traeger, A., Wright, C.P., Zadok, E.: Versatile, portable, and efficient OS profiling via latency analysis. In: Proceedings of the Twentieth ACM Symposium on Operating Systems Principles, SOSP 2005, pp. 1–14. ACM, New York (2005)
17. Kulkarni, A., Lumsdaine, A., Lang, M., Ionkov, L.: Optimizing latency and throughput for spawning processes on massively multicore processors. In: Proceedings of the 2nd International Workshop on Runtime and Operating Systems for Supercomputers, ROSS 2012, pp. 6:1–6:7. ACM, New York (2012)
18. Martin, P., Moir, M., Steele, G.: Dcas-based concurrent deques supporting bulk allocation. Technical report, Sun Microsystems Laboratories (2002)
19. Massalin, H., Pu, C.: A lock-free multiprocessor OS kernel. Technical report, Department of Computer Science, Columbia University (1991)
20. Mellor-Crummey, J.M., LeBlanc, T.J.: A software instruction counter. In: Proceedings of the Third International Conference on Architectural Support for Programming Languages and Operating Systems, ASPLOS III, pp. 78–86. ACM, New York (1989)
21. Mellor-Crummey, J.M.: Concurrent queues: practical fetch-and-ϕ algorithms. Technical report 229, Computer Science Deptartement, University of Rochester (1987)
22. Michael, M.M.: Hazard pointers: safe memory reclamation for lock-free objects. IEEE Trans. Parallel Distrib. Syst. **15**(6), 491–504 (2004)
23. Michael, M.M., Scott, M.L.: Simple, fast, and practical non-blocking and blocking concurrent queue algorithms. In: Proceedings of the Fifteenth Annual ACM Symposium on Principles of Distributed Computing, PODC 1996 (1996)
24. Molnar, I.: Modular scheduler core and completely fair scheduler [CFS] (1997). http://lwn.net/Articles/230501/

25. Moura, A.L.D., Ierusalimschy, R.: Revisiting coroutines. ACM Trans. Program. Lang. Syst. **31**(2), 6:1–6:31 (2009)
26. Muller, P.J.: The active object system design and multiprocessor implementation. Ph.d. thesis, Swiss Federal Institute of Technology Zurich (ETH Zurich) (2002)
27. Sun Microsystems. Multithreading in the Solaris(TM) Operating Environment (2002)
28. Valois, J.D.: Implementing lock-free queues. In: Proceedings of the Seventh International Conference on Parallel and Distributed Computing Systems, PDCS 1994 (1994)
29. Wirth, N.: The programming language Oberon. Softw. Pract. Exp. **18**(7), 671–690 (1988)

Scheduling for Better Energy Efficiency on Many-Core Chips

Chanseok Kang, Seungyul Lee, Yong-Jun Lee, Jaejin Lee,
and Bernhard Egger$^{(\boxtimes)}$

Department of Computer Science and Engineering,
Seoul National University, Seoul, Korea
{chanseok,seungyul,yongjun,jaejin,bernhard}@csap.snu.ac.kr

Abstract. Many-core chips are especially attractive for data center operators providing cloud computing service models. With the advance of many-core chips in such environments energy-conscious scheduling of independent processes or operating systems (OSes) is gaining importance. An important research question is how the scheduler of such a system should assign the cores to the OSes in order to achieve a better energy utilization. In this paper, we demonstrate that many-core chips offer new opportunities for extremely light-weight migration of independent processes (or OSes) running bare-metal on the many-core chip. We then show how this intra-chip migration can be utilized to achieve a better performance per watt ratio by implementing a hierarchical power-management scheme on top of dynamic voltage and frequency scaling (DVFS). We have implemented and tested the proposed techniques on the Intel Single Chip Cloud Computer (SCC). Combining migration with DVFS we achieve, on average, a 25–35% better performance per watt over a DVFS-only solution.

Keywords: Scheduling · Process migration · DVFS · Performance per watt

1 Introduction

The recent trend to integrate more and more cores onto a single chip, so called chip multiprocessors or CMPs [2,19], has led to chip-level power and thermal constraints becoming one of the primary design constraints and performance limiters [1]. A higher power consumption not only leads to increased energy cost but the higher die temperatures adversely affect chip reliability and lifetime.

Dynamic voltage and frequency scaling (DVFS) allows to lower the operating voltage and frequency of a core to meet its required performance. For current multi-core systems, each core can be controlled individually, however, for CMPs the required logic for individually controlling the voltage and frequency for each core is becoming too costly [12]. Cores are logically clustered into voltage and frequency domains that share a common setting [8,21]. Researchers have proposed numerous techniques for individually-controllable and clustered cores [4,5,10,20].

© Springer International Publishing AG 2017
N. Desai and W. Cirne (Eds.): JSSPP 2015/2016, LNCS 10353, pp. 46–68, 2017.
DOI: 10.1007/978-3-319-61756-5_3

With the ongoing server consolidation, an ever increasing number of cores per chip, and the overhead associated with maintaining a coherent global shared memory, it is more and more common to run several completely independent (sequential or parallel) applications alongside each other on the same physical many-core chip without a common underlying OS [3]. Instead, the independent OSes or applications have full control over the assigned hardware resources and are responsible for scheduling the work on the assigned cores and managing the allocated physical memory. Hosting providers, for example, providing access to bare-metal hosts can execute independent OSes on the different physical cores of a CMP. Existing power management solutions for CMPs are built for a single operating system kernel managing all running (groups of) tasks. To the best of our knowledge, no solutions for CMPs running independent OSes have been proposed.

In this paper, we propose an extremely light-weight OS migration method for independent OSes running on CMPs and show that the scheduler can exploit this OS migration to significantly increase the effectiveness of DVFS policies for CMPs. We have implemented an energy-aware scheduler exploiting light-weight OS migration in the Linux operating system running on the Intel Single-chip Cloud Computer (SCC) [9]. Compared to a state-of-the-art hierarchical power management with DVFS but no OS migration [10], the proposed approach achieves 25–35% better performance per watt ratio over a wide range of workloads.

The remainder of this paper is organized as follows: Sect. 2 presents related work. Section 3 introduces the many-core architecture. Section 4 describes the implementation of the light-weight OS migration in detail. In Sect. 5, the integration of OS migration into an energy-aware scheduler with hierarchical power management for many-core chips is discussed. Section 6 presents the experimental setup, and Sect. 7 discusses the experimental results. Section 8, finally, concludes the paper.

2   Related Work

There is a significant amount of work focusing on the design and implementation of power management techniques for CMPs. Our focus lies on independent OSes executing directly on the hardware in a space-shared manner on the CMP and on exploiting the hardware capabilities of existing and future many-core systems with regard to coarse-grained voltage and/or frequency domains.

One line of related work considers heterogeneous CMP designs in order to consume less power with no or minimal performance loss. Kumar et al. [13] propose heterogeneous CMPs composed of cores supporting the identical ISA but consuming more or less energy depending on the core architecture. Ghiasi [7] proposes CMPs with cores executing at different frequencies. Both works show that such systems offer improved power consumption and thermal management. Our work differs in that our approach modifies the voltage/frequency of cores dynamically, without being bound to certain hardware heterogeneity.

Another line of research has focused on exploiting idle periods. Meisner et al. propose PowerNap [16] and DreamWeaver [17]. Both assume hardware support for quick transitions between on- and off-states; the latter work batches wake-up events to increase the sleep periods. Our work is orthogonal to such approaches, with one limitation: applying DVFS may lead to a longer execution time which in turn reduces the potential to sleep.

A number of researchers have proposed heterogeneous power management techniques for CMPs [5,10,11,14,15,18,20]. Li et al. [14] provide an analytical model and experiments to show to what extent parallel applications can be parallelized given a power-budget. Isci et al. [11] apply different DVFS policies under a given power budget and show that their best policy performs almost as good as an oracle policy having limited knowledge of the future. Meng et al. [18] proposes an adaptive power saving strategy that adheres to a global chip-wide power budget through run-time adaptation of configurable processor cores. Rangan et al. [20] propose ThreadMotion, a technique that moves threads around in order to improve power consumption. Their approach requires hardware support to quickly move threads from one core to another. Our approach is similar, but can be implemented on available CMPs without extra hardware support. Cai et al. [5] propose to identify critical threads by measuring the slack of threads at fork-join barriers; non-critical threads can then be executed at reduced speed. In our work, we focus on independent OSes as opposed to threads within parallel applications. Ma et al. [15] propose a scalable solution aiming at a mixed group of single-threaded and multi-threaded applications. Unlike our approach with is best-effort, they aim at minimal performance reduction while maintaining a global power budget.

The work most closely related to ours is a hierarchical power manager for the Intel SCC presented by Ioannou et al. [10]. We show that by adding OS migration a significantly improved performance/watt ratio can be achieved.

3   Many-Core Architectures

Many-core architectures exhibit a number of typical characteristics [22] in order to effectively manage and utilize the large number of cores. In particular, many-core architectures feature an interconnection network to enable on-chip communication between the cores. This network is also employed when accessing shared resources such as memory. Atomic operations are provided to enable efficient synchronization of multiple cores.

The technique described in this paper does not require any special hardware support and is thus in principle applicable to any many-core architecture. We provide a working implementation on Intel's Single-Chip-Cloud Computer (SCC) [9] as a proof of concept. We leverage the SCC's two-level address translation (see next section) to implement zero-copy OS migration, but the same effect can be achieved – although with some additional overhead – by directly modifying a core's memory translation tables. The remainder of this section describes the architecture of the Intel SCC in more detail.

3.1   The Intel Single-Chip Cloud Computer

Architecture Overview. The Intel SCC is a concept vehicle created by Intel Labs as a platform for many-core research. It consists of 48 independent cores interconnected by a routed network-on-chip (NoC). The cores are Intel P54C Pentium® cores with bigger L1 caches (16 KB) and additional support for managing the on-chip scratchpad memory, the so-called *message passing buffer* (MPB). The Intel SCC provides no cache coherence for the core-local L1 and L2 caches. Always two cores are grouped together to form a *tile*; the 24 tiles are organized on a 6 by 4 grid. Four memory controllers in the four corners of the chip provide access to up to 64 GBs of memory. A system FPGA provides the interface between the CMP and the management-console PC (MCPC). Figure 1 shows the SCC block diagram. For better readability, not all cores are shown.

Memory Addressing. Each core provides the standard virtual-physical memory translation; all addresses leaving the core are 32-bit physical addresses. 32-bit addresses are not wide enough to address the entire 64-GB address range; to allow access to a total of 4 GB of memory located somewhere in the SCC's 64 GB address space, an additional address translation takes place.

The address translation from core (physical) addresses to system addresses is provided by a core-local lookup table (LUT). Each LUT has 256 entries and is indexed by the top eight bits of the 32-bit core address. Without going into much detail, a LUT entry contains an 8-bit destination ID `destID` designating one of the four memory controllers (MC), and 10 address bits that are prepended to the remaining 24 bits of the core address to form a 34-bit address. One LUT entry thus maps 16 GB of memory. Together with the memory controller designation, this translation allows to access the entire 64 GB memory space of the SCC.

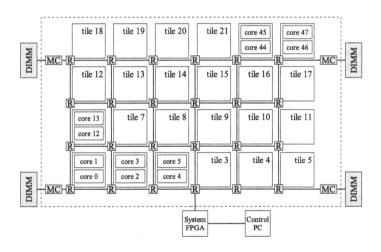

Fig. 1. Intel SCC block diagram

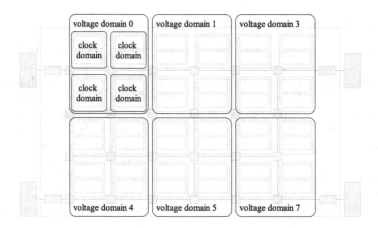

Fig. 2. Voltage and clock domains on the Intel SCC

DVFS Capabilities. The SCC provides voltage and frequency control over the cores and the NoC. The frequency can be controlled *per tile*, that is, the two cores located on the same time always run at the same frequency and constitute a clock domain (CD). The voltage can be regulated for a group of four tiles, i.e., a voltage domain (VD) comprises a total of eight cores. Figure 2 illustrates the clock and voltage domains on the SCC. Voltage domains 2 and 6 are not shown in the figure; they are logically the same and regulate the NoC and the system interface.

Voltage and frequency are controlled and queried through registers. Each tile has specific registers to set/read the tile's frequency; voltage changes are similarly controlled through a register interface. Frequency changes happen almost immediately, however, measurements on the SCC revealed that voltage changes may take up to 100ms to complete (this value was obtained by comparing the progress of two cores, one control core running on a unchanged voltage domain, and one running on the domain whose voltage was changed). In addition, voltage change requests can only affect a single domain; requests for several domains must be serialized.

The SCC supports seven different supply voltage levels, however, only four are of practical interest: $1.1\,V$ to run at a frequency of $800\,\text{MHz}$, $0.9\,V$ to run at $533\,\text{MHz}$, $0.8\,V$ for $400\,\text{MHz}$, and $0.7\,V$ for frequencies below $400\,\text{MHz}$. The frequency is set by writing a divisor between 2 and 16 for the $1600\,\text{MHz}$ clock resulting in core frequencies from 800 to $100\,\text{MHz}$.

Power Measurement. The SCC provides a number of voltage and ampere meters on-board. The total power consumed by the SCC chip is obtained by multiplying the (constant) supply voltage with the supply current for the entire SCC chip. The power consumption of individual voltage domains cannot be computed because only the per-domain supply voltage is available but not the current consumed by the domain. We thus always report the total chip power in our experiments in Sect. 7.

The sensors and meters can be read by the management console via telnet from the system FPGA or by directly querying the system FPGA from a core in the SCC. We chose the latter approach because of its comparatively low overhead.

4   Zero-Copy OS Migration

In order to optimize the execution of workloads on a CMP towards a specific goal, the scheduler is often required to move workloads from one core to another. Such goals include but are not limited to even heat dissipation and adherence to a given power budget. In the first case, busy and idle workloads are distributed evenly over the cores of the CMP to even out the sources of the heat generation. The second case is motivated by the need to cluster workloads with similar performance requirements in voltage and/or frequency domains to achieve optimal results when applying DVFS.

A workload in this context can refer to anything from a thread of a parallel application to an entire operating system running exclusively on a core. Clustering threads or processes in the presence of an operating system with shared memory amounts to re-scheduling them on a different core is straightforward. For applications exhibiting periodic behavior and fork-join parallel programs, special techniques allow accurate estimation of the expected performance requirements and thus more aggressive DVFS policies [10,15,20].

For independent programs (such as a Linux kernel) running bare-metal on the assigned cores, migration is not trivial. In this section, we describe the technical details on how such kernels can be migrated from one core to another, the scheduler's *migration policies* are discussed in the section on power management (Sect. 5).

4.1   Cooperative vs. Transparent Guest OS Migration

Moving an OS from one physical core to another can be implemented with or without cooperation of the migrated OS. In a co-operative setting, the OS enters a safe state in which it is moved to the newly assigned core and then resumed. The OS itself takes care of changed memory mappings and the like. Transparent OS migration, on the other hand, happens without any interaction or knowledge of the migrated OS.

The main caveat is how to deal with the volatile state, i.e., the assigned memory of the workload and values currently held in registers inside the CPU core. If the CMP implements a global shared address space, the assigned memory does not have to be moved physically; the same physical addresses are still valid on the new core. Since such designs cannot provide total isolation of independently running workloads, CMPs often implement an additional step in the memory translation process from physical to system addresses. The physical-to-system address translation operates in almost the same way virtual-to-physical translation works: instead of per-process page tables, the CMP provides per-core translation tables indexed by the higher part of the core address (see Sect. 3.1). We exploit this additional translation step to realize an extremely light-weight migration of OSes.

The volatile state of the OS also includes the data values kept in the registers of the CPU core. Similar to a preemptive task switch, these register values need to be saved on the source core and restored on the destination core. If the CMP provides the means to read and write the register file of physical cores, migration can be implemented without any cooperation from the migrated OS. To this day, however, no many-core chip we are aware of provides such a feature. As a consequence, a minimal amount of cooperation from the OS is necessary.

The following sections describe the necessary steps and the implementation on the SCC in more detail.

4.2   Migration Steps

In the proposed implementation, zero-copy OS migration is orchestrated by a migration manager that is part of the global scheduler. The steps are illustrated in Fig. 3. It reveals that migration is, in fact, rather a *circular swap* of two (or more) OSes rather than a unidirectional migration from one core to another. Since we require a minimal amount of cooperation from all involved cores, we assume that a cooperative OS runs on all (including the currently unused) cores. The migration signal is sent by the migration manager in form of an interrupt to the affected cores. This interrupt is handled by the cooperative OS' interrupt handler which saves the necessary registers into a per-core designated memory area. After all registers have been saved, the affected cores signal completion to the migration manager and completely flush their caches. The migration manager

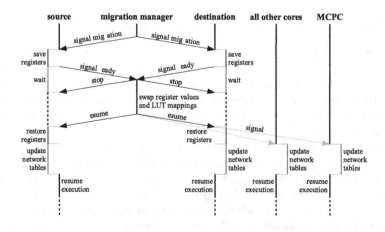

Fig. 3. OS migration steps

then stops all cores involved in the migration by gating their clock, and swaps the cores' register values and the memory mappings. Next, the migration manager signals completion of the migration by resuming the clock on the migrated cores. The cores proceed by restoring the (new) register values from memory, exit the interrupt handler and resume operation. In addition, all cores, including the MCPC need to update internal network routing tables to reflect the new locations of the cores (see Sect. 4.4 below).

4.3 Migrating Volatile State

The migrated cores save/restore register values to a designated memory area in a custom interrupt handler. In principle, exactly the same registers need to be saved/restored as when performing a context switch in a preemptive multitasking system. After saving the registers, the migrated cores flush all caches and enter a busy loop. It is impossible to flush a core's cache externally; as a consequence the code of the busy loop will reside in a migrated core's instruction cache. In addition, it is impossible to set the program counter immediately after resuming the clock since we do not know what instruction of the busy loop the core was executing when the clock was gated. However, we can ignore this technical difficulty by assuring that the busy loop, including the code to save and restore the registers, is located at identical virtual addresses on all migrated cores. Since we currently only use a modified version of the sccLinux OS, this condition is always met. If several different OSes are involved in migration, it may be necessary to turn off virtual-to-physical memory translation temporarily and re-enable it once the new page table base register has been set.

4.4 Networking

Cores on a CMP communicate with other cores through the NoC. IP addresses are translated to the destination core's x/y coordinates on the grid in the data link layer of the network stack. Migrated OSes keep their IP addresses, hence additional steps are necessary to update the IP to link-layer translation tables in all cores on the chip.

On the SCC, two separate networks exist: one network for on-chip networking, and a subnet for communication with the MCPC. Data packets sent on-chip from one core to another are first stored in the MPB (see Sect. 3.1) on the sender side. The sender then signals the receiver with an interrupt, and the receiver fetches the message data directly from the sender's buffer. For migrated cores the location of their MPB remains unchanged; storing/retrieving network packets from the buffer is thus unaffected by migration. However, the target core of a network interrupt is identified by its physical core ID which corresponds to the x/y-coordinates of the core on the grid. In the original sccLinux the interrupt target ID is computed from the core ID. In order to support migration, a table containing the IP-to-coreID mappings is added and kept up-to-date by each core. After each migration, the migration manager thus notifies *all* cores about the changes to the IP-to-coreID mapping table.

A very similar data structure is maintained by the MCPC to route data packets from external sources to each of the individual cores. The migration manager notifies the MCPC through the system interface about migrations taking place such that the MCPC can keep an up-to-date list of IP-to-coreIDs.

These two simple modifications are enough to keep networking, including open connections, alive across migrations. DMA is not supported, and no other devices exist on the SCC; input/output, including access to permanent storage, are routed through the network.

5   Hierarchical Power Management

In order to remain scalable, power management techniques for many-core CMPs are either organized in a hierarchical manner [10,11,15] or operate with independent local agents [6]. Our goal is to apply OS migration in order to improve the effectiveness of DVFS which necessitates a hierarchical design. This section describes the organization of the hierarchical power manager and the DVFS and migration policies in detail.

5.1   Organization

The structure of the hierarchical power manager reflects the structure of the SCC with its different voltage and frequency domains. At the lowest level in the hierarchy is a single core because individual cores exhibit different performance values. The next level represents a tile which comprises two cores and represents a clock domain. Decisions about which clock frequency to run at are made at this level. One level up is the voltage domain. A voltage domain consists of four tiles and represents the unit where voltage changes can be initiated. The highest level models the entire chip.

5.2   Local Performance Monitoring and Prediction

On each active core, a local agent monitors the current performance of the core. Depending on the load factor, it requests a higher, the same, or a lower frequency from the next-higher level in the hierarchy. The local agent uses the core's performance monitoring unit (PMU) to gather statistics about the number of executed and memory-bound instructions. At regular intervals the local agent predicts the load of a core based on a weighted average of sampled PMU data. When the core is not fully utilized, the optimal operating frequency can be analytically computed. For purely CPU-bound benchmarks, for example, and a utilization of 50% at 800 MHz we expect 100% load at 400 MHz. Frequency values are discreet, the computed frequency is thus always rounded up to the next higher available frequency.

If the core is fully utilized, however, it is not clear by how much the frequency should be increased. We have experimented with three policies: step-up one, step-up two, and half-way step-up. The first two policies increase the operating frequency by one and two steps, respectively, while the half-way step-up computes the requested frequency by adding half the difference of the current frequency to the maximal frequency. Experiments have shown that in our framework the performance and power consumption are indifferent in regard to the three policies.

Performance is measured periodically; experiments have shown that values between 0.5 and one second are short enough to quickly react to changing performance requirements, but long enough to avoid too much noise in the signal.

5.3 Domain Managers

Each domain, clock, voltage, and global, maintains its own domain manager. Each level only communicates directly with the level above or below, i.e., the clock domain manager interacts with the voltage domain manager, the voltage domain manager interacts downstream with the clock domain, and upstream with the global domain manager. The functionality of the different domain managers is elaborated in more detail in the following sections.

Clock Domain Manager. For each clock domain, its clock domain manager computes and sets the appropriate frequency. The frequency of a clock domain is constrained by the current voltage level of the corresponding voltage domain and computed based on the performance counters reported by the local agents and the currently active DVFS policy (see Sect. 5.4 below). Each clock domain manager maintains sorted lists of the current and requested frequencies for all of its cores. The clock domain managers communicate with their voltage domain manager by periodically sending the list of requested frequencies. The voltage domain manager signals changes in the voltage level.

Voltage Domain Manager. The voltage domain manager computes and sets the operating voltage of a voltage domain. Due to the nature of DVFS, voltage changes must happen in close collaboration with frequency changes: before lowering the voltage, all frequencies must be lowered to a values supported by the lower voltage. Similarly, for higher voltages, the voltage must be increased before the frequencies can be raised. Similar to the clock domain managers, voltage domain managers also maintain sorted lists of the current and requested voltages per clock domain. The voltage domain managers communicate with the global manager by periodically sending the list of requested frequencies and voltages upstream.

Global Domain Manager. The global manager gathers the sorted voltage/ frequency requests from the domain managers and determines which cores to migrate based on the migration policy. After migration has completed, the global domain managers informs the voltage domain managers of the migration such that the voltage may be changed immediately. This is not absolutely necessary since the information will eventually be sent from the local agents to the voltage domain managers, however, giving the voltage domain managers a chance to react immediately to migration leads to better results.

5.4 Scheduler Power Management Policies

The goal of the scheduler's power management policy is to optimize the *performance per watt* ratio of the overall chip. Other policies, such as, for example, even heat dissipation or adhering to a given power budget, are part of future work.

The power management policy is implemented in the global domain manager. The core migration and DVFS algorithms are invoked at regular intervals by the scheduler. The DVFS and migration policy, though the former depends on the latter, are completely separated in order to be able to freely combine different migration and DVFS policies. The following sections describe our DVFS and migration policies in detail.

OS Migration Policy. Without migration OSes are pinned to their cores. For voltage domains containing both very busy cores and idle cores there is no optimal voltage setting: if the voltage is too low, idle cores run at the optimal frequency but the performance of busy cores is severely affected because the low voltage prevents the frequency domain manager from selecting the required frequency. On the other hand, if the voltage is set high enough to satisfy the performance needs of busy cores, idle cores waste energy because they operate at a higher than necessary voltage.

OS migration enables consolidation of cores with similar performance requirements into one voltage/frequency domain. This allows setting the voltage/frequency of the domain to a value that is close to the optimal value for most involved cores.

A naïve algorithm is to sort the OSes by their performance requirements and then assign them in order to the voltage and frequency domains. While the resulting allocation of cores to domains is optimal for one time quantum, this algorithm fails to consider the overhead of OS migration. The actual live migration of an OS is very quick ($\leq 3\,ms$), each time an OS is migrated it will experience a lot of cold misses in the local instruction and data caches which will lead to both a performance reduction as well as increased memory traffic. The migration algorithm must thus also consider the current positions of the OSes and minimize the number of migrations.

We currently employ a buyer-seller heuristic where domain managers for a given target frequency put up cores for sale that are expected to require a lower than the given target frequency. A market manager then matches the sellers to buyers. At the moment, the market manager has knowledge of all voltage domains; however, a hierarchical model is possible if the number of voltage domains prohibits a global analysis. A limitation of the current heuristic is that

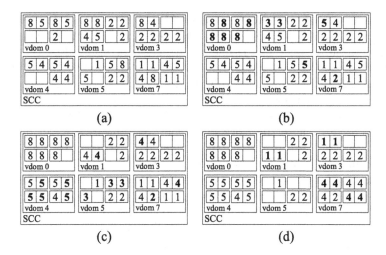

Fig. 4. Buyer-seller algorithm: (a) initial configuration, (b) configuration after running the first round for $v = 8$, (c) configuration after running the second round for $v = 5$, (d) final configuration after running the last round for $v = 4$. Bold values represent tiles/cores migrated in that iteration.

it does not consider the location of a core's data. Developing a memory-location and contention aware OS migration policy is part of future work.

Figure 4 shows the effect of our heuristic. Figure 4 (a) displays the estimated frequencies for each core before the buyer-seller algorithm starts. Figures 4 (b)-(d) show the layout after each repetition for $v_i = 8, 5$ and 4, respectively; (d) represents the final configuration.

The heuristic returns the instructions to perform the actual migration in form of several circular lists of cores that are to be migrated. This list is then processed by the migration manager as discussed in Sect. 4.2.

DVFS Policies. We implement two DVFS policies that are similar to policies used in the hierarchical power manager for CMPs proposed by Ioannou et al. [10]. Their work has been implemented on the Intel SCC chip and thus provides a good reference point. The policies proposed in [10] and reproduced here are:

- `Allhigh`: this policy runs all cores within a voltage domain at the highest requested frequency.
- `Tile`: grants the requested frequency to each clock domain and sets the voltage accordingly. Within each clock domain, the higher of the requested frequencies is chosen. Note: in [10] this policy is denoted `Simple`.

We have not implemented the `Alllow` and `Allmean` policies since they sacrifice too much performance in return for power savings.

For both policies the voltages of the voltage domains are computed such that all clock frequencies of the associated clock domains can be satisfied, i.e., $v_{VD} = \max_i v(f_{CDi})$. $v(f)$ for a given frequency f is a simple table lookup.

Phase Ordering and Frequency Considerations. In order to achieve maximum power savings, migration should occur before applying DVFS. The frequency of migration, voltage, and frequency changes is determined by the cost of these operations: the time for migration is largely unaffected by the number of cores being migrated because all involved cores can store/restore the volatile state in parallel. Migrated cores are stopped and have their caches flushed while unaffected cores continue to run during migration operations. Voltage changes are quite expensive because the clock of all affected cores is stopped during the rather long voltage adjustment. Frequency changes, on the other hand, are almost instantaneous and can thus be performed often. On the SCC specifically, we have measured the following latency: $\leq 3\,\mathrm{ms}$ for migration and $\leq 10\,\mathrm{ms}$ for voltage changes. On this particular architecture, migration is cheaper than voltage changes. In addition, the SCC only supports one voltage change at a time; i.e., different domains cannot change the voltage in parallel. Nevertheless, for our server/desktop benchmark scenarios with rather slow changes in the CPU load, migration and voltage changes can be performed at every step. Section 7 discusses the benchmarks and results in more detail.

6   Experimental Setup

All experiments were conducted on an Intel Single-chip Cloud Computer. The scheduler runs on a dedicated core in voltage domain 3 on the SCC itself. All cores from the other voltage domains run a modified version of the sccLinux.

In addition to the scheduler we also run a few monitoring and logging processes on dedicated cores in voltage domain 3. In order not to pollute the migration algorithm with these processes, voltage domain 3 is excluded from the hierarchical power management. However, the reported results show the *total chip power* and therefore also include the power consumed by vdom3.

A benchmark scenario comprises a number of OSes with distinct workloads and an initial placement of the different OSes onto the SCC's cores.

The workloads running on the cores are either synthetic workloads used to demonstrate the operation of the proposed scheduler or represent profiled workloads that we have gathered by profiling 20 desktop and development computers of graduate students over a period of several months.

The baseline of the experiments is obtained by running the benchmark scenario on the SCC at full speed (800 MHz) with no power management enabled. Unlike the work in [10] we do not use a phase-detector based on message passing since we are aiming at independent OSes running on a CMP. Instead, we apply the workload prediction method based on a weighted average. We compare the DVFS policies of [10] without OS migration, Allhigh and Tile, against the same policies with OS migration.

7   Results

We have conducted a wide range of experiments on the proposed scheduler. To show the effect of OS migration on DVFS, we first present the results of a synthetic periodic workload. The second example details the results of applying the proposed method on a workload pattern obtained from desktop machines of our graduate students. We conclude this section with the overall results over all benchmark scenarios.

Synthetic Periodic Workload. The setup and the results of this workload are shown in Fig. 5. The load pattern is shown in Fig. 5(a) and consists of two simple periodic synthetic workloads that alternate between 10% and 90% CPU load. The second workload s2 is slightly time-shifted compared to s1. The initial OS distribution onto the different voltage domains of the SCC is shown in the left chart of Fig. 5(b). Each domain initially contains three or four OSes running one of the load patterns.

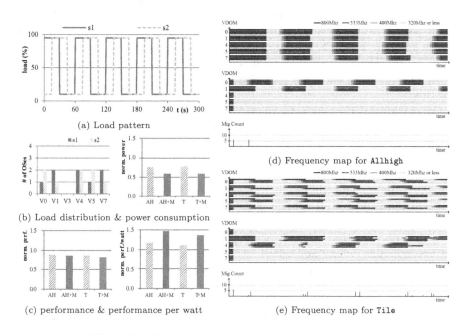

(a) Load pattern

(b) Load distribution & power consumption

(c) performance & performance per watt

(d) Frequency map for Allhigh

(e) Frequency map for Tile

Fig. 5. Results for a simple alternating synthetic load

The results of running this benchmark scenario are shown in Fig. 5(b) and (c). The right-hand of Fig. 5(b) and (c) show the normalized power consumption, performance, and performance per watt, respectively, for the Allhigh and the Tile policy, denoted AH and T, without and with (appended +M postfix) OS migration.

We observe that both DVFS only and DVFS+migration suffer from a performance loss. In the case of DVFS only, there are two reasons for this loss: first, a voltage change operation of an island stops execution on all cores, adjusts the voltage, and then resumes the core clock. This process is implemented in hardware and takes about 10ms per voltage change. The second reason for reduced performance is observed when the workload prediction model fails to predict a sudden raise in the load and selects a too low operating frequency for a workload. OS migration incurs additional overhead: migration requires stopping and resuming all involved cores. Additionally, the changes in the routing tables are propagated to all active OSes through external interrupt; processing these interrupts on the individual cores also causes a minimal performance overhead.

Nonetheless, as can be seen from the normalized power consumption in Fig. 5(b) on the right-hand side, the reduction in power by far outweighs the loss in performance. In terms of performance per watt (right-hand of Fig. 5(c)), both DVFS only and DVFS+migration show better results. In particular, the proposed method of combining DVFS with OS migration achieves about a 30% improved performance per watt compared to DVFS-only policies.

Figures 5(d) and (e), finally, visualize the effect of DVFS only and DVFS+migration on the individual voltage domains' frequency settings for the two DVFS policies Allhigh and Tile. The frequency over time is shown for each voltage domain for DVFS only (upper part) and DVFS+migration (middle part of the figure). Higher frequency (and thus voltage) settings are represented by darker levels of gray. The lower part of the chart shows the number of migrations over time.

Comparing DVFS and DVFS+migration with the Allhigh DVFS policy (Fig. 5(d)) clearly shows how migration is able to group OSes with similar performance characteristics together and thus select voltages that are closer to the optimal value. In the Allhigh policy in particular, if only one core in a particular voltage domain requests a frequency of 800 MHz and thus the highest voltage setting, the entire domain will run at $1.1V$. Since in this artificial example the OSes are evenly spread over all voltage domains, without OS migration all domains run at maximum voltage most of the time. In comparison to DVFS+migration, we clearly observe that the migration policy first migrates all OSes into the first two domains, vdom0 and vdom1. About 30 s into the benchmark, the OSes running load pattern s1 drop to 10% load which causes another batch of migrations and results in grouping the OSes running the same load pattern together. After this, the OSes running in the same voltage domain observe similar load patterns and no more migrations are necessary. The DVFS policy can select the appropriate voltage and frequency for the first two domains.

For the Tile DVFS policy we observe a similar pattern (Fig. 5(e)). Here, the frequency can be set on a tile-basis. Again, DVFS only cannot consolidate OSes with similar load patterns, resulting in voltage settings that are too high for most cores in a domain. DVFS+migration, on the other hand, groups all OSes into vdom1 and vdom4. We see that migration fails to group the OSes running identical load patterns into distinct domains at first which causes some migration activity after about one third of the benchmark's runtime. From then on, the two load patterns are nicely separated. Even though the load patterns are perfectly synchronized at the beginning of the run, the overhead of DVFS and migration causes them to drift apart slowly which then again triggers migrations.

Profiled Workload. Figure 6 shows the results of a scenario based on actual, measured workloads patterns. Seven different load patterns obtained from profiling data of graduate students' computers, s1 to s7, are assigned to a total of 40 OSes and initially placed onto the different voltage domains.

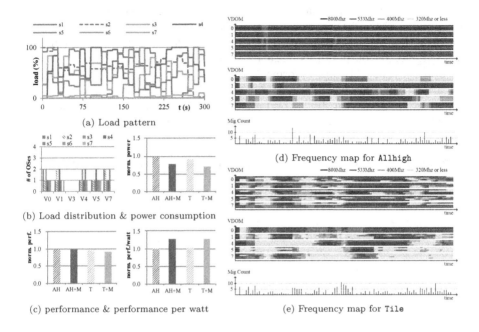

Fig. 6. Results for a profiled load pattern

Compared to the synthetic workload, the performance loss (left-hand in Fig. 6(c)) is much less severe (1% and 2.5% for AH and AH+M, and 3% and 8% for T and T+M, respectively). This is because profiled workloads exhibit smoother workload changes; the local performance prediction is thus much more accurate. The DVFS-only policies cannot group OSes with similar workload characteristics together, and all voltage domains run at maximal voltage during most of the benchmark (upper-hand VDOM charts in Figs. 6(d) and (e)). As a consequence only minimal total energy savings are obtained (1% and 7% for AH and T).

With OS migration, however, the scheduler is able to group workloads exhibiting similar load patterns into voltage domains as shown by the lower-hand VDOM charts in Figs. 6(d) and (e). The total energy savings are significant (23% and 26% for AH+M and T+M) and lead to a much better performance per watt increase compared to DVFS only (1% and 4% for DVFS only, 26% and 26% for DVFS+migration).

Overall Results. Table 1, finally, displays the normalized power, performance, and performance per watt over the baseline, respectively, for the Allhigh and the `Tile` policy, denoted `AH` and `T`, without and with (appended `+M` postfix) OS migration for three different benchmark scenarios all based on profiled workload patterns (details the benchmark scenarios are given in Appendix A).

Independent of the workload at hand, migration OSes before applying a DVFS policy results in a significantly reduced power consumption at the expense of a very moderate performance degradation. Taking the DVFS-only policy as the baseline, `Allhigh+Migration` achieves a 36% better power-per-watt energy efficiency than `Allhigh` at a relative performance loss of only 1.3%. Similarly, `Tile+Migration` outperforms `Tile` by 28.4% at a performance loss of 3.4%. We observe that `Tile` outperforms `Allhigh` without migration whereas with migration they achieve similar performance. The reason is that OS migration is able to group OSes with similar performance requirements into voltage domains such that the superior `Tile` DVFS policy has less effect.

Table 1. Normalized power, performance, and performance per watt (PPW)

BM	AH			AH+M			T			T+M		
	Power	Perf	PPW	Power	Perf	PPW	Power	Perf	PPW	Power	Perf	PPW
1	99.2	99.9	100.8	77.2	97.7	126.5	73.6	97.4	104.0	74.2	93.5	126.0
2	88.2	98.8	112.0	62.6	96.3	153.8	80.3	96.6	120.2	62.2	94.0	151.2
3	92.1	99.5	108.0	63.7	100	157.2	84.9	97.8	115.3	62.5	96.4	154.1
4	98.1	99.9	101.9	77.1	98.6	127.9	91.9	96.5	105.0	71.7	90.7	126.6
Avg.	**94.4**	**99.5**	**105.7**	**70.2**	**98.2**	**141.4**	**82.7**	**97.1**	**111.1**	**67.7**	**93.7**	**139.5**

8   Conclusion

In this work, we show that energy-aware space-shared scheduling of independent programs running on a CMPs is feasible and the potential to achieve significantly energy savings. We provide a working implementation on the Intel Single-chip Cloud Computer where the individual OSes run bare-metal on the assigned cores, and the global scheduler communicates with cores through interrupts.

Techniques for reducing power consumption of CMPs rely on well-known DVFS techniques. The special organization of CMPs into frequency and voltage domains makes direct application of previous work difficult. We employ zero-copy OS migration implemented in a energy-aware scheduler to consolidate OSes with similar workloads onto the same frequency and voltage domains, thereby allowing DVFS policies to achieve a larger power reduction at the cost of a minimal performance penalty.

The proposed energy-aware scheduler with its integrated hierarchical power management supporting intra-core live migration is put to a test with a wide range of workloads. Experimental results conducted on a real system show that, on average, the proposed techniques achieve an improvement of the performance per watt by 25–35% over previous DVFS approaches.

Acknowledgments. This work was supported, in part, by BK21 Plus for Pioneers in Innovative Computing (Dept. of Computer Science and Engineering, SNU) funded by the National Research Foundation (NRF) of Korea (Grant 21A20151113068), the Basic Science Research Program through NRF funded by the Ministry of Science, ICT & Future Planning (Grants NRF-2015K1A3A1A14021288 and NRF-2008-0062609), and by the Promising-Pioneering Researcher Program through Seoul National University in 2015. ICT at Seoul National University provided research facilities for this study.

Appendix

A   Profiled Workload Benchmark Scenarios

This appendix describes the details of the benchmarks evaluated in this work. Each benchmark scenario consists of two parts:

– Two or more workload pattern that describe how the workload changes over time.
– An initial assignment of the workloads to the 48 cores of the exercised Intel SCC.

Each workload pattern (WL), denoted S{1–7} in the tables below, lists the CPU workload for every epoch (10 or 15 s, depending on the benchmark) for the duration of one period (300 s). A workload never stops, it keeps repeating the workload pattern period after period. Note that all workloads are pure CPU-based workloads; memory-based workloads are part of future work.

The core assignment tables below show what workload pattern are assigned to which cores when the experiment starts. In our setup, voltage domain 3 runs various logging and monitoring services and is thus not available for user benchmarks. The power measurements include the power consumed by **vdom3** because power is only reported for the entire chip and not for individual voltage domains.

A benchmark ends after a predefined number of seconds (in our example after 300 s). The total progress of each workload is measured externally and thus includes all overheads caused by migration, voltage changes or slowdowns cause by too low frequency settings.

A.1   Synthetic Benchmark Scenario based on Periodic Workloads

The synthetic benchmark consists of two identical workload patterns shifted in time. Each voltage domain contains workloads of both patterns. The purpose of this benchmark is to demonstrate the potential of combining DVFS with OS migration. The results of this benchmark are shown in Fig. 5.

Workload patterns:

WL	Epoch (1 epoch = 15 s)																				
	0	1	2	3	4	5	6	7	8	9	10	11	12	13	14	15	16	17	18	19	20
S1	95	95	10	10	95	95	10	10	95	95	10	10	95	95	10	10	95	95	10	10	10
S2	10	95	95	10	10	95	95	10	10	95	95	10	10	95	95	10	10	95	95	10	10

Core assignment:

vdom0		vdom1		vdom3		vdom4		vdom5		vdom7	
-	-	-	-	n/a	n/a	-	-	-	-	-	-
S2	-	S2	-	n/a	n/a	S2	S2	S2	-	S2	-
-	-	-	-	n/a	n/a	-	-	-	-	-	
S1	S2	S1	S1	n/a	n/a	S1	S1	S1	S2	S1	S1

A.2　Benchmark Scenarios based on Profiled Workloads

The following four benchmarks are based on the usage patterns of Linux and Windows desktop computers. Initially, each voltage domain is loaded with different workload patterns. These benchmarks demonstrate the effect of the proposed technique when applied to a multi-user setup (i.e., virtual desktops of employees on a server machine).

The detailed result of the first benchmark are shown in Fig. 6, and Table 1 lists the combined results for all four benchmark scenarios shown here.

Benchmark 1 (BM1)

Workload patterns:

WL	Epoch (1 epoch = 10 s)																														
	0	1	2	3	4	5	6	7	8	9	10	11	12	13	14	15	16	17	18	19	20	21	22	23	24	25	26	27	28	29	30
S1	27	49	31	32	62	77	80	44	0	6	1	1	8	73	87	81	80	91	100	99	89	67	13	52	0	0	10	46	27	86	63
S2	69	57	68	60	55	66	61	63	69	58	56	57	63	59	62	58	57	67	68	64	61	71	78	63	71	82	69	14	0	2	4
S3	28	84	41	12	83	48	55	0	35	69	42	59	17	46	59	49	51	2	46	47	80	40	4	73	41	53	47	18	100	42	45
S4	27	49	31	32	62	77	80	44	0	6	1	1	8	73	87	81	80	91	100	99	89	67	13	52	0	0	10	80	66	56	32
S5	71	53	26	9	34	25	23	38	37	26	96	92	34	41	89	100	100	12	17	30	27	21	31	35	41	84	89	63	100	96	84
S6	0	0	0	0	0	0	0	0	0	0	0	0	0	0	0	0	27	96	63	100	27	0	0	0	0	0	0	0	0	0	0
S7	5	4	5	7	2	4	5	6	6	4	100	6	2	4	1	1	0	1	2	2	4	2	2	4	6	6	6	5	2	10	5

Core assignment:

vdom0		vdom1		vdom3		vdom4		vdom5		vdom7	
S4	S6	S4	S4	n/a	n/a	S5	S5	S5	S6	S5	S5
S3	S3	S3	S7	n/a	n/a	S3	S3	S4	S4	S2	S2
S2	S5	S2	S2	n/a	n/a	S2	S6	S2	S7	S3	S4
S1	S1	S1	S5	n/a	n/a	S1	S4	S1	S3	S1	S1

Benchmark 2 (BM2)

Workload patterns:

WL	Epoch (1 epoch = 10 s)																														
	0	1	2	3	4	5	6	7	8	9	10	11	12	13	14	15	16	17	18	19	20	21	22	23	24	25	26	27	28	29	30
S1	27	49	31	32	62	77	80	44	0	6	1	1	8	73	87	81	80	91	100	99	89	67	13	52	0	0	10	46	27	86	63
S2	82	39	55	42	96	42	100	33	53	20	20	10	11	14	13	11	13	13	1	5	1	0	23	45	61	42	83	83	20	15	3
S3	28	84	41	12	83	48	55	0	35	69	42	59	17	46	59	49	51	2	46	47	80	40	4	73	41	53	47	18	100	42	45
S4	27	49	31	32	62	77	80	44	0	6	1	1	8	73	87	81	80	91	100	99	89	67	13	52	0	0	10	10	15	30	27
S5	71	53	26	9	34	25	23	38	37	26	96	92	34	41	89	100	100	12	17	30	27	21	31	35	41	84	89	63	100	96	84
S6	53	21	52	48	33	92	89	100	39	38	29	41	48	4	64	45	36	31	42	41	42	35	15	80	93	62	10	23	48	32	0

Core assignment:

vdom0		vdom1		vdom3		vdom4		vdom5		vdom7	
-	-	-	-	n/a	n/a	-	-	-	-	-	-
S5	S6	S5	S6	n/a	n/a	S3	S6	S4	S5	S4	S5
-	-	-	-	n/a	n/a	-	-	-	-	-	-
S1	S4	S1	S2	n/a	n/a	S1	S2	S2	S3	S1	S3

Benchmark 3 (BM3).

Workload patterns:

WL	Epoch (1 epoch = 10 s)																														
	00	01	02	03	04	05	06	07	08	09	10	11	12	13	14	15	16	17	18	19	20	21	22	23	24	25	26	27	28	29	30
S1	42	77	25	11	34	36	30	14	33	26	22	58	100	52	30	13	15	0	21	39	48	43	40	41	40	42	41	40	39	36	35
S2	45	15	6	27	25	9	64	55	27	28	18	51	46	100	56	20	25	25	12	0	0	0	0	0	0	0	0	0	0	0	0
S3	71	53	26	9	34	25	23	38	37	26	30	23	34	41	39	29	29	12	17	30	27	21	31	35	41	84	89	63	100	96	2
S4	11	22	20	10	27	12	45	100	22	9	4	14	9	43	19	6	17	18	14	21	5	5	5	6	25	16	7	0	0	0	0
S5	42	66	40	67	57	67	66	71	75	72	31	38	59	54	86	80	68	55	95	100	89	85	86	77	64	0	0	0	0	0	0

Core assignment:

vdom0		vdom1		vdom2		vdom4		vdom5		vdom7	
S5	-	-	-	n/a	n/a	S5	-	S5	-	S5	-
-	-	S5	-	n/a	n/a	S4	-	S4	-	S4	-
S2	S4	S2	S4	n/a	n/a	-	S3	S2	S3	S2	-
S1	S3	S1	S3	n/a	n/a	S1	S2	S1	-	S1	S3

Benchmark 4 (BM4).

Workload patterns:

WL	Epoch (1 epoch = 10 s)																														
	0	1	2	3	4	5	6	7	8	9	10	11	12	13	14	15	16	17	18	19	20	21	22	23	24	25	26	27	28	29	30
S1	27	49	31	32	62	77	80	44	0	6	1	1	8	73	87	81	80	91	100	99	89	67	13	52	0	0	10	46	27	86	63
S2	82	39	55	42	96	42	100	33	53	20	20	10	11	14	13	11	13	13	1	5	1	0	23	45	61	42	83	83	20	15	3
S3	8	20	21	30	80	100	24	50	36	54	83	92	91	73	27	1	0	1	1	1	1	0	1	1	10	1	21	17	33	5	7
S4	27	49	31	32	62	77	80	44	0	6	1	1	8	73	87	81	80	91	100	99	89	67	13	52	0	0	10	10	15	30	27
S5	53	21	52	48	33	92	89	100	39	38	29	41	48	4	64	45	36	31	42	41	42	35	15	80	93	62	10	23	48	32	0

Core assignment:

vdom0		vdom1		vdom2		vdom4		vdom5		vdom7	
-	-	-	-	n/a	n/a	-	-	-	-	-	-
S3	S4	S3	S4	n/a	n/a	S3	S4	S3	S4	S3	S4
-	S5	-	S5	n/a	n/a	-	S5	-	S5	-	S5
S1	S2	S1	S2	n/a	n/a	S1	S2	S1	S2	S1	S2

References

1. Agerwala, T., Chatterjee, S.: Computer architecture: Challenges and opportunities for the next decade. IEEE Micro **25**(3), 58–69 (2005)
2. Barroso, L.A., Gharachorloo, K., McNamara, R., Nowatzyk, A., Qadeer, S., Sano, B., Smith, S., Stets, R., Verghese, B.: Piranha: a scalable architecture based on single-chip multiprocessing. In: Proceedings of the 27th Annual International Symposium on Computer Architecture, ISCA 2000, pp. 282–293. ACM, New York (2000)
3. Borkar, S.: Thousand core chips-a technology perspective. In: Proceedings of the 44th Annual Design Automation Conference, DAC 2007, pp. 746–749. ACM, New York (2007)
4. Burd, T.D., Brodersen, R.W.: Energy efficient CMOS microprocessor design. In: Proceedings of the Twenty-Eighth Hawaii International Conference on System Sciences, vol. 1, pp. 288–297 (1995)

5. Cai, Q., González, J., Magklis, G., Chaparro, P., González, A.: Thread shuffling: combining DVFS and thread migration to reduce energy consumptions for multi-core systems. In: Proceedings of the 17th IEEE/ACM International Symposium on Low-power Electronics and Design, ISLPED 2011, pp. 379–384. IEEE Press, Piscataway (2011)

6. Ebi, T., Faruque, M., Henkel, J.: Tape: Thermal-aware agent-based power econom multi/many-core architectures. In: IEEE/ACM International Conference on Computer-Aided Design - Digest of Technical Papers, ICCAD 2009, pp. 302–309 (2009)

7. Ghiasi, S.: Aide De Camp: asymmetric multi-core design for dynamic thermal management. PhD thesis, Boulder, CO, USA (2004). AAI3136618

8. Herbert, S., Marculescu, D.: Analysis of dynamic voltage/frequency scaling in chip-multiprocessors. In: 2007 ACM/IEEE International Symposium on Low Power Electronics and Design (ISLPED), pp. 38–43, August 2007

9. Howard, J., Dighe, S., Hoskote, Y., Vangal, S., Finan, D., Ruhl, G., Jenkins, D., Wilson, H., Borkar, N., Schrom, G., Pailet, F., Jain, S., Jacob, T., Yada, S., Marella, S., Salihundam, P., Erraguntla, V., Konow, M., Riepen, M., Droege, G., Lindemann, J., Gries, M., Apel, T., Henriss, K., Lund-Larsen, T., Steibl, S., Borkar, S., De, V., Van der Wijngaart, R., Mattson, T.: A 48-core IA-32 message-passing processor with DVFS in 45 nm CMOS. In: IEEE International Solid-State Circuits Conference Digest of Technical Papers (ISSCC), 2010, pp. 108–109, February 2010

10. Ioannou, N., Kauschke, M., Gries, M., Cintra, M.: Phase-based application-driven hierarchical power management on the single-chip cloud computer. In: Proceedings of the 2011 International Conference on Parallel Architectures and Compilation Techniques, PACT 2011, pp. 131–142. IEEE Computer Society, Washington, DC (2011)

11. Isci, C., Buyuktosunoglu, A., Cher, C.Y., Bose, P., Martonosi, M.: An analysis of efficient multi-core global power management policies: maximizing performance for a given power budget. In: Proceedings of the 39th Annual IEEE/ACM International Symposium on Microarchitecture, MICRO 39, pages 347–358. IEEE Computer Society, Washington, DC, USA (2006)

12. Kim, W., Gupta, M.S., Wei, G.Y., Brooks, D.: System level analysis of fast, per-core DVFS using on-chip switching regulators. In: IEEE 14th International Symposium on High Performance Computer Architecture (HPCA 2008), pp. 123–134, February 2008

13. Kumar, R., Tullsen, D.M., Ranganathan, P., Jouppi, N.P., Farkas, K.I.: Single-ISA heterogeneous multi-core architectures for multithreaded workload performance. In: Proceedings of the 31st Annual International Symposium on Computer Architecture, ISCA 2004, p. 64. IEEE Computer Society, Washington, DC, USA (2004)

14. Li, J., Martinez, J.F.: Power-performance implications of thread-level parallelism on chip multiprocessors. In: IEEE International Symposium on Performance Analysis of Systems and Software (ISPASS 2005), pp. 124–134, March 2005

15. Ma, K., Li, X., Chen, M., Wang, X.: Scalable power control for many-core architectures running multi-threaded applications. In: Proceedings of the 38th Annual International Symposium on Computer Architecture, ISCA 2011, pp. 449–460. ACM, New York (2011)

16. Meisner, D., Gold, B.T., Wenisch, T.F.: Powernap: Eliminating server idle power. In: Proceedings of the 14th International Conference on Architectural Support for Programming Languages and Operating Systems, ASPLOS XIV, pp. 205–216. ACM, New York (2009)

17. Meisner, D., Wenisch, T.F.: Dreamweaver: architectural support for deep sleep. In: Proceedings of the Seventeenth International Conference on Architectural Support for Programming Languages and Operating Systems, ASPLOS XVII, pp. 313–324. ACM, New York (2012)

18. Meng, K., Joseph, R., Dick, R.P., Shang, L.: Multi-optimization power management for chip multiprocessors. In: Proceedings of the 17th International Conference on Parallel Architectures and Compilation Techniques, PACT 2008, pp. 177–186. ACM, New York (2008)

19. Olukotun, K., Nayfeh, B.A., Hammond, L., Wilson, K., Chang, K.: The case for a single-chip multiprocessor. In: Proceedings of the Seventh International Conference on Architectural Support for Programming Languages and Operating Systems, ASPLOS VII, pp. 2–11. ACM, New York (1996)

20. Rangan, K.K., Wei, G.Y., Brooks, D.: Thread motion: fine-grained power management for multi-core systems. In: Proceedings of the 36th Annual International Symposium on Computer Architecture, ISCA 2009, pp. 302–313. ACM, New York (2009)

21. Rotem, E., Mendelson, A., Ginosar, R., Weiser, U.: Multiple clock and voltage domains for chip multi processors. In: Proceedings of the 42nd Annual IEEE/ACM International Symposium on Microarchitecture, MICRO 42, pp. 459–468. ACM, New York (2009)

22. Vajda, A.: Multi-core and many-core processor architectures. Programming Many-Core Chips, pp. 9–43. Springer, New York (2011)

Data Driven Scheduling Approach for the Multi-node Multi-GPU Cholesky Decomposition

Yuki Tsujita$^{(\boxtimes)}$ and Toshio Endo

Tokyo Institute of Technology, Tokyo, Japan
`tsujita.y.aa@m.titech.ac.jp`

Abstract. Recently large scale scientific computation on heterogeneous supercomputers equipped with accelerators is receiving attraction. However, traditional static job execution methods and memory management methods are insufficient in order to harness heterogeneous computing resources including memory efficiently, since they introduce larger data movement costs and lower resource usage. This paper takes the Cholesky decomposition computation, which is an important linear algebra kernel, as the target for optimization. And we describe a scalable data-driven scheduling method and a heterogeneous memory management method in order to improve resource utilization and reduce amount of data movement. Through the performance evaluation on TSUBAME2.5, which is a heterogeneous supercomputer with NVIDIA GPUs, we demonstrate the efficiency of the proposed task scheduling method and data replacement strategies considering data reusability.

1 Introduction

Recently general purpose graphic processing unit (GPGPU) computing, technology that harnesses GPUs for generic computation including scientific computing, is gathering attraction in high performance computing area, for GPUs' high computation throughput and memory bandwidth. In the latest Top 500 supercomputers ranking [1], the Titan supercomputer ranked as world No. 2 is equipped with 18,688 GPUs to accelerate its performance and improve the power performance ratio. Also the TSUBAME2.5 supercomputer [2] at Tokyo Institute of Technology embodies 4,224 NVIDIA K20X GPUs.

GPGPU has been used for applications from various areas, including numerical optimization applications. In this paper, we take SDPARA software [12], a high performance solver for semi-definite programs (SDP) as the target for optimization. SDPARA's important computation kernel is the Cholesky decomposition for a dense large matrix, which already harnesses multiple GPUs in the recent version. It has achieved peta-scale computation speed of 1.7 PFlops by using 4,080 GPUs on TSUBAME2.5 [10,11]. For this application, it is required to support larger scale problems, which produces the larger matrix to be decomposed. In order to support larger matrix than the aggregate capacity of device

© Springer International Publishing AG 2017
N. Desai and W. Cirne (Eds.): JSSPP 2015/2016, LNCS 10353, pp. 69–82, 2017.
DOI: 10.1007/978-3-319-61756-5_4

memory among GPUs, we put the matrix on host memory, which has larger capacity. On the other hand, a typical, synchronous implementation suffers from larger amount of data movement between GPUs and CPUs. Although this issue is partially mitigated by parameter tuning such as block sizes [9], we will require further optimization toward future supercomputer architectures on which data movement will be more expensive relatively.

In this paper, we introduce data driven scheduling approach for the optimization of the multi-node multi-GPU Cholesky decomposition. Unlike the synchronous approach, the algorithm is expressed as a task dependency graph, where a single task corresponds to an update kernel of a small block of the matrix, which takes approximately 1 to 10 ms. The matrix is distributed among the multiple nodes, and the task graph includes dependencies between tasks on different nodes. Our distributed fine-grained task scheduling method has the following properties:

- The scheduling method is scalable in order to support more than 1 M tasks
- The scheduling method is aware of memory hierarchy that consists of GPU device memory, local host memory and remote host memory. It is designed to minimize the data movement between the hierarchy.
- Our implementation supports overlapping of computation and data movement to improve the overall performance.

Through the performance evaluation on TSUBAME2.5 supercomputer, we demonstrate that the amount of data movement between CPUs and GPUs are reduced largely, and we have achieved 13.9 TFlops on 16 nodes.

2 Background

2.1 GPGPU and PCIe Communication

GPGPU(General Purpose Graphics Processing Unit) is a technique to use computing resources of GPU (Graphics Processing Unit) for a general-purpose calculation as well as image processing. GPUs are processors originally designed for image processing, and mainly equipped by video cards and connected to the host computer via the PCI Express (PCIe) bus. Current GPUs can not work by themselves but works under the control of the host CPUs. Compared with CPUs, GPUs are designed to make throughput of computation higher; thus, they have been successful in parallel computations with regular structures, including matrix operations. Programmers can use GPGPU with dedicated programming tools, such as CUDA, OpenCL and OpenACC. In this paper, we use CUDA programming environment designed for NVIDIA GPUs, however, the proposed techniques are applicable to other environments.

While GPUs have higher computation throughput and memory bandwidth, they have limitations on memory size. The memory region that is directly accessible from GPU cores is called device memory, which is attached on the graphic card. Currently the device memory size is limited to several gigabytes (6 GB on

NVIDIA K20X GPUs, used in our evaluation), while the host memory can be expanded more easily (54 GB on the TSUBAME nodes).

Therefore in order to support larger scale computation, we can harness the capacity of host memory in addition to device memory. However, we should consider the amount of data movement between CPUs and GPUs (hereafter we call it PCIe communication). Since the bandwidth of PCIe, 8 GB/s in our case, is much smaller than device memory bandwidth (250 GB/s on K20X), we have to reduce the amount of PCIe communication in order to achieve high performance. We take the Cholesky decomposition as the target computation, and introduce task scheduling methods that are aware of memory access locality, in order to reduce PCIe communication cost.

2.2 Cholesky Decomposition

The Cholesky decomposition takes a symmetric positive definite matrix A, whose size is $N \times N$. We assume A is a dense matrix. Then it decomposes A into the product of a lower triangle matrix L and its transposition, where $A = LL^T$.

Here we describe a typical parallel algorithm in the ScaLAPACK parallel linear algebra library [7]. The matrix A is divided into blocks with a uniform size $n_b \times n_b$, and the blocks are distributed among processes in two-dimensional block cyclic method. The algorithm consists of an outermost loop; at the k-th iteration of the loop, the sub matrix $A^{(k)}$ of size $n \times n$, where $n = N - k \times n_b$, is transformed into $L^{(k)}$ in place as follows.

$$
\begin{pmatrix} A_{11} & A_{21}^T \\ A_{21} & A_{22} \end{pmatrix} = \begin{pmatrix} L_{11} & 0 \\ L_{21} & L_{22} \end{pmatrix} \begin{pmatrix} L_{11}^T & L_{21}^T \\ 0 & L_{22}^T \end{pmatrix}
$$
$$
= \begin{pmatrix} L_{11}L_{11}^T & L_{11}L_{21}^T \\ L_{21}L_{11}^T & L_{21}L_{21}^T + L_{22}L_{22}^T \end{pmatrix}
$$

Here A_{11} is a single block of the $n_b \times n_b$ size, A_{21} is a $(n - n_b) \times n_b$ matrix and A_{22} is a $(n - n_b) \times (n - n_b)$ matrix as shown in Fig. 1. In a single iteration, we calculate the Cholesky decomposition of A_{11}, L_{11} first. Then the rest part of $L^{(k)}$ is obtained as follows.

$$
L_{21} \longleftarrow A_{21}(L_{11}^t)^{-1}
$$
$$
\tilde{A_{22}} \longleftarrow A_{22} - L_{21}L_{21}^t = L_{22}L_{22}^t
$$

The ScaLapack routine executes this decomposition as follows.

1. PDPOTF2: The process which has A_{11} performs the Cholesky decomposition.

$$
A_{11} \longrightarrow L_{11}L_{11}^t
$$

2. PDTRSM: L_{11} is send to all the processes which have A_{21} and they calculate L_{21}.

$$
L_{21} \longleftarrow A_{21}(L_{11}^t)^{-1}
$$

3. PDSYRK: L_{21} is sent to all the processes and transposed. Then each process
has L_{21} and L_{21}^t. They update a part of A_{22} using them.

$$\tilde{A}_{22} \longleftarrow A_{22} - L_{21}L_{21}^t$$

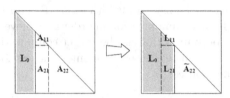

Fig. 1. The snapshot of the block Cholesky decomposition from Fig. 5 in J. Choi
et al. [7]

2.3   Simple Implementation on GPUs and Its Problem

The existing SDPARA GPU version uses a simple extension of this ScaLapack
algorithm [11]. In order to support matrix larger than the aggregated capacity of
device memory of GPUs, the matrix A is distributed among the compute nodes
and allocated on host memory. In order to accelerate computation, each process
executes the following work at each kernel routine. We copy the partial matrix,
which is divided so that it fits in the device memory, from host to device via
PCIe. And then we let the GPU compute for it by using high performance BLAS
routines, and the copy back the result into the host memory. The computation
on GPUs and PCIe communication are overlapped with each other.

This GPU implementation has the following problems:

Lower utilization of computing resources: The current ScaLapack based
implementation is based on a synchronous style. For example, while a single
process is calculating L_{11}, other processes tend to be idle, which degrades
the total performance. We could improve the GPU utilization by introducing
asynchronous execution, while we need to keep necessary data dependency.

More PCIe communication: The current implementation assumes that all
the matrix data is available on host memory after each kernel finishes. With
this method, we suffer from the cost of PCIe communication; the amount is
$O(N^3/n_b)$. We could reduce it if the matrix data can reside in device memory
over several iterations of the outer loop.

Larger memory consumption: ScaLapack uses the rectangular matrix data
format, although only a triangular part is necessary for Cholesky decomposition. Thus memory consumption on host memory is twice than that is really
required. We could support larger matrices by changing the data format.

2.4   Motivation for Data Driven Execution

The above discussion motivates us to adopt the data driven implementation similar to DAGuE [5] or StarPU [3]. Here we describe the basic execution method. First, we change the data format for the matrix. Instead of the rectangular format, we let each process maintain several blocks, each of which is an array of $n_b \times n_b$ size. Thus we can reduce memory consumption.

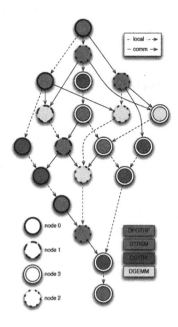

Fig. 2. Direct Acyclic Graph(DAG) of the Cholesky decomposition from Fig. 2 in G. Bosilca et al. [6]

Next, when we consider the data dependency in the block level, we could harness more parallelism than in the synchronous style. Therefore we consider the computation of a single block as a task, and we consider the dependency among the tasks. Also we introduce task scheduling methods of these fine grained tasks, while conforming the dependency, as described later. If a task execution requires input blocks that resides on remote processes, MPI communication is involved. Also we have to consider the memory hierarchy of device memory and host memory. If the input block is not available on the device memory, PCIe communication is involved. After all the input blocks are available on the device memory, we can execute the task. If the device memory is already full, some blocks are swapped out to the host memory. Also our scheduler is designed so that computation, MPI communication and PCIe communication are overlapped with each other.

By using this method, the utilization of computing resources is expected to be improved, and the PCIe communication amount is reduced.

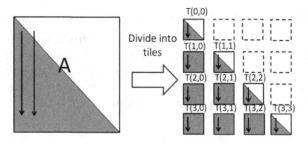

Fig. 3. Tile division

3   Our Scheduling Method

This section explains the implementation of the block Cholesky decomposition. After describing the basic data driven scheduling method, we discuss strategies for selecting runnable tasks and for GPU memory sweeping.

First, we divide the input matrix data A into the units called "tiles", each of which has $n_b \times n_b$ size. The tiles are distributed among MPI processes (we do not distinguish MPI processes and computing nodes in this discussion) in a two-dimensional block cyclic style. Instead of holding all the tiles included in A, we hold only tiles for the lower triangular part of A as shown in Fig. 3, because Cholesky decomposition assumes A as a symmetric matrix. In the initial state, the tile data is put on the host process.

We regard each computation kernel for a tile as a task, which is executed by the owner process of the target tile (owner computing rule). Each task can be executed if all the precedent tasks in the task graph has been finished. Unlike the synchronous execution method, tiles may be updated step by step independently. Thus each tile maintains a variable to express its current running step.

Also each tile is in one of the following three states:

RUNNABLE: The next task for this tile is runnable, since all the precedent tasks are finished.

SLEEP: In order to proceed the next task for this tile, we have to wait for precedent tasks.

FINISHED: All tasks for this tile have been finished. No more update is required.

In our implementation, an MPI process consists of several (two or three typically) worker threads and a ignition thread. We introduce multiple calculation threads in order to achieve overlapping of calculation, PCIe communication and MPI communication in a simple implementation. Each process has its task queue, shared by all its threads, in order to manage the runnable tasks on the process.

Each worker thread performs the following steps, task select, localize, execute, and finalize, continuously.

Task select: It takes out a runnable task from the task queue if exists; we let T be the target tile of the task. If the task queue is empty, the calculation is blocked.

Localize: Generally, execution of a task requires the result data of the precedent tasks as inputs. We let T_{i1}, T_{i2} be the result tiles of the precedent tasks[1]. Then the worker thread checks the state of tiles T, T_{i1}, T_{i2} and executes the corresponding operations as follows.

1. if the tile data is on device memory, nothing is required.
2. if the tile data is not on device memory, but on the local host memory, the tile data is copied to device memory via PCIe bus. This may involve *swapping out* operation, as described below.
3. if the tile data is neither on device memory nor on local host memory, the thread issues `MPI_Recv` in order to receive the tile data from its owner process. After the data arrival, we execute as in Case 2.

Execute: Now all the required tile data are available on GPU; thus we execute the calculation task, which is typically invocation of a BLAS function on GPU.

Finalize: When a task is finished, the worker thread performs operations for the following tasks, which need the result of this task. The operations involve inter-process messages of two types as shown in Fig. 4. First, the calculation thread sends *notice messages* to processes that have following tasks, which may eventually make the following tasks runnable. In the current implementation, we send the data of tile T to the receiver immediately. To avoid blocking the worker thread long, we use non-blocking communication, `MPI_Isend`, for sending notice messages and tile data.

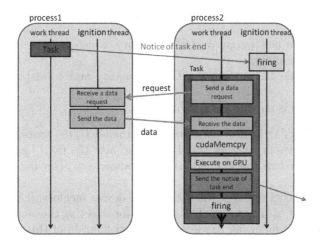

Fig. 4. MPI Communication pattern when a task is finalized

---

[1] In Cholesky decomposition, each task depends on two tasks or less.

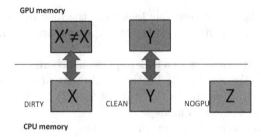

Fig. 5. The association state of CPU memory and GPU memory

The ignition thread continuously checks arrivals of notice messages that notify information of finishing tasks. If the ignition thread finds the notice message makes a local task runnable, it adds the task into the process's task queue[2].

With this described method, we can execute the whole computation in a data driven style. This method reuse data of tile on the GPU device memory if possible; this can reduce PCIe communication between CPUs and GPUs.

3.1   Memory Management

In our implementation, each process put data of all the tiles owned by the process on the host memory. On the other hand, the smaller GPU device memory is used like a "cache" of the host memory.

When a process copies a tile data to GPU, it needs to evict other tile if the capacity is full. In this time, the data on GPUs has to be copied back if it is newer than data on host memory (the data is dirty). In order to maintain consistency, each tile has an additional variable expressing the state of the cached data on GPU as shown in Fig. 5. Each tile is in one of the following three states.

DIRTY: The tile has a copy on GPU memory, which may be different from data on host memory.
CLEAN: The tile has a copy on GPU memory, and consistent with host memory.
NOGPU: There is no copy on GPU memory.

When the DIRTY tile is swapped out from the GPU, the process copies back the tile to host memory, copies the data of the new tile from host memory to device memory. When the CLEAN tile is swapped out, copying back can be omitted.

When the process replaces the data of the device memory, it chooses a tile to be swapped out as the victim. The strategy for selecting the victim can affect the performance of following processes. In the evaluation of this paper, we use LRU strategy. In LRU strategy, we select a tile that has not been used for a long time. To implement this, we maintain a list of tiles and move tiles that are used for task execution into the tail of the list.

---

[2] Note that the input tile data is received by a work thread, not by the ignition thread.

3.2 Task Selection Strategies

As previously described, we manage the runnable tasks by using the task queue per process. Since a task queue may contain several runnable tasks, we need to make strategies to select a task to be executed. We compare the following four strategies.

FIFO strategy: We take the oldest task from the queue.

Random strategy: We take one of runnable tasks randomly.

Greed strategy: We prefer a task that can be executed with less data movement. When a worker thread is going to take a task, we traverse tasks in the task queue to see how much data movement will be required in the "Localized" step described above. If we find a task whose required tiles data are already available on the device memory, we take the task for execution immediately. This strategy is expected to improve the access locality and reduce total PCIe communication costs.

ByIJ strategy: This strategy is also expected to improve the access locality, and takes the property of the Cholesky decomposition into account. In this computation, the tiles that reside in the same row or the same column tend to have strong relations with each other. In this strategy, we track a last task that has been finished. When the task of $T(i, j)$, a tile in the i-th row and j-th column, finishes, the next task is chosen as follows.

1. If the queue has a task of the tile in the same column $T(\cdot, j)$, it is taken out. If not, we proceed the next step.
2. If the queue has a task of the tile in the same row $T(i, \cdot)$, it is taken out. If not, we proceed the next step.
3. A task of the top of the queue is taken out.

4 Performance Evaluation

To evaluate the performance of our implementation (called "NEW") with data driven scheduling, we have conducted the performance measurement. The NEW implementation includes several strategies for task selection in memory swapping as described in the previous section. Our implementation is compared with a synchronous implementation used in the existing SDPARA version [10,11], which is called "OLD" in this section. OLD has recorded 1.7 PFlops on the TSUBAME 2.5 supercomputer with 4080 GPU.

4.1 Experimental Condition

For the experiment we have used the TSUBAME 2.5 supercomputer at the Global Scientific Information and Computing Center at Tokyo Institute of Technology. TSUBAME 2.5 is a GPU-accelerated supercomputer, and its total peak performance reaches 5.7 PFlops. Table 1 represents the hardware specification of the node used in the evaluation.

Table 1. Hardware specification of TSUBAME 2.5 node

CPU Memory	Intel Xeon X5670 2.93 GHz (6 cores) x 2 54 GiB
GPU	NVIDIA Tesla K20X x 3
GPU Peak Performance	1.31 TFlops per GPU
GPU Memory	6GiB per GPU

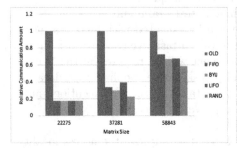
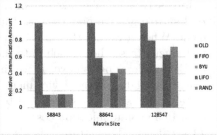

Fig. 6. Relative communication amount of PCIe on one node

Fig. 7. Relative communication amount of PCIe on four nodes

We have used a GPU per node and conducted all the performance evaluation with four work threads. We have fixed the tile size at 2048 × 2048. For GPU management, we used NVIDIA CUDA 6.0, and used CUBLAS 6.0 as basic linear algebra library on each GPU.

4.2 PCIe Communication Amount

First we have measured the amount of data movement between CPUs and GPUs. We have performed it with the OLD implementation and several versions of NEW implementation. For NEW implementation, we measured with each task selection strategy. The measurement is done with varying matrix sizes; with the smallest case, the matrix data can be fully allocated on (aggregated) GPU memory, and the other matrix sizes are larger than the GPU memory capacity. The results are shown in Fig. 6 (one node cases) and Fig. 7 (four nodes cases). The PCIe communication amounts are normalized to one with OLD implementation.

The figures exhibits the communication amount between CPU and GPU greatly decreased in NEW implementations, for all the combinations of strategies. If the matrices are small, we have reduced it to about 17% on one node and 15% on four nodes. Here the strategies do not affect the performance, since data reuse is fully successful if the matrix data fits the GPU memory. PCIe communication is limited to the beginning and the end of the Cholesky decomposition. On the other hand, OLD invokes PCIe communication on every kernel routine that causes redundant communication.

With larger matrices than GPU memory, we also observe the reduction of PCIe communication, though the reduction is mitigated as the matrix gets larger.

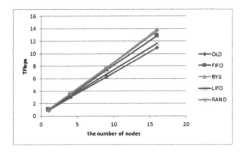

Fig. 8. Weak scalability

On four nodes, NEW with BYIJ strategy reduces it to 37% with matrix size of 88,641. Among the task selection strategies, the BYIJ strategy greatly reduces the communication amount by using the reusability of data, as expected.

4.3 Weak Scalability

Figure 8 represents the weak scalability study. This matrix size is scaled up accordingly to the number of nodes to keep the data size per a node constant. The minimum matrix size is 58,843 with one node and the maximum one is 247,131 with 16 nodes. We observe that all the implementations exhibits good scalability. Among them, BYIJ achieves the best performance, 13.92 TFlops with 16 nodes (16 GPUs). We observe the every NEW versions shows better performance than OLD version. We consider the reason is as follow; the reduction of the PCIe communication amount improved performance as planned. But, with LIFO strategy, we cannot get much performance for PCIe communication amount. We will further investigate this point in future.

4.4 Strong Scalability

Figure 9 represents the strong scalability study. The matrix size is fixed at 47142, and the number of nodes varies from one to 16. Compared with weak scalability

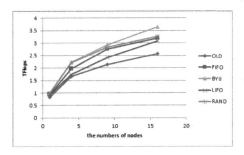

Fig. 9. Strong Scalability

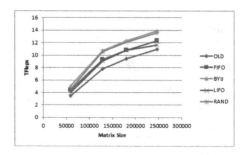

Fig. 10. Performance with varying matrix sizes on 16 nodes

case, the scalability is milder, especially with FIFO and RAND strategy. But BYIJ and LIFO strategy are a little better scalability than other strategies. As the number of nodes increases, the NEW strategies give much better performance than the OLD strategy. This seems due to the followings; increase of the number of the nodes cause the matrix data assigned to the node to be smaller than the GPU memory capacity.

4.5 Varying Matrix Sizes

We have conducted the performance evaluation with varying matrix sizes from 58,843 to 247,131. The number of nodes is fixed at 16, and the results are shown in Fig. 10. When we compare the various strategies, we see similar results to Fig. 8; the ByIJ strategies show the best performance and the RAND version comes next. The BYIJ strategy achieves 13.92 TFlops with the 247131×247131 matrix.

5   Related Work

Our data driven scheduling method is strongly influenced by DAGuE/PaRSEC by Bosilca et al. [4,5]. They have presented a direct acyclic graph (DAG) scheduler for distributed environments with GPUs, and demonstrated that the scheduler can execute applications including the Cholesky decomposition efficiently. We also use their methodology of tiling algorithm. On the other hand, to our knowledge, it is not clear how DAGuE/PaRSEC treats memory objects when GPU memory is full. Our focus is to reduce the amount of data movement between host and GPUs, by introducing task selection strategy that is aware of data locality and memory swapping strategy. In future, we are planning to compare our methods and DAGuE/PaRSEC in detail. Also we could embed our strategies in their implementation.

StarPU [3] is a DAG scheduling framework for heterogeneous environments. It allows for each task to run either on CPUs or GPUs according to the resource utilization, in order to improve the performance of execution of the whole task graph. It also maintains data consistency, while mitigating data movement between CPUs and GPUs. However, StarPU has been basically designed for a single node, while our target is distributed environments. Although the recent version is integrated to MPI communication, the programming model for distributed task dependency is different from local dependency.

In order to harness memory hierarchy of GPU memory and CPU memory in a transparent style, authors have proposed a runtime library called hybrid hierarchical runtime (HHRT) [8]. HHRT uses an oversubscription model; each GPU is shared by multiple processes, and when GPU memory is full, data of some processes are automatically swapped out. This methodology is successful for stencil based applications, however, we did not adopt it for the Cholecky decomposition. One of the reasons is that using MPI communication between processes on the same node degrades the overall performance for this computation. Also the memory consumption would be increased because of the lack of the mechanism for sharing memory objects among processes. After these problems are solved, we could integrate HHRT and the scheduling methods in this paper.

6   Conclusion and Future Work

We have described data driven scheduling approach for the optimization of the multi-node multi-GPU Cholesky decomposition. With our implementation, the communication amount between CPU and GPU is reduced by scheduling tasks appropriately and replacing the data considering its reusability. Compared with the synchronous implementation, the amount of PCIe communication is reduced by more than 80% with smaller matrices than GPU memory size, and for larger matrices, it is reduced by 40 to 60% with the best strategies. The implementation is scalable and achieved 13.9 TFlops with 16 GPUs on 16 nodes.

Among the described strategies, the "BYIJ" task selection strategy shows the best performance both for communication reduction and the speed performance. It shows we can get better performance by adopting the property of the computation for scheduling.

Also we are going to measure the performance with O(1000) nodes of TSUB-AME, in order to evaluate the scalability in peta-scale environments in order to accelerate the solution of large scale SDP problems with more than 2,000,000 constraints.

Acknowledgment. This research was supported by the Japan Science and Technology Agency (JST), the Core Research of Evolutionary Science and Technology (CREST) research project.

References

1. Top500. http://www.top500.org/
2. Tsubame2.5. http://tsubame.gsic.titech.ac.jp/
3. Augonnet, C., Thibault, S., Namyst, R., Wacrenier, P.A.: Starpu: a unified platform for task scheduling on heterogeneous multicore architectures. In: Concurrency and Computation: Practice and Experience, pp. 187–198, 23 Februaly 2011

4. Bosilca, G., Bouteiller, A., Danalis, A., Faverge, M., Herault, T., Dongarra, J.: PaRSEC: exploiting heterogeneity to enhance scalability. IEEE Comput. Sci. Eng. **15**(6), 36–45 (2013)
5. Bosilca, G., Bouteiller, A., Danalis, A., Herault, T., Lemarinier, P., Dongarra, J.: DAGuE: a generic distributed DAG engine for high performance computing. Parallel Comput. **38**, 27–51 (2012)
6. Bosilca, G., Bouteiller, A., Danalis, A., Herault, T., Lemarinier, P., Dongarra, J.: DAGuE: a generic distributed DAG engine for high performance computing. Technical report ICL-UT-10-01, Innovative Computing. Laboratory 11 April 2010
7. Choi, J., Dongarra, J., Ostrouchov, S., Petitet, A., Walker, D., Whaley, R.C.: The design and implementation of the ScaLAPACK LU, QR, and Cholesky factorization routines. In: Technial report UT CS-94-246, LAPACK Working Note 80, September 1994
8. Endo, T., Jin, G.: Software technologies coping with memory hierarchy of GPGPU clusters for stencil computations. In: Proceedings of IEEE Cluster Computing (CLUSTER2014), pp. 132–139 (2014)
9. Endo, T., Nukada, A., Matsuoka, S., Maruyama, N.: Linpack evaluation on a supercomputer with heterogeneous accelerators. In: Proceedings of IEEE/ACM International Parallel and Distributed Processing Symposium (IPDPS 2010), pp. 1–8 (2010)
10. Fujisawa, K., Sato, H., Matsuoka, S., Endo, T., Yamashita, M., Nakata, M.: High-performancd general solver for extremely largescale semidefinite programming problems. In: Proceedings of IEEE/ACM International Conference for High Performance Computing, Networking, Storage and Analysis (SC12), pp. 1–11 (2012)
11. Fujisawa, K., Endo, T., Yasui, Y., Sato, H., Matsuzawa, N., Matsuoka, S., Waki, H.: Peta-scale general solver for semidefinite programming problems with over two million constraints. In: Proceedings of the International Conference on Parallel and Distributed Processing Symposium 2014 (IPDPS2014), p. 10 (2014)
12. Yamashita, M., Fujisawa, K., Kojima, M.: SDPARA: semidefinite programming algorithm parallel version. Parallel Comput. **29**, 1053–1067 (2003)

Real-Life Experience with Major Reconfiguration of Job Scheduling System

Dalibor Klusáček[1,2], Šimon Tóth[2(✉)], and Gabriela Podolníková[2]

[1] CESNET a.l.e., Zikova 4, Prague, Czech Republic
[2] Faculty of Informatics, Masaryk University,
Botanická 68a, Brno, Czech Republic
{xklusac,toth,xpodoln}@fi.muni.cz

Abstract. This work describes the goals and impacts of a large reconfiguration of the job scheduling system, used in the Czech National Grid and Cloud infrastructure MetaCentrum, which was implemented in early 2014. MetaCentrum, as a "long-tail" oriented provider, serves a varied user-base consisting of both individual users and research groups. This imposes strict requirements on the robustness of job scheduling algorithms being employed, as the system must be capable of assigning a highly heterogeneous set of workloads to a similarly heterogeneous set of computational resources. Primary goals for MetaCentrum were always to provide efficient and fair resource utilization with respect to different users in the system. During the last few years, MetaCentrum has gone through a period of rapid growth (1,500 CPU cores in 2009 vs. 10,600 CPU cores in 2014) forcing us to re-evaluate our scheduling approaches, as the "old" configuration no longer satisfied our utilization and fairness demands. This re-evaluation was supported by a significant body of research, which included the proposal of new scheduling approaches as well as detailed simulations based on real-life complex workload traces. First of all, a new multi-resource aware fair-sharing algorithm (based on our recent research) was deployed, with the goal of improving fairness with respect to the growing heterogeneity of resources and users' workloads. Second, the queue configuration of the entire system was completely reworked in order to decrease resource fragmentation and improve the utilization and the impact of fairness policies. This paper summarizes the effects of these changes using real-life data from the production system. Moreover, we publish complex workload traces from MetaCentrum that were used in this paper, since they represent a valuable source of data concerning a highly heterogeneous production system. Last but not least, we also present our advanced job scheduling simulator which is routinely used for testing of new scheduling strategies prior their deployment in the real system.

Keywords: Scheduling · Fairness · Queue · Workload · Heterogeneity

© Springer International Publishing AG 2017
N. Desai and W. Cirne (Eds.): JSSPP 2015/2016, LNCS 10353, pp. 83–101, 2017.
DOI: 10.1007/978-3-319-61756-5_5

1   Introduction

MetaCentrum serves various users and research groups. During the last 5 years, MetaCentrum has grown from approximately 1,500 CPU cores (2009) to almost 11,000 CPU cores (2014), with the number of processed jobs matching this growth curve (see Fig. 1). The system is divided into two separate pools of resources, each managed by a different job scheduler. The smaller pool ($\sim$4, 900 CPUs) is managed by a custom-developed scheduler which uses planning (instead of queues) [7] while the larger pool ($\sim$6, 100 CPUs) is managed by a queue-based scheduler based on TORQUE resource manager. While the plan-based scheduler has been heavily optimized in the past, the original "historic" scheduling approaches used in the queue-based scheduler—which remained mostly the same for a decade—were becoming clearly inefficient and had to be revised to better reflect growing heterogeneity of both hardware resources and users' workloads. In this work, we focus on the queue-based scheduler which manages the major part of MetaCentrum computing resources.

The goal of this work is to share our real-life experience with a major reconfiguration of a production system as it was a unique opportunity to apply "theoretical" results in practice. Therefore, we summarize our previous efforts and describe how the newly proposed modifications were evaluated and applied in practice, i.e., we provide new results showing the improvement of system performance achieved through a newly defined scheduling setup.

In case of MetaCentrum, there were two main issues with the historical setup: an obsolete (unfair) fair-sharing mechanism and a rather inefficient queue configuration. When solving these issues, we are building upon our earlier "theoretical" works where new multi-resource aware fair-sharing mechanisms were proposed [9] and the impact and interactions of various system-specific policies were described [10]. It is worth noticing that the improvement was solely achieved by the newly configured queues and new fair-sharing mechanism, while the actual scheduling algorithm remained unchanged. Furthermore, we also provide detailed information concerning MetaCentrum *infrastructure and users' workloads* that were used both for the development of the new system configuration as well as for later analysis of the suitability of the new solution [13]. They represent valuable source of data, especially in terms of heterogeneity of system resources and users' workloads. Last but not least, we have prepared a largely extended

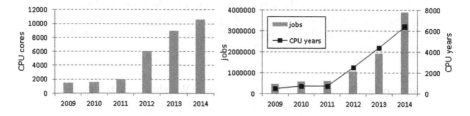

Fig. 1. Available CPU cores (left) and the number of jobs and used CPU years (right).

version of our jobs scheduling simulator *Alea* [2], which was heavily used when developing the new system setup and provides advanced simulation capabilities compared to its previous releases [8].

This paper is organized as follows. Applied modifications of the scheduling system are presented in the following section. Section 2.1 describes the queue reconfiguration, discussing differences between previous and current queue setup. Section 2.2 presents the new mechanism used to guarantee user-to-user fairness subject to heterogeneous users' requests. Next, the impact of queue reconfiguration on the overall performance is analyzed and the influence and suitability of the new fair-sharing mechanism is discussed in Sect. 3. Complex MetaCentrum workloads and the advanced job scheduling simulator Alea are presented in Sects. 4 and 5 respectively. Section 6 concludes the paper and discusses the future work.

2 Reconfiguration of MetaCentrum Scheduling System

Production resource management systems need to satisfy the constraints imposed by resource providers, the expectations of users and must be robust enough to deal with short term fluctuations in the user base, its workloads and resource outages. In our previous work [10], we have discussed the complexities of configuring a production resource management system, such as PBS Pro and Torque, to satisfy all three of these requirements. The issue at the root of this problem is that production software is generally configured in a bottom-up fashion, meaning that the desired behavior is achieved through a combination of various policies.

The search for a new efficient setup of a resource management system is then particularly problematic as relatively straightforward configuration changes can have highly unexpected side effects arising from the interactions between individual policies. The choice of queue configuration can have significant effect on the way the scheduling algorithm selects jobs for execution [11], fair-sharing mechanisms that establish fair job order may be seriously diluted by both the scheduling algorithm [5] and the queue configuration [10], and too generous or too restrictive queue limits may either cause resource fragmentation or excessive resource saturation [16].

In this section we describe how we established the new queue configuration to enable higher job throughput and fairer scheduling (Sect. 2.1). Also, we briefly describe the newly applied multi-resource aware fair-sharing mechanism that reflects heterogeneity of resources and users' requests (Sect. 2.2).

2.1 Queue Reconfiguration

Detailed description of the queue reconfiguration, including the analysis of the historical setup, design and verification of a new configuration was already presented in our previous work [10]. Therefore, in this section we will only provide a summary of the core ideas that are required for the remainder of this paper and we kindly invite the reader to seek out our previous work for more details.

Mainstream resource management systems generally utilize the concept of queues to allow fine control over the systems behavior. Queue specific policies include per-user, per-group and per-queue limits [1,17] concerning the maximum number of running jobs and/or utilized amount of a particular resource type (e.g., CPU cores). Queues can also be configured to have access to only a subset of available resources, e.g., limiting a queue to a particular cluster of machines. This allows the establishment of resource pools, in which several queues compete for a limited set of resources, thus preventing a (potentially dangerous) saturation of the entire system. Of course, queues and their configuration can increase resource fragmentation [5] as each job is limited to a single pool of resources. This may however be necessary to deal with different classes of users and/or jobs accessing the system. We need to be very careful and avoid saturating the system with single class of jobs, as for example, saturating the system with long running jobs (i.e., jobs with expected runtime of several weeks) will lead to great deterioration in performance characteristics of the system, e.g., huge wait times for shorter jobs will be inevitable since they would have to wait until those long jobs would complete and free some resources.

Historical Queue Configuration. For nearly a decade, MetaCentrum used one configuration, that only underwent small tweaks through the years. This configuration was originally designed manually by experts to fit the users' workloads at the time. The configuration was designed in a self-balancing manner, using overlapping resource pools with different sizes that were balanced out by queue priorities, with the highest priority queue having access to only the smallest resource pool. To achieve this, the system utilized three major queues (long, normal, short) each with a different maximum walltime limitation (30 days, 24 h, 2 h), different priorities (70, 50, 60) and different limits defining the maximum allowed number of concurrently running jobs of one user (70, 300, 250). Later (2010), a low priority (20) queue called backfill has been introduced, that only accepted single node jobs (max limit per user is 1000) that run up to 24 h. It was designed for undemanding jobs and increases system utilization during off-peak hours. To provide a fair access to the system, jobs in these queues were dynamically ordered using priorities based on fair-share [5]. Next, queues were traversed one-by-one by the scheduling policy, starting with the highest priority queue (long). The scheme of the historical setup is shown in Fig. 2 (left).

After analyzing the behavior of this setup under the current users' workloads, we have determined that the major problem with this setup is the congestion of the long queue. To understand the reason we first must understand the self-balancing nature of the original setup. The long queue had to be limited to a relatively small pool of resources (1440 CPU cores) as increasing this pool would immediately lead to complete saturation of these resources with long jobs due to the high priority of the long queue. It was the combination of the small resource pool and the fact that the long queue was the only one accepting jobs

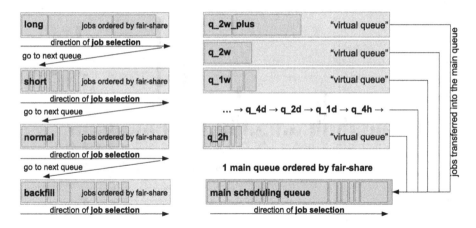

Fig. 2. Historical setup of queues (left) and the newly applied configuration (right).

longer than 1 day, that lead to the new inefficiency observed in the system. The users' workloads have shifted enough that the majority of the CPU time was now consumed by the long queue, despite the resource pool limitation. Shorter jobs are much more frequent, as can be seen in Fig. 3, which shows job arrivals (top) and CPU time distribution (bottom) with respect to queues and time (on a weekly basis)[1]. As was observed, long queue only contained 2.75% of all jobs but produced 51.5% of overall CPU utilization. It was then very clear, that it should not have the smallest pool of available CPUs, but at the same time we could not simply increase the resource pool (for reasons mentioned above).

Applied Queue Reconfiguration. Several proposals of new queue configuration have been considered and experimentally evaluated in a simulator [10]. The main goal was to increase the pool of available CPUs for longer jobs in a safe fashion. In the first step, long queue has been refined into 5 queues. The one with the longest maximum job walltime limit is called q_2w_plus (up to 30 days) and has the maximum priority. Next, there are q_2w, q_1w, q_4d, q_2d with decreasing priorities and walltime limits (2 weeks, 1 week, 4 days and 2 days, respectively). Normal and short queues are now called q_1d and q_2h while q_4h is a new queue with walltime limit being 4 h. Once the long queue has been replaced with several new queues it was possible (and safe) to increase the number of available CPUs for selected newly created queues.

When setting up the new per-queue limits, several rules were applied that were based either on simulation results or our empirical knowledge. The first rule was that the number of available CPUs for a given queue should be—in general—inversely proportional to the maximum walltime limit of a given queue. In another words, it is safe to assign a large pool of resources to a queue

---

[1] Only major queues in the main system pool are considered. Auxiliary and specialized queues are omitted as well as all results coming from the second scheduler.

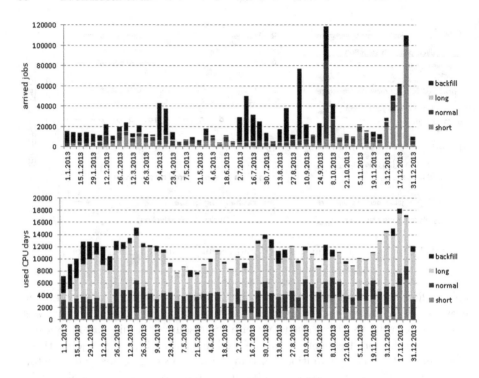

Fig. 3. Job arrivals (top) and used CPU time (bottom) per week and queue.

that only executes short jobs, since those CPUs—if necessary—will be free soon (short jobs completes early). Also, the actual workload indicates that short jobs having their walltime ≤1 day are in fact the most common jobs in MetaCentrum (see Fig. 4 (top)). On the other hand, it is very important to choose a rather conservative limit for long jobs as those may execute for weeks or even months, thus blocking resources over a long time period. Still, this "conservative" limit should be as high as acceptable, since long jobs are responsible for the majority of system utilization, at least this is the case in MetaCentrum (see Fig. 4 (bottom)). Last but not least, it is known that excessive number of queues with dedicated resources may cause resource fragmentation [5], leading to a low system utilization and large wait times. Therefore, whenever it was possible, resources were not dedicated exclusively to a given queue. Instead, several queues were allowed to compete for the same set of resources as their pools were overlapping. In such cases, it was observed that per-queue limits and fair-share are sufficient to balance "queue-sharing" of resources.

At the same time, the *effect of newly added queues on fairness* was considered as well. Using our complex workloads, we have performed detailed simulations which revealed that multiple queues with fixed ordering are very unfair and practically eliminate the impact of the fair-sharing algorithm. For example, if a job has a low priority (due to the fair-share) but ends up in a high priority

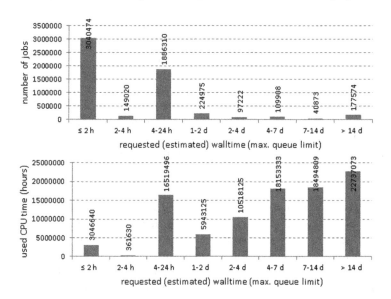

Fig. 4. Number of jobs according to their requested walltime (top) and corresponding used CPU time (bottom) wrt. to requested walltime during 2013–2014 period.

queue (due to its expected walltime) it will often start much earlier than a high priority job residing in a low priority queue. Clearly, this is highly unfair. Therefore, the applied solution uses a little trick, where the queues are only used to (1) *maintain resource limits* and (2) *provide information on job's maximum walltime* (if not specified directly by a user). Otherwise, all (major) queues have the same priority, i.e., the ordering in which a job is being selected for execution is now solely based on the priority of a given user which is established by fairshare. Therefore, those queues are now only "virtual" and the actual scheduling process is performed over *one single queue* ordered by fair-share, which contains all jobs from those "virtual" queues. Figure 2 (right) depicts the new setup of queues.

2.2 Multi-resource Aware Fair-Sharing

MetaCentrum serves the scientific community and provides its resources for free. Therefore, *money cannot be used* to define the order in which users and their (pending) workload will use the resources [19]. Instead, user-to-user fairness is maintained by the well known *fair-sharing* [5] approach, which dynamically establishes fair user ordering.

Historical Fair-Sharing Algorithm. Originally, the fair-sharing algorithm considered only single resource (allocated CPU time) and then calculated users priorities using the popular *max-min* approach [4], i.e., it assigned high priority to a user with low CPU time utilization and vice versa. As discussed in the literature, single-resource based fair-sharing is (highly) unfair for (highly) heterogeneous systems and workloads [4,6,9], which is the case of MetaCentrum. The most critical problem regarding the original CPU time-based fair-sharing was that users with memory demanding workloads (and small CPU demands) were constantly favored by the scheduler, causing serious blocking of memory-heavy machines, poor fairness and low CPU utilization of large machines [9]. Therefore, the original single-resource aware fair-sharing algorithm was reply a newly developed multi-resource aware solution that also reflects the consumption of RAM memory.

Applied Multi-resource Aware Fair-Sharing Algorithm. Technical details as well as a detailed comparison with other existing techniques has been already published in our recent work [9]. Therefore, we will only briefly mention the main features of the newly applied solution. The new mechanism determines a user priority F_u based on CPU and RAM requirements of that user's (previously completed) jobs. F_u is computed by aggregating weighted walltimes of all jobs (J_u) of given user u (see Formula 1). Each job $walltime_j$ is weighted by so called job penalty P_j and machine speed factor S_j, which is used to reflect the influence of machine speed on resulting walltime of a completed job. S_j normalizes a job walltime such that job executed on a slow machine is not additionally penalized by its longer walltime (execution time), and vice versa. Job penalty P_j expresses the amount of allocated CPU and RAM resources (see Formula 2).

$$F_u = \sum_{j \in J_u} P_j \cdot walltime_j \cdot S_j \tag{1}$$

$$P_j = \min_{m \in M_j} \left(\max \left(\frac{cpu_j}{cpu_m}, \frac{ram_j}{ram_m} \right) \cdot cpu_m \right) \tag{2}$$

P_j penalty extends the well known Processor Equivalent (PE) metric [5], eliminating some serious problems related to job and resource heterogeneity. The major difference is that instead of calculating the penalty according to machines assigned to a given job (actual "price"), it calculates what is the minimal possible price (ideal price) according to the set of all suitable machines (M_j) and job requests (cpu_j, ram_j). Simply put, for each job the set of all suitable machines is constructed (M_j) and the "price" of executing that job is calculated for each machine in M_j. Finally, P_j is set to the minimal found price. Then P_j is independent of scheduler decisions and users have no reason to complain or cheat as they are guaranteed to obtain the best price. Once F_u priorities are calculated for all users, they are then ordered in the *lowest F_u first* order[2]. The actual implementation also *reflects aging* [5] by periodically decreasing all recorded consumption using the so called decay factor [1]. Using it we put higher emphasis on a more recent resource consumption.

---

[2] To be more precise, not users but their jobs in a queue are then ordered according to corresponding F_u values.

3 Results

This section analyzes the impact of queue reconfiguration on the overall performance of the MetaCentrum system and the influence and suitability of the new multi-resource aware fair-sharing mechanism.

3.1 Impact of Queue Reconfiguration

The new queue setup has been evaluated by comparing several statistical indicators using historical workload data from two consecutive time periods. The first period (October–December 2013) represented the old queue configuration while January–March 2014 period represented the new configuration. Both time periods lasted 92 days and the underlying infrastructure was identical during that time. We could not have used longer time periods, since those would contain several occasions when either old clusters were removed from the system or new ones were included. Obviously, such resource fluctuation would make the analysis less reliable. On the other hand, we do acknowledge that by comparing two setups of a production system in two distinct time periods, we inherently include differences in the underlying workloads, which could skew the presented results. Yet, we believe that the presented results are representative, as not only the metrics have shown improvements but also user feedback was positive.

We start with a comparison of the number of processed jobs which has increased significantly. During the October–December 2013 period, 513,976 jobs have been completed in MetaCentrum while in the January–March 2014 period (new queue configuration) 854,972 jobs were completed, representing an increase of 66.3%. At the same time, the overall CPU utilization has increased significantly (43.2%) as can be seen by the naked eye in Fig. 5, which shows the utilized CPU hours before and after queue reconfiguration. For simplicity, the average CPU time usage in those two periods is highlighted in the figure using dashed lines.

Figure 6 (top) presents a closer look on the distribution of utilized CPU time. It reveals that the largest increase in utilized CPU time is visible for jobs having their walltime in the interval of 4 h–14 days. It confirms that the newly introduced queues are being used regularly and users of the system are able to recognize their benefits, e.g., larger pools of resources associated with these shorter queues[3].

Beside the overall utilization we have also analyzed job wait times which are an important factor, especially for the users of the system. It would not be surprising if the higher throughput and utilization caused that jobs are actually waiting longer. This is a real-life phenomenon originating from the fact that the system is more saturated, while users submit more jobs as they see the improved performance. However, as we have observed, even with a significantly larger throughput and utilization, job wait times remained decent. In fact, they

---

[3] As was explained in Sect. 2.1, q_2w, q_1w, q_4d, q_2d, etc. queues now have larger pools of available resources compared to the original long queue.

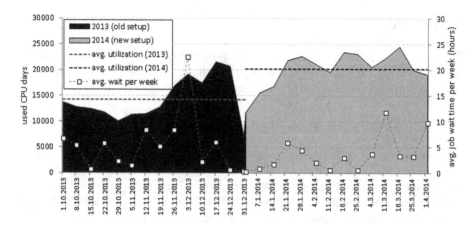

Fig. 5. Comparison of used CPU days (in a given week) before and after queue reconfiguration (left axis) and the average wait time per week (right axis).

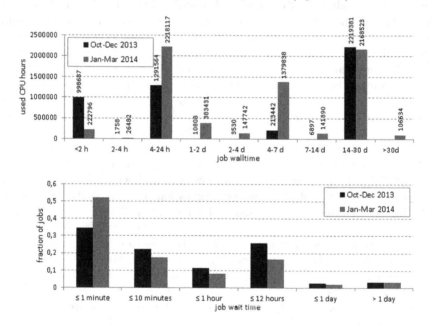

Fig. 6. Comparison utilized CPU hours wrt. to job walltime (top) and the distribution of job wait times before/after queues were reconfigured (bottom).

were—on average—decreased by 17.9% (4.4 vs. 3.6 h). A more detailed view is available in Fig. 5, where the average job wait time per week is shown (with the scale on the right side of the chart) along with the previously discussed average used CPU time. As we can see, the average wait time is bellow 5 h on 11 occasions during January–March 2014. At the same time, there were only six weeks during October–December 2013 when the average wait time was bellow 5 h.

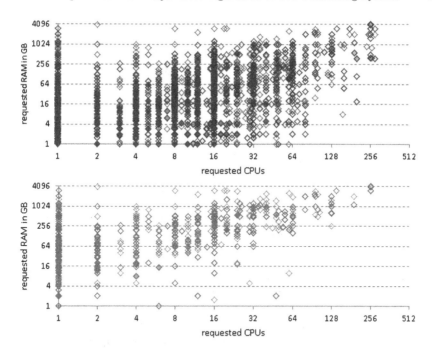

Fig. 7. The distribution of jobs requirements during January–March 2014 (top) and the corresponding jobs affected by the new fair-sharing mechanism (bottom).

Certainly, this is a important finding which shows that the new configuration allows for higher throughput and utilization while keeping the wait times in an acceptable level. Another detailed view is presented in Fig. 6 (bottom). It shows how jobs are distributed with respect to their wait times. As we can see, the new queue configuration leads to a shorter wait times for majority of the jobs.

3.2 Impact of Multi-resource Aware Fair-Sharing

In the next step, we have analyzed the influence of the new fair-sharing mechanism. Again, we have used historical workload traces from the October–December 2013 (old, single-resource fair-sharing) and January–March 2014 (new, multi-resource aware fair-sharing) periods.

First of all, we have plotted all jobs coming from the January–March 2014 period according to their CPU and memory requirements, as shows Fig. 7 (top). For better visibility, both the x-axis and the y-axis are in log. scale. As can be seen, the workload from MetaCentrum is truly heterogeneous. For example, a job requesting 1 CPU may have its memory requirements anywhere between 1 GB and 2 terabytes of RAM[4]. Figure 7 (top) demonstrates the huge heterogeneity

---

[4] Jobs requesting less than 1 GB of RAM are not shown in Fig. 7 as they would end up "bellow" the baseline of the log. scale-shaped graph.

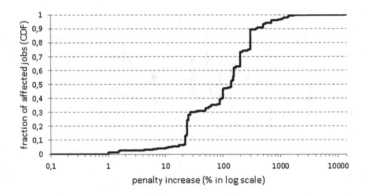

Fig. 8. The CDF showing the increase of penalty value (P_j) for affected jobs according to the new fair-sharing mechanism.

of job requirements, which was the reason why the historic single-resource based fair-sharing was impractical, i.e., extremely unfair.

In the second step, we have analyzed the workload from January–March 2014 period and selected *all jobs that were affected* by the new fair-sharing algorithm, i.e., their "fair-sharing penalty" P_j was different when computed according to the new multi-resource aware scheme. Those *affected jobs* are shown in Fig. 7 (bottom). As we can see, the new multi-resource aware penalty function works as ones intuition would suggest, i.e., higher penalties are assigned to those jobs that request large amounts of RAM compared to their CPU requirements. With a few exceptions[5], the new fair-sharing algorithm targets jobs lying "above the main diagonal", i.e., those that have high RAM to CPU ratio, which is the expected behavior.

We have also analyzed the increase of penalty values. For this purpose we took jobs affected by the new penalty $P(j)$ and measured the resulting percentage increase of $P(j)$ value with respect to the old, CPU-based version. Figure 8 shows the resulting distribution using the cumulative distribution function (the x-axis is in log. scale). In this case, the CDF is a $f(x)$-like function showing the probability that the percentage increase of $P(j)$ for a given job j is less than or equal to x. In another words, the CDF represents the fraction of jobs having their $P(j)$ increased by at most x percents. As can be seen, the improvement is often significant. For example, nearly 60% of affected jobs have their $P(j)$ at least two times higher (penalty increase $\geq 100\%$).

In the next step, we have analyzed the impact of the new multi-resource aware fair-sharing mechanism on the performance of affected jobs. This time, we have compared those two time periods: October–December 2013 (old fair-sharing) and January–March 2014 (new fair-sharing). Again, we have selected those jobs

---

[5] Those exceptions are jobs lying under the main "diagonal", i.e., in the lower central/right part of the plot. Such exceptions were expected as the new fair-sharing scheme may also (rarely) assign smaller penalties compared to the original single-resource aware mechanism.

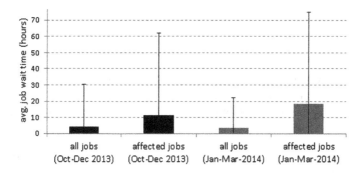

Fig. 9. Comparison of avg. wait times wrt. the old and the new fair-sharing mechanism.

that were affected by the new multi-resource aware fair-sharing scheme[6]. Then we have computed the average wait time (and its standard deviation) of such affected jobs for both periods, i.e., before and after the new fair-sharing was deployed.

Figure 9 shows the results of such a comparison. Apparently, with the new multi-resource aware fair-sharing algorithm the average wait time of affected jobs is significantly larger (18.3 vs. 11.4 h). At the same time, standard deviations of wait times are similar in both situations which indicates that the overall increase of wait times is not accidental (a result of few extremes), instead it is a common tendency. It means that the new fair-sharing is working as intended, appropriately assigning higher penalties to (memory) demanding jobs, thus prolonging their wait times.

3.3   Summary

The evaluation presented above was based on real-life data coming from Meta-Centrum. So far, the results indicate that the two applied modifications, i.e., queue reconfiguration and new fair-sharing algorithm work as intended. First of all, thanks to the newly configured queues the overall throughput and utilization have increased significantly. At the same time, the average wait times were decreased. Also, the new multi-resource aware fair-sharing mechanism works better than the original mechanism, since RAM demanding jobs now obtain appropriate penalties as the consumption of RAM memory is considered when computing a user priority. Unlike in the old fair-share, RAM intensive jobs are now penalized similarly to CPU demanding jobs, resulting in a more fair behavior of the system. So far, no significant comments concerning the new fair-sharing approach were recorder from either the users or the management team of Meta-Centrum.

---

[6] In case of the earlier period (October–December 2013)—which did not use the new fair-sharing mechanism—these affected jobs were detected using the Alea job scheduling simulator which is capable of emulating the new fair-sharing method.

4   MetaCentrum Workload Traces

One of the contributions of this paper is that we are offering the scientific community a complex workload trace from the MetaCentrum system. This workload starts in January 2013 and represents 2 years of job execution in MetaCentrum, containing 5.8 millions jobs.

We believe that this workload may be valuable for several reasons. First of all, MetaCentrum is a very heterogeneous environment. It contains variety of resources, starting with small nodes (8 cores with 16 GB of RAM per node) and going up through moderate nodes (16–64 cores with 64–256 GB of RAM per node) to large and RAM-heavy machines (80–384 cores with 0.5–6.0 TB of RAM). Beside common clusters, MetaCentrum also provides 3 GPU-enabled clusters (*konos*, *doom* and *gram*) for CUDA-like computations. We have prepared a detailed resource description file, which contains information about each cluster. Here we specify the number of nodes, number of CPU cores per node, the amount of RAM per node and the results of the Standard Performance Evaluation Corporation's SPEC CPU2006 benchmark (CFP2006 suite/fp_rate_base2006). Furthermore, the availability of MetaCentrum's clusters is provided too.

Similarly, jobs in the workload vary accordingly. The majority of jobs (71%) is sequential while parallel jobs represent 29% of all jobs. On the other hand, sequential jobs represent only 10% of used CPU time as parallel jobs use 90% of CPU time. A more detailed view showing how jobs and CPU time are spread over existing queues with respect to job parallelism is presented in Fig. 10, where x-axis represents job parallelism and y-axis represents number of jobs and used CPU time, respectively. The y-axis is in log scale in both cases. Figure 10 (top) shows that the "shape" of distribution of job parallelism is similar for all queues, and most jobs (88%) belong to "short" queues (walltime ≤ 24 h). On the other hand, Fig. 10 (bottom) shows that "long" (walltime > 24 h), parallel jobs are those that are responsible for the majority of used CPU time. The distribution of jobs and CPU time with respect to walltimes (i.e., queues) can be found in Fig. 4, showing that "long" jobs—which represent only 12% of all jobs—are responsible for 80% of used CPU time. Finally, an example of the variability of job CPU and RAM requirements is shown in Fig. 7 (top).

The job workload is presented in more than usual detail. Beside common parameters that are routinely provided, e.g., in the Standard Workload Format (SWF) [3], we provide additional job specifications that influence job scheduling and allow for more detailed simulations and analysis. Here we use input parameters of the `qsub` command. For example, `2:ppn=4:x86:linux:cl_minos` input parameters mean that the job is requesting 2 nodes, with 4 processors per node (ppn). Both nodes must be operated by linux-like OS, lie within *minos* cluster and have x86 architecture. Similarly, `1:ppn=1:gpu=1:cl_gram` means that the job can only be executed on cluster *gram* and requires 1 node with 1 CPU and 1 GPU card[7].

---

[7] A detailed description of `qsub` semantics is available at: https://wiki.metacentrum. cz/wiki/Running_jobs_in_scheduler.

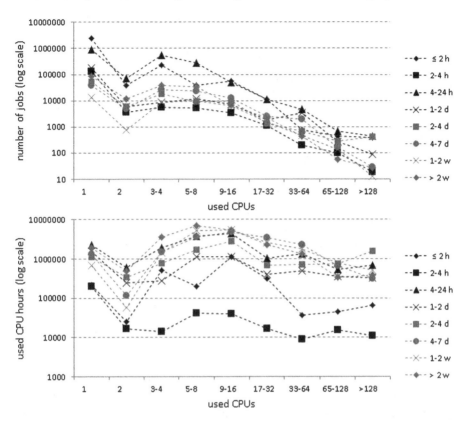

Fig. 10. The number of jobs per queue (top) and the utilized CPU time per queue (bottom) with respect to job parallelism.

Last but not least, information about queues, their priorities and per-user CPU limits are provided as well. The whole job workload formatted in an extended SWF format as well as related information concerning resources and queues can be obtained at: http://www.fi.muni.cz/~xklusac/jsspp/.

5 Job Scheduling Simulator

Designing a well working scheduler for HPC, Cloud or a Grid-like system is a complex task. One needs not only to consider the workloads the system will need to process, but is also constrained by the requirements of the resource providers and users. Simulators can simplify this task by allowing fast iterations over different system configurations.

In MetaCentrum, simulations are used regularly for testing new setups and features of the scheduling system as well as for designing new scheduling algorithms. For this purpose, *Alea job scheduling simulator* [8] based on GridSim [21]

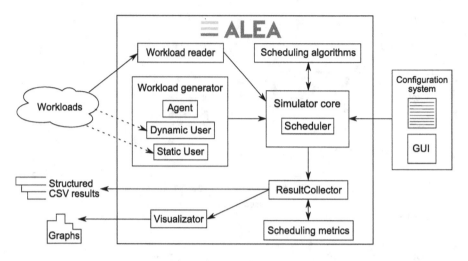

Fig. 11. The structure of the Alea simulator.

has been developed and is continuously upgraded [18]. It provides advanced features that allow for detailed simulations. A high-level scheme of the structure of the simulator is shown in Fig. 11.

The major role is played by the *scheduler* entity which represents the centralized scheduler. The scheduler holds current simulation data, handles communication and delegates scheduling decisions to a chosen scheduling algorithm. Variety of scheduling algorithms is provided, including trivial First Come First Served and its prioritized versions such as Shortest Job First, Earliest Deadline First, etc. Also policies using backfilling are supported, including aggressive backfilling (no reservations), EASY backfilling [20] and Conservative backfilling [15].

Of course, a simulator cannot work properly unless it is supplied with an appropriate workload. Therefore, parsers for common workload formats are provided. However getting access to a historical workload that fits the expected workload of the system is often a complicated process. One possible solution to the problem of finding a matching workload is to simply generate one. Solutions for generating workloads, with varying degrees of complexity, have been available for some time [14]. From models based on statistical analysis [12] that generate jobs fitting a particular parameter distribution to dynamic models that react to the behavior of the evaluated scheduler [22]. Alea takes a step ahead and provides a *dynamic workload generator* which extends existing approaches further and concentrates on modeling the behavior of users in the system using *user agents*. Agents have access to scheduling information and therefore react to stimuli, such as a completion of a job. This allows us to model different user behavior from very batch-oriented users that submit sets of jobs and wait for the entire batch to complete, to interactive users that submit one job at a time, wait for its completion, process the results and then submit a new job. Realistic modeling of day-night and week-weekend cycles is matter of course. This approach allows for more thorough testing of scheduling setups, but also enables testing of hypothetical scenarios. Determining how the system will behave if we add, e.g., another user, becomes a matter of modifying a configuration file.

During the simulation, the *result collector* entity collects the data and—using either default or user-provided metrics—stores results into CSV files and (optionally) uses them for visualization. Importantly, Alea supports various fair-sharing policies allowing for simulations where fairness is of importance. Also, various queues including limits as well as complex job specifications (see Sect. 4) are supported, resulting in much more realistic simulations.

This complexity of simulation capabilities resulted in a newly designed configuration system [18]. In a user-friendly fashion, it allows to adjust parameters of simulations by providing an intuitive way how to choose different data sets, scheduling algorithms, measured metrics as well as additional features, e.g., the type of fair-sharing algorithm. Alea is freely available at GitHub [2].

6   Conclusion and Future Work

In this paper we are sharing our experience with a *major reconfiguration* of the job scheduling system in MetaCentrum. Our analysis measures the impact of two major modifications—the queue reconfiguration and the new multi-resource aware fair-sharing algorithm. Both the results and the feedback from the users of the system indicate that the reconfigured system is more efficient than it was previously. First of all, thanks to the new queue setup the throughput is now much larger while job wait times remained decent. Concerning the new fair-sharing algorithm, the results revealed that it works as intended, assigning higher penalties to jobs with large requirements concerning RAM. The effect of increased penalties was observed as well, i.e., wait times of RAM-heavy jobs have increased compared to the period when single-resource based fair-sharing was used. Last but not least, we are presenting our jobs scheduling simulator and the complex workload traces from MetaCentrum to the scientific community.

Still, our work has some limitations. Although we have mentioned some general rules (see Sect. 2.1), values of several (important) parameters such as queue-related limits are currently based on an empirical knowledge or an (hand-tuned) expert assessment. In the future we would like to develop more rigorous methods that would allow for a (semi)automatic identification of proper and efficient system setups. For starters, it would be very helpful to have some method that—given a current workload—would perform a dynamic adaptation of various queue-related limits.

Acknowledgments. We highly appreciate the support of the Grant Agency of the Czech Republic under the grant No. P202/12/0306. The support provided by the programme "Projects of Large Infrastructure for Research, Development, and Innovations" LM2010005 funded by the Ministry of Education, Youth, and Sports of the Czech Republic is highly appreciated. The access to the MetaCentrum computing facilities and workloads is kindly acknowledged.

References

1. Adaptive Computing Enterprises, Inc., Maui Scheduler Administrator's Guide, version 3.2, January 2014. http://docs.adaptivecomputing.com
2. Alea job scheduling simulator, February 2015. https://github.com/aleasimulator/
3. Chapin, S., et al.: Benchmarks and standards for the evaluation of parallel job schedulers. In: Feitelson, D.G., Rudolph, L. (eds.) JSSPP 1999. LNCS, vol. 1659, pp. 67–90. Springer, Heidelberg (1999). doi:10.1007/3-540-47954-6_4
4. Ghodsi, A., Zaharia, M., Hindman, B., Konwinski, A., Shenker, S., Stoica, I.: Dominant resource fairness: fair allocation of multiple resource types. In: 8th USENIX Symposium on Networked Systems Design and Implementation (2011)
5. Jackson, D., Snell, Q., Clement, M.: Core algorithms of the maui scheduler. In: Feitelson, D.G., Rudolph, L. (eds.) JSSPP 2001. LNCS, vol. 2221, pp. 87–102. Springer, Heidelberg (2001). doi:10.1007/3-540-45540-X_6
6. Joe-Wong, C., Sen, S., Lan, T., Chiang, M.: Multi-resource allocation: fairness-efficiency tradeoffs in a unifying framework. In: 31st Annual International Conference on Computer Communications (IEEE INFOCOM), pp. 1206–1214 (2012)
7. Klusáček, D., Chlumský, V., Rudová, H.: Planning and optimization in TORQUE resource manager. In: High Performance and Distributed Computing (HPDC). ACM (2015)
8. Klusáček, D., Rudová, H.: Alea 2 - job scheduling simulator. In: 3rd International ICST Conference on Simulation Tools and Technique (ICST) (2010)
9. Klusáček, D., Rudová, H.: Multi-resource aware fairsharing for heterogeneous systems. In: Cirne, W., Desai, N. (eds.) JSSPP 2014. LNCS, vol. 8828, pp. 53–69. Springer, Cham (2015). doi:10.1007/978-3-319-15789-4_4
10. Klusáček, D., Tóth, Š.: On interactions among scheduling policies: finding efficient queue setup using high-resolution simulations. In: Silva, F., Dutra, I., Santos Costa, V. (eds.) Euro-Par 2014. LNCS, vol. 8632, pp. 138–149. Springer, Cham (2014). doi:10.1007/978-3-319-09873-9_12
11. Lawson, B.G., Smirni, E.: Multiple-queue backfilling scheduling with priorities and reservations for parallel systems. In: Feitelson, D.G., Rudolph, L., Schwiegelshohn, U. (eds.) JSSPP 2002. LNCS, vol. 2537, pp. 72–87. Springer, Heidelberg (2002). doi:10.1007/3-540-36180-4_5
12. Lublin, U., Feitelson, D.G.: The workload on parallel supercomputers: modeling the characteristics of rigid jobs. J. Parallel Distrib. Comput. **63**(11), 1105–1122 (2003)
13. MetaCentrum workload logs, February 2015. http://www.fi.muni.cz/xklusac/workload/
14. Parallel workload models, February 2015. http://www.cs.huji.ac.il/labs/parallel/workload/models.html
15. Mu'alem, A.W., Feitelson, D.G.: Utilization, predictability, workloads, and user runtime estimates in scheduling the IBM SP2 with backfilling. IEEE Trans. Parallel Distrib. Syst. **12**(6), 529–543 (2001)
16. Ohio Supercomputer Center. Batch Processing at OSC, February 2014. https://www.osc.edu/supercomputing/batch-processing-at-osc
17. PBS Works. PBS Professional 12.1, Administrator's Guide, January 2014. http://www.pbsworks.com
18. Podolníková, G.: Configuration and presentation system of job scheduling simulator, Bachelor's thesis (2014). http://is.muni.cz/th/396214/fi_b/Gabriela_Podolnikova_BP.pdf

19. Sempolinski, P., Thain, D.: A comparison and critique of Eucalyptus, OpenNebula and Nimbus. In: Proceedings of the 2010 IEEE Second International Conference on Cloud Computing Technology and Science (CLOUDCOM 2010), pp. 417–426. IEEE Computer Society (2010)
20. Skovira, J., Chan, W., Zhou, H., Lifka, D.: The EASY — loadleveler API project. In: Feitelson, D.G., Rudolph, L. (eds.) JSSPP 1996. LNCS, vol. 1162, pp. 41–47. Springer, Heidelberg (1996). doi:10.1007/BFb0022286
21. Sulistio, A., Cibej, U., Venugopal, S., Robic, B., Buyya, R.: A toolkit for modelling and simulating data grids: an extension to gridsim. Concurr. Comput. Pract. Exp. **20**(13), 1591–1609 (2008)
22. Zakay, N., Feitelson, D.G.: Preserving user behavior characteristics in trace-based simulation of parallel job scheduling. In: 22nd Modeling, Analysis & Simulation of Computer & Telecommunication System (MASCOTS), pp. 51–60 (2014)

EVALIX: Classification and Prediction of Job Resource Consumption on HPC Platforms

Joseph Emeras[1]($\boxtimes$), Sébastien Varrette[2], Mateusz Guzek[1],
and Pascal Bouvry[2]

[1] Interdisciplinary Centre for Security Reliability and Trust,
Luxembourg, Luxembourg
{Joseph.Emeras,Mateusz.Guzek}@uni.lu
[2] Computer Science and Communications (CSC) Research Unit,
6, rue Richard Coudenhove-Kalergi, 1359 Luxembourg, Luxembourg
{Sebastien.Varrette,Pascal.Bouvry}@uni.lu

Abstract. At the advent of a wished (or forced) convergence between High Performance Computing HPC platforms, stand-alone accelerators and virtualized resources from Cloud Computing CC systems, this article unveils the job prediction component of the EVALIX project. This framework aims at an improved efficiency of the underlying Resource and Job Management System RJMS within heterogeneous HPC facilities by the automatic evaluation and characterization of the submitted workload. The objective is not only to better adapt the scheduled jobs to the available resource capabilities, but also to reduce the energy costs. For that purpose, we collected the resource consumption of all the jobs executed on a production cluster for a period of three months. Based on the analysis then on the classification of the jobs, we computed a resource consumption model. The objective is to train a set of predictors based on the aforementioned model, that will give the estimated CPU, memory and IO used by the jobs. The analysis of the resource consumption highlighted that different classes of jobs have different kinds of resource needs and the classification of the jobs enabled to characterize several application patterns of the users. We also discovered that several users whose resource usage on the cluster is considered as too low, are responsible for a loss of CPU time on the order of five years over the considered three month period. The predictors, trained from a supervised learning algorithm, were able to correctly classify a large set of data. We evaluated them with three performance indicators that gave an information retrieval rate of 71% to 89% and a probability of accurate prediction between 0.7 and 0.8. The results of this work will be particularly helpful for designing an optimal partitioning of the considered heterogeneous platform, taking into consideration the real application needs and thus leading to energy savings and performance improvements. Moreover, apart from the novelty of the contribution, the accurate classification scheme offers new insights of users behavior of interest for the design of future HPC platforms.

Keywords: RJMS · HPC · Classification · Machine learning

© Springer International Publishing AG 2017
N. Desai and W. Cirne (Eds.): JSSPP 2015/2016, LNCS 10353, pp. 102–122, 2017.
DOI: 10.1007/978-3-319-61756-5_6

1   Introduction

Many organizations have departments and workgroups that benefit (or could benefit) from High Performance Computing HPC resources to analyze, model, and visualize the growing volumes of data they need to run their business. The size of the largest HPC platforms has dramatically evolved to attain hundreds of thousands of processors nowadays. Providing the energy and the cooling infrastructure to sustain such large systems is now more than ever a challenge. These tasks are becoming even more complex, as most of the current facilities comprise heterogeneous resources nowadays, either due to acquisitions at diverse period of time, or by the completion of the existing nodes with specialized hardware (GPU or CPU accelerators, FPGAs etc.) to achieve superior throughput for some specific workloads. Moreover, with the advent of the Cloud Computing CC paradigm and the widespread availability of virtualized computing resources, the classification and prediction of the most appropriate target for a given job is key to achieve a better efficiency and reduced energy costs. In this context, this paper presents the basic brick of the EVALIX project, which aims at the automatic evaluation and characterization of HPC workload and user patterns to identify the jobs that may benefit from the underlying heterogeneity of the platform. For that purpose, we collected the resource consumption of all the jobs from a production HPC system operated within the University of Luxembourg UL on a period of three months. The analysis of these traces permitted to develop a model that link the profile of the submitted jobs with their actual usage pattern, whether in terms of CPU, memory or IO load. Another contribution of this article is the definition and implementation of a supervised machine-learning approach based on Support Vector Machines SVM to characterize incoming jobs according to that model.

This paper is organized as follows: Sect. 2 reviews the context and motivations in the origin of the EVALIX project. In particular, we demonstrate from the analysis of Resource and Job Management System RJMS logs within a production HPC platform the necessity to carry on a deeper characterization of users' jobs resource consumption. Then, the method used to collect and classify these usage patterns is presented in Sect. 3.1. A supervised learning approach is detailed in Sect. 4 to deduce the above classification for incoming jobs. A performance evaluation of the designed predictors is also provided. Section 5 reviews the related works. Finally, Sect. 6 concludes the paper and provides some future directions and perspectives opened by this study.

2   Context and Motivations

The performance of an HPC system is obviously determined by the unitary performance of the subsystems that compose it, but also by the efficiency of their interactions and management by the middleware. In these kind of systems, a central component called the RJMS is in charge of managing the users' jobs on the system's computing resources. The RJMS has a strategic position in the whole HPC software stack as it has a constant knowledge of both workload

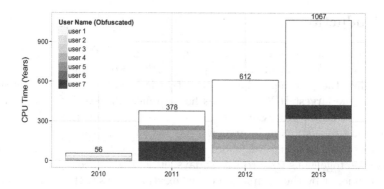

Fig. 1. Platform yearly utilization and top users contributions.

and resources. In order to improve the scheduling and resource management strategies, the workload of such systems has been widely studied and led to the construction of various models, as proposed by Lublin et al. in [1] and Feitelson in [2]. These models, were later used as a basis in scheduling techniques evaluations and optimization studies, such as [3,4]. However the aforementioned works were based on the study of the resources allocation to the jobs and not on their actual usage. We already discovered that allocation and usage often mismatch [5]. In order to have a more efficient scheduling of the jobs and a better resource management, it becomes necessary to get a better insight of the actual resource usage of the jobs. We have once again observed this divergence on a production HPC facility operated since 2007 by the UL. Users of this facility are people from three faculties and two Interdisciplinary centers within the UL, which cover various research topics such as bio-medicine, material science or security. An overview of the platform, its configuration together with its management is proposed in [6]. In this paper we study the usage of the *Gaia* cluster, the largest and most used of the UL HPC facilities. Composed of 151 nodes for a total of 2004 computing cores at the time of writing, it provides to more than 200 users a total computing power of 21.178 TFlops and relies upon the OAR [7] RJMS. During the last two years, *i.e.* between 2012 and end of 2013, almost three million jobs were launched, which gives an average throughput of one job every 23 s. Still in the same period, the average run time of jobs was about 33 min and many of them have a run time below the minute. The most frequent requested allocations are, by order of frequency: 1 core, 1 node, half a node (*i.e.* one socket) for single node allocations and 4 nodes, 2 nodes and 3 nodes for multi-node allocations. An average user has submitted more than 5,000 jobs to the RJMS and 9 users have more than 10,000 jobs.

As suggested in a previous study on user behavior [8], not all users have the same impact on an HPC infrastructure. In this work the authors classified users in three groups regarding their level of importance based on their utilization of the platform, assuming that top users were the most productive ones. This difference of importance between users on the UL HPC platform is well visible in Fig. 1, which presents the yearly CPU time allocated to jobs. For each year, the

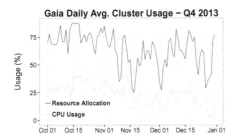

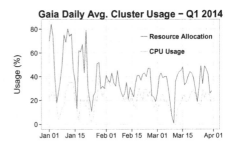

Fig. 2. Resource allocation vs. actual CPU usage. Over this time period 2 of the top users are responsible for 38% of total job area and a low CPU usage.

Fig. 3. Resource allocation vs. actual CPU usage. Time periods with different relative CPU usage patterns highlight the presence of different users.

3 largest users in terms of job area (number of resources × run time) and their relative usage are presented. What is very remarkable is that since the launch of the platform the computational area of these large users is very large regarding the total year's area. For example in 2013, 3 users from the same laboratory are responsible for 41% of the whole platform utilization. This confirms the previous idea [8] of the existence of a class of a few top users who consume a large part of the computing power. In the study by Feitelson et al. [9] of nine logs taken from the Parallel Workload Archive PWA [10], it was found that in many cases the activity of a few individual users can dominate all other activity in the system. e.g. in the HPC2N log, one single user was responsible for 57.8% of the whole log activity and in the SDSC and LANL logs, the number of jobs produced by few users could be 5 to 10 times the average weekly total, but this only for a short period. However one might wonder if these really use the platforms in reasonable ways and if their jobs are efficient enough or if they waste some computational power. Indeed, the time consumed by them is the CPU time allocated to the jobs and not their actual CPU usage. In a previous work [5], we showed that the jobs' actual CPU usage was in many cases very different from the CPU allocation, even for jobs that are supposed to be CPU intensive.

In order to verify what is the actual CPU utilization, we reconstruct the CPU usage of the jobs in function of CPU allocation on the UL HPC platform. From RJMS logs, we compute the percentage of platform's CPU resources allocated to the jobs (taking into account failures and resource absence). To estimate the actual CPU usage on the computing nodes at this level, the data collected by the Ganglia monitoring system were used[1]. We measured the average system noise generated on the nodes by the Ganglia daemon as being negligible, i.e. less than 0.05% over one hour. Information retrieved this way is thus well representative of jobs CPU usage on the nodes. This information is retrieved at node level, so when several jobs share the same node we cannot say much about their respective CPU usage. However, this gives us a general tendency of the utilization vs. allocation. Figures 2 and 3 present the difference between CPU allocation by the RJMS and

---

[1] Later on, another monitoring tool named *Colmet* [11] will be used.

the actual CPU usage of the jobs. The darkest curve presents the percentage of CPU allocated by the RJMS regarding the total number of resources available in the system at this time. The lightest curve presents the aggregated CPU usage as reported by Ganglia. Thus the height difference between the two curves gives the relative CPU usage, which is frequently far from being 100% of what is allocated. Also, there exists periods with different CPU usage patterns. For instance in Fig. 2, two users are responsible for 38% of job area, for a CPU usage of about 30%. These users belong to the top 3 users of the year 2013. If we take shorter time periods with different CPU usage patterns, for example in Fig. 3 from *2014-01-01* to *2014-01-15* and *2014-02-01* to *2014-02-15*, we can observe the impact of the presence of particular users. In the first time period we have two peaks of high CPU allocation (around 80% of the full platform) with a CPU usage around 40%. During this period, two users are responsible for 45% of total job area. These are the same users that were predominant in Fig. 2. On the contrary in the second time period the CPU allocation is lower (varying between 20% to 40%) for a high relative CPU usage. During this time period the two users account for 34% of total job area and a single user accounts for more than 43%. Not surprisingly these two are still the same ones as before and the user who has the largest job area is also one of the year 2013 top 3 users. This phenomenon is not isolated and other periods where these 3 top users are present have the same pattern (e.g. beginning vs. end of March 2014).

In the light of this observation, it seems that the presence of some particular users can have a strong impact on the platform usage pattern. Moreover it is also well visible that users have different resource consumption patterns, depending on the applications they run. This raises the following questions: *are there some typical user profiles that we could extract from the observation of the jobs?* and *could we benefit from this knowledge to predict users' future needs in terms of resources depending on the jobs they run?*

Answering these questions is central in the EVALIX project, which aims at the automatic evaluation and characterization of HPC workload and user patterns to better adapt to heterogeneous resources. Detailing this project is clearly out of the scope of this paper. Here, we propose to look deeper into job's internals and measure what they use in terms of physical resources. Then based on the history of jobs consumption, a machine-learning approach is proposed to predict the expected resource consumption from incoming jobs upon submission. Obviously, the proposed supervised algorithm is the first step in the design of a framework able to cover EVALIX goals. We now detail the analysis performed to classify the jobs consumption of the *Gaia* cluster over the considered 3-month period.

3   Job Consumptions Data Collection and Classification

3.1   Data Collection

Following the previous work on jobs consumption collection initiated in [5], we choose a monitoring of all the jobs processes, managed at the node level. In our previous work, we used the Linux */proc* virtual filesystem to gather information of resource consumption of all the processes that composed a job. Carefully polling the filesystem for collecting counters information at a one minute frequency enabled us to capture and analyze a 9 month trace on two production clusters at little cost. In this paper, we perform the monitoring of jobs consumption with a dedicated tool named *Colmet* [11], provided as a testing software by the OAR RJMS development team. Unlike Ganglia which is designed for monitoring a whole machine, Colmet is able to evaluate a set of processes. More precisely, it relies on Linux *taskstats* accounting feature coupled with the *cgroup* [12] kernel isolation mechanism to retrieve at low cost jobs consumption counters. Collected data is stored on a dedicated node in a file structured in Hierarchical Data Format v5 HDF5. This storage type enables to process large volumes of data easily. The evaluation of this tool is not the topic in this work. However to give an insight, we measured the overhead induced by *Colmet* when monitoring resources by running some carefully selected benchmarks representative of HPC workloads (NAS Parallel Benchmarks NPB [13] version 3.3.1 for instance). Our evaluation demonstrates a performance overhead below 0.1% for the considered benchmarks, even with a frequency of 1 s between each data collection step. This is by far the least intrusive tool we are aware of, for monitoring a given set of processes at a few seconds frequency and that provides such a large file storage capability. We collected a 3-month trace on *Gaia* cluster, from *2014-05-22* to *2014-08-19*. This trace is composed of 51859 jobs, belonging to 84 different users. The size of the trace stored in compressed HDF5 is about 10 GB and contains 6.05×10^{-9} values from the different metrics retrieved by taskstats.

In order to compare *Gaia*'s workload with what is observable in other HPC sites we analyzed 8 of the most recent cluster logs of various size from the PWA. In Table 1, we present some of their characteristics along with our cluster's 3-month trace characteristics. We also provide the robust data dispersion indicators: Median Absolute Deviation MAD and Inter-Quartile Range IQR, to estimate the differences between *Gaia* and these other systems. Despite its humble size when compared to large platforms such as CEA Curie or ANL Intrepid, we can see that *Gaia* still has a good job throughput and a relatively fair core utilization. Moreover its job mix is relatively close to what is visible in other systems and we can assume that our analysis and learning approach could also benefit to such other systems.

3.2 Analysis of Jobs Consumption

As *Colmet* collects temporal data, it would be possible to analyze job patterns during their execution. This kind of analysis is definitely worth doing, however due to the complexity of performing the learning with time series data, we will first focus on the average job consumption patterns. Thus, this work aims at the coarse grain analysis of jobs resource consumption and does not focus on temporal data for the moment. The analysis of the time series shall be done in further works. To process and analyze this large amount of data, we first aggregate it on the job duration and allocated resources. This means that for each

Table 1. Comparison of the UL HPC Platform 3-month trace statistics with various other systems listed in the PWA [10].

Platform	#cores	#users	Throughput (jobs/h)	Job size mode (cores)	Avg. utilization (%)
ULHPC Gaia	2,004	84	32.3	12	45.4
Metacentrum	806	147	25	1	36.3
LLNL-uBGL	2,048	62	21.1	1024	56.1
PIK IPLEX	2,560	225	25.6	1	38
LLNL-Thunder	4,008	283	35.7	4	87.9
RICC	8,192	176	122	1	87.2
LLNL-Atlas	9,216	132	12.7	8	64.1
CEA Curie	93,312	722	82.2	1	29.3
ANL intrepid	163,840	236	12	2048	59.6
Median			25.6	4	56.1
MAD			15	4.4	26.8
IQR			14.6	11	26.1
			General statistics		

job we have its average CPU and memory usage, maximum memory reached, average disk IO reads and writes per second. The averages are given per allocated core. Thanks to the use of lightweight isolation mechanism, *Colmet* monitoring takes into account all the processes and threads that belong to a given job and thus ensures the completeness of the job's usage data. In OAR RJMS, depending on the user application needs, a job can belong to one of the following classes:

- **besteffort** jobs are preemptible, low constrained multi-parametric jobs that are supposed to be CPU-intensive. A besteffort job will always be considered as being part of the besteffort class, regardless its number of allocated core.
- **interactive** jobs are for debugging purpose, they provide to the user a direct shell to his allocated machines.
- **serial** jobs are jobs requesting only one core.
- **parallel** jobs are traditional HPC jobs that request several cores.

In order to visualize jobs that may be comparable, Fig. 4 exhibits jobs consumption statistics grouped by class of job. Figure 4a presents the jobs average consumption for each metric: CPU, memory (average and maximum) and IO (reads and writes) along with the proportion of jobs per class. If we focus on this last metric (bottom right figure), we can see that most of the jobs are parallel or besteffort. However, even though besteffort jobs account for 30% of total number of jobs, their area is much lower. In fact, they represent only 4.05% of the total job area while interactive jobs account for a relative area of 1.04% and the area of serial job is 5%. Thus *Gaia* workload is mainly composed of parallel jobs.

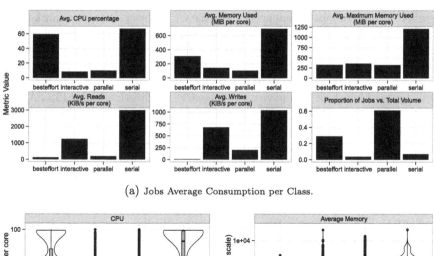

(a) Jobs Average Consumption per Class.

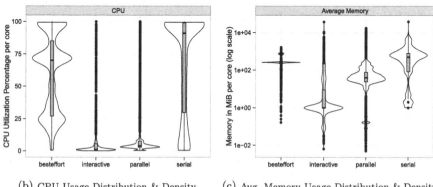

(b) CPU Usage Distribution & Density.   (c) Avg. Memory Usage Distribution & Density.

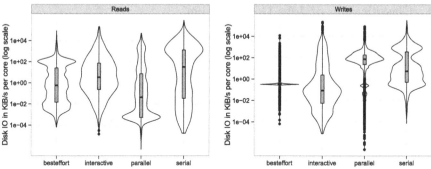

(d) Disk I/O Reads Distribution & Density.   (e) Disk I/O Writes Distribution and Density.

Fig. 4. Jobs consumption analysis for the workload scheduled on the *Gaia* cluster between May 22th, 2014 and August 19th, 2014.

Figures 4b, c, d and e present violin plots, *i.e.* box plots with jobs probability densities. Violins are given per consumption metric and for each job class. The plot relative to the maximum memory usage is not shown as its data distribution is quite similar to the average memory usage. In Fig. 4b, we observe that besteffort and serial jobs consume the most the CPU power. We also remark three distinct patterns in besteffort jobs corresponding to the largest job densities: around 25%, 75% and 100%. These patterns most probably come from different types of application. As expected, interactive jobs tend to have a very low CPU utilization. However what we were not suspecting is the low CPU utilization of parallel jobs. Almost all jobs have an average CPU utilization under 15%. Above that are only some outliers. In Fig. 4c, we note that only interactive jobs have a low memory usage. In this figure, the average memory usage is given per allocated core thus the global memory used by the job is depending on its size. We also observe that besteffort jobs have a very stable and predictable memory usage (on the order of 100MiB per core) while parallel and serial jobs have more variations. Finally from Figs. 4d and e, we can spot that disk IO and in particular reads accesses have a very wide scale and spread distribution. We also witness that parallel jobs have the higher IO write values for median and density but lower IO read values. Thus parallel jobs tend to write more than others but read less.

Overall, the jobs that use the most the resources belong to the serial class. A very high proportion of these use around 100% of CPU but also a fairly high amount of memory (on the order of the GiB). What is quite surprising is the relatively low CPU utilization of parallel jobs. For a vast majority of the jobs, this value is around 5%. This is counterbalanced by a relatively high memory usage (on the order of the 100th of MiB per core) and for a lot of them, a high rate of disk writes. Moreover, this analysis exhibits the importance of the user factor: as little as 8 users among the 56 that ran parallel jobs during the considered period, account for an area of 80% of parallel jobs.

3.3   Classification of Jobs Consumption

As job consumption values distribution takes various forms from centered around the median to really sparse and with a wide range, we prefer here to adopt *first* a classification approach instead of using regression techniques to train the EVALIX predictor. This preliminary step is expected to make the training easier with a better accuracy of the predictions. Each consumption metric will be divided into several classes of values and thus, the learning will be done on these classes and not on the continuous values. For the clustering of data, we chose to divide each consumption metric into four classes as depicted in Table 2.

Table 2. Clustering classes for consumption metrics.

	CPU	Memory	Disk IO
Class 1	0 to 25%	Up to 10 MiB	Up to 10 KiB/s
Class 2	25 to 50%	From 10 to 100 MiB	From 10 to 100 KiB/s
Class 3	50 to 75%	From 100 to 1 GiB	From 100 to 1 MiB/s
Class 4	75 to 100%	Above 1 GiB	Above 1 MiB/s

The CPU consumption data was clustered linearly regarding its level CPU usage. For memory consumption, we applied a logarithmic clustering of the average and maximum memory usage; same for disk IO consumption (reads and writes) but given on average per second. Moreover, an expert knowledge based approach was chosen instead of automatic clustering algorithms since it was giving a stronger semantic meaning to classes. In particular, the logarithmic approach enables to compare the jobs based on their order of magnitude for memory usage or disk access, which is more suitable regarding the distribution of the resource usages. We compared our approach with three unsupervised learning classification methods: k-means, hierarchical trees clustering and gaussian mixtures. None of them was satisfying enough compared to our naive manual clustering approach: *Hierarchical trees clustering* gives although too much (over 10, leading to poor prediction results in the learning phase) or too few classes (only 2), depending on the level of intra-class heterogeneity chosen. *Gaussian mixtures* led to similar problem and when the number of classes is limited to a reasonable number (between 4 to 8), a few very dense classes are produced while others are very sparse. Finally, the *k-means clustering* also reproduces the same problem with very sparse classes.

To get back at our first initial question: *are there some typical user profiles that we could extract from the observation of the jobs?* It is now easy to detect some classes of users that have always the same usage pattern. We define that, if on average a user belongs to classes 3 or 4 for a given consumption metric, he uses intensively the resource. However, if the maximum class attained in all this user's jobs is 1 or 2, we define his use of the resource as low. Thus a user highly relying on several resources will be marked as so and a user consuming lowly all the resources will be categorized as having a low resource usage. We have to be careful not to take into account interactive jobs, these being debugging or setup jobs, they do not reflect an application behavior. Applying this methodology on the jobs consumption classes gives us the user classification presented in Table 3. What is satisfying is that among 84 active users, 30 of them have a stable behavior and can be classified very simply. It is also interesting that a total of 10 users were identified as lowly using all the resources. The area of their jobs only accounts for 3.12% of the total job area but with an average CPU usage of 18% which cause a loss in CPU time of more than 5 years. As for the 54 users that could not be classified with the above methodology, either they have a stable behavior but their jobs are mixed between different resources consumptions or they run applications with different resource usage patterns. For instance, the top 3 users on the year 2013 fall into this *"Unclassified"* category yet we are now able to better understand their profile. Concerning the first two users who had an overall low CPU usage, one of them has most of his jobs being composed of a medium to low consumption on all the metrics and few jobs with a high CPU usage. On the data observed from this user's jobs we could not see any correlation between the CPU usage and memory or disk usage. What is the most probable is that his jobs are not belonging to one particular class but correspond to a mixed usage patterns. The second user seems to have two kinds of jobs, one

Table 3. User classification based on average resource usage over the jobs monitoring period (84 active users) excl. interactive jobs.

User average consumption	# of users
CPU intensive	11
CPU and memory intensive	7
CPU and IO intensive	1
Memory intensive	15
Memory and IO intensive	3
IO intensive	4
All resources intensive	1
Low resource usage	10
Medium usage – unclassified users	54

with a very high CPU usage and a moderately high memory usage, and another type, which represent most of his workload, shows a very low CPU and memory usage pattern. In all his jobs, the volume of disk reads and writes is very small. What is very interesting with this user's jobs profile is that their memory usage is directly correlated with their CPU usage. We can be quite confident that we are in presence of a user whose workload is composed of two distinct types of jobs. For the third user who was showing a high CPU usage on Fig. 3, there are probably more than two job classes. For the CPU usage, 60% of his jobs belong to class 1 and 32% of his jobs are of class 4, but despite the CPU class we also witness different memory usage patterns (with low and high usage) that are not correlated with the CPU usage. However, what is well visible for this user is the temporal correlation of the consumption. Indeed, this user's jobs that are submitted within a short time frame tend to have a very similar CPU or memory usage. This is a very interesting property that could be useful in an online classification. More generally, we need a more advanced mechanism to assort the *Unclassified* jobs consumption, in particular to take into account not only the user name but also all the job input parameters. That's the object of the machine-learning approach proposed in the next section, with the idea that by perusing the history, we will be able to predict all future job consumption classes based on user query to the RJMS.

4   A Supervised Learning Algorithm for the Complete Prediction of Job Resource Consumption

Several supervised learning techniques coexist in the literature. Among the most used ones are Neural Networks and SVM algorithm [14]. Although they differ in their mechanism, they can both be used for data classification and regression analysis. In [15], the comparison between both techniques revealed that SVM is generally more efficient. More precisely, at the price of a higher computation time, SVM is able to compute models that generate predictions with a lower error rate. As the training of our models is done offline from a trace extraction, models computing time is not a constraint and we prefer the approach that gives the best results. To perform the supervised learning and train the SVM-based predictors on jobs consumption data, we choose the reference implementation proposed in the *libsvm* [16] library (version 2.6).

4.1 Metrics for Machine Learning Performance Assessment

In our previous classification of jobs consumption, a classification of data within four classes has been chosen to have a finer evaluation of the consumption. Indeed, a two-class classification seemed too restrictive as it would only tell if a given resource usage was either *high* or *low*. With four classes we have the possibility to express more precisely at which level is the resource consumption. Nevertheless, SVM is originally designed for binary classification problems. In consequence, our considered multiclass classification problem needs to be transformed to a form of binary classification. Generally this is done either with a *one-against-one* or a *one-against-all* voting scheme. The first method decomposes the original problem into several two-class classification problems. The second one treats each class separately and data either belongs to the class or not the class (i.e. any of the other classes). In a study comparing multiclass SVM problems for machine learning [17], it was shown that among several voting scheme, the *one-against-one* technique is commonly seen as the most suitable. Consequently, this approach has been considered for EVALIX predictors. Also, the usual classification performance indicators are not useful. For example sensitivity, specificity and likelihood are meant to be calculated for two classes only. In [18], the authors proposed three performance indicators that can be used for the evaluation of multiclass classifiers:

1. **Accuracy**, which gives the proportion of observations that were correctly classified. Derived from the confusion matrix, the multiclass accuracy is the average of the accuracies obtained from each class. This metric provides the **information retrieval rate** performed by the learning.
2. **Area Under the ROC Curve (AUC)** which comes from the radiologic community to judge the discrimination ability of statistical methods. The AUC measures the **probability to correctly classify a random sample**.
3. **Cohen's kappa** measure of agreement. This indicator aims to compensate for classifications that may be due to chance. In [19], the use of Kappa is proposed as a standard meter for measuring the accuracy of all multi-valued classification problems. A kappa value over 40% is generally considered to be a moderate agreement and over 60% a good agreement.

In the context of EVALIX predictors, the above three metrics were considered as *complementary* performance measures. On the one hand, while the accuracy remains the most widely used indicator due to its simplicity, it was showed in [20] that this metric alone can be misleading under skewed class distribution, which is the case for some data in the present study. On the other hand, the kappa metric suffers from several undesirable effects: first, kappa may be low even though there are high levels of agreement and that individual ratings are accurate [21]. Then, and that's more problematic in our case, its value is influenced by data distribution and as a result, kappa values should not be compared across studies [22]. As regards the AUC evaluation, we use a generalized pairwise comparison approach as proposed in [23]. Given the inherent advantages of this metric [24] (better standard error as the number of test samples increases etc.), AUC will remain our most important evaluation criterion with precedence over the accuracy and kappa indicators.

4.2 Training and Evaluating the Models

Input Data Selection. Mandatory information to submit a job in OAR RJMS is: user name, submission queue, number of resources asked, maximum time requested (or walltime), type of job (interactive or batch). Using the information on OAR configuration on the cluster, we are able to determine also the class of the job (besteffort, interactive, parallel or serial) so we can add this information in the training. Iteratively we tested the prediction results in function of the job characteristics used as input in the learning. The best results obtained, which are presented later in this article, used as learning input the **user name**, the job **submission queue**, the **number of resources reserved**, the job **walltime**, the **job type**, whether the job was an **advance reservation** or not and the **job class**. For instance, the job name (which is optional in OAR) was of no interest for the training. Actually we got worse results with the trainings that included this information than the ones that did not. The explanation is quite simple: 26% of the jobs have no name, and for those who have, these names reflect for many user either the version of the code run or the application input parameters. This means that many jobs have different names that slightly differ but actually correspond to the same job with different input parameters. In consequence, this information disrupts the learning process. Based on the information given by the user at submission time, we train one predictor per consumption metric. This means that from the history of the input parameters of each job, associated with their resource consumption, we compute the support vectors and the models that will describe this relationship. Thus we will have five consumption models: CPU utilization, average memory, maximum memory, disk IO reads and writes; each computed from jobs input parameters.

Finding the Best Training Parameters. The performance of SVM is very dependent on the choice of parameters [25]. To ensure a good learning of the consumption data we evaluated two of the most used kernels: polynomial and RBF (radial), and for each of them using a grid search to determine the best hyper-parameter set. For both kernels we evaluated the error rate and dispersion with a gamma between $10^{(-3:3)}$ and a cost between 1 to 5. For polynomial kernel we tested a degree between 1 to 3. With the best parameter sets for each kernel and for each model, we found that the polynomial kernel performed better than

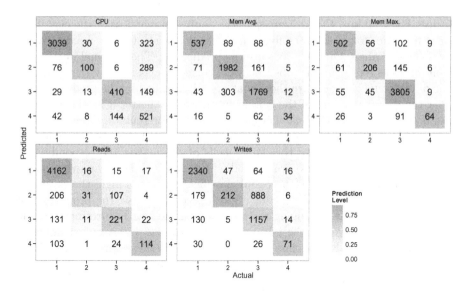

Fig. 5. Test data confusion matrices.

Table 4. Accuracy values of trained models and test data prediction scores.

		Test data		
Model	10-fold accuracy	Accuracy	AUC	kappa
CPU	79.4%	78.5%	75.6%	60.8%
Mem. Avg	83.4%	87.3%	81.1%	73.2%
Mem. Max	88.3%	93.8%	78.4%	68.8%
Writes	71.3%	72.9%	78.1%	57.5%
Reads	87.0%	87.3%	70.6%	53.4%

RBF during the prediction evaluation (slightly better Accuracy, but 1 to 2% better AUC and Kappa). Thus we present only the results for the polynomial kernel. The best parameter set for our classification problem was thus a degree 3 polynomial kernel, with a gamma value of 1 and a cost of 2. This set gave us an error rate of 0.179 and a dispersion of 0.007. Since our data sample is relatively large (over 50,000 samples), a test set of 10% of data size and a cross-validation technique at training phase is recommended [26] to ensure a low variance of the results. Thus for the training of our models we first extract randomly 10% of data that will be used as test data. Then, using the best parameters we train our models on the remaining 90% using a 10-fold cross validation with a validation set of 10% at each fold, then we also compute the predictive accuracy of the models on their respective test sets. This gives the results presented in Fig. 5 and Table 4. The 10-fold cross validation ensures statistically stronger results than the test evaluation itself as the process of selecting a test data set and comparing it with a train data set is done 10 times on disjoint sets.

Models Evaluation. Figure 5 presents the confusion matrices of the classification of test data for each of the five consumption models. On the x-axis are the actual classes values. On the y-axis are the predictions. The diagonal in the confusion matrices represent the jobs that were correctly classified by the predictor while off-diagonal elements are those that are misclassified by the predictor. The higher the diagonal values of the confusion matrix the better it is, since it indicates many correct predictions. The prediction level presents in a scale of grey, for a given class the rate of job classifications. What we observe is that generally the predictions are accurate: the darker cells of the matrix (corresponding to the higher classification rates) are located on the diagonal. However, we can also observe that even though the successful classification rate is high, the reverse is not always true. This means that for a given predicted class, the proportion of jobs that actually were belonging to this class can be low. For example, in the Disk Writes model, over all the jobs predicted as class 2, 179 were belonging to class 1, 212 to class 2, 888 to class 3 and 6 to class 4. In this example, only 16.5% of the jobs that were predicted as class 2 were actually belonging to class 2.

In order to perform the evaluation of the models taking into account this phenomenon, instead of simply looking at the confusion matrices, we also use the earlier defined performance indicators, with the results depicted in Table 4. It shows the model accuracies of the 10-fold cross validations along with test data evaluation. Even though the 10-fold cross validation is statistically stronger, the evaluation on test data is also interesting as it enables to compute not only the model accuracies but also the other performance indicators AUC and kappa. The cross validation shows a good accuracy for the five models, around 80 to 88% of the jobs are correctly classified. The best accuracies are for the Memory and disk Reads models, while the CPU and disk Writes show a slightly worse accuracy. The accuracies computed from test data are, for all the models except CPU, seemingly higher than the ones obtained from the cross validation, this illustrates why the cross validation is very important for a stronger evaluation of the model. Test data AUC values are quite good, the probability to correctly classify a sample from this set is around 80% for Memory and Disk Writes, 75% for CPU and 70% for disk Reads. It could be counter-intuitive that disk Reads has the lowest probability even though it has one of the highest accuracies. In fact this comes from many jobs from the test data set belong to class 1 and were actually classified as class 1, this gives a very good diagnostic rate for the class 1. However this is not necessarily the case for the other classes, in particular class 2 and class 3. This is an example of the influence of data distribution skewness on the accuracy value. It is the same phenomenon for CPU that also shows a high density of jobs in class 1 correctly classified but class 4 shows a less good diagnostic rate. This perfectly highlights the interest of AUC over the sole accuracy as a performance indicator. For the kappa indicator, the best performance is obtained from the CPU and Memory models. Performance indicators for the different models evaluated on test data showed quite good results. Accuracy, AUC and kappa were giving fair to good scores for each model and the 10-fold cross validation accuracies were still remaining good. As the statistical properties of the cross validation ensures a more reliable accuracy evaluation, we will compute the others indicators with the same method from the full data set.

4.3   Evaluating the Predictions on the Full Data Set

To evaluate deeper the performance of the models computed in the previous section and to ensure a stronger statistical result, we split the initial data set into 10 extracts of 10% of its size.

Each of these extracts will be used as different test sets to evaluate the prediction performance. By this means we will mimic the 10-fold cross validation process that was used in the predictor training phase. Thus the performance evaluation of the predictions is not computed from a test set extract as was done for the training validation, but on different subsets that cover the full data. For each test set and for each metric we compute the Accuracy, AUC and kappa. The result of the performance indicator averages along with the 95% confidence intervals obtained are presented in Fig. 6. On average the model accuracies are very good: either close to or above 80%, except for Disk Writes model that shows a lower accuracy of 71%. This corresponds to an information retrieval of 71% to 89%, computed solely from the information given at the submission time of the job. For CPU and Memory models the Cohen's kappa indicator is above 60% which is considered as a good value. For Disk Reads and Writes, the value is lower than for the others but is still over 40% which is considered as an acceptable kappa value. In the same time for each of the five models, the AUC indicator shows a fair to good probability to correctly predict the resource consumption class of the jobs. We remind that, for multiclass problems the AUC shows interesting statistical properties and lower dispersion regarding other indicators. This holds particularly when dealing with large samples, as is our case. This is why we chose this indicator as our main evaluation criterion.

For the CPU, Memory and disk Writes models the multiclass AUC is larger than 75% which corresponds to a good prediction score. For the disk Reads

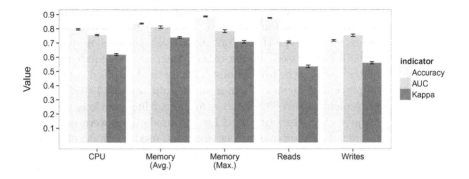

Fig. 6. Model prediction evaluation scores.

model the AUC is 70% which is still a fair value. Considering the fact that we are dealing with a multiclass problem and that we have four possible classes, a random prediction would give a probability of 0.25 for each class. Thus, a probability of having an accurate prediction being between 0.7 and 0.8 is a good score. We evaluated our five multiclass models with three different criteria: the accuracy which gives the amount of information correctly predicted, Cohen's kappa that compensates for predictions made by chance and the AUC which gives the probability to correctly classify a random sample. The three performance indicators gave us a good overall performance of our consumption models. The Disk Reads model in spite of a high accuracy is the one that shows the lowest prediction score considering the AUC (71%) and kappa (54%) values but is still considered as having a fair prediction score. Based on these observations we can say that the information provided by the user at job submission time is already a reliable source of information to predict the resource consumption of a job, which raises many scheduling optimization possibilities.

5   Related Work

The idea of using machine learning techniques, regressions and history analysis to predict the jobs characteristics based on their input parameters as already been addressed in several works.

In [27], two bioinformatics applications were used as benchmarks for an empirical assessment of the suitability of several machine learning techniques for the prediction of the size and time used by the jobs. In [28], Tsafrir et al. used predictions of job runtimes to correct user estimations. They showed that using the user estimated runtime of the job as a kill-time and using their proposed predictions as a runtime estimate, enabled to propose a simple scheduler respecting FCFS and EASY properties but with significant improvements in performance, predictability and accuracy. The generated prediction of job runtime was simply an average of the runtimes of the last two jobs by the same user. They also highlighted the importance of using recent data for predictions rather than a long history. In a similar work by Smith et al. [29], four workloads from the PWA were used to study the characteristics of the jobs resource requirements to the RJMS to predict application runtimes. The jobs characteristics used for the predictions were the job type (batch or interactive), submission queue, user name, number of nodes requested, among others, then used a genetic algorithm to find job templates used for the predictions. This method resulted in prediction errors of 40 to 60 percent of mean run times on the four workload studied which was a good improvement (14 to 60% lower error) regarding previous works [30] where classifying jobs characteristics used for the predictions were user name, parallelism level and submission queue. The approach used by Smith et al. using more criteria for the predictions was more efficient.

However, in spite of a wide literature on job runtimes prediction based on the jobs characteristics at submission time, very few job address the study of the prediction of jobs resource consumption. In [31], the authors used four application benchmarks, each corresponding to a particular resource consumption pattern: CPU, Memory, IO, Network. With the profiling of these applications, using the Ganglia monitoring system and ran within a Virtual Machine VM, they trained a 3-Nearest Neighbor classifier. This classifier is to be used later to categorize a given application into CPU-bound, IO-bound, Network-bound or Idle. Based on this, around ten real world applications and benchmarks are classified and this classification is used as an input to an ad-hoc scheduler on a small cluster of workstation. They showed that the knowledge of the applications resource requirements enabled the scheduler to perform a better system throughput of about 22% by not scheduling applications with the same consumption pattern on the same nodes. Our work differs from this as we did not use a set of few benchmarks for the training of the predictor but we analyzed a real 3-month trace of our own users' job consumption. To the best of our knowledge, the only analysis of the jobs resource consumption on a large trace from a production HPC cluster was from our previous work [5]. By using the analysis of the workload coming from our own facility instead of using benchmarks, we remove the bias of training with applications unadapted to our users' workloads. We also guarantee that data used for classification and prediction is realistic while more accurate predictions of the future jobs consumption are ensured.

6   Conclusion

In this work and in the context of the EVALIX project, we collected, analyzed and classified a trace of all the jobs resource consumptions during a period of three months on a production HPC cluster. The outcome of this work is threefold. First, the analysis of the resource usage by the jobs depending on their class enabled to differentiate different kind of resource needs. Interactive jobs have a very low CPU and memory usage but can have high IO usage, besteffort jobs are very CPU intensive with few IO and medium memory usage and serial jobs are using the resources quite intensively.

Then, the classification of the jobs regarding the CPU, memory and disk IO consumption enabled to characterize the activity of 20 of the users active at that period (24% of the total number), whose applications are always of the same type. We classified these users as being intensive in one or several of these metrics: CPU, memory, disk IO. We also identified 10 users (or 12% of the total number) that always use very few resources. The CPU time loss caused by the activity of these accounts is in terms of years.

Last, we build a consumption model based on the classification and trained a set of predictors based on the jobs input parameters. We validated our prediction models with the comparison of three criteria and showed that the information retrieval rate is between 71% and 89%, and the probability of predicting the correct class is quite high: from 0.7 to 0.8.

These results lead to several optimizations of the RJMS and the scheduling. Firstly, the most immediate optimization is to benefit from the knowledge of the class of the job to make a scheduling aware of jobs resource needs, as proposed in [31]. The principle was simply to not schedule applications with the same consumption pattern on the same nodes and this enabled to perform a better system throughput. By not scheduling several serial jobs on the same resources, or by mixing on the same resources interactive and besteffort jobs (which show complementary patterns), this will positively impact the jobs. Moreover, the preliminary classification of the jobs is done based on an expert knowledge approach, however it will be interesting as a future direction to evaluate fuzzy logic algorithms to better handle uncertainties that come from the data dynamics.

Secondly, the prediction of the consumptions at job submission time will enable to refine the scheduling aware of jobs resource needs. With the prediction, the scheduling will be able to load balance the jobs on the heterogeneous resources to obtain a better performance and energy efficiency. The predictor needs to be updated frequently and integrate a two-level prediction. First compute a prediction from a consumption model derived from the recent activity on the cluster, i.e. from the last months or weeks. Then for jobs that cannot be predicted by this means, to use a larger model containing an annual history of jobs consumptions.

Finally, with the analysis of the job resource consumptions, one can compute the real cost of the jobs of the users on the platform. Moreover, most recent schedulers embedded in the RJMS use fair-sharing strategies to avoid the monopoly of the resources by the largest users or to grant more resource hours or higher priorities to a certain group of users. This real usage cost must be balanced by the resource request provided by the user at submission time. This would give usage information that, integrated into the fairness score, will enable the user to pay the right price for his computation and to get a feedback of his behavior on the platform.

With the ability to automatically evaluate and characterize HPC workload and user patterns, and with a model of the cost of jobs, the EVALIX framework will provide a highly efficient usage in terms of resources and infrastructure costs, along with a better adaptation of the jobs to heterogeneous resources. More precisely, our study offers new insights to guide the future partitioning of the computing platform: it is now possible to define in an accurate manner several sets of computing resources that will fit the analyzed heterogeneous usage patterns. Coupled with a wrapper at the RJMS level that schedules the incoming jobs according to their corresponding partition, substantial gains can be obtained, whether at the level of the computing of energy efficiency. Our first experiments based on a naive trace replay simulator reveal a potential energy efficiency improvement between 5 to 10%. Part of our short-term perspective for this work consists in consolidating these results and integrating the proposed classification/prediction scheme within the RJMS of our HPC platform to evaluate experimentally its effectiveness. Another mid-term objective is related to the extension of our work to a more accurate temporal analysis of the collected traces, to better take into account the user pattern changes over sliding period of time.

Acknowledgments. The experiments presented in this paper were carried out using the HPC facility of the University of Luxembourg. Many thanks are also due to all those who participated in collecting and distributing the logs available through the PWA and used in Table 1.

References

1. Lublin, U., Feitelson, D.: The workload on parallel supercomputers: modeling the characteristics of rigid jobs. J. Parallel Distrib. Comput. **63**, 1105–1122 (2001)
2. Feitelson, D.G.: Workload modeling for performance evaluation. In: Calzarossa, M.C., Tucci, S. (eds.) Performance 2002. LNCS, vol. 2459, pp. 114–141. Springer, Heidelberg (2002). doi:10.1007/3-540-45798-4_6
3. Feitelson, D.G., Jettee, M.A.: Improved utilization and responsiveness with gang scheduling. In: Feitelson, D.G., Rudolph, L. (eds.) JSSPP 1997. LNCS, vol. 1291, pp. 238–261. Springer, Heidelberg (1997). doi:10.1007/3-540-63574-2_24
4. Cao, J., Zimmermann, F.: Queue scheduling and advance reservations with cosy. In: Parallel and Distributed Processing Symposium, p. 63 (2004)
5. Emeras, J., Ruiz, C., Vincent, J.-M., Richard, O.: Analysis of the jobs resource utilization on a production system. In: Desai, N., Cirne, W. (eds.) JSSPP 2013. LNCS, vol. 8429, pp. 1–21. Springer, Heidelberg (2014). doi:10.1007/978-3-662-43779-7_1
6. Varrette, S., Bouvry, P., Cartiaux, H., Georgatos, F.: Management of an academic HPC cluster: the UL experience. In: Proceedings of the 2014 HPCS Conference (2014)
7. Capit, N., Costa, G.D., Georgiou, Y., et al.: A batch scheduler with high level components. In: CCGrid, pp. 776–783 (2005)
8. Wolter, N., McCracken, M.O., Snavely, A., et al.: What's working in HPC: Investigating HPC user behavior and productivity. CTWatch Q. **2**, 9–17 (2006)
9. Feitelson, D.G., Tsafrir, D., Krakov, D.: Experience with using the parallel workloads archive. J. Parallel Distribut. Comput. **74**(10), 2967–2982 (2014)
10. Feitelson, D.: Parallel workload archive
11. Colmet. https://github.com/oar-team/colmet
12. Linux Kernel: https://www.kernel.org/, Taskstats: https://www.kernel.org/doc/Documentation/accounting/taskstats.txt, Cgroups: https://www.kernel.org/doc/Documentation/cgroups/cgroups.txt
13. Bailey, D.H.: NAS parallel benchmarks. In: Padua, D. (ed.) Encyclopedia of Parallel Computing. Springer, Heidelberg (2011)
14. Cortes, C., Vapnik, V.: Support-vector networks. Mach. Learn. **20**(3), 273–297 (1995)
15. Duan, R., Nadeem, F., Wang, J., Zhang, Y., Prodan, R., Fahringer, T.: A hybrid intelligent method for performance modeling and prediction of workflow activities in grids. In: Proceedings of the 2009 CCGRID Conference, pp. 339–347 (2009)
16. Chang, C.C., Lin, C.J.: Libsvm: a library for support vector machines. ACM Trans. Intell. Syst. Technol. **2**(3), 27: 1–27: 27 (2011)
17. Hsu, C.W., Lin, C.J.: A comparison of methods for multiclass support vector machines. IEEE Trans. Neural Netw. **13**(2), 415–425 (2002)
18. Szollosi, D., Denes, D.L., Firtha, F., Kovacs, Z., Fekete, A.: Comparison of six multiclass classifiers by the use of different classification performance indicators. J. Chemometr. **26**(3–4), 76–84 (2012)
19. Ben-David, A.: Comparison of classification accuracy using cohen's weighted kappa. Expert Syst. Appl. **34**(2), 825–832 (2008)

20. Provost, F.J., Fawcett, T., et al.: Analysis and visualization of classifier performance: comparison under imprecise class and cost distributions. KDD **97**, 43–48 (1997)
21. Uebersax, J.S.: A generalized kappa coefficient. Educ. Psychol. Meas. **42**(1), 181–183 (1982)
22. Feinstein, A.R., Cicchetti, D.V.: High agreement but low kappa: I. the problems of two paradoxes. J. Clin. Epidemiol. **43**(6), 543–549 (1990)
23. Hand, D., Till, R.: A simple generalisation of the area under the roc curve for multiple class classification problems. Mach. Learn. **45**(2), 171–186 (2001)
24. Bradley, A.P.: The use of the area under the ROC curve in the evaluation of machine learning algorithms. Pattern Recognit. **30**(7), 1145–1159 (1997)
25. Duan, K., Keerthi, S., Poo, A.N.: Evaluation of simple performance measures for tuning SVM hyperparameters. Neurocomputing **51**, 41–59 (2003)
26. Guyon, I.: A Scaling Law for the Validation-Set Training-Set Size Ratio. AT&T Bell Laboratories (1997)
27. Matsunaga, A., Fortes, J.A.B.: On the use of machine learning to predict the time and resources consumed by applications. In: CCGrid (2010)
28. Tsafrir, D., Etsion, Y., Feitelson, D.: Backfilling using system-generated predictions rather than user runtime estimates. IEEE Trans. Parallel Distrib. Syst. **18**(6), 789–803 (2007)
29. Smith, W., Foster, I., Taylor, V.: Predicting application run times using historical information. In: Feitelson, D.G., Rudolph, L. (eds.) JSSPP 1998. LNCS, vol. 1459, pp. 122–142. Springer, Heidelberg (1998). doi:10.1007/BFb0053984
30. Gibbons, R.: A historical application profiler for use by parallel schedulers. In: Feitelson, D.G., Rudolph, L. (eds.) JSSPP 1997. LNCS, vol. 1291, pp. 58–77. Springer, Heidelberg (1997). doi:10.1007/3-540-63574-2_16
31. Zhang, J., Figueiredo, R.: Application classification through monitoring and learning of resource consumption patterns. In: IPDPS, April 2006

Influence of Dynamic Think Times on Parallel Job Scheduler Performances in Generative Simulations

Stephan Schlagkamp$^{(\boxtimes)}$

Robotics Research Institute, TU Dortmund University,
Dortmund, Germany
stephan.schlagkamp@udo.edu

Abstract. The performance of parallel schedulers is a crucial factor in the efficiency of high performance computing environments. Scheduler designs for practical application focusing on improving certain metrics can only be achieved, if they are evaluated in realistic testing environments. Since real users submit jobs to their respective system, special attention needs to be spent on their job submission behavior and the causes of that behavior. In this work, we investigate the impact of dynamic user behavior on parallel computing performances and analyze the significance of *feedback* between system performance and future user behavior. Therefore, we present a user-based dynamic workload model for generative simulations, which we use to analyze the impact of dynamically changing think times on simulations. We run several such simulations with widely known scheduling techniques *FCFS* and *EASY*, providing first insights on the influence of our approach on scheduling performances. Additionally, we analyze the performances by means of different metrics allowing a discussion on user satisfying performance measures.

Keywords: Workload · Generative simulation · User behavior · Feedback

1 Introduction and Related Work

So far, a common technique to compare performances of different schedulers is achieved by simulations using previously recorded workload traces. There are many studies on analyzing properties of workloads, e.g., [9], resampling workload, e.g., [16], or prediction of future workload, e.g. [2].

According to Schwiegelshohn, this technique does not suffice to gain practical performance measures. Schwiegelshohn describes a gap between scheduling in theory and its practical application [10]. According to him, there is a need to "prevent misunderstanding between researchers and practitioners", e.g., by comprehensible interpretations and conclusions from analyses. Additionally, he describes the necessity of workload models including a simulation of interaction

© Springer International Publishing AG 2017
N. Desai and W. Cirne (Eds.): JSSPP 2015/2016, LNCS 10353, pp. 123–137, 2017.
DOI: 10.1007/978-3-319-61756-5_7

of users and the system due to the spreading of the parallel computing concept. In this work, we address both discussed aspects: We develop a simulation framework for generative simulations of users interacting with a parallel computing system giving the opportunity to test schedulers in a real world simulation environment.

We present and analyze the results of a generative simulation and argue why such simulations must be of dynamic fashion. Since the process of users submitting jobs to a computing environment and receiving a response once their job was computed is based on user behavior. Users may react to sparse resources changing the workload or submit times, which are then faced by a certain scheduler. Testing scheduler performances by using earlier recorded workload traces suffers from a lack of these interactive effects. Shmueli and Feitelson investigated a crucial impact in performance measure when applying *feedback* in form of statistically sampled think times [11].

Since Feitelson describes a correlation between response times and think times [4], we model a dynamic and interactive simulation environment focusing on such user behavior. The system performance is an outcome of a generative process. Regarding this idea, each recorded workload trace is only one instantiation of a dynamic interaction process.

We can think of many different forms of feedback between users and a parallel computing environment:

- People could start their daily work earlier or finish later, if the system does not offer satisfying performances.
- Contrary, they could begin their work later, or finish earlier, if the responsiveness of the system is *good*.
- In a system with poor performances, people could tend to work on weekends, to find it less utilized, assuming that they prefer working on weekdays.
- Users could tend to change the characteristics of jobs they submit. Job parameters (size, length, etc.) may be adapted to get results faster or to use resources more efficiently.
- In case further resources advance the system, job characteristics might be adjusted accordingly.
- Runtime estimates can have a major influence on scheduling performances [14]. We can also think of them being *tuned* by users, to receive more satisfying results.

So far, little or none dynamic simulations were conducted in the context of parallel scheduler evaluations. Although we discussed different possible forms of feedback, we want to focus on *think times*, which is the interval between response and submission of two consecutive jobs. This form of feedback is analyzed in different works, e.g., [4].

Feitelson describes the reaction of users to system performances as "a mystery" [6, p. 414]. The workload submitted by users and the system performance should meet in a *stable state*. A growing demand leads to poorer system performance (cf. Fig. 1). This result can be obtained in a performance test with increasing workload. Nevertheless, the actual user reaction is an open question.

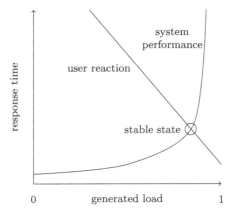

Fig. 1. Supply-and-demand curves crossing in stable state [6, p. 414].

Our simulations are based on the *teikoku Scheduling framework* [1] which is extended by a workload generation module simulating dynamic user behavior. Future work can adapt this model to simulate further forms of feedback. We measure the performance by four different metrics, which we interpret to have an impact on user satisfaction. Results from simulations as provided in this paper can justify certain goals of optimization in applied scheduling strategies to make results more comprehensible for practitioners.

This work is structured as follows. In the next section, we present the dynamic user model as the basis of the simulation and discuss different feedback functions in Sect. 2. In Sect. 3, we present the simulation setup and discuss the influence of dynamic think times. We close this study with a conclusion in Sect. 4.

2   User Model and Feedback

To develop our simulation environment, we make three a priori assumptions. First, submission times and working habits are based an a weekly pattern, e.g., described in [6, p. 394]. Regularly, people work from Monday to Friday followed by the weekend from Saturday to Sunday. We assume that this observation holds for the work with HPC environments to some extend, as well. Second, users do not work all day long. We suppose that they start at a certain point in time and finish work later, according to different days of the week. Third, we choose to model submission behavior as a submission of consecutive batches. Feitelson gives an overview of different works, which analyze or model user activity as sessions and batches [6, p. 396ff].

These assumptions lead to the framework of our simulation. Given a weekly structure as the global frame of user behavior, our simulation can run for an adjustable number of n_w weeks. Furthermore, we model n_u individual users $u \in U$ in the set of all users U participating in a simulation run. Users might be more or less active, as Feitelson and Shmueli have analyzed [12]. We take care of this fact by introducing the *activity ratio*

$$p_{a,u} \in [0,1], \tag{1}$$

which is the percentage chance of a user being active in a certain week.

After describing this main structure of the simulation, we can now focus on attributes describing the submission behavior of a single user. To model different activity at different days of the week, we introduce a distribution describing this activity

$$p_{d,u} \in [0,1] \quad \forall d \in D = \{mon, tue, \ldots, sun\}, \forall u \in U,$$
$$\sum_{d \in D} p_{d,u} = 1 \quad \forall u \in U. \tag{2}$$

Every user has a certain point in time to start and to end his or her day. Additionally, we introduce variables

$$t_{b,u} \in [0, 86400], \tag{3}$$
$$t_{e,u} \in [0, 86400] \quad \forall u \in U, \tag{4}$$
$$t_{b,u} < t_{e,u}$$

describing an individual start and end of their working day in seconds. In case the submit time of a new job is not between $t_{b,u}$ and $t_{e,u}$, it is delayed until the next day begins. Additionally, we focus on job characteristics. We restrict the number of processors per job to powers of two, as other numbers of requested processors are fairly uncommon [4]. The number of requested processors of a job and its running time are not correlated over different systems [4]. However, we assume that jobs in different applications tend to have the same characteristics regarding their sizes and running times, or that the same user submits jobs of the same type. Therefore, we model a correlation of job characteristics according to each user. For each user u, we give the probability of choosing a certain number of processors for his job

$$p_{u,m_j} \in [0,1],$$
$$\sum_{m_j} p_{u,m_j} = 1 \quad \forall u \in U, m_j \in \{2^i \mid i \in \mathbb{N}\}. \tag{5}$$

The normal distributions of running times for a given number of processors

$$\mu_{u,m_j}, \tag{6}$$
$$\sigma_{u,m_j} \quad \forall u \in U, m_j \in \{2^i \mid i \in \mathbb{N}\}, \tag{7}$$

are set for each user respectively.

We add a *parallelity factor*, to respect batch-wise job submissions. After a job is sampled, another job is sampled with probability

$$p_{p,u} \in [0,1].$$

Furthermore, we model interarrival time t_{in} to be the time between submissions of jobs of the same batch.

Keeping the model simple, we introduce a linear think time function. Two variables represent each user's specific think time behavior. Variables $tt_{u,m}$ and $tt_{u,b}$ are used in the linear function

$$tt_u(r_{j_i}) = tt_{u,m} \cdot r_{j_i} + tt_{u,b}, \tag{8}$$

giving the think time according to the response time r_{j_i} of the last finishing job of the current batch named j_i submitted by user u. Note that we do not model user sessions in detail, due to the difficulty of extracting session information from workload traces [15]. In this work, sessions are an implicit outcome of the described behavior. Figure 2 depicts an overview of the described process.

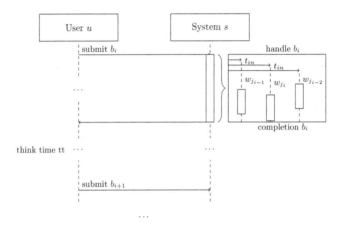

Fig. 2. Job submission workflow of user u.

Now we can analyze some situations for which we set up a set of users in a certain system. Therefore, we consecutive extract data from existing workload traces to run feedback-aware simulations. Although not all users might fit in the proposed model due to different working habits, e.g., there might be people starting their work one day and working over midnight to finish next day, we hope that the simulation is a first step towards user-aware simulation.

We arbitrarily choose six workload traces to learn parameters $tt_{u,m}$, and $tt_{u,b}$. Traces LANL CM5, KTH-SP2, OSC Cluster, HPC2N, ANL Intrepid, and SDSC SP2 range from 213–437 users with 28, 489–527, 371 jobs, and 100–163, 840 cores [5]. Figure 3 depicts a plot of the think times in the chosen traces. Only jobs j_i having a subsequent job j_{i+1} of the same user are considered. They must not overlap, i.e., the beginning of j_{i+1} must be after j_i finished. Furthermore, only think times of less than 8 h are considered: $0 < s_{i+1} - r_i < 28{,}800$ s, with submit time s_{i+1} of job j_{i+1} and response time r_i of job i. Fitting a linear function to the provided data, we receive $tt_{u,m} = 0.4826$, and $tt_{u,b} = 1779$, when least-squares is applied.

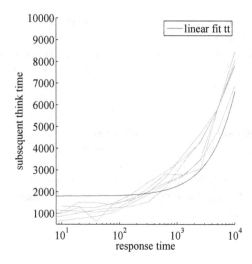

Fig. 3. Linear fit of think times in different workload traces.

3   Generative Simulations

We are interested in the effect on the following different measurements of performances (cf. [3]). We consider the following four metrics.

– *Average Response Time (ART)*: The sum of all response times (time passing from job submission to receiving of the result) divided by the number of jobs

$$\text{ART} = \frac{\sum_{j \in J} r_j}{|J|}.$$

– *Average Weighted Response Time (AWRT)*: The response time of each job is weighted by its size and divided by the number of jobs submitted in total,

$$\text{AWRT} = \frac{\sum_{j \in J} p_j \cdot m_j \cdot r_j}{\sum_{j \in J} p_j \cdot m_j}.$$

– *Average Waiting Time (AWT)*: All waiting times (time passing from job submission to actual processing) are normalized by the number of jobs

$$\text{AWT} = \frac{\sum_{j \in J} w_j}{|J|}.$$

– *Average Slowdown (ASD)*: The slowdown is defined as the response time normalized by the running time. We sum up all slowdowns and take the average

$$\text{ASD} = \frac{\sum_{j \in J} \frac{r_j}{p_j}}{|J|}.$$

We choose these metrics for the following reasons. Since we model the think time as a function of response time, we implicitly assume that different time measures of a job have a certain impact on users. The ART is the time a user has to wait in total for a result and is therefore considered. Furthermore, the AWRT takes the size of a job into consideration and might also be of interest for certain user behavior. Additionally, we focus on the waiting time. While AWT expresses the waiting times users face, SD expresses the proportional running time according to the processing time (and therefore indicates on the proportional waiting time).

In this work, we choose two commonly known scheduling techniques for comparison.

- *First Come First Serve (FCFS)*: Using FCFS, jobs are computed in order of arrival at the system.
- *EASY backfilling (EASY)* [8]: If running times of jobs are known or at least an estimation is given, queued jobs are preferred iff jobs will not violate the reservation made for the first queued job.

In our simulations, EASY has an optimal working environment due to perfectly known running times at forehand. Clearly, this is an advantage for the performance of this scheduling technique. Future analyses may also consider mistakes in runtime estimations, as they are not necessarily of good quality in practice [7].

3.1 Simulation Setup

We want to analyze potential differences and finding out how far the performance of scheduling strategies is influenced according to the previously discussed metrics. Therefore, we find parameters to the introduced user model. Instead of clustering users into certain groups, e.g. suggested by Talby [13], we choose an averaging user model in this study. We analyze the KTH SP2 trace [5] and generate the following user archetype:

We suppose that each user would regularly work from 9 a.m. to 5 p.m. ($u_b = 32400$, $u_e = 61200$). In the KTH trace, we find the following activity distribution regarding the number of submitted job

$$p_{mon,u} = 0.15624, \quad p_{tue,u} = 0.17744,$$
$$p_{wed,u} = 0.18432, \quad p_{thu,u} = 0.18625,$$
$$p_{fri,u} = 0.15536, \quad p_{sat,u} = 0.06560,$$
$$p_{sun,u} = 0.07480.$$

Analyzing the distributions of cores and runtimes, the trace provides the following averages.

$$p_1 = 0.33 \qquad\qquad \mu_1 = 10232.73$$
$$p_2 = 0.18 \qquad\qquad \mu_2 = 5053.17$$
$$p_4 = 0.18 \qquad\qquad \mu_4 = 5982.80$$
$$p_8 = 0.17 \qquad\qquad \mu_8 = 12364.73$$
$$p_{16} = 0.08 \qquad\qquad \mu_{16} = 10668.04$$
$$p_{32} = 0.04 \qquad\qquad \mu_{32} = 9582.56$$
$$p_{64} = 0.02 \qquad\qquad \mu_{64} = 8870.41$$

Furthermore, we find an interarrival time t_i of 240.73 s, a probability of a further job submission of $p_p = 0.54$ and an activity ratio of $p_a = 0.18$.

As we want to investigate whether there is a difference when linear think time is present, we compare it to constant behavior. Therefore, we choose the following four different think time functions:

- Constant: 20 min, $tt_{u,c20}(r_j) = 1200$
- Constant: 120 min, $tt_{u,c120}(r_j) = 7200$
- Constant: 240 min, $tt_{u,c240}(r_j) = 14400$
- Linear: linear think time model,
  $tt_{lin}(r_j) = m_u \cdot r_j + b_u$, $m_u = 0.4826$, $b_u = 1779$ (cf. Sect. 2)

Furthermore, we define three setups, named *less*, *regular* and *more*. The regular setup contains 60 users, which is the number of users responsible for 80% of the workload plus an estimation of the users responsible for the other 20%. The KTH trace contains 214 users, of which 165 users (72.9%) only submit 20% of workload, i.e., 49 users represent 80% of the workload. We replace these 165 users by 11 users representing the otherwise missing 20%. To simulate different load situations, we decrease the number of users by one third, for the more setup we add one third of users, i.e., 40 are in the less and 80 users are in the more simulation, respectively. Each setup is repeated for 150 consecutive weeks.

These users submit jobs to a system s of size $m_s = 100$, which is the size of KTH. Job sampling and submission is fulfilled according to the described parameters and one certain think time function. Whenever a user would sample a job, which is greater than the currently simulated system size, the job size is reduced to system size, i.e., $m_j \leftarrow \min\{m_s, m_j\}$. Furthermore, each simulation is performed with schedulers FCFS and EASY (cf. Sect. 2).

Summarizing, one simulation run has the following attributes:

- System size $m_s = 100$
- Scheduler: FCFS or EASY
- Think time model: tt_{c20}, tt_{c120}, tt_{c240}, or tt_{lin}
- Simulation of 150 weeks

All parameters describing a single user are summarized in Table 1. To create convincing data, which is less affected by outliers, we repeat each simulation configuration for 25 times.

Table 1. Basic parameters defining all users in the artificial simulation setup.

Parameter	Value						
Start of day t_b	32400						
End of day t_e	61200						
Interarrival time t_i	240.73						
Parallelity factor p_p	0.54						
Activity ratio p_a	0.18						
Activity within week	mon	tue	wed	thu	fri	sat	sun
	0.16	0.18	0.18	0.19	0.16	0.07	0.07
Job attributes							
Cores m_j	1	2	4	8	16	32	64
Dist. p_{m_j}	0.33	0.18	0.18	0.17	0.08	0.04	0.02
μ_{m_j}	10232.73	5053.17	5982.80	12364.73	10668.04	9582.56	8870.41
Think times		Parameter tt	c_{20}	c_{120}	c_{240}	lin	
		Think time $tt_{u,m}$	0.0	0.0	0.0	0.48	
		Think time $tt_{u,b}$	1200.0	7200.0	14400.0	1779.0	

Influence of Different Think Time Functions. We cannot distinguish whether the working habits and type of work performed by users cause the length of think times or if there is some psychological reason for such behavior. However, these experiments will give arguments on positive or negative effects on the metrics considered. Furthermore, we can analyze which metrics are influenced more than others, which might allow us to draw conclusions on the effects of user behavior in parallel computing environments. Comparing the four different think time models we also have to take the processed workload into account. Taking the workload into consideration allows clearer comparisons as of the nature of the analyzed problem: in a less utilized system the chance of better scheduling results according to certain metrics might be easier. We measure the workload in *processor hours*, which describe the amount of workload processed on the system. All running times of all cores are summed up.

The results of each simulation are presented in Figs. 4 and 5. Each row of box plot charts represents one user population (less, regular, more). Each row depicts the values for the three metrics AWRT, AWT, and ASD, as well as the processed workload for all four different think time functions named c20, c120, c240, and lin. The figure does not consider ART, because of the job sampling process. The average job size converges and ART and AWT differ by almost a constant. A single box plot is the graphical representation of all metric or workload values gained at the 25 simulation runs.

At the first glance, we can see that the processed workload decreases for increasing constant think times. The longer a user waits between job submissions, the less workload must be handled by the system in the simulated 150 weeks interval.

For both schedulers, FCFS and EASY, the metric values decrease according to the decrease in workload for constant think times c20, c120, and c240. Furthermore, we see an expectable outcome that the metric values increase for the increase of load, e.g., for c120 AWRT increases from 16290 (less), to 20395 (regular), and 24594 (more) for FCFS and from 15769 (less), to 19099 (regular), and 22360 (more) for EASY. Comparing the results for the linear think time to constant think times, the median of workload is located between the median workload of c20 and c120.

Interestingly, the results of the considered metrics are not always located between the results of c20 and c120. The influence of the linear think time model is significant, as the following detailed analyses show.

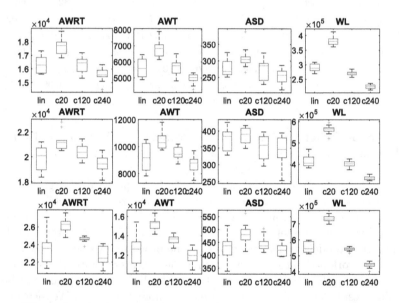

Fig. 4. Results for simulation setups less, reg, and more with FCFS

We compare the results gained for both schedulers for all three different load conditions. Since the median workload of the linear think time is greater than c120, but smaller than c20, we compare the result from simulations with linear think time to the results of c120 to eliminate positive effects from less handled workload. We use Table 2 to analyze differences in performances.

In this table, the median value depicts the performance of different runs of simulations for two different think time models. Additionally, we highlight the difference in percentage between both simulations. We use three different ways to emphasize this difference in percentage: In case the first think time model is better than the second, the percentage value is bold. We use italic writing in case the difference is less than the processed workload, e.g., 2% more workload is processed but the value for a certain metric is only larger by 1%. Otherwise, the value is not emphasized.

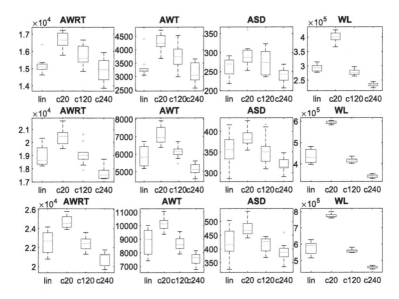

Fig. 5. Results for simulation setups less, reg, and more with EASY

The differences in all metric values are at least relatively better for the linear think time model compared to c120, except for ASD when FCFS is applied to regular workload, which is worse by 6.78% at an increase of workload of only 0.77%.

For FCFS we see a decrease in workload from less to more and performances measured by AWRT and AWT increases. The increase ranges from −1.03% to −4.56% for AWRT and from −3.27% to −8.34% for AWT. This means, the impact of feedback in form of linear think time does not seem to be much different for different load situations.

For ASD, the results are different. Performances range between −6.63% to 6.78% compared to c120. In comparison, we do not see such diverging results for EASY, where ASD ranges between −2.91% to 1.82% in different load situations.

Performance of AWRT and AWT decrease for increasing load. For AWT we see the greatest difference between the less and more setup from −15.85% to 4.70% at almost the same workload. The result for the more setup is still relatively better, but EASY does not seem to be affected as much as FCFS for AWRT and AWT when workload increases.

Summarizing, a linear think time model seems to influence system performance more for a FCFS strategy, than an EASY strategy. Nevertheless, both scheduling strategies are significantly influenced.

Comparison FCFS and EASY. The results allow a comparison between FCFS and EASY. Again, we choose the results obtained with the linear and the c120 think time model. Regarding the workload submitted by the user model, we see that when choosing EASY, 1.61% to 7.72% more workload was handled

Table 2. Performances of FCFS and EASY with constant think time c120 and linear think time.

		FCFS			EASY		
		Less	Regular	More	Less	Regular	More
AWRT	lin	16288.70	20095.50	23560.10	15103.71	18633.92	22694.13
	c120	16456.53	20385.91	24634.64	15581.23	19023.41	22402.40
		−1.03%	**−1.45%**	**−4.56%**	**−3.16%**	**−2.09%**	*1.29%*
AWT	lin	5591.77	9182.48	12625.58	3230.84	5835.65	8992.57
	c120	5774.56	9432.35	13678.10	3742.86	6166.18	8570.19
		−3.27%	**−2.72%**	**−8.34%**	**−15.85%**	**−5.66%**	*4.70%*
ASD	lin	267.98	384.44	437.01	269.94	356.78	415.25
	c120	285.74	358.37	436.85	274.14	350.30	427.32
		−6.63%	6.78%	*0.04%*	**−1.56%**	*1.82%*	**−2.91%**
WL	lin	288544.95	404789.29	544911.61	293323.09	431047.95	590471.88
	c120	271372.21	401689.01	542332.83	275815.78	417931.71	559622.24
		5.95%	**0.77%**	**0.47%**	**5.97%**	**3.04%**	**5.22%**

underlining the overall influence of performance on workload submitting in the designed model. The difference in performance according to the three metrics is also significant.

Regarding AWRT, the difference between EASY and FCFS drops from −7.85% to −3.82% with a linear think time model. While workload increases at the same scale from 1.63% to 7.72%, we cannot reason whether the greater user population causes the difference or not. For c120, we see that EASY outperforms FCFS by up to 9.96%. The more users submit jobs to the system, the greater the difference becomes.

For AWT a similar analyses holds. The gap between performance decreases for the linear model, while it increases when constant think time is applied. We observe the greatest differences of up to 73.07%. For the analyzed user model and the chosen parameters, EASY outperforms FCFS most.

Applying linear think time, we cannot see a clear tendency in the influence of the user model on the difference in performance of FCFS and EASY. Besides, all values are at least relatively better ranging from −7.75% to 0.73%. For constant think time, we see a slight increase from −4.23% to −2.23%.

We conclude, that AWT is the most significantly affected metric comparing FCFS and EASY in the analyzed setup. The influence of linear think time seems to decrease for an increase of the size of the user population (Table 3).

Resulting Think Times. We also report on the resulting think times, since this is a main feature of this simulation. Figure 6 shows the think times in the KTH SP2 log, as well as in two simulations. The simulations cover a regular setup with FCFS an EASY scheduler. A moving averages filter (window size = 50)

Table 3. Comparison of results obtained for FCFS and EASY.

	FCFS/EASY lin			FCFS/EASY c120		
	Less	Regular	More	Less	Regular	More
AWRT	16288.70	20095.50	23560.10	16456.53	20385.91	24634.64
	15103.71	18633.92	22694.13	15581.23	19023.41	22402.40
	−7.85%	**−7.84%**	**−3.82%**	**−5.62%**	**−7.16%**	**−9.96%**
AWT	5591.77	9182.48	12625.58	5774.56	9432.35	13678.10
	3230.84	5835.65	8992.57	3742.86	6166.18	8570.19
	−73.07%	**−57.35%**	**−40.40%**	**−54.28%**	**−52.97%**	**−59.60%**
ASD	267.98	384.44	437.01	285.74	358.37	436.85
	269.94	356.78	415.25	274.14	350.30	427.32
	0.73%	**−7.75%**	**−5.24%**	**−4.23%**	**−2.30%**	**−2.23%**
WL	288544.95	404789.29	544911.61	271372.21	401689.01	542332.83
	293323.09	431047.95	590471.88	275815.78	417931.71	559622.24
	1.63%	**6.09%**	**7.72%**	**1.61%**	**3.89%**	**3.09%**

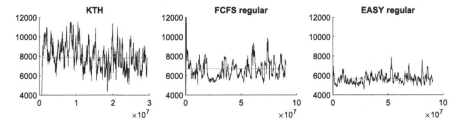

Fig. 6. Think times in different traces: Original KTH log, simulation with FCFS (regular), and simulation with EASY (regular).

smoothens the plots to improve the readability. The horizontal line indicates the mean value in each plot.

We find that the KTH plot is more volatile than the simulated ones. One main reason for this probably is the fixed runtimes in the simulation setup. Greater variance in runtimes should lead to greater volatility in think times, since think time is linearly dependent on these runtimes. Beside different volatility, the resulting average think times differ significantly from the original trace. While the average think time in the KTH SP2 log is 7841.4 s, it is 6697.2 s for the FCFS setup. The average reduces for the EASY setup to 5644.7 s, which is 15.7% less. Choosing more complex parameter sets and modeling different users independently will decrease the gap between observed think times and the original trace. Furthermore, the batch sampling process might influence the results. Applying a strategy, which analyzes user- or batch-wise correlations between job characteristics will probably lead to further changes in results.

Discussion. A linear think time model impacts the performances of both scheduling strategies, FCFS and EASY, significantly. We investigated an increase in performance compared to constant think times regarding AWRT, AWT, and ASD when comparable workload is processed. Dynamic think times seem to have a *balancing* influence on the distribution of workload, since we investigated not just an overall increase in performance, but impacts on performance are greater for simulations using FCFS than for simulations using EASY.

Nevertheless, metrics are affected differently. We suggest to always considering different types of ways to rate a system quality, when performing feedback-aware simulations.

The resulting think times already show some volatility, but they are not close to those of the KTH trace. This is probably due to the simplifying assumptions made for both, model and parameters.

In a situation of high demand and many queued jobs, favoring certain jobs and delaying others allows to influence the think time function and therefore manipulation of the balancing effect. This would mean that some users are treated less fair than others compared to a first come first serve based policy, but the metrics considered would be affected in a positive way. In how far this is an appropriate outcome remains discussable. Choosing think time as a metric of performance prevents such strategy.

4   Conclusion

We introduced a generative simulation environment to analyze feedback effects. We modeled user reactions to system performances in form of dynamic think times. In several analyses, we showed that the dynamic reaction leads to results, which outperform the results obtained with static behavior. We conclude, that modeling feedback effects is essential for simulation of user-system interaction in high performance computing. The resulting think times are not as volatile as from the original trace. Future work should consider more sophisticated job sampling processes. The results must be verified in further studies and more work of this type is important to simulate feedbacks appropriately. Even psychological research should focus on the presented aspects to understand human behavior in HPC environments more deeply.

References

1. teikoku Grid Scheduling Framework (2012). http://forge.it.irf.tu-dortmund.de/projects/teikoku/. Accessed 12 Nov 2014
2. Di, S., Kondo, D., Cirne, W.: Host load prediction in a Google compute cloud with a Bayesian model. In: Proceedings of the International Conference on High Performance Computing, Networking, Storage and Analysis, SC 2012, pp. 1–11, Los Alamitos, CA, USA. IEEE Computer Society Press (2012)
3. Feitelson, D.G.: Metrics for parallel job scheduling and their convergence. In: Feitelson, D.G., Rudolph, L. (eds.) JSSPP 2001. LNCS, vol. 2221, pp. 188–205. Springer, Heidelberg (2001). doi:10.1007/3-540-45540-X_11

4. Feitelson, D.G.: Looking at data. In: IPDPS 2008, pp. 1–9 (2008)
5. Feitelson, D.G.: Parallel Workloads Archive (2008). http://www.cs.huji.ac.il/labs/parallel/workload/. Accessed 12 Nov 2014
6. Feitelson, D.G.: Workload Modeling for Computer Systems Performance Evaluation (2014). http://www.cs.huji.ac.il/~feit/wlmod/wlmod.pdf. Accessed 12 Nov 2014
7. Lee, C.B., Snavely, A.: On the user-scheduler dialogue: studies of user-provided runtime estimates and utility functions. In: International Journal of High Performance Computing Applications, vol. 20, pp. 495–506 (2006)
8. Lifka, D.A.: The ANL/IBM SP scheduling system. In: Feitelson, D.G., Rudolph, L. (eds.) JSSPP 1995. LNCS, vol. 949, pp. 295–303. Springer, Heidelberg (1995). doi:10.1007/3-540-60153-8_35
9. Mishra, A.K., Hellerstein, J.L., Cirne, W., Das, C.R.: Towards characterizing cloud backend workloads: insights from google compute clusters. SIGMETRICS Perform. Eval. Rev. **37**(4), 34–41 (2010)
10. Schwiegelshohn, U.: How to design a job scheduling algorithm. In: Cirne, W., Desai, N. (eds.) JSSPP 2014. LNCS, vol. 8828, pp. 147–167. Springer, Cham (2015). doi:10.1007/978-3-319-15789-4_9
11. Shmueli, E., Feitelson, D.: Using site-level modeling to evaluate the performance of parallel system schedulers. In: 14th IEEE International Symposium on Modeling, Analysis, and Simulation of Computer and Telecommunication Systems. MASCOTS 2006, pp. 167–178, September 2006
12. Shmueli, E., Feitelson, D.G.: On simulation and design of parallel-systems schedulers: are we doing the right thing? IEEE Trans. Parallel Distrib. Syst. **20**(7), 983–996 (2009)
13. Talby, D.: User modeling of parallel workloads. Ph.D. thesis, Hebrew University of Jerusalem (2006)
14. Tang, W., Desai, N., Buettner, D., Lan, Z.: Analyzing and adjusting user runtime estimates to improve job scheduling on the blue gene/p. In: IEEE International Symposium on Parallel Distributed Processing (IPDPS), pp. 1–11, April 2010
15. Zakay, N., Feitelson, D.G.: On identifying user session boundaries in parallel workload logs. In: 16th Workshop on Job Scheduling Strategies for Parallel Processing (JSSPP), pp. 216–234 (2012)
16. Zakay, N., Feitelson, D.G.: Workload resampling for performance evaluation of parallel job schedulers. Concurrency Comput. Pract. Exp. **26**(12), 2079–2105 (2014)

JSSPP 2016

Automatic Co-scheduling Based on Main Memory Bandwidth Usage

Jens Breitbart$^{(\boxtimes)}$, Josef Weidendorfer, and Carsten Trinitis

Department of Informatics, Chair for Computer Architecture,
Technical University Munich, Munich, Germany
{j.breitbart,josef.weidendorfer,carsten.trinitis}@tum.de

Abstract. Most applications running on supercomputers achieve only a fraction of a system's peak performance. It has been demonstrated that co-scheduling applications can improve overall system utilization. In this case, however, applications being co-scheduled need to fulfill certain criteria such that mutual slowdown is kept at a minimum. In this paper we present a set of libraries and a first HPC scheduler prototype that automatically detects an application's main memory bandwidth utilization and prevents the co-scheduling of multiple main memory bandwidth limited applications. We demonstrate that our prototype achieves almost the same performance as we achieved with manually tuned co-schedules in previous work.

1 Introduction

Most applications running on supercomputers achieve only a fraction of a system's peak performance, even though carefully optimized applications are able to get close to this limit. It seems unlikely that code written by non-experts will provide higher system utilization in the foreseeable future, especially with computer architecture permanently evolving, making it a moving target for optimizations. Furthermore, expected trends such as increased core counts, specialization and heterogeneity will make it even more difficult to exploit available resources.

A possible way to increase overall system utilization without optimizing the code itself is co-scheduling, i. e., running multiple applications with different resource demands on the same node[1]. Such an approach may reduce single application performance. However, it increases overall application throughput of the whole system and thereby produces more results with a given time frame or energy budget. A major challenge for efficient co-scheduling is the detection of an application's resource requirements and predicting the applications performance when co-scheduled with another application.

It is obviously not feasible for HPC compute centers to run every possible application combination to decide on optimal co-schedules. As a possible solu-

---

[1] A node is one endpoint in the network topology of an HPC system. It consists of general purpose processors with access to shared memory. Optionally, a node may be equipped with accelerators such as GPUs.

N. Desai and W. Cirne (Eds.): JSSPP 2015/2016, LNCS 10353, pp. 141–157, 2017.
DOI: 10.1007/978-3-319-61756-5_8

tion, we present a mechanism to detect application memory bandwidth requirements at runtime and use Linux control groups (cgroups[2]) to suspend applications if multiple applications require a high amount of main memory bandwidth. These mechanisms are implemented in a prototype application scheduler. We present a set of schedules with various applications and benchmarks and demonstrate that for these applications our scheduler works as expected and co-scheduling can increase performance and save energy. For energy measurements we present measurements of a whole node using a node-external power distribution unit (PDU). The PDU, a MEGWARE[3] Clustsafe unit, takes the complete system power consumption including power supply into account. The results are almost identical to manually tuned co-scheduling results we presented previously [1].

The paper is organized as follows: First, Sect. 2 gives a detailed overview of the hardware used for our measurements, followed by an introduction to our test applications in Sect. 3. Section 4 analyzes the used applications and shows that depending on the application characteristics using all cores does not necessarily guarantee an optimal result. The following section (Sect. 5) discusses shared hardware resources in an HPC node. Sections 6 and 7 introduce our new library and scheduler. The next section discusses the results achieved with our scheduler. The paper finishes with an overview on related work and conclusions, in Sects. 9 and 10, respectively.

2   Hardware Overview

In this section we will give a brief overview of the hardware used in this paper and how energy consumption measurements were carried out.

All benchmarks were run on a 2 socket NUMA system. The system is equipped with two Intel Xeon E5-2670[4] CPUs, which are based on Intel's Sandy Bridge architecture. Each CPU has 8 cores, resulting in a total of 16 CPU cores in the entire system. One CPU core has support for two hardware thread contexts (HTC, often called Hyperthreading) resulting in a total of 32 HTCs for the whole system. The L3 cache is shared among all CPU cores. The base frequency of the CPU is 2.6 GHz, however, the CPU typically changes the frequency of its cores based on the load of the system. Therefore, clock frequencies can vary between cores at the same time. When a core is idle, the operating system (OS) puts it into sleep state, which significantly reduces power consumption. In case only a fraction of its cores are used, the CPU can increase core clock frequencies (Intel Turbo Boost) up to 3.3 GHz. This is typically done to increase the performance of applications not being able to utilize all available CPU cores, as the CPU is less power efficient at higher frequencies. The so-called thermal design

---

[2] https://www.kernel.org/doc/Documentation/cgroup-v1/cgroups.txt

[3] http://www.megware.com/

[4] http://ark.intel.com/products/64595/Intel-Xeon-Processor-E5-2670-20M-Cache-2_60-GHz-8_00-GTs-Intel-QPI

power (TDP) of each CPU in our system is 115 W, i.e. the CPU consumes about 115 W on average when all 8 cores are active.

Each CPU has its own set of memory controller with its own dedicated DRAM memory, yet there is only a single memory address space. Each core can access every memory location. Accesses to memory of a remote CPU, however, have a higher latency and can lead to contention. Memory is distributed among the CPUs by the OS using a first touch policy, which is the default on Linux (i.e. a memory page is allocated as close as possible to the core first writing to it). The location of the memory page is not changed unless explicitly requested by the OS or the user application. Our system is equipped with a total of 128 GB of RAM (64 GB per CPU). Furthermore there are both a QDR Infiniband network card and an Ethernet network card in the system, however these were idle during our measurements. All data required for the benchmark were stored on a local SSD.

Our energy measurements were carried out using a MEGWARE Clustsafe, which measures the energy consumed by the entire system. Clustsafe is a PDU developed by the MEGWARE company and typically used in their HPC system installations to monitor and control the power consumed by the system. Further, accumulated energy consumption can be provided to developers and system administrators by one counter per PDU outlet which can be queried across the network. According to MEGWARE, Clustsafe measures energy consumption with an accuracy of ±2%. We use Clustsafe to measure the energy consumption on the primary side comprising all components of the system including cooling, network devices and storage.

3   Test Applications

We used two example applications and two benchmarks in this paper:

- a slightly modified version of MPIBlast 1.6.0[5],
- an example application using the CG solver algorithm provided by the LAMA [2] library,
- the PRACE[6] application proxy benchmark Hydro, and
- the heat benchmark developed at Technische Universität München.

3.1   MPIBlast

MPIBlast is an application from computational biology. Using MPI-only, it is a parallel version of the original BLAST (Basic Local Alignment Search Tool) algorithm for heuristically comparing local similarity between genome or protein sequences from different organisms. To this end, the program compares input sequences to sequence databases and calculates the statistical significance

---

[5] http://mpiblast.org/
[6] http://www.prace-ri.eu/

of matches. BLAST is used to infer functional and evolutionary relationships between sequences as well as help identify members of gene families.

Due to its embarrassingly parallel nature using a nested master-slave structure, MPIBlast allows for perfect scaling across tens of thousands of compute cores [3]. The MPI master processes hand out new chunks of workload to their slave processes whenever previous work gets finished. This way, automatic load balancing is applied. MPIBlast uses a two-level master-slave approach with one so-called super-master responsible for the whole application and possibly multiple masters distributing work packages to slaves. As a result, MPIBlast must always be run with at least 3 processes of which one is the super-master, one is the master, and one being a slave. The data structures used in the different steps of the BLAST search typically fit into L1 cache, resulting in a low number of cache misses. The search mostly consists of a series of indirections resolved from L1 cache hits. MPIBlast was pinned using the compact strategy, i. e., the threads are pinned closely together filling up CPU after CPU.

Our modified version of MPIBlast is available on GitHub[7]. In contrast to the original MPIBlast 1.6.0 we removed all `sleep()` functions calls that were supposed to prevent busy waiting. On our test-system, this resulted in underutilization of the CPU. Removing sleeps increased performance by about a factor of 2. Furthermore, our release of MPIBlast updated the Makefiles for the Intel Compiler to utilize inter-procedural optimization (IPO) which also resulted in a notable increase in performance.

In our benchmarks we used MPIBlast to search through the DNA of a fruit-fly (Drosophila melanogaster)[8]. The DNA was queried with 4056 snippets created from itself.

3.2 LAMA

LAMA is an open-source C++ library for numerical linear algebra, emphasizing on efficiency, extensibility and flexibility for sparse and dense linear algebra operations. It supports a wide range of target architectures including accelerators such as GPUs and Intel MIC by integrating algorithm versions using OpenMP, CUDA and OpenCL at a node level, and MPI to handle distributed memory systems. We used the latest development version of LAMA committed to its development branch on Sourceforge (commit 43a7ed[9]).

Our test application concentrates on LAMA's standard implementation of a conjugate gradient (CG) solver for x86 multi-core architectures. This purely exploits multi-threading (no MPI), taking advantage of Intel's MKL library for basic BLAS operations within the step of the CG solver. Each solver iteration involves various global reduction operations, resulting in frequent synchronization of the threads. However, static workload partitioning is sufficient for load balancing among threads. Due to the nature of a CG solver, there is no way

---

[7] https://github.com/jbreitbart/mpifast

[8] ftp://ftp.ncbi.nlm.nih.gov/blast/db/FASTA/drosoph.nt.gz

[9] http://sourceforge.net/p/libama/git/ci/43a7ed

to exploit caches by tiling or blocking. As involved data structures (vectors and sparse matrices) do not fit into processor caches for reasonable use cases (which is also the case in our setting), performance is fundamentally limited by main memory bandwidth and inter-core/node bandwidth for reduction operations. Often, off-chip bandwidth capacity of multi-core CPUs can already be fully exploited by 2 or 3 cores. Thus, for a CG solver implementation for such a multi-core CPU, we expect to obtain the best performance with only a few cores, as using more, only would result in higher congestion regarding memory accesses. We use scattered pinning for the CG solver, i. e., threads were distributed equally among the CPUs. This allows the CG solver to use the memory bandwidth of both CPUs with less threads.

The CG solver of LAMA was applied on a matrix generated with LAMA's matrix generator. The sparse matrix has a size of $2000 * 2000$ elements and is filled with a 2-dimensional 5-point stencil.

3.3 HYDRO

HYDRO is not a low-level benchmark, but an application proxy benchmark that is being used to benchmark European Tier-0 HPC systems. HYDRO serves as a proxy for RAMSES[10] [4], which is a Computational Fluid Dynamics application developed by the astrophysics division in CEA Saclay. HYDRO contains all performance relevant algorithms and communication patterns of the original application, but it is simplified and trimmed down to only about 1500 lines of code (compared to about 150,000 lines of code of the original RAMSES). Subsequently, HYDRO was ported to various programming languages and parallel programming models including Fortran, C/C++, OpenMP, MPI, hybrid MPI/OpenMP, CUDA, OpenCL and OpenACC [5]. Our experiments are based on the hybrid MPI/OpenMP C99 implementation. HYDROS' performance, similarly that of LAMAs CG solver is limited by main memory bandwidth, as its data typically does not fit into L3 cache. For our tests we use two processes, i. e., one per CPU package, and increase the number of threads for each process as this results in optimal performance for the benchmark.

3.4 Heat

Heat is a benchmark providing various implementations of an iterative Jacobi method for solving the heat dissipation problem on a regular 2-D square domain. The basic parallel implementation (called algorithm 2) uses OpenMP and two simple loops to iterate across the matrix. As a result, it is inherently main memory bandwidth limited. In contrast, algorithm 9, a more sophisticated version of this benchmark, uses cache-oblivious diamond tiling [6] and as a result is not limited by main memory bandwidth, but compute bound.

---

[10] http://www.itp.uzh.ch/~teyssier/ramses/RAMSES.html

4   Application Analysis

Figure 1 shows the scalability of all applications/benchmarks on our test-system. The figure shows that the CG solver provides the best performance with 11 threads (42.7 s), however there is hardly any benefit compared to running with 8 threads (44.0 s). Overall, the CG solver only scales linearly up to 2 threads. Hydro and heat – algorithm 2 behave almost identical with a minimum runtime at 12 cores (Hydro) and 10 cores (heat – algorithm 2), but both hardly increase performance with more then 8 cores (Hydro) and 6 cores(heat – algorithm 2). MPIBlast scales almost linearly up to 16 CPU cores and heat – algorithm 9 scales almost linear up to 11 cores, but than hardly increases performance any

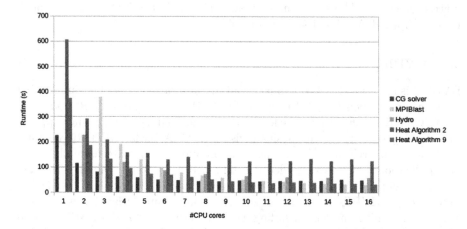

Fig. 1. The scalability of our test applications. We only use one HTC per core.

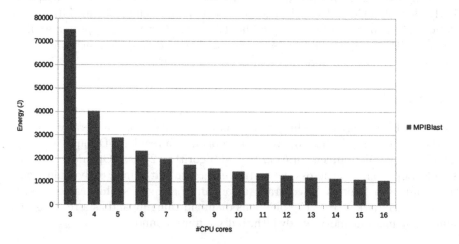

Fig. 2. Power required while running MPIBlast (Watts) and the energy required for one run (Joule).

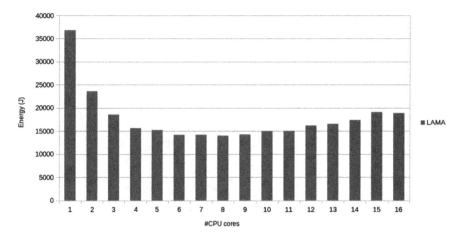

Fig. 3. Energy required for one LAMA CG solver run (Joule). We only use one HTC per core.

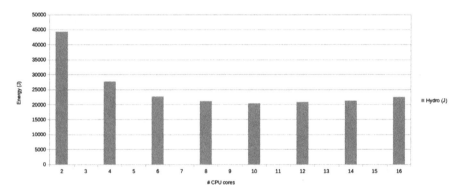

Fig. 4. Energy required for one Hydro run (Joule). We only use one HTC per core.

further. We only show even number of CPU cores for Hydro, as we use two processes with equal number of threads.

Figure 3 shows both the average power used during the scalability runs in Watt and the energy required to complete a single run of the CG solver in Joule. The Watts measured by the different sensors are indicated by lines, and the total energy integrated over the time required to complete a single run of the CG solver (often called *energy-to-solution*) is indicated by bars. It should be noted that the minimum energy-to-solution is not obtained when the CG solver provides the best performance, but with 8 cores, instead. Again Hydro (see Fig. 4) behaves almost identically, as well as heat – algorithm 2 (see Fig. 5).

Figure 2 shows the same information for MPIBlast. MPIBlast scales well, and the minimal energy-to-solution is obtained when using 16 CPU cores. Heat – algorithm 9 again has an optimal energy-to-solution at the point where it performs best. Figure 6 shows energy-to-solution for heat – algorithm 9.

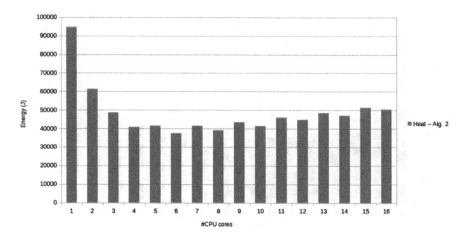

Fig. 5. The energy required for one heat – algorithm 2 run (Joule). We only use one HTC per core.

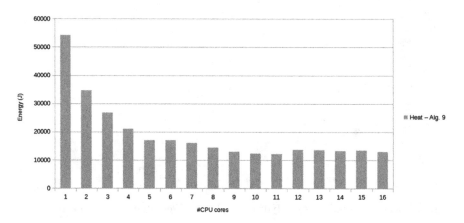

Fig. 6. The energy required for one heat – algorithm 9 run (Joule). We only use one HTC per core.

5   Shared Hardware Resources Within an HPC Node

In this section we discuss the various shared hardware resources that can limit co-scheduling performance.

At **core level**, each HTC has its own set of registers, but shares the instruction pipeline and both L1 and L2 caches with the second HTC of the same core. The instruction pipeline has dedicated hardware for floating point, integer and SIMD instructions, which can be co-issued with various constrains. As a result, co-scheduling an integer and floating point heavy application can potentially increase the utilization of the CPU core, as we have demonstrated before [1].

All cores on the same **package** share the L3 cache, the interconnect between CPU packages and main memory bandwidth. Co-scheduling multiple applications with a large L3 cache working set results in a high number of L3 cache misses and drastically reduces performance [7]. The same holds true for main memory bandwidth. Co-scheduling multiple applications with high main memory bandwidth requirements drastically reduces the performance of both applications. Based on our experience, the inter-package interconnect is typically not a limiting factor for co-scheduling.

Overall, based on our experience both main memory bandwidth and L3 cache usage conflicts can degrade co-scheduling performance up to a point at which overall system throughput is worse than dedicated scheduling. Co-scheduling different applications on a single CPU core can increase performance further, but is not essential. As a result, for all shown measurements in this paper we only use one HTC per CPU core. We leave out L3 working set detection for future work, as Intel has just recently introduced its Cache Allocation Technology (CAT)[11] that can be used to detect L3 cache working sets via hardware support, but is not supported at our test system. Main memory bandwidth usage is the main topic of this paper moving forward.

6   Main Memory Bandwidth Utilization (libDistGen)

Unfortunately current x86 CPUs do not provide any direct way to measure main memory bandwidth utilization, i. e., there is no performance counter that provides this information. As a result, we must deduce this information from other measurements. We leverage the fact that with co-scheduling an application never uses all CPU cores and we can use the other cores to run small benchmarks.

In previous work [7], we showed that effective co-scheduling can be predicted based on stack reuse histograms[12]. Stack reuse histograms can be used to (estimate) the cache working set as well as if an application is main memory bandwidth limited. However, computing such a histogram typically results in multiple orders of application slowdown, as the we must simulate a whole application and analyze every memory access. As a result, we introduced a micro-benchmark called DistGen that can be used to get similar results. DistGen can be configured to produce memory accesses with certain stack reuse patterns. When co-scheduled with an application, we can detect peaks in the stack reuse histogram of the application based on the slowdown of DistGen. A detailed analysis can be found in [7], however all previous work was designed for off-line analysis.

Based on the original DistGen, we now introduce libDistGen, a library designed to be incorporated into schedulers or agents that collect on-line information to be used by the scheduler. libDistGen's interface is simple and consists of just three functions:

---

[11] https://www-ssl.intel.com/content/www/us/en/communications/cache-monitoring-cache-allocation-technologies.html

[12] The *Stack Reuse Distance*, introduced in [8], is the distance to the previous access to the same memory cell, measured in the number of distinct memory cells accessed in between. For the first access to an address, the distance is infinity.

distgen_init() is called to initialize the library. The system must be idle when this function is called, as we run various benchmarks to assess the maximum performance of the system. Depending on the numbers of cores in the system and the available memory bandwidth, this function call can take up to a few minutes to complete.

distgen_membw_available() estimates the percentage of the currently available main memory bandwidth for a given set of CPU cores compared to maximum available memory bandwidth of these CPU cores. The runtime of this function call is less than a second.

distgen_membw_max() is mainly available for debugging purposes. It returns the maximum available memory bandwidth for a given set of CPU cores of the system in GB/s.

distgen_membw_available() is implemented by processing an array with the CPU cores for which the available main memory bandwidth should be estimated. The array is larger than the L3 cache of the CPUs, so all accesses go to main memory. We measure the runtime of the accesses to the array and compare these to measurements made during *distgen_init()*. It is important to note, that these memory accesses will eventually complete, even if all other cores are running memory bandwidth limited code. As a result, we will never directly measure an available memory bandwidth of 0%, but memory bandwidth is typically equally distributed among the cores at hardware level if all cores execute memory bandwidth limited code. *distgen_membw_available()* is designed to consume as much main memory bandwidth as possible by doing hardly any computation and only accessing one byte per cache-line. These characteristics have to be considered when interpreting the return value of *distgen_membw_available()* in a scheduler.

libDistGen is available as open source on GitHub[13].

7 Poor Mans Co-Scheduler (poncos)

The Poor Mans Co-Scheduler (poncos) is our scheduler prototype built on top of libDistGen and libponci[14], which is a small wrapper for Linux control groups (cgroups). Cgroups can be used to limit which CPU cores a set of applications are allowed to use as well as transparently freeze and restart these applications. Cgroups provide plenteous of other options and are typically used to implement containers (like e. g., Docker[15]), but we only use the functionality named before.

For now, poncos reads a job queue from a file using a straightforward co-scheduling algorithm to run the applications listed in this file. Our algorithm briefly follows a scheme of:

1. start the first application on a subset of the available CPU cores
2. wait until the initialization phase of that application has completed (see description below)

---

[13] https://github.com/lrr-tum/libdistgen
[14] https://github.com/lrr-tum/ponci
[15] https://www.docker.com/

3. use *distgen_membw_available()* on the remaining free CPU cores to detect the available memory bandwidth for the free cores
4. start the next application in the queue
5. wait until the initialization phase of the new application has ended
6. pause the old application (using cgroups)
7. use *distgen_membw_available()* on the CPU cores of the paused application to detect of available memory bandwidth
8. restart the old application
9. decide if both applications can be co-scheduled based on the available memory bandwidth
    (a) yes: wait until one application has completed
    (b) no: pause the new application and resume it after the old one has been completed
10. continue with 4. until the queue is empty

The current form of the algorithm expects a uniform behavior of the application during runtime. This is not true for all HPC applications, but seemingly for a large fraction of them, as other tools like for example [9] rely on the same behavior and work fairly well. In general, phase detection in applications should not be done via libDistGen as this requires the application to be paused, but phase detection should be done using hardware performance counters as demonstrated by Chetsa et al. [10]. However, libDistGen can also be used to provide information per application phase (if the phase is long enough) and this information can be used to decide if co-scheduling should be applied. For example, one could decide to only co-schedule applications if at maximum one of them has a memory bandwidth limited application phase.

We currently do not detect the end of the initialization phase, but rely on a timer that fits well with our test applications. However, in general this can be done via the mechanisms described by Chetsa et al. [10] as well.

As mentioned before, *distgen_membw_available()* will never return 0% memory bandwidth available and one has to be careful when interpreting the return value. When calling *distgen_membw_available()* to estimate the available memory bandwidth on half of the system's CPU cores, 50^{16}% means that there is memory bandwidth limited code running on the other half of the available CPU cores and one should not co-schedule another memory bandwidth limited application. Our scheduler currently prevents co-scheduling if the sum of all applications' memory bandwidth estimations is above 90%. We use 90% instead of 100%, as we already noticed a decrease in performance once congestion on main memory gets closer to the maximum. However, this is expected behavior as the current hardware does not guarantee fair resource distribution and slowing down a particular core can decrease overall application performance due to synchronization.

Poncos is available as open source on GitHub[17].

---

[16] The theoretical minimum of distgen is at about 33%, as distgen only reads from main memory and the other half can issue both reads and writes.

[17] https://github.com/lrr-tum/poncos/tree/one-node-only

8 Evaluation

For our evaluation we split our test system in two scheduling domains each consisting of 4 CPU cores per socket, i. e., a total of 8 cores. We choose this setup, as memory bandwidth limited applications can typically not efficiently use more than half of the cores of a socket. More cores only adds to the congestion on the memory controller and decreases performances, as discussed in Sect. 4.

In general, libDistGen works as expected with each possible pair of the applications and benchmarks listed in Sect. 3. Table 1 lists the estimated available main memory bandwidth required for the application, and based on the algorithm described in the previous section, we can deduce that poncos will prevent the co-scheduling of

- Hydro
- Lama
- Heat with algorithm 9

with each other, whereas all other combinations are fine. The resulting schedules based on our setup is rather straight forward and we only show the results of 2 input queues.

The first queue only consists of the two heat variants:

- heat – algorithm 2 (`heat -r 9000 -i 5000 -a 2 -t 8`)
- heat – algorithm 9 (`heat -r 9000 -i 5000 -a 9 -t 8`)
- heat – algorithm 9 (`heat -r 9000 -i 5000 -a 9 -t 8`)
- heat – algorithm 2 (`heat -r 9000 -i 5000 -a 2 -t 8`)
- heat – algorithm 9 (`heat -r 9000 -i 5000 -a 9 -t 8`)
- heat – algorithm 9 (`heat -r 9000 -i 5000 -a 9 -t 8`)

Figure 7 shows the runtime of queue one. In co-scheduling we only show the critical path of the scheduling. The whole schedule was completes after both runs of heat – algorithm 2 have ended, as all runs with heat – algorithm 9 could be co-scheduled with an run of heat – algorithm 2. As we can see, co-scheduling in this case increases overall application throughput, even though heat – algorithm 2 itself runs slower. The total energy consumption (see Fig. 8) of co-scheduling is

Table 1. The main memory bandwidth available for half of the cores according to libDistGen, while the other half is running the listed application. Estimated usage for the application is compute via $1 - (distgen\_membw\_available() - 0,33)/(1 - 0,33)$.

Application	$distgen\_membw\_available()$	Estimated usage for the application
Hydro	52.7	70.5
Lama	46.6	79,7
MPIBlast	92.5	11.1
Heat – Algorithm 2	41.0	88.1
Heat – Algorithm 9	76.5	35.1

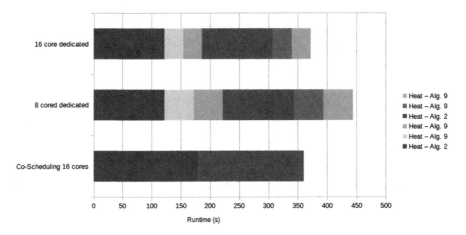

Fig. 7. The runtime of queue 1 with both dedicated scheduling and co-scheduling.

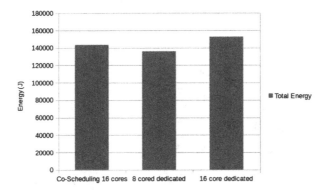

Fig. 8. The energy consumption of scheduling queue 1 with both dedicated scheduling and co-scheduling.

also better than dedicating all 16 cores to the individual applications, but just dedicating 8 cores provides a better energy-to-solution.

Our second example queue consists of:

- LAMA CG solver
- MPIBlast
- LAMA CG solver

The Figs. 9 and 10 show the total runtime and energy-to-solution of the schedules of queue 2. In Fig. 9 we again only show the runtime of the critical path, i.e., at the beginning LAMA is running by itself while we wait for the initialization phase to be completed and than run our measurements. After that MPIBlast is started and runs until the completion of the queue. Both LAMA runs are finished before the MPIBlast run is complete. We see a notable decrease in both runtime and energy consumption when co-scheduling MPIBlast and

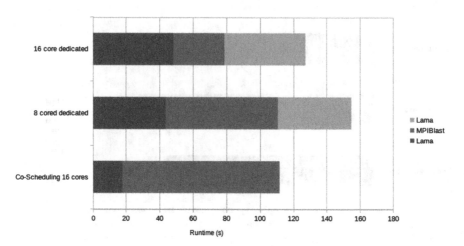

Fig. 9. The runtime of queue 2 with both dedicated scheduling and co-scheduling.

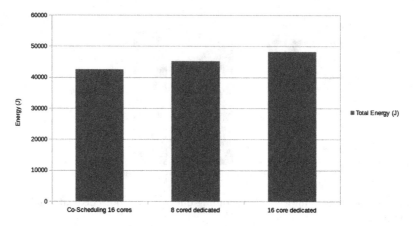

Fig. 10. The energy consumption of scheduling queue 2 with both dedicated scheduling and co-scheduling.

LAMA. These results match well with our previous manual fine tuning of the MPIBlast/LAMA co-schedule previously published in [1].

Both queues have been selected so that co-scheduling is possible. In case the queue does not allow for co-scheduling, we expect to see a small decrease in performance and a small increase in energy consumption due to the additional measurements. However, these effects seem to be within the order of measurements noise, as we could not directly measure any clear overhead.

9   Related Work

On server and desktop systems with multiple cores or hardware thread contexts simultaneous scheduling of different applications is the norm. However, in

HPC systems, most larger compute centers hardly apply any co-scheduling. Co-scheduling is typically used only for purely sequential jobs which cannot utilize all cores in a single node.

A different approach with the same goal as co-scheduling is to use power capping and dynamic voltage frequency scaling (DVFS) to reduce the power consumption of existing systems. Such an approach can obviously not increase the overall throughput of an HPC system, but increase its energy efficiency. For example Wang et al. [11] discuss a scheduling heuristic that uses DVFS to reduce overall system power consumption. The Adagio [12] tool uses DVFS to reduce the idle time of the system by analyzing the time spent in blocking MPI function calls and decreases the performance of CPU cores accordingly.

The Invasive Computing research project [13] works on an approach to have applications dynamically react to changes of their resource requirements and potential request additional resources or return resources that are no longer used. Schreiber et al. [14] for example present applications that automatically balance their work load.

Another approach to increase system efficiency is to work on the infrastructure used in the HPC centers. Auweter et al. [15] give an overview of this area and describe how a holistic approach including monitoring the various jobs can help to improve efficiency without modifying the applications itself.

Characterizing co-schedule behavior of applications by measuring their slowdown against micro-benchmarks is proposed by different works. MemGen [16] is focussing on memory bandwidth usage, similar to Bandwidth Bandit [17] which is making sure not to additionally consume L3 space. Bubble-Up [18] is similar tool accessing memory blocks of increasing size. All these tools are not designed for optimizing the schedule at runtime.

10   Conclusions and Future Work

In this paper we presented a library for on-line application analysis to guide co-scheduling and present a basic prototype scheduler implementation, which shows that this information can actually be used to implement co-scheduling. Our approach works well with all tested applications and overall system throughput and energy consumption with co-scheduling varies based on the input.

In this paper, we only concentrated on main memory bandwidth, but other resources like L3 cache usage are also important to identify if co-scheduling should be applied. In future work, we will concentrate on L3 cache usage. Furthermore, this work only explores co-scheduling on a single node. We plan to extend our experiments to a multi-node setup.

As part of the FAST project[18] we plan to integrated our approach with an improved Slurm[19] scheduler that uses predetermined application statistics and runtime measurements to co-schedule applications.

---

[18] http://www.fast-project.de/
[19] http://slurm.schedmd.com/

Acknowledgments. We want to thank MEGWARE, who provided us with a Clustsafe to measure energy consumption. The work presented in this paper was funded by the German Ministry of Education and Science as part of the FAST project (funding code 01IH11007A).

References

1. Breitbart, J., Weidendorfer, J., Trinitis, C.: Case study on co-scheduling for HPC applications. In: 44th International Conference on Parallel Processing Workshops (ICPPW), pp. 277–285 (2015)
2. Kraus, J., Förster, M., Brandes, T., Soddemann, T.: Using lama for efficient amg on hybrid clusters. Comput. Sci. Res. Dev. **28**(2–3), 211–220 (2013)
3. Lin, H., Balaji, P., Poole, R., Sosa, C., Ma, X., Feng, W.-C.: Massively parallel genomic sequence search on the blue gene/p architecture. In: International Conference for High Performance Computing, Networking, Storage and Analysis. SC 2008, pp. 1–11. IEEE (2008)
4. Teyssier, R.: Cosmological hydrodynamics with adaptive mesh refinement-a new high resolution code called ramses. Astron. Astrophys. **385**(1), 337–364 (2002)
5. Lavallée, P.-F., de Verdière, G.C., Wautelet, P., Lecas, D., Dupays, J.-M.: Porting and optimizing HYDRO to new platforms and programming paradigms lessons learnt (2012). http://www.prace-project.eu/IMG/pdf/porting_and_optimizing_hy dro_to_new_platforms.pdf
6. Bertolacci, I.J., Olschanowsky, C., Harshbarger,B., Chamberlain, B.L., Wonnacott, D.G., Strout, M.M.: Parameterized diamond tiling for stencil computations with chapel parallel iterators. In: Proceedings of the 29th ACM on International Conference on Supercomputing, pp. 197–206. ACM (2015)
7. Weidendorfer, J., Breitbart, J.: Detailed characterization of HPC applications for co-scheduling. In: Proceedings of the 1st COSH Workshop on Co-Scheduling of HPC Applications, p. 19, January 2016
8. Bennett, B.T., Kruskal, V.J.: LRU stack processing. IBM J. Res. Dev. **19**, 353–357 (1975)
9. Klug, T., Ott, M., Weidendorfer, J., Trinitis, C.: Automated optimization of thread-to-core pinning on multicore systems. In: Stenström, P. (ed.) Transactions on High-Performance Embedded Architectures and Compilers III. LNCS, vol. 6590, pp. 219–235. Springer, Heidelberg (2011). doi:10.1007/978-3-642-19448-1_12
10. Tsafack Chetsa, G.L., Lefèvre, L., Pierson, J.-M., Stolf, P., Da Costa, G.: Exploiting performance counters to predict and improve energy performance of HPC systems. Future Gener. Comput. Syst. **36**, 287–298 (2014). https://hal.archives-ouvertes. fr/hal-01123831
11. Wang, L., Von Laszewski, G., Dayal, J., Wang, F.: Towards energy aware scheduling for precedence constrained parallel tasks in a cluster with DVFS. In: 2010 10th IEEE/ACM International Conference on Cluster, Cloud and Grid Computing (CCGrid), pp. 368–377. IEEE (2010)
12. Rountree, B., Lownenthal, D.K., de Supinski, B.R., Schulz, M., Freeh, V.W., Bletsch, T.: Adagio: making DVS practical for complex HPC applications. In: Proceedings of the 23rd International Conference on Supercomputing, ser. ICS 2009, pp. 460–469. ACM, New York (2009). http://doi.acm.org/10.1145/1542275. 1542340

13. Teich, J., Henkel, J., Herkersdorf, A., Schmitt-Landsiedel, D., Schröder-Preikschat, W., Snelting, G.: Invasive computing: an overview. In: Hübner, M., Becker, J. (eds.) Multiprocessor System-on-Chip, pp. 241–268. Springer, New York (2011)
14. Schreiber, M., Riesinger, C., Neckel, T., Bungartz, H.-J., Breuer, A.: Invasive compute balancing for applications with shared and hybrid parallelization. Int. J. Parallel Program. 1–24 (2014)
15. Auweter, A., Bode, A., Brehm, M., Huber, H., Kranzlmüller, D.: Principles of energy efficiency in high performance computing. In: Kranzlmüller, D., Toja, A.M. (eds.) ICT-GLOW 2011. LNCS, vol. 6868, pp. 18–25. Springer, Heidelberg (2011). doi:10.1007/978-3-642-23447-7_3
16. de Blanche, A., Lundqvist, T.: EnglishAddressing characterization methods for memory contention aware co-scheduling. Engl. J. Supercomput. **71**(4), 1451–1483 (2015)
17. Eklov, D., Nikoleris, N., Black-Schaffer, D., Hagersten, E.: Bandwidth bandit: Quantitative characterization of memory contention. In: 2013 IEEE/ACM International Symposium on Code Generation and Optimization (CGO), pp. 1–10 (2013)
18. Mars, J., Vachharajani, N., Hundt, R., Soffa, M.L.: Contention aware execution: online contention detection and response. In: Proceedings of the 8th Annual IEEE/ACM International Symposium on Code Generation and Optimization, ser. CGO 2010, pp. 257–265. ACM, New York (2010)

Adaptive Space-Shared Scheduling for Shared-Memory Parallel Programs

Younghyun Cho, Surim Oh, and Bernhard Egger$^{(\boxtimes)}$

Department of Computer Science and Engineering,
Seoul National University, Seoul, Korea
{younghyun,surim,bernhard}@csap.snu.ac.kr

Abstract. Space-sharing is regarded as the proper resource management scheme for many-core OSes. For today's many-core chips and parallel programming models providing no explicit resource requirements, an important research problem is to provide a proper resource allocation to the running applications while considering not only the architectural features but also the characteristics of the parallel applications.

In this paper, we introduce a space-shared scheduling strategy for shared-memory parallel programs. To properly assign the disjoint set of cores to simultaneously running parallel applications, the proposed scheme considers the performance characteristics of the executing (parallel) code section of all running applications. The information about the performance is used to compute a proper core allocation in accordance to the goal of the scheduling policy given by the system manager.

We have first implemented a user-level scheduling framework that runs on Linux-based multi-core chips. A simple performance model based solely on online profile data is used to characterize the performance scalability of applications. The framework is evaluated for two scheduling policies, balancing and maximizing QoS, and on two different many-core platforms, a 64-core AMD Opteron platform and a 36-core Tile-Gx36 processor. Experimental results of various OpenMP benchmarks show that in general our space-shared scheduling outperforms the standard Linux scheduler and meets the goal of the active scheduling policy.

1 Introduction

Modern operating systems (OSes) are still based on time-shared scheduling techniques originally developed for single-core machines where – despite local run queues – one system kernel maintains the entire information about the system and manages all running tasks in the same manner. At the same time, current parallel programming models such as OpenMP [11], TBB [23], Cilk [7], or OpenCL [16] assume that each application can utilize all physically available hardware resources without considering the current system workload.

In such a disjoint runtime model, OSes lack good scheduling policies when multiple parallel programs are executed simultaneously. Averse effects of this approach include not only a low cache utilization caused by cache cold misses

© Springer International Publishing AG 2017
N. Desai and W. Cirne (Eds.): JSSPP 2015/2016, LNCS 10353, pp. 158–177, 2017.
DOI: 10.1007/978-3-319-61756-5_9

due to context switches of an oversubscription of threads to single cores but also performance interference caused by scheduling threads in a time-shared manner. For example, the standard Linux scheduler, the Completely Fair Scheduler (CFS), provides the same execution chances for each task [21]. Each task's virtual (execution) time is accumulated in proportion to the task priority. This per-task resource management can cause severe performance interference between applications comprising a large number of threads.

A promising approach to address this issue is space-shared resource allocation [28]. In the OS community, several research groups have introduced experimental OS prototypes [5,18,30]. The presented prototypes commonly follow the principle of space-partitioning for scalable many-core resource management. In this new model, the role of the OS is divided into two parts. The *coarse-grained resource manager* provides space-shared resource multiplexing while the application-specific *fine-grained resource manager* manages an application's resource management such as, for example, assigning the application's tasks to the allocated cores. Although the space-shared OSes introduced new OS design principles, the scheduling and resource allocation schemes have lots of open issues to be solved. For traditional parallel job scheduling, a lot of space-shared scheduling schemes such as First-come First-served or Backfilling [14,17,20] have been proposed. However, the prior art mostly focuses on supercomputers or distributed systems where the resource requirements of parallel jobs are typically explicit. For today's many-core chips and parallel programming models that provide no explicit resource requirements, an important research issue of space-shared scheduling is thus to provide a proper resource allocation to the running applications while considering not only the architectural features but also the characteristics of the parallel applications.

In this paper, we introduce a space-shared scheduling strategy for shared-memory parallel programs. Many parallel applications exhibit varying resource requirements and performance characteristics during the execution lifetime of the application. It is therefore increasingly important to consider an application's dynamically changing workload. The proposed scheduling scheme considers all parallel code section of an application. To properly assign the core resources, the scheduler considers the performance characteristics of the currently executing parallel code sections of all running applications. Based on profiled performance information, the scheduler allocates the core resources in accordance with the active scheduling policy which is given by the system manager.

We have first implemented a user-level scheduling framework that performs the proposed scheduling strategy for OpenMP programs on Linux-based many-core systems. In shared-memory systems, the memory access contention is one of the major limiting factor of performance scalability. By extracting the shared-memory access patterns, a simple performance model is used to characterize the performance scalability of running applications. In this work, we implement two Quality-of-Service (QoS) based scheduling policies: Equalizing QoS, and Maximizing QoS. The scheduling framework is evaluated for various OpenMP benchmark scenarios on two different many-core platforms, a 64-core AMD Opteron

NUMA system and a 36-core Tile-Gx36 processor. The empirical studies in this paper show that our space-sharing scheme outperforms the current Linux standard scheduler and confirm space-sharing has potential as a resource management scheme for current and future many-core systems.

The remainder of this paper is organized as follows. Section 2 discusses related work. In Sect. 3, we introduce our approach to dynamic space-shared scheduling. Section 4 describes our scheduler framework including the performance model and the scheduling algorithm. In Sect. 5, we evaluate our scheduling and show how our performance model and scheduling scheme meet the requirements of the active scheduling policy. Section 6 discusses where we see additional room for further performance improvement and the research direction towards better scheduling. Finally, we conclude this paper in Sect. 7.

2   Related Work

For shared-memory many-core systems several empirical scheduling techniques have been proposed that consider applications' performance characteristics.

Moore and Childers [19] introduce a utility model to characterize an application's scalability and performance interference between multi-threaded applications based on offline training. Their model finds the performance plateau of an application and uses the information to choose the thread counts for multi-threaded applications. Grewe et al. [15] decide thread counts of OpenMP applications based on prediction. The prediction relies on machine learning for the selected performance features. Both works decide the proper thread count when a parallel program is launched, but they do not consider varying workloads in an application, and their techniques rely on additional efforts for offline training.

For more fine-grained resource management, Raman et al. [22] propose Parcae, a compiler-assisted dynamic tuning system. Their compiler generates flexible codes for data- and pipeline-parallelism such that they can change the degree of parallelism at runtime. They find the proper thread count by iteratively trying different thread configurations based on a hill-climbing algorithm. However, the hill-climbing approach often fails to find globally optimal thread counts. Emani et al. [13] use a machine learning technique and compiler-assisted information to predict better OpenMP thread counts. On the other hand, Creech et al. [10] introduce SCAF that decides the proper thread count of OpenMP parallel applications when it enters a parallel region. The scalability of an OpenMP application is determined by creating and running a serial process concurrently with the parallel section. An online profiler then compares the progress of the serial process to that of the multi-threaded process based on the instructions per cycle count. Since SCAF does not change the parallelism once the number of threads has been determined, their method is useful for iterative programs in that the serial process is executed once when a parallel section is first executed. These works aim at improving system performance by dynamically tuning the parallelism, but the techniques require application runtime support to dynamically manage the degree of parallelism. For HPC (High Performance Computing) systems, Breitbart *et al.* [8] perform co-scheduling of multiple applications on a multi-core node. To maximize system throughput their scheduler automatically detects an application's main memory bandwidth utilization. On the other hand, we focus on a spatial mapping of parallel programs for managing QoS of applications and do not consider changing active thread counts of applications.

Sasaki *et al.* [24] consider the scalability of multiple multi-threaded applications and perform a spatial partitioning without offline information. The work also focuses on balancing performance of co-located applications via spatial partitioning. To understand the performance scalability of applications, they run the same application on three different core allocations at runtime and measure how the application's IPS (Instructions Per Second) changes for the different resource configurations. In addition, they detect applications' phases to deal with varying workload characteristics. Our scheduling scheme, on the other hand, require a communication API between the space-shared scheduler and the application runtimes. We also aim to characterize the application's performance scalability without runtime reconfiguration and adaptively change the scheduling goals according to the input given by the system manager.

3 The Space-Shared Scheduling Strategy

In this section, we introduce a space-shared scheduling strategy for scheduling multiple shared-memory parallel applications. It is obvious that, even when strictly adhering to a space-shared resource allocation scheme, the allocations are of temporal nature and must be re-evaluated in order to efficiently utilize the given hardware and achieve satisfactory performance. In general, applications can start and end at any given time which will require a re-computation of the current resource allocation. More importantly, the resource requirements of a parallel application are likely to vary over the course of its execution. For example, in sequential sections, one core should be sufficient whereas the different parallel regions of the application may each exhibit divergent characteristics and will thus require a different resource allocation. Assigning the correct amount of resources to all applications at any given time while satisfying both the overall system's and each application's performance goals is thus undoubtedly a challenging problem.

3.1 Interaction with Application Runtimes

Parallel applications consist of several parallel and sequential regions, and the different parallel applications typically posses divergent characteristics [4]. To consider the varying performance characteristics of parallel applications, we propose an approach in which the space-shared scheduler interacts directly with the parallel programming model runtimes of the applications.

A naïve but easy approach is to use synchronous communication between the scheduler and the application runtimes. Figure 1(a) illustrates the approach. System-wide resource re-allocation is performed whenever an application enters

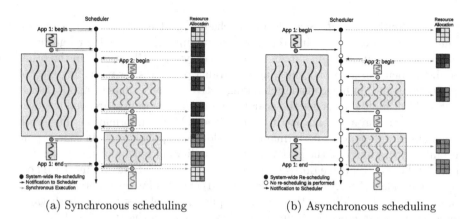

(a) Synchronous scheduling   (b) Asynchronous scheduling

Fig. 1. Adaptive space-shared scheduling scheme.

or exits a parallel region. However, this synchronous scheduling model suffers from a number of problems. The synchronous communication model serializes accesses of parallel applications to the scheduler, thereby effectively limiting parallelism. In addition, re-evaluating the resource allocations whenever one of the concurrently executing parallel applications enters or exits a (possibly very short) parallel region leads to an unacceptably high overhead of the scheduler.

A better approach is to perform asynchronous communication and scheduling as illustrated in Fig. 1(b). In this scheme, parallel applications communicate with the scheduling runtime by sending their status (i.e., events about entering and exiting parallel regions) to the scheduler and asynchronously execute their jobs. The scheduler periodically wakes up to re-evaluate the current resource allocation of the simultaneously running application. Since re-scheduling and re-allocating resources to applications are comparatively expensive operations, re-scheduling is not performed at every wake-up but only if the system state is stable for a long enough period of time. Without that condition, an application executing a short parallel regions in a loop might trigger a system-wide re-scheduling of resources. Section 5 discusses the wake-up frequency and defines what we consider to be a stable system state. The proposed scheduling approach does not limit progress of parallel applications thanks to the asynchronous communication model and, at the same time, is able to reduce frequent inefficient resource re-allocations.

We need to define a method to communicate with the applications or the application-specific runtimes. Applications have to notify the global scheduler about their state. A parallel application is either executing a sequential code section or in one of its parallel sections. We do not distinguish between different sequential code sections, however, the scheduler considers the different parallel sections of an application. The *execution state* of an application from the viewpoint of the scheduler is defined as (a) *sequential* or (b) by the *unique identifier of a parallel section*.

The calls to the scheduler can be inserted manually or automatically in to the source code, made by a customized parallel programming runtime library, or by intercepting the application's calls to the runtime through dynamic library interpositioning. In this paper, we have implemented the last approach for OpenMP applications, dynamic library interpositioning, because it is automatic and neither requires access to the application's source code nor modifications to the parallel runtime library. An easy way to uniquely label parallel sections is to use the address of the parallel code section. Section 4.2 elaborates the details of this approach.

3.2 Application Runtimes and Programming Malleability

Since no application shares core resources with any other application in a space-shared approach, we first need to reclaim the cores from an application before redistributing them to other applications. This functionality has to be implemented without much runtime overhead in order to be beneficial.

To add or reclaim cores from an application, we need to consider what programming model is used. The most prominent parallel programming models are thread-based fork-join model (e.g., OpenMP), task-parallel models (e.g., Cilk, TBB, or OpenMP 3.0) and data-parallelism (e.g., OpenCL, CUDA).

In the OpenMP fork-join model, it is impossible to reduce or increase the number of parallel threads once the worker threads have been created and assigned with a portion of the workload at the entrance of a parallel region unless additional compiler or runtime support is provided. On the other hand, task-parallel models and data-parallel models present opportunities to reclaim and reassign resources during the execution of a parallel section. For example, task-parallel programming models such as Cilk or TBB have a scheduler which distributes tasks for all cores. Also, data parallel programming models such as OpenCL, a possibly large number of work units (termed *work groups* in the OpenCL model) are distributed to a pool of worker threads by the OpenCL work group scheduler. For those programming models, increasing or decreasing the number of active worker threads is easily achieved.

In this paper, we tackle the OpenMP programming model and thus focus on scheduling a fixed number of threads. Instead of adjusting the number of threads, we employ a thread-migration based approach. We allow different applications to share core resources temporarily during a migration phase until the required migrations have finished. Changing the thread count during execution is outside of the scope of this paper and part of future work.

3.3 Performance Model and Scheduling Policies

A space-shared scheduler needs to provide sufficient resources to all running applications while considering each application's characteristics and hardware features at the same time. Also, the resource manager should be able to compute a proper resource allocation according to the specific scheduling policy. In order to do so, the scheduler needs information about the applications' runtime profiles.

There are some important features that affect an application's performance scalability. Memory access patterns, inter-core communication patterns, and the (dynamic) working set input size can all affect the scalability of an application. To understand the performance characteristics of parallel applications, prior works usually employ offline training, [19], machine learning [13,15], extracted information through static program analysis [29], runtime resource reconfiguration [10,22,24], or analytical approaches such as, for example, resource contention modeling [26,27].

In this work, we implement a performance model that solely relies on online profile data. The model assumes that the memory access contention is the major limiting factor of performance scalability. Section 4.3 shows this assumption is valid to capture the trend of an application's scalability. More sophisticated shared resource contention modeling and additional performance information from applications' annotation or static analysis can potentially obtain more accurate and versatile performance models and allow implementation of more sophisticated scheduling policies. Better analysis techniques and policies are part of future work.

4   The Scheduling Framework

In this section, we discuss the details of the proposed scheduling framework that performs dynamic space-shared resource allocation as outlined in Sect. 3. The framework is implemented on Linux-based many-core platforms and performs scheduling for GNU-OpenMP applications. Other parallel programming models can be easily supported by defining and implementing the communication interface into the respective parallel programming library.

Figure 2 illustrates the system software stack of the framework. We explain each component in the subsections below.

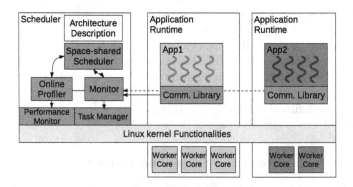

Fig. 2. The scheduling framework.

4.1   Core Mapping Scheme

In our scheduling framework, the scheduler allocates a `cluster` (a set of computing cores that share a common last-level cache (LLC)) as the default scheduling granularity. Exceptions are allowed in two cases: (1) when a serial section is scheduled or (2) when the number of running applications is bigger than the number of `clusters` in the system. This is sensible because each application can benefit from cluster-level management in terms of LLC sharing.

Furthermore, the core allocator tries to maintain shapes of minimal perimeter inside each `cluster`. This has a positive effect on inter-core communication and also reduces the number of migrations at runtime caused by resource reallocations. For some architectures, especially mesh-style NoCs, the overhead of the cache coherence protocol is high if the communication distance is long.

4.2   Communication Library

The runtime environment manager is implemented in a component called *monitor* (Fig. 2). This *monitor* module runs as a daemon and interacts with the application runtimes, the space-shared scheduler and the online profiler. The monitor periodically tries to perform system-wide scheduling if all running applications execute in a specific parallel/serial code region for a sufficiently long enough time. The wake-up frequency of the scheduler is an parameter that depends on the target architecture platform.

Our scheduler needs to keep track of the contexts of all running applications. In other words, the scheduler requires information whether a given application is currently executing in a sequential or a parallel section. Since different parallel sections exhibit different performance characteristics, it also needs to distinguish between the different parallel sections.

In our implementation, the current context of an application is stored to a global memory region that is shared with the scheduler. An OpenMP application calls `GOMP_parallel_start` and `GOMP_parallel_end` when it enters and exits a parallel region, respectively. Our framework intercepts these calls through library interpositioning. The function pointer of the parallel section provided to the `GOMP_parallel_start` upon entering a parallel code section is used to distinguish between different parallel sections.

4.3   Online Profiler

A proper performance model is required in order to compute resource allocations to the different parallel applications with respect the current scheduling policy. Our online profiler collects important performance features by monitoring the hardware's performance counters and computes a performance model for each encountered parallel code section of every application.

Our model is based on the idea that shared resource contention among threads is one of important factors that affect applications' performance scalability. Tudor *et al.* [27] introduced an analytical memory contention model for shared-memory parallel programs. In their work, the authors show that shared-memory resource contention can be modeled using an M/M/1 queue. We apply this idea to efficiently characterize the performance characteristics of the concurrently executing applications.

Memory Contention Performance Model. The performance (i.e., speedup) model is organized as follows. The specific amount of work that a parallel section of an application performs is denoted by the *work cycles* W. If a parallel section uses N cores then the work cycles are divided by N. If the threads are completely independent, i.e., in the absence of inter-core communication or access to shared resources, the application's parallel section speedup becomes N. Most applications, however, access shared resources such as memory. The shared-resource contention is denoted by $C(N)$. In our model, we currently consider only memory-level contention. We also don't take into account other features such as load-imbalance and data dependencies because experiments with OpenMP benchmarks (especially in a parallel section) exhibit a much larger sensitivity to the contention in memory accesses $C(N)$.

To estimate the speedup, we measure the per-core last-level cache miss rate of each application, denoted LLC. In addition, we compute LLC_ALL, the sum of the total LLC miss rates from all applications running in parallel. If N cores are assigned to an application, the speedup model is given as follows:

$$SpeedUp(N, LLC, LLC\_ALL) = \frac{W + C(1)}{W/N + C(N)} \qquad (1)$$

To compute the shared memory contention overhead $C(N)$, we first estimate how many memory accesses happen during the given work cycles $(W/N * LLC)$. Then we can compute the total number of cycles required to finish the given work cycles by multiplying the expected memory service time $(T(N))$ (i.e., latency cycles) as shown below:

$$C(N) = \frac{W}{N} * LLC * T(N) \qquad (2)$$

The service time is modeled by an M/M/1 queuing model. In this work, we assume that if the system contains a number of memories, the memory accesses are evenly distributed (interleaved) to each memory. We further assume that the memory service times are the same regardless of the distance between memory controllers and cores in the interleaved allocation scheme. The memory latency cycles without any contention are modeled as L and the number of memories is represented by M.

$$T(N) = \frac{1}{service\ rate - request\ rate} = 1/(\frac{1}{L} - \frac{LLC\_ALL}{M}) \qquad (3)$$

This model efficiently generates a logarithmic scalability curve by modeling the increased contention overhead. However, this model is not theoretically valid for our problem. Foremost, the model assumes an infinite number of resource competitors, but we only have a finite number of cores. This possibly incurs negative or impractically large estimated latency cycles because the simple regression ($LLC * N$ in Eq. 3) increases LLC without considering the service response (the response time reduces the LLC miss rate of a queuing competitor). In addition, in modern memory architectures, there are a number of distributed contention points. To overcome this limitation, we use a threshold for the delay. Once the estimated latency reaches the pre-determined threshold in memory-intensive applications, the estimated latency is fixed to the threshold and the scalability curve becomes linear.

Examples of the Performance Model. Figure 3 shows some examples of the model. The baseline in Fig. 3(a) is obtained by running the applications with a varying number of cores on the target machine, a 64-core AMD architecture. Each benchmark is then executed standalone on all available cores and the LLC miss-rate is obtained by monitoring the performance counters. The modeled performance scalability is depicted in Fig. 3(b). Linear performance scalability in the graph is caused by the capping the maximum service delay with a threshold as outlined above.

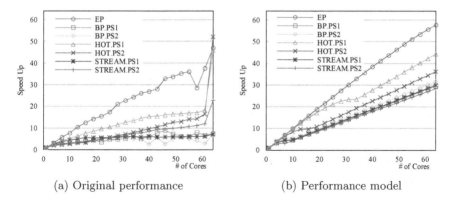

(a) Original performance   (b) Performance model

Fig. 3. Examples of the performance model. EP is taken from NPB3.3 [25], the others (BP-backpropagation, HOT-hotspot, STREAM-streamcluster) are from Rodinia [9]. We show the results of benchmarks containing one or two parallel sections (PS).

The performance model does not capture various performance features such as data dependencies, inter-core communication or synchronization patterns. However, as long as the relation between the different applications' scalabilities are predicted correctly, the absolute error of the model is not of great importance in order to compute a resource allocation.

Performance Counter Measurement. The performance indicators required by the performance model are obtained by monitoring the hardware performance counters. We measure LLC miss events and total cycles.

Our framework is tested on a 64-core AMD Opteron platform and the Tile-Gx36 platform. For the AMD platform [3], the LLC miss event counters are provided on the AMD NorthBridge and we can obtain the count using the "NBPMCx4E1 L3 Cache Misses" [12] as an event descriptor. The total number of cycles is a generalized CPU event which is already defined and measured in the Linux kernel. On the other hand, the Tile-Gx36 does not have a specific last-level cache. Instead, the architecture uses DDC (Dynamic Distributed Cache) techniques [2] in which local cache misses try to fetch their data from distributed caches. For the Tile-Gx36 NoC architecture, we consider local cache misses (from local cache to memory) and remote cache misses (from remote cache to memory) at the same time. LLC is computed as the sum of the two.

4.4   Scheduling Algorithm

The main advantage of the performance model is that we can design different scheduling algorithms to accommodate for specific scheduling policies. In this work, our scheduling policies are based on the QoS which we define as the normalized speedup compared to executing the application on fully-available hardware resources without co-located applications. QoS is computed as follows:

$$QoS = \frac{SpeedUp\ On\ Given\ Resources}{SpeedUp\ Executed\ Standalone} \tag{4}$$

To maintain a polynomial-time algorithm, the scheduler implements greedy-pareto policies (e.g., maximize QoS, balancing QoS). The algorithm first reserves at least one allocation unit to each application. Whenever the scheduler reserves a new allocation unit, it takes the best (pareto) solution according to the scheduling policy.

Algorithm 1 decides the proper amount of core resources based on the balancing QoS policy. The computational complexity is $O(N^2M)$ where N is the number of applications and M is the number of allocation units. This is an acceptable overhead because the number of executed applications is usually small. Also, we allocate `cluster` as a default allocation granularity (refer Sect. 4.1) which reduces the complexity as well.

After the core resources for all applications have been reserved, we consider core clustering among applications when more than two applications are packed into one `cluster`. For example, the Tile-Gx36 has 36 tiles in a single chip because the machine has no specific LLCs. In addition, on the tiled architecture, the clustering benefits from dynamic distributed caching technique because it can reduce the cost of maintaining cache coherence.

Another important consideration is to reduce the number of thread migrations (i.e., re-assignment to a different core) caused by the system-wide rescheduling. In this work, we have implemented a rather simplistic approach in which the scheduler always allocates the cluster/core resources to applications in the same order in order to minimize the number of migrations.

Algorithm 1. Scheduling Policy: Balancing QoS

N = # of applications in the system
M = # of computing cores in the system
CPU[N] = # of reserved cores for each application, initialized to 1
LLC[N] = per-core LLC miss rate of each application

while $sum(CPU) < M$ **do**
    best_app = −1
    min_variance = ∞
    for $i = 0$ to $N − 1$ **do**
        QoS[N] = estimated QoS for each applications
        LLC_ALL = summation of LLC miss rate from all applications
        for $j = 0$ to $N − 1$ **do**
            if $i == j$ **then**
                LLC_ALL += LLC[j]*(CPU[j]+1)
            else
                LLC_ALL += LLC[j]*CPU[j]
        for $j = 0$ to $N − 1$ **do**
            if $i == j$ **then**
                QoS[j] = $SpeedUp$(CPU[j]+1, LLC[j], LLC_ALL) / $SpeedUp$(M, LLC[j], LLC[j]*M)
            else
                QoS[j] = $SpeedUp$(CPU[j], LLC[j], LLC_ALL) / $SpeedUp$(M, LLC[j], LLC[j]*M)
        if $variance(QoS) < min\_variance$ **then**
            min_variance = $variance$(QoS)
            best_app = i
    CPU[best_app] += 1

4.5 Task Manager

Another important consideration is the application of internal task scheduling in the application-specific runtime. To assign an application's tasks to specific cores, the framework comprises a special kernel module. As our main concern is not application-specific resource management but space-shared mapping, we utilize the Linux kernel's processor affinity mask to define the set of cores that can be utilized by the threads of an application. The standard Linux scheduler is responsible for thread allocation to the assigned cores and load-balancing. In this way, we can focus on coarse-grained resource allocation techniques and leave the application-specific fine-grained thread-to-core assignment to the Linux kernel.

5 Evaluation

5.1 Target Architectures

The scheduling framework has been evaluated on a 64-core AMD Opteron 6380 server platform [3] and the Tile-Gx36 platform [1]. The AMD Opteron server represents a multi-socket multi-core NUMA system, and the Tile-Gx36 platform is a representative of a mesh-style many-core processor. The main features for performance evaluation of the two architectures are shown in Table 1.

5.2 Target Applications

For the evaluation, we selected several OpenMP applications which have specific characteristics from known benchmark suites. The three OpenMP applications

Table 1. Target Architecture.

Architecture	AMD64	Tile-Gx36
Processor	Opteron6380	Tile-Gx8036
Clock frequency	2.5 GHz	1.2 GHz
Memory size	128 GB	32 GB
Total cores	64	36
# of cores per processor	8	36
# of NUMA nodes	8	2
Linux kernel	3.13	2.6.40
Scheduling frequency	33 Hz	13 Hz
Scheduling steady state	2 periods	2 periods

(EP, CG, MG) from SNU-NPB3.3 [25], Freqmine from Parsec 3.0 [6] and Stream-cluster from the Rodiana [9] benchmark suite all exhibit different characteristics: EP is CPU intensive, CG issues irregular memory accesses, MG is a memory-intensive benchmark, Freqmine is CPU-intensive with a long sequential part, and Streamcluster is also a memory-intensive benchmark. Execution information about each benchmark is shown in Table 2. The standalone execution and speedup values in the table are obtained by executing the benchmarks standalone on the AMD Opteron platform. For Tile-Gx36, we use the same benchmarks but adjust the working set sizes because the Tile-Gx8036 processor has less processing power than the AMD Opteron6380 processor.

Table 2. Target application (A-AMD64, T-Tile-Gx36).

Application	Description	Serial time	Standalone execution (Speed Up)
EP	Embarrassingly parallel	-	A-21.4s(47.1) T-43.6(34.1)
CG	Conjugate gradient	-	A-11.6s(9.3) T-40.1(34.2)
MG	Multi-grid	-	A-17.2s(10.7) T-32.2(23.9)
F.M (Freqmine)	FP-growth method	A-5.8s T-7.1s	A-25.5s(17.8) T-34.0(4.4)
S.C (Streamcluster)	clustering	-	A-15.8s(7.7) T-34.7(15.2)

One benchmark scenario comprises several parallel application benchmarks executed simultaneously. The 10 benchmark scenarios are composed of different application benchmarks representing different workload patterns in order to show the broad applicability of the proposed method.

There are some considerations of the applications' executions with respect to evaluation of performance. First of all, the working set size (execution time) is an important factor for performance evaluation. For example, if the working set sizes are too different between applications, then the normalized performance may vary too much. Therefore, we manually adjust the working set sizes for the target applications to have a similar turnaround time when they are executed standalone on the target architecture. We further use the system's memory interleaving option (using *numactl* tool to manage NUMA settings) such that memory allocations are evenly distributed across the available memory controllers.

To evaluate the scheduling performance for simultaneous applications, we measure the performance for each application and compute the summation of the performance metrics (QoS, speedup, and turnaround time) from simultaneous applications. We also compute the standard deviation for each performance metric to quantify how balanced the applications' performances are.

5.3 Scheduling Policies

To evaluate the space-shared scheduling policies, we compare the scheduling performance with not only the time-shared scheduler but also other simple space-shared scheduling policies. In these experiments, the different schedulers/scheduling policies are as follows.

- CFS - the Linux standard time-shared scheduler.
- Static Equal Partition - static equal core partitioning for each application. In this scheme, system resource re-allocation is not performed (not even when an application finishes execution).
- Dynamic Equal Partition - dynamic equal core partitioning: perform dynamic scheduling whenever an application starts or finishes execution.
- Dynamic Equal QoS - our space-shared scheduling scheme where we perform fine-grained resource management and strive to balance the QoS among applications whenever a core resource is reserved.
- Dynamic Max QoS - our space-shared scheduling scheme. The scheduling policy is set to maximize the sum of the QoS of all applications.

5.4 Scheduling Scenario

We execute every combination of three applications from the five target applications as shown in Table 2 for each scheduling policy. Thus, the overall scheduling runs comprise ten sets of applications. We provide the benchmark results of the scheduling set for five different policies both on AMD64 and the Tile-Gx36 platform. In each scenario, each application creates as many threads as physical cores are available in the system, and the thread count is not changed during an application's lifetime.

64-Core AMD Opteron Platform. Figure 4 shows the performance of the framework on the 64-core AMD Opteron platform. The first graph in the figure represents the summation of QoS among applications. The second graph shows its speedup, and the last graph shows the turnaround time among applications.

An important consideration is the variance of the three target applications' performances. We show the standard deviation of the performance of three simultaneous applications on the top of each bar. Longer lines indicate a bigger standard deviation; a good scheduler should provide low standard deviations.

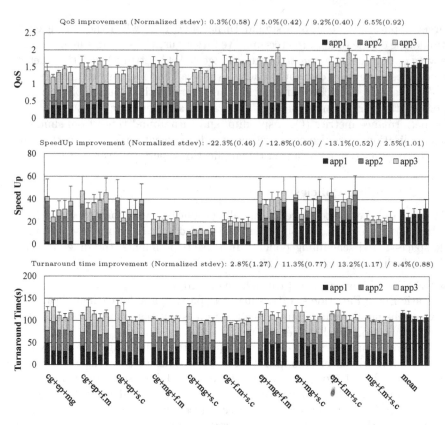

Fig. 4. Benchmark result: 64 core AMD Opteron platform. The five bars for each scheduling scenario represent the results in the order CFS, Static Equal Partition, Dynamic Equal Partition, Equal QoS, and Max QoS. The four values on the top of each graph compare the performance (and standard deviation) of each scheduling policy to CFS in terms of the performance metric from left (Static Equal Partition) to right (Max QoS).

For the QoS analysis, higher is better. QoS is an important metric, because if a scheduler only considers maximum speedup then the scheduler may allocate a large number of cores to the application which has the best scalability while starving the others. In such a scenario, only one application would achieve a good scalability and a high QoS. To increase the overall QoS among applications, the scheduler eventually needs to be aware of the application's scalability in advance.

For example, consider the first scenario (app1: CG, app2: EP, app3: MG): In the QoS graph, CFS provides a good QoS for EP, the most CPU-intensive application in our target application set. However, the other applications starve and fail to get a good QoS. This effect is also visible in the second (SpeedUp) graph. Here, EP achieves the biggest speedup, whereas MG and CG do not achieve satisfactory performance. On the other hand, the Equal QoS policy or the Equal Partition policy provide more CPU time (physical cores) for CG and MG,

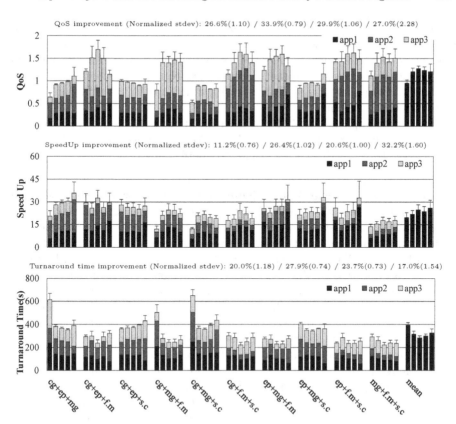

Fig. 5. Benchmark result: 36 core Tile-Gx36 platform. The layout of the benchmark results is equal to that in Fig. 4.

and as a consequence, the speedup of the two applications CG and MG increases. Since CG and MG are less scalable than EP, the overall speedup of the Equal-QoS policy is smaller than that of CFS. However, the overall QoS is increased and the QoS becomes more balanced. We observe that the Equal-Partition and the Equal-QoS policies manage to reduce the variance (i.e., standard deviation) of the results.

The static policy provides a static allocation of cores to each application for its entire lifetime and thus achieves a good resource isolation. As a consequence, cores that become available when one of the application finishes early cannot be reallocated to the running ones, which in turn causes a reduced overall performance. The last scheduling policy, Max-QoS shows similar characteristics as the Linux scheduler. The reason is that the Max-QoS policy determines that EP achieves the best increase in QoS.

Across the scheduling scenarios, there is no scheduling policy that always achieves the best performance; each scheduling policy shows a slightly different behavior. However, in the general case, the space-shared scheduling schemes outperform the Linux scheduler in terms of our performance metrics. The last five bars in each graph show the average (geometric mean for QoS and speedup, arithmetic mean for turnaround time) of the summation of three application performances. We have found that in general the equal QoS policy is well suited to meet the requirements of QoS among parallel applications on our 64-core AMD Opteron machine.

The third graph in Fig. 4 shows the sum of the turnaround times of each application, i.e., lower is better. We observe that all space-shared policies outperform the CFS scheduler with Equal QoS performing best.

36-Core Tile-Gx36 Platform. Figure 5 shows the performance of scheduling policies on the Tile-Gx36 platform for the same experimental scenarios.

Overall, all space-shared policies outperform the standard Linux scheduler with the dynamic Equal partition policy performing best. This is in contrast to the AMD64 NUMA platform where our scheduling policies performed better.

The reason is twofold: first, the lower computational power of the Tile-Gx36 platform causes less contention, and the speedups of the different applications become similar. Second, while the overhead caused by the periodic re-allocation of the resources is not an issue on the AMD machine, the effect is noticeable on the slower Tile-Gx36 chip. Dynamic equal partition policy requires re-computations only when an application starts or finishes.

An interesting observation is that Tile-Gx36 benefits by a significantly larger performance improvement from space-partitioning compared to the results from AMD64. The reason is that each core in the AMD system is a highly-efficient super-scalar processor on which multiple threads from multiple applications can be efficiently scheduled by using advanced hardware technologies. However, the trend of many-core architectures suggests that future many-core chips will comprise simpler but many more cores in a single chip. Therefore, we believe that space sharing will be an indispensable scheduling component for future many-core resource management.

6   Discussion

Although the evaluations show that our scheduling policies can outperform Linux's time-shared scheduling in terms of QoS, speedup, and turnaround time for simultaneous parallel applications, there are still lots of issues to be solved and room for improvement. Here we discuss our research direction for improved space-shared scheduling based on the experience of this work.

First, for scheduling OpenMP applications, our evaluation is fixed to the default setting where every (OpenMP) parallel application is executed with the same default number of threads (i.e., $\#threads = \#cores$). However, Linux and OpenMP runtime systems may apply different resource management schemes in dependence of the number of an application's internal tasks. We also need to consider other situations where application thread counts are not equal to the number of physical cores in the system (e.g., when an application requests a bigger number of threads than physically available cores, or vice-versa).

Second, although a space-shared scheduler requires sophisticated performance models to characterize various performance features with high accuracy, the performance model used in this paper is not accurate and captures only the scalability trend. In addition, we used multi-socket multi-core NUMA systems for the evaluation but did not consider NUMA-related performance issues in this work. The advanced performance modeling and understanding how application's performance is varied according to the active NUMA policy are our future work.

Third, an important issue of space-shared resource allocation is how to manage the degree of parallelism (thread counts). Especially for data-parallel programming models (OpenCL, Hadoop) or task-parallel runtimes (Intel TBB, Cilk) we can reclaim and reassign resources in a more flexible way. We expect that by avoiding thread overcommitment, we can achieve additional performance improvements. The mechanism for efficiently changing the parallelism from an application runtime is our research consideration. We also further consider to dynamically manage the parallelism even for the thread-based OpenMP programming model by exploiting runtime and compiler support.

Lastly, our scheduling framework aims at providing (fine-grained) resource allocation while considering a dynamically changing workload. However, known parallel application benchmarks are usually based on a monotonous workload, i.e., their behavior does not change enough for the benefits from a fine-grained resource management scheme to become apparent. We consider to use various real-world applications composed of several phases exhibiting different performance characteristics.

7 Conclusion

In this paper, we introduce an adaptive space-shared scheduling strategy for shared-memory parallel applications to efficiently handle dynamically changing workload characteristics. We have implemented a space-shared scheduling framework with several scheduling policies such as achieving balanced or maximal performance when simultaneously executing several OpenMP applications. Based on a simple performance model that uses the last-level cache miss rates as its main metric, our scheduler dynamically recomputes core resource allocations.

The analysis of the results on our implementations for two different many-core platforms, a 64-core AMD architecture and the Tile-Gx36, shows that, in general, space-shared scheduling schemes provide better QoS compared to the standard Linux time-shared scheduler. As a the main contribution of this work, we show that the space-shared scheduling approach has a lot of potential on current and future many-core systems.

The experiences gained from this work provide important guidelines towards better space-sharing. As part of our future work we plan to investigate other space-shared scheduling policies and to improving the performance model in order to capture various application and architecture characteristics better. Also, in this work, we have only focused on coarse-grained scheduling issues and left the fine-grained task-to-core mapping to the Linux scheduler. To increase the performance further, dynamically managing the active thread counts (i.e., control the amount of parallelism) of applications is a logical next step of this research.

Acknowledgments. This work was supported, in part, by BK21 Plus for Pioneers in Innovative Computing (Dept. of Computer Science and Engineering, SNU) funded by the National Research Foundation (NRF) of Korea (Grant 21A20151113068), the Basic Science Research Program through NRF funded by the Ministry of Science, ICT & Future Planning (Grant NRF-2015K1A3A1A14021288), and by the Promising-Pioneering Researcher Program through Seoul National University in 2015. ICT at Seoul National University provided research facilities for this study.

References

1. Tile-Gx36 Processor. http://www.mellanox.com/related-docs/prod_multi_core/PB_TILE-Gx36.pdf. Accessed 28 Feb 2016
2. UG130: Architecture manual. Tilera Corp
3. AMD. AMD Opteron 6300 Series Processors. http://www.amd.com/en-us/products/server/opteron/6000/6300. Accessed 28 Feb 2016
4. Asanovic, K., Bodik, R., Catanzaro, B.C., Gebis, J.J., Husbands, P., Keutzer, K., Patterson, D.A., Plishker, W.L., Shalf, J., Williams, S.W., Yelick, K.A.; The landscape of parallel computing research: a view from berkeley. Technical Report UCB/EECS-2006-183, EECS Department, University of California, Berkeley, December 2006
5. Baumann, A., Barham, P., Dagand, P.-E., Harris, T., Isaacs, R., Peter, S., Roscoe, T., Schüpbach, A., Singhania, A.: The multikernel: a new os architecture for scalable multicore systems. In: Proceedings of the ACM SIGOPS 22Nd Symposium on Operating Systems Principles, SOSP 2009, pp. 29–44. ACM, New York (2009)
6. Bienia, C., Kumar, S., Singh, J.P., Li, K.: The parsec benchmark suite: characterization and architectural implications. In: Proceedings of the 17th International Conference on Parallel Architectures and Compilation Techniques, pp. 72–81. ACM (2008)
7. Blumofe, R.D., Joerg, C.F., Kuszmaul, B.C., Leiserson, C.E., Randall, K.H., Zhou, Y.: Cilk: an efficient multithreaded runtime system. J. Parallel Distrib. Comput. **37**(1), 55–69 (1996)
8. Breitbart, J., Weidendorfer, J., Trinitis, C.: Automatic co-scheduling based on main memory bandwidth usage. In: Proceedings of the 20th Workshop on Job Scheduling Strategies for Parallel Processing (JSSPP), JSSPP 2016, May 2016
9. Che, S., Boyer, M., Meng, J., Tarjan, D., Sheaffer, J.W., Lee, S.-H., Skadron, K.: Rodinia: a benchmark suite for heterogeneous computing. In: IEEE International Symposium on Workload Characterization. IISWC 2009, pp. 44–54. IEEE (2009)
10. Creech, T., Kotha, A., Barua, R.: Efficient multiprogramming for multicores with scaf. In: Proceedings of the 46th Annual IEEE/ACM International Symposium on Microarchitecture, pp. 334–345. ACM (2013)
11. Dagum, L., Enon, R.: Openmp: an industry standard API for shared-memory programming. IEEE Comput. Sci. Eng. **5**(1), 46–55 (1998)
12. Advanced Micro Devices. BIOS and kernel developer's guide (BKDG) for AMD family 15h models 00h–0fh processors (2012)

13. Emani, M.K., Wang, Z., O'Boyle, M.F.P.: Smart, adaptive mapping of parallelism in the presence of external workload. In: 2013 IEEE/ACM International Symposium on Code Generation and Optimization (CGO), pp. 1–10. IEEE (2013)

14. Feitelson, D.G., Rudolph, L., Schwiegelshohn, U.: Parallel job scheduling—a status report. In: Feitelson, D.G., Rudolph, L., Schwiegelshohn, U. (eds.) JSSPP 2004. LNCS, vol. 3277, pp. 1–16. Springer, Heidelberg (2005). doi:10.1007/11407522_1

15. Grewe, D., Wang, Z., O'Boyle, M.F.P.: A workload-aware mapping approach for data-parallel programs. In: Proceedings of the 6th International Conference on High Performance and Embedded Architectures and Compilers, pp. 117–126. ACM (2011)

16. Khronos Group: The open standard for parallel programming of heterogeneous systems. https://www.khronos.org/opencl/. Accessed 28 Feb 2016

17. Lifka, D.A.: The ANL/IBM SP scheduling system. In: Feitelson, D.G., Rudolph, L. (eds.) JSSPP 1995. LNCS, vol. 949, pp. 295–303. Springer, Heidelberg (1995). doi:10.1007/3-540-60153-8_35

18. Liu, R., Klues, K., Bird, S., Hofmeyr, S., Asanović, K., Kubiatowicz, J.: Tessellation: space-time partitioning in a manycore client OS. In: Proceedings of the First USENIX Conference on Hot Topics in Parallelism, HotPar 2009, p. 10. USENIX Association, Berkeley (2009)

19. Moore, R.W., Childers, B.R.: Using utility prediction models to dynamically choose program thread counts. In: ISPASS, pp. 135–144 (2012)

20. Mu'alem, A.W., Feitelson, D.G.: Utilization, predictability, workloads, and user runtime estimates in scheduling the IBM SP2 with backfilling. IEEE Trans. Parallel Distrib. Syst. 12(6), 529–543 (2001)

21. Pabla, C.S.: Completely fair scheduler. Linux J. 2009(184), 4 (2009)

22. Raman, A., Zaks, A., Lee, J.W., August, D.I.: Parcae: a system for flexible parallel execution. SIGPLAN Not. 47(6), 133–144 (2012)

23. Reinders, J.: Intel Threading Building Blocks: Outfitting C++ for Multi-core Processor Parallelism. O'Reilly Media, Inc (2007)

24. Sasaki, H., Tanimoto, T., Inoue, K., Nakamura, H.: Scalability-based manycore partitioning. In: Proceedings of the 21st International Conference on Parallel architectures and Compilation Techniques, pp. 107–116. ACM (2012)

25. Seo, S., Kim, J., Jo, G., Lee, J., Nah, J., Lee, J.: SNU NPB Suite (2011). http://aces.snu.ac.kr/software/snu-npb/. Accessed 28 Feb 2016

26. Tudor, B.M., Teo, Y.M.: A practical approach for performance analysis of shared-memory programs. In: 2011 IEEE International Parallel & Distributed Processing Symposium (IPDPS), pp. 652–663. IEEE (2011)

27. Tudor, B.M., Teo, Y.M., See, S.: Understanding off-chip memory contention of parallel programs in multicore systems. In: 2011 International Conference on Parallel Processing (ICPP), pp. 602–611. IEEE (2011)

28. Vajda, A.: Programming Many-Core Chips, 1st edn. Springer Publishing Company, Incorporated, New York (2011)

29. Wen, Y., Wang, Z., O'Boyle, M.: Smart multi-task scheduling for OpenCL programs on CPU/GPU heterogeneous platforms. In: High Performance Computing (HiPC) (2014)

30. Wentzlaff, D., Gruenwald III, C., Beckmann, N., Modzelewski, K., Belay, A., Youseff, L., Miller, J., Agarwal, A.: An operating system for multicore and clouds: mechanisms and implementation. In: Proceedings of the 1st ACM Symposium on Cloud Computing, pp. 3–14. ACM (2010)

Batsim: A Realistic Language-Independent Resources and Jobs Management Systems Simulator

Pierre-François Dutot[1,2], Michael Mercier[1,2,3], Millian Poquet[1,2(✉)], and Olivier Richard[1,2]

[1] Univ. Grenoble Alpes, LIG, 38000 Grenoble, France
[2] Inria, CNRS, LIG, 38000 Grenoble, France
{pierre-francois.dutot,michael.mercier,millian.poquet,
olivier.richard}@inria.fr
[3] Atos, Bezons, France

Abstract. As large scale computation systems are growing to exascale, Resources and Jobs Management Systems (RJMS) need to evolve to manage this scale modification. However, their study is problematic since they are critical production systems, where experimenting is extremely costly due to downtime and energy costs. Meanwhile, many scheduling algorithms emerging from theoretical studies have not been transferred to production tools for lack of realistic experimental validation. To tackle these problems we propose Batsim, an extendable, language-independent and scalable RJMS simulator. It allows researchers and engineers to test and compare any scheduling algorithm, using a simple event-based communication interface, which allows different levels of realism. In this paper we show that Batsim's behaviour matches the one of the real RJMS OAR. Our evaluation process was made with reproducibility in mind and all the experiment material is freely available.

Keywords: RJMS · Scheduling · Simulation · Reproducibility

1 Introduction

Resources and Jobs Management Systems (RJMSs) play a critical role in modern high performance computing (HPC) infrastructures, simultaneously maximizing the efficiency of the platform and fairly sharing its capacities among all their users. Thus, the job scheduling algorithms that are used need to be effective in multiple domains. On the way to exascale computing, large scale systems become harder to study, to develop or to calibrate because of the costs in both time and energy of such processes. It is often impossible to convince managers to use a production cluster for several hours simply to test modifications in the RJMS. Moreover, as the existing RJMS production systems need to be highly reliable, each evolution requires several real scale test iterations. The consequence is that

© Springer International Publishing AG 2017
N. Desai and W. Cirne (Eds.): JSSPP 2015/2016, LNCS 10353, pp. 178–197, 2017.
DOI: 10.1007/978-3-319-61756-5_10

scheduling algorithms used in production systems are mostly outdated and not customized correctly.

The most efficient way to tackle these problems is coarse-grained simulation. Simulation of these large scale systems is faster by multiple orders of magnitude than real experiments. The savings in computing time and energy consumption allow a much larger variety of scenarios to be tested. This unlocks new research avenues to explore, and possibly leads to scientific discoveries and industrial innovations.

Furthermore, recent algorithms developed in scheduling theory are impossible to compare in realistic conditions, because of the lack of simple and extensible simulators. There is a vast literature on possible theoretical improvements, proved in different theoretical job and platform models which are generally not yet transferred to production schedulers in real environments.

The research field around RJMS and scheduling in large scale systems in general would greatly benefit from a simple – yet realistic – validated scheduling simulator that is modular enough to be used with any theoretical or production algorithm implementation in order to truly compare all of them in a scientific way. Currently existing RJMS simulators are based on too simple models. Most of them only rely on delays for job modeling or on network models that are either minimalistic or not scalable enough to test really large scale systems.

From this assessment, we propose Batsim (for BATch scheduler SIMulator). It is based on SimGrid [7], a state-of-the-art distributed platform simulator with realistic network and computation models. Batsim allows different levels of realism depending on the user's needs, uses a simple message interface to achieve language independence, uses an easily expandable workload input format and provides readable and analysable outputs with jobs and scheduling details. For comprehension's sake, a simple Gantt chart visualisation tool is provided separately.

Batsim was also created to achieve experiment reproducibility. We are well aware that hardware suffers from a great variability. This is the main barrier to achieve experiment reproducibility in computer science. But in the case of simulation, those constraints do not exist anymore because the result of the simulation can be deterministic with respect to the simulation's inputs (parameters and input data). That is why simulation experiments are much easier to reproduce if the simulation environment and inputs are provided by the authors, which is rarely the case [29]. There can be several reasons for this, as explained in [31]:

- Restrictive licence or any intellectual property problem
- Complexity of the usually homemade simulation tool
- Missing experimental plan: used parameters are not provided
- Input data and/or results are not provided
- No access to the experimental environment (like the testbed or computer Grid)

Despite the intellectual property problem, which by definition prevents the reproducibility, all the aforementioned problems could be addressed by some good practice and appropriate tools:

1. Use reusable and proven simulators
2. Provide environments
3. Provide experiment plan, design and workflow
4. Provide inputs and results

Batsim was made to implement the first of these solutions. In fact, most published articles use ad hoc simulators which are not expected to be used after the articles' publications. Furthermore, simulators kept on-the-shelf are not proven to be accurate. In order to validate simulation results, the simulator must be assessed theoretically, and also experimentally if possible. Batsim aims at improving repeatability in this domain which is widely affected by the problems mentioned above.

The rest of this paper is organised as follows. Section 2 presents related work in the field of RJMS simulation. Section 3 gives an overview of how Batsim works. Section 4 develops the underlying models of Batsim. Section 5 gives more detailed explanations on Batsim's mechanics. Batsim's evaluation process is presented in Sect. 6, and its results in Sect. 7. Section 8 gives technical details on how to repeat our evaluation process. Section 9 concludes the paper and outlines our future work.

2   Related Work

Many simulators can be found in the literature which can be used to simulate a RJMS. Unfortunately, most implementations are either not available online or depend on outdated softwares and libraries which are themselves not available anymore. Thus, we chose to focus on simulators whose source code could be found.

To the best of our knowledge, most scheduling simulators are either very specific to one domain (e.g. Realtss) or do not primarily focus on realism of results, since comparisons to real existing systems are hardly ever done. This can be easily explained by the financial and ecological cost of such evaluations.

The approach which is closest to ours may be Alea [21]. This simulator is based on the GridSim simulation toolkit and allows to compare different scheduling algorithms. We chose the same approach of building our scheduling simulator on top of a simulation framework. However, Batsim's approach and Alea's differ in their modularity since Batsim allows to connect any scheduling algorithm, written in any programming language, whereas the supplied Alea API only allows new schedulers to be written in Java inside the project source code, with a queue-oriented API. Moreover, at the best of our knowledge, this simulator has not been validated in a real environment yet.

Another interesting approach can be found in article [26]. This approach consists in using the INSEE [27] fine-grained network simulator offline, in order to obtain the execution time of any configuration the job can run in. Article [26] proposes job placement policies that guarantee that no network interference can occur between the jobs, allowing to use offline execution times while simulating an online workload. However, this approach cannot be used accurately when jobs can interfere with each other.

A previous initiative of building a scheduling simulator on top of SimGrid has been done in Simbatch [5]. However, as far as we know, the project has been left unmaintained since 2007 and cannot be used easily with current SimGrid versions. Moreover, Simbatch has not been developed in the perspective of connecting real RJMSs into it, nor to allow separation of concerns regarding system simulation and scheduling algorithms.

3   Batsim General Description

Batsim is an open source platform simulator that allows to simulate the behaviour of a computational platform on which a workload is executed according to the rules of a scheduling algorithm. In order to obtain sound simulation results and to broaden the scope of the experiments that can be done thanks to Batsim, we did not choose to build it from scratch but on top of the SimGrid simulation framework instead.

Batsim allows separation of concerns since it decouples the platform simulation and the decisions in two clearly separated components, represented in Fig. 1. The Batsim component is in charge of simulating the computational resources behaviour whereas the Decision component is in charge of taking scheduling or energy-related decisions. The scheduling decisions include executing a job or rejecting it. The energy-related decisions include changing the power state of a machine – i.e. to change its DVFS mode – or switching a machine ON or OFF.

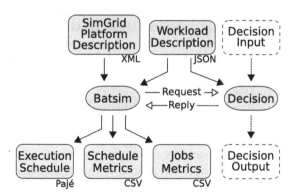

Fig. 1. The two *real* processes involved in a Batsim simulation, their network communication pattern and their inputs and outputs.

The components are instantiated as processes (within the meaning of Operating System processes) and communicate via a Unix Domain Socket.

The communication protocol used is a simple synchronous one which follows the request-reply pattern. The simulation runs in the Batsim component and as soon as an event occurs, Batsim stops the simulation and reports what happened to the Decision component. Batsim then waits for the Decision component's reply, then continues the simulation by applying the Decision component's choices. Protocol details can be found in [34].

Splitting the simulation workflow into two separated components in this way allows the Decision component to be implemented in any programming language which can communicate through a Unix Domain Socket. Thus, existing event-based scheduling algorithm implementations would not be hard to adapt in order to connect them with the Batsim component.

4   Models

This section describes the simulation models used by Batsim by giving a simplified overview of SimGrid in Sect. 4.1 then by detailing the models specific to Batsim in Sect. 4.2.

4.1   SimGrid Models

Since Batsim uses SimGrid internally, a brief – and simplified – overview of the SimGrid models that were used is given for sake of clarity. A **host** is a resource that can compute floating-point operations (flop). Hosts are connected via a network whose **links** have a latency (in seconds) and a bandwidth (in bytes per second). Links are hyperedges which can either represent a network link (a connection between two nodes) or a network node (a switch or a router). Hosts and links compose a platform that can be of virtually any topology.

Several SimGrid **processes** can be run on any SimGrid host. A SimGrid process can only be on one host at a time. These SimGrid processes – which will simply be called processes from now on – are user-given source code executed within the simulation. These processes can execute **tasks** and communicate with each other with **messages**. For simplicity's sake, we will assume that such messages are sent to processes.

Hence, a SimGrid-based simulator is composed by a set of processes which compute user-given functions. The user-given functions are executed within the simulator whereas the execution of tasks and the communications are simulated. Please note that user-given functions can spawn processes on which user-given functions are executed. SimGrid orchestrates, at any time, which processes are executed and which ones are not. SimGrid may change the running processes whenever they enter a state that implies a simulation time increase. For example, computing a task, sending a message or entering a sleep state implies a simulation time increase.

SimGrid allows us to create parallel tasks which combine computations and communications. To do so, we can build tasks with a computation vector (or row matrix) c where each c_k represents the amount of computation (in number of floating-point operations) that must be computed on the kth host on which the parallel task is run and a square communication matrix C in which each element $C[r, c]$ represents the amount of communication (in number of bytes) from the rth to the cth hosts involved in computing the task.

The SimGrid energy consumption model only takes computation hosts into account at the moment and is described in the following paragraph. Each host h has a set of power states P_h where each power state $p \in P_h$ has a computational power cp_p (in number of floating-point operations per second), a minimum electrical power consumption $ep_p^\wedge$ (in W) and a maximum electrical power consumption $ep_p^\vee$ (also in W). The SimGrid model which simulates the execution of activities on simulated resources computes the computational load $l_h(t)$ of each host h at any simulation time t. The load is a real number in $[0, 1]$ where 0 represents an idle host and 1 a host computing at maximum computational power. Let $p_h(t)$ be the power state in which host t is at simulation time t. The instant electrical consumption of host h at time t is noted $P_h(t)$ and is determined by $p_h(t)$ and $l_h(t)$. $P_h(t)$ is computed as the linear interpolation between $ep_{p_h(t)}^\wedge$ and $ep_{p_h(t)}^\vee$ in function of $l_h(t)$: $P_h(t) = ep_{p_h(t)}^\wedge + (ep_{p_h(t)}^\vee - ep_{p_h(t)}^\wedge) \cdot l_h(t)$ and is expressed in watts. The energy consumption of host h is then given by $E_h = \int P_h(t)dt$ and is expressed in joules.

4.2   Batsim Models

The computation platforms used by Batsim are theoretically as broad in scope as SimGrid ones and can be of virtually any topology. However, only a subset of SimGrid platforms are valid Batsim platforms. Indeed, we chose to use a dedicated SimGrid host – that may be also be referred to as *computational resource* from now on – referred as the *Master host* to compute the resource management processes. In order to be able to run a job on computational resources, the platform must allow messages to be exchanged between the Master host and the other computational resources. Moreover, if jobs are parallel and must be run on different computational resources, the platform must allow the set of computational resources allocated to the job to communicate with each other.

Moreover, we enhanced the SimGrid energy model by adding explicit sleep and transition power states. We chose to split the set P_h of power states of the host h into three disjoint sets: P_h^c is the set of **computation** power states, P_h^s is the set of **sleep** power states and P_h^t is the set of **transition** power states. The computation power states are the only ones which can be used to compute jobs. A sleep power state represents the state of one machine which cannot instantaneously compute something *e.g.* ACPI S1, S3, S4 or S5 states. A Batsim host can switch from one computation power state to another instantaneously. However, entering into one sleep power state s or leaving it can take some time and cost some energy. Transition power states are *virtual* power states which are only used to simulate the transition into and from sleep power states. To do so, the amount of computation done in one transition is fixed to 1 flop. If one transition t should take time t_t (in seconds) and consume e_t energy (in joules), the corresponding virtual power state p_t should have a computational power

$cp_{p_t} = \frac{1}{t_t}$ and electrical power consumption bounds $ep_{p_t}^{\wedge} = ep_{p_t}^{\vee} = \frac{e_t}{t_t}$. If Batsim is run with energy enabled, the platform used must fulfill all SimGrid energy requirements and define, for each host h each sleep power state $s_h \in P_h^s$, the transition power state $v_{s_h}^{\downarrow}$ used to switch into s_h and the transition power state $v_{s_h}^{\uparrow}$ used to leave s_h.

Batsim workloads are divided into two parts: one set J of jobs and one set P of profiles. Each job $j \in J$ must have a unique job number id_j, a submission time sub_j (the time at which the job is submitted into the system), a walltime $wall_j$ (the user-specified execution time bound such that j is killed if its execution time exceeds $wall_j$), the number of requested resources res_j (rigid at the moment but moldable jobs can trivially be added into our architecture if needed) and the **profile** $prof_j$ the job executes. One profile describes how a job is computed. The profile information has been separated from the jobs because 1. it avoids data duplication when many jobs are computed in the same way 2. it makes workload generation easier and more modular.

At the moment several atomic profile types are available: **Delay** profiles are fixed amounts of time, **msg** profiles compute a vector c and a communication matrix C and **smpi** profiles simulate the execution of one SimGrid MPI time-independent trace within Batsim. Moreover, non-atomic profile types exist such as the **msg_homogeneous** profile type that wraps the msg profile type and simplifies its usage by forcing homogeneity to the underlying computation vector and communication matrix. As another non-atomic profile type, we can think of the **sequence** profile type, which is composed of a list of other profiles it must execute in sequence a certain number of times. The sequence profile type can be used to model Bulk Synchronous Parallel jobs for example. Our architecture allows to implement new profile types quite easily and the JSON format used in workload description allows modularity since any user can add any field to jobs or profiles to match their needs. For example, we used the same workloads to compare Batsim's behaviour to a real platform's by simply specifying how each profile should be run on the real platform.

5   Batsim Inner Mechanics

Batsim is a C++ program developed using the SimGrid C library. SimGrid allows us to simulate the behaviour of a computation platform on which concurrent SimGrid processes are run. We will use the phrase "real process" to talk about a process which is directly run by the user on a given Operating System. For example, the Batsim real process and the Decision real process. A SimGrid process (which will simply be referred to as a *process* from now on) is a process simulated within Batsim. The main Batsim processes and their interactions are shown in Fig. 2.

The **Jobs Submitter** process is in charge of reading one workload and submitting the jobs at the right simulation time. To do so, it simply iterates over the jobs in ascending submission time order and sends a message to the Server process as soon as a job has been submitted. If the next job submission time is

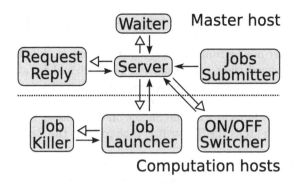

Fig. 2. The different processes within Batsim. The Job Launcher, Job Killer, and ON/OFF Switcher processes are executed on the computational resources whereas the other processes are run on a dedicated resource called the Master host. Filled arrows represent message transmissions and hollow arrows stand for a process execution.

strictly after the current simulation time, this process enters a sleep phase until the aforementioned job is submitted. Once all the jobs of its appointed workload have been submitted, the Jobs Submitter process tells the Server it has finished then ends. Several Jobs Submitters may be instantiated in the same simulation, which can be useful to simulate internally (within Batsim) the behaviour of concurrent users. These processes are executed on the Master host.

The **Request Reply** process's role is to manage the Unix Domain Socket to communicate with the Decision real process. Its lifespan is short: It is launched by the Server process on the Master host, it sends a network message to the Decision real process, then waits for its reply. It then parses the received message according to the Batsim protocol. The received message is composed of a sequence of events. In order to simulate the impact of real decision algorithms, which may take some decisions before returning the control flow, a simulation time is associated to each event (potentially the same for all events). The Request Reply process parses and transmits those events to the Server process one by one in the given chronological order. Just as the Jobs Submitter process, the Request Reply process enters a sleep phase between events to respect the received simulation times at which the events should have occured. Once all events have been sent to the Server, the process tells the Server the message has been managed, then ends.

The **Server** is the main Batsim process. It orchestrates the simulation: It knows when jobs are submitted, chooses when the Decision real process should be requested – ensuring that only one Request Reply process can be executed at the same time – and follows the orders dictated by the Decision real process (received from the Request Reply process). Depending on the received order, the Server process might launch a Job Launcher process to run a job, or launch a ON/OFF Switcher process to either boot or shutdown a computational resource, or launch a Waiter process if the Decision real process wants to be awaken at a specific time. The Server process ends its execution if and only if the following conditions are met. 1. All Jobs Submitters must have finished their executions. 2. All submitted jobs must have been either processed or rejected. 3. The Request-Reply process must not be running at the current time. 4. All ON/OFF Switchers must have finished their executions. 5. There should be at least one Jobs Submitter connected – to ensure that the simulation starts.

The **Waiter** process is used to wake the Decision real process at a specific time. To do so, it is launched by the Server on the Master host, sleeps for the right amount of time, tells the Server it is time to wake the Decision real process then ends.

The **ON/OFF Switcher** process is in charge of simulating what happens when a computational resource is booted or shut down. It is executed on the computational resource whose state is requested to change.

The **Job Launcher** process is in charge of executing a job on a set of computational resources R. The process is executed on one computational resource $r \in R$. Jobs are then computed according to their profiles. If the profile type is Delay, the process is simply put into a sleep state for the right amount of time. If the profile type is MSG, the computation vector and the communication matrix are generated into memory then computed on the given set of computational resources R. If the profile type is Sequence, the different subjobs are computed sequentially according to previously given rules for the requested number of times. Finally, if the profile type is SMPI, the given MPI trace is replayed on R. To respect the walltime of non-SMPI jobs, the Job Launcher process executes the **Job Killer** process. The Job Killer process is in charge of waiting for the walltime amount of time. For each walltime-constrained job j there is a double $p_j = (launch_j, kill_j)$ where $launch_j$ is the Job Launcher process in charge of job j and $kill_j$ is the Job Killer process associated to $launch_j$. The first process to finish its task in p_j (either the job computation or the sleep) cancels the other process's task. This leads to $kill_j$ finishing its execution and $launch_j$ sending a message to the Server process to tell it j has been computed (successfully or not) then finishing its execution too.

6   Batsim Evaluation Experiment

In order to evaluate whether Batsim's behaviour is similar to real RJMSs', we set up an experiment comparing Batsim to OAR [6]. OAR is a RJMS – or batch scheduler – notably known for being used in the Grid'5000 [1] infrastructure. We chose OAR over other RJMSs – e.g. SLURM – because the modular design of OAR allows its scheduling part to be decoupled from the other parts of the system very easily. We tested Kamelot [35], a conservative backfilling scheduling algorithm implemented in OAR by executing it on real OAR-managed resources on Grid'5000 and by plugging it to Batsim. Since the same scheduling algorithm is used both in reality and in simulation, this allows us 1. to demonstrate that Batsim's architecture can be used to test production schedulers 2. to check Batsim's behaviour's soudness.

Our experimental process can be simplified in two major parts: 1. workload generation 2. schedule comparison between real and simulated workload executions. The first major part requires real programs, their instrumentation and a methodology to create jobs in our different job models. This is detailed in Sect. 6.1. Subsequently, the way the jobs are put together to form workloads is explained in Sect. 6.2. The second major part is described in Sects. 6.3 and 6.4.

Using a realistic simulator means using a realistic platform. Fortunately, the Graphene cluster situated in the Nancy Grid'5000 site [13] has already been calibrated so we chose to use this cluster for our real and simulated experiments. Thus, all our real experiments were done on the Grid'5000 Graphene cluster, reserving the nodes below one switch each time.

6.1 Profile Generation

In order to execute a scheduling algorithm, workloads must be generated. However, the jobs of our workloads must fulfill some requirements to be executed both in a real platform and in simulation. Batsim allows different levels of realism depending on the profile models used in the workload, which makes the workload generation process more complex. Indeed, the msg model needs realistic computation vectors and communication matrices to make sense. Furthermore, the smpi model requires MPI traces in order to be used.

In order to obtain realistic values for our profile models, we chose to execute real jobs from the MPI version of the NAS Parallel Benchmarks (NPB)[1] and to instrument them to obtain execution traces. We have selected the three benchmarks IS, FT and LU. We chose to compile and execute them for all available processor sizes – powers of two from 1 to 32 – and for tiny to medium data sizes – B to D depending on the benchmark. Considering NPB limitations, we were able to compile 47 different MPI programs.

First, in order to obtain the real execution times of our programs, we run them in a sequence (one by one, to avoid network influence of one program to another) without instrumentation. This allowed us to directly generate delay profiles.

We then instrumented the jobs using Extrae [2], which gave us heavy execution traces. In order to get time-independent traces – required by SimGrid – from the format used by Extrae, we used a script, courtesy of Lucas Schnorr [33]. Time-independent traces contain, for each processor, a sequence of events describing how many flops the processor computed or the MPI functions it called with the associated data amount. Unfortunately, the conversion script we used is a work in progress and was not able to capture all MPI messages, which added a profile calibration phase in our experiment process.

Since SimGrid does not allow – at the moment – the concurrent execution of several SMPI applications at the same time, we were not able to validate the smpi profile type in the present article. On the other hand, we aggregated the time-independent traces into computation vectors and communication matrices

---

[1] NPB 3.3.1 available here [25].

to obtain msg profiles. These msg profiles have been calibrated such that their execution times match those of the previously obtained delay profiles. The main advantage of the calibrated msg profiles over the delay ones is that their execution time may vary depending on resources' computational power, network bandwidth or network contention. On the contrary, delay profiles have a fixed execution time that strongly depends on the platform they were executed on, and cannot take network contention into account. This difference makes this type of profile more appropriate for heterogeneous experiments.

6.2   Workload Generation

The workload generation algorithm that we decided to use is described in this paragraph and was inspired by Chap. 9.6 of book [12]. Please note that our workload generation method is not intended to be sound for comparing scheduling heuristics, but only to evaluate how Batsim behaves compared to a real RJMS. The algorithm generates $N = 800$ jobs iteratively. The interarrival submission times of the jobs is computed randomly with a Weibull distribution of shape parameter $k = 2$ and scale parameter $\lambda = 15$. Since the job sizes (the rigid number of resources a job requests) of the real jobs at our disposal are powers of 2 (from 1 to 32), the size of each job is computed with the formula $2^{\lfloor u \rfloor}$ where u is a lognormal variate of parameters $\mu = 0.25$ and $\sigma = 0.5$. Only variates such that $\lfloor u \rfloor$ is in $[0, log_2(32) = 5]$ are used to match the sizes at our disposal. The generation of those workloads depends on a random seed, simply referred as *seed* in the remainder of this article.

We chose to generate nine different workloads and to execute each of them once below two different switches of the Graphene cluster. We chose two different switches to obtain more representative simulation results. Indeed, both the computation nodes and the switches are homogeneous in Graphene and are described in the exact same way in the simulated platform. However, in practice, little differences exist between nodes that are supposed to be identical and we hope that these differences will be more noticeable this way.

6.3   Executing Workloads in a Real Platform

In order to execute the workloads we generated on Graphene, we used a reproducible methodology which is described in Sect. 8. This methodology includes the installation and the configuration of OAR within the nodes we reserved in Graphene. We configured OAR such that it uses the Kamelot scheduler and implemented a replay tool that reads a Batsim workload, then launches real OAR submissions at the times dictated by the workload. The OAR submissions launch the MPI programs which were previously generated.

6.4   Executing Workloads in Simulation

Executing the workloads in simulation simply consists in running the Kamelot scheduler on Batsim with the aforementioned calibrated platform file. To do so, we created an adaptor between Batsim and OAR which will be used later to test the different algorithms implemented in OAR.

7   Results

The nine different workloads we generated have been executed twice on a real platform (on identical machines and network, but not on the exact same machines), and twice in simulation (with Delay and MSG profile types). This section presents the different results and analyses them.

An overview of the execution of all the workloads can be found on Fig. 3. First of all, Fig. 3 shows that the MSG and the Delay simulation results are very close to each other. The execution times of MSG jobs depends on where the jobs are allocated and depends on the network saturation. However, in this experiment, the platform is highly homogeneous and very low contention has been observed during the jobs' execution, which explains why the results are so close. Furthermore, Fig. 3 shows that the difference between two real executions of the same workload is not negligible.

7.1   Similarities

Many similarities exist between the schedules resulting from the simulated and real executions of the workloads we defined.

Figure 3 allows to see the makespan and the mean bounded stretch of real and simulated executions of all the workloads we generated. The closer the points of a given color, the more similar the real and simulated executions are. For most

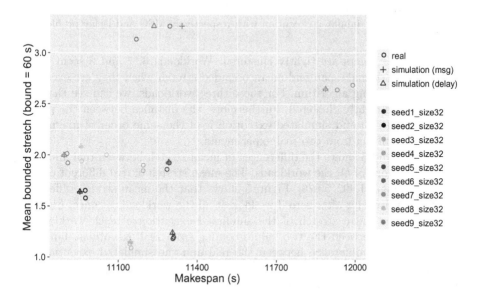

Fig. 3. Mean bounded stretch against the makespan of all workload executions. Each point represents one workload execution. Circles are executions on the real platform, triangles and crosses are simulated executions with respectively Delay and MSG profiles. Each workload is associated with one color.

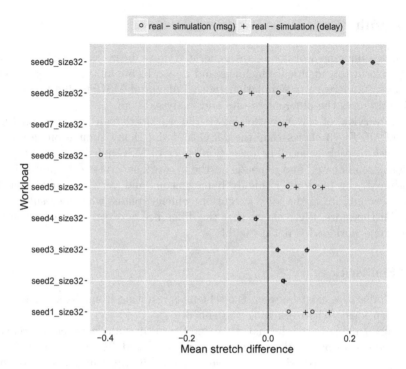

Fig. 4. Mean stretch difference between real and simulated executions of each workload. Different workloads are plotted on different lines. Circles and crosses represent the difference from the simulated execution with respectively MSG and Delay profiles.

workloads, the points are tightly clustered. Workloads 6, 7 and 8 seem to be unstable in both makespan and mean bounded stretch when they are executed with this scheduling algorithm. For these three workloads, we can see that the points are less tightly clustered. Furthermore, the distance between the points resulting from real and simulated execution is of the same order of magnitude as the one resulting from two real experiments.

Figures 4 and 5 shows the differences in mean stretch between real and simulated executions of all the workloads. The mean stretch of real different executions is in range $[1.492, 5.876]$. Figure 5 shows that the mean stretch difference is centered a little bit after zero if we look at all the workloads at once. Figure 4 shows that the mean stretch of the simulated execution of each workload is not necessarily between the two values coming from real executions, but that the mean stretch difference between the real and the simulated executions of one workload is of the same order of magnitude as the mean stretch difference between the two real executions of the same workload.

7.2 Differences

Figure 6 shows that simulated workload executions are almost always below real executions, which means that Batsim underestimates the waiting time of jobs.

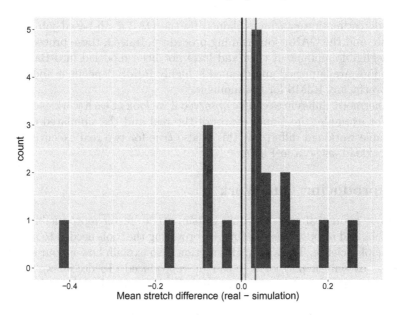

Fig. 5. Distribution of the mean stretch difference between real and simulated (with MSG profiles) executions of all workloads. The black vertical line is on zero. Red and green vertical lines are respectively the mean and median of the mean stretch difference among all workloads. (Color figure online)

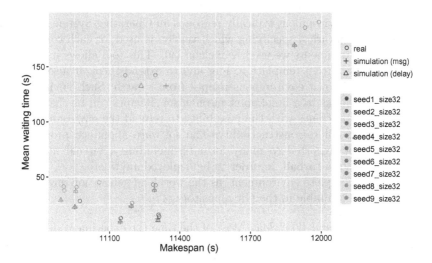

Fig. 6. Mean waiting time against the makespan of all workload executions. Each point represents one workload execution. Circles are executions on the real platform, triangles and crosses are simulated executions with respectively Delay and MSG profiles. Each workload is associated with one color.

This underestimation can be explained by the OAR's ssh-based job launching procedure and the OAR's job cleaning procedure. Indeed, these procedures take a non-negligible amount of time and have not been modeled into Batsim. The way the jobs are launched and cleaned is highly RJMS-dependent and we chose not to overfit any RJMS for the moment.

Furthermore, differences can be observed if we look at each workload at a finer grain. For example, the Gantt charts of the real and the simulated executions of the same workload differ, but this is also true for two real executions of the same workload, as seen in Fig. 7.

8 Reproducing Our Work

One of our main goal while creating Batsim was to foster reproducibility in the field of jobs and resources scheduling, by providing the tools needed to make more reproducible science. The aim of this section is to explain how all our evaluation process – or only a part of it – can be reproduced. To do so, we provide a complete environment to use Batsim and the different schedulers which run on top of it.

All the experiment tools mentioned below (Batsim, Kameleon, Execo, Grid'5000) are necessary to repeat the experiments we done. Of course, other tools exist to achieve reproducibility but we describe the ones we chose for our experiments.

Environments. An environment can be seen as an object that fixes a software context. Such an environment typically regroups an Operating System and a set of programs and libraries, specifying which version is used for each component. To build our environments we used Kameleon [30]. This tool allows its users to build environments from template recipes and to extend them. It also allows a user to write their own environment recipes from scratch. Such environments handle failures thanks to a breakpoint mechanism. Recipes can be shared using Git, and Kameleon comes with the possibility to rebuild the environment from cache to achieve full re-constructibility. The software appliance produced by Kameleon can be exported to many formats, including a virtual machine, a docker container or a tarball, in order to be deployed anywhere.

The Batsim complete environment, as the workload generation environment recipes, are both available in the Git repository [17].

Experiment Design and Workflow. Most of the time the experiment design consists in one or more documents that describe the purpose and the experiment with some details and some dedicated scripts. Some domain specific tools exist to compute the experiment on a grid from a user-defined workflow [37], but it is not well suited for computer science experiments, which also need to select the underlying software stack and OS. Hopefully, computer scientists dedicated testbeds exist, like Grid'5000 which allows this level of management.

Batsim's evaluation experiment has been made using Execo [19], a tool which completely automates the experiment workflow. Execo is a tool which allows

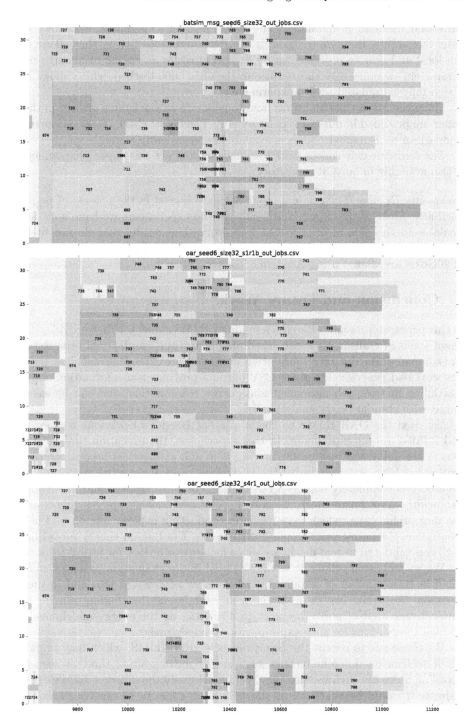

Fig. 7. Final section of the Gantt charts of the executions of workload *seed* = 6. The uppermost gantt chart is a simulated execution while the other two are real executions. Workload *seed* = 6 is the least stable workload in makespan.

Grid'5000 users to programmatically describe their experiment workflows in order to compute them on the grid. It is a Python toolbox library that allows to run local and remote processes easily. It also provides an engine to manage the parameters sweeping and an interface to the Grid'5000 testbed, which allows to design fully automated sets of experiments.

Moreover, the scripts and tools used to generate all the figures present in this paper are provided in our Git repository [18]. The Gantt chart visualisation and comparison tools named *Evalys* is available independently [15].

The complete experiment workflow made to conduct this paper's experiment is also available in our Git repository [18].

Inputs and Results. The original input data are crucial in the process of reproducibility. Most of the inputs and results of the experiments we have done are available in the aforementioned Git repository. The results that do not fit in the repository because of their size – notably the MPI instrumentation traces ($\simeq$20Go) – are shared using Academic Torrent [24].

9   Conclusion and Future Work

In this paper we presented Batsim, a modular RJMS simulator that provides different levels of realism, on which scheduling algorithms can be easily connected and compared. Batsim JSON-formatted workloads are extensible and allow painless workload generation. Batsim CSV outputs provide clear information about scheduling metrics, job placement and energy consumption, and can be easily linked with standard data analysis tools.

We used the OAR RJMS to check whether Batsim's behaviour is close to real RJMSs' in our experiment. In this experiment, the execution times of the jobs in the delay and msg profile models were almost identical because no contention has been observed during the experiment, and because the platform that we used was completely homogeneous both in computing power and in network bandwidth. As a future work, we can think of a validating process concerning the msg profile type, which may focus on conducting experiments on real heterogeneous platforms for example. Furthermore, the Batsim energy model has not been validated in real machines yet, which opens a door for future work.

We are well aware that the workloads used in our evaluation process remain small in their number of resources, their number of different jobs and in their duration. We would like to do larger scale experiments but finding funding to conduct this kind of study becomes problematic, as the energy and financial costs of reservations for such experiments would skyrocket.

We chose not to overfit the behaviour of a given RJMS, which may impact result realism on different metrics such as the mean waiting time, as seen in Sect. 7.2. Since our architecture allows to model finely the different RJMS's procedures, it would be beneficial to allow Batsim's users to parametrize how the different procedures should be done in order to improve accuracy.

At the moment, Batsim allows a production scheduler to be used in simulation. To do so, Batsim is in charge of simulating the RJMS whereas the scheduling component of the real RJMS makes the decisions. An interesting future work would be to allow the opposite type of connection: The real RJMS would run normally but it would communicate with a Batsim-compatible algorithm to make scheduling decisions. This would simplify greatly the production launch of theoretical scheduling algorithms.

Even if Batsim is fully operational as we wrote this article, we would like to improve its capabilities in several way. For example, we would like to implement the possibility to concurrently run several SMPI application within SimGrid in order to use those applications within Batsim. Moreover, we are also interested in IO-related problems for big data workload simulation. Eventually, we want to implement a user model to take user reactions into account during the ongoing scheduling execution.

As we want to promote experiment reproducibility, all the materials necessary to understand and reproduce our evaluation experiments are provided online.

Batsim is an open source [16] project and we encourage any researcher or engineer that has to deal with resources and jobs scheduling to use it. Besides, we would be pleased to collaborate with anyone who wants to port an existing scheduling algorithm to Batsim. This would enhance the list of supported algorithms which may be studied and compared in the same context, in order to make more reproducible and better science.

References

1. Balouek, D., et al.: Adding virtualization capabilities to the grid'5000 testbed. In: Ivanov, I.I., Sinderen, M., Leymann, F., Shan, T. (eds.) CLOSER 2012. CCIS, vol. 367, pp. 3–20. Springer, Cham (2013). doi:10.1007/978-3-319-04519-1_1
2. Barcelona Supercomputing Center: Extrae, February 2016. https://www.bsc.es/computer-sciences/extrae
3. Bedaride, P., Degomme, A., Genaud, S., Legrand, A., Markomanolis, G., Quinson, M., Stillwell, M., Suter, F., Videau, B.: Toward better simulation of MPI applications on ethernet/TCP networks, November 2013. https://hal.inria.fr/hal-00919507/document
4. Bell, W.H., Cameron, D.G., Millar, A.P., Capozza, L., Stockinger, K., Zini, F.: Optorsim: a grid simulator for studying dynamic data replication strategies. Int. J. High Perform. Comput. Appl. **17**(4), 403–416 (2003)
5. Caniou, Y., Gay, J.-S.: Simbatch: an API for simulating and predicting the performance of parallel resources managed by batch systems. In: César, E., et al. (eds.) Euro-Par 2008. LNCS, vol. 5415, pp. 223–234. Springer, Heidelberg (2009). doi:10.1007/978-3-642-00955-6_27
6. Capit, N., Da Costa, G., Georgiou, Y., Huard, G., Martin, C., Mounié, G., Neyron, P., Richard, O.: A batch scheduler with high level components. In: IEEE International Symposium on Cluster Computing and the Grid, 2005. CCGrid 2005, vol. 2, pp. 776–783. IEEE (2005)
7. Casanova, H., Giersch, A., Legrand, A., Quinson, M., Suter, F.: Versatile, scalable, and accurate simulation of distributed applications and platforms. J. Parallel Distrib. Comput. **74**(10), 2899–2917 (2014). http://hal.inria.fr/hal-01017319

8. Clauss, P.N., Stillwell, M., Genaud, S., Suter, F., Casanova, H., Quinson, M.: Single node on-line simulation of MPI applications with SMPI, May 2011. https://hal. inria.fr/inria-00527150/document

9. Diaz, A., Batista, R., Castro, O.: Realtss: a real-time scheduling simulator. In: 4th International Conference on Electrical and Electronics Engineering, 2007. ICEEE 2007, pp. 165–168. IEEE (2007)

10. Dutot, P.-F., Poquet, M., Trystram, D.: Communication models insights meet simulations. In: Hunold, S., et al. (eds.) Euro-Par 2015. LNCS, vol. 9523, pp. 258–269. Springer, Cham (2015). doi:10.1007/978-3-319-27308-2_22

11. Estrada, T., Flores, D., Taufer, M., Teller, P.J., Kerstens, A., Anderson, D.P., et al.: The effectiveness of threshold-based scheduling policies in BOINC projects. In: Second IEEE International Conference on e-Science and Grid Computing, 2006. e-Science 2006, p. 88. IEEE (2006)

12. Feitelson, D.G.: Workload Modeling for Computer Systems Performance Evaluation. Cambridge University Press, Cambridge (2015). https://cds.cern.ch/record/2005898

13. Grid5000: Nancy: Home - Grid5000, February 2016. https://www.grid5000.fr/mediawiki/index.php/Nancy:Home

14. Imbert, M., Pouilloux, L., Rouzaud-Cornabas, J., Lébre, A., Hirofuchi, T.: Using the EXECO toolbox to perform automatic and reproducible cloud experiments, December 2013. https://hal.inria.fr/hal-00861886

15. Inria: InriaForge: Evalys: Projet Home. https://gforge.inria.fr/projects/evalys

16. Inria: BatSim Homepage, February 2016. http://batsim.gforge.inria.fr/

17. Inria: InriaForge: Batsimctn: Project Home, February 2016. https://gforge.inria.fr/projects/simctn/

18. Inria: InriaForge:expe_batsim: Project Home, February 2016. https://gforge.inria.fr/projects/expe-batsim

19. Inria: Welcome to execo–execo v2.5.3, February 2016. http://execo.gforge.inria.fr/doc/latest-stable/

20. Jones, W.M., Ligon III, W.B., Pang, L.W., Stanzione, D.: Characterization of bandwidth-aware meta-schedulers for co-allocating jobs across multiple clusters. J. Supercomput. **34**(2), 135–163 (2005)

21. Klusáček, D., Rudová, H.: Alea 2: job scheduling simulator. In: Proceedings of the 3rd International ICST Conference on Simulation Tools and Techniques, p. 61. ICST (Institute for Computer Sciences, Social-Informatics and Telecommunications Engineering) (2010)

22. Legrand, A.: Simgrid Usages, January 2016. http://simgrid.gforge.inria.fr/Usages.php

23. Lucarelli, G., Mendonca, F., Trystram, D., Wagner, F.: Contiguity and locality in backfilling scheduling. In: 2015 15th IEEE/ACM International Symposium on Cluster, Cloud and Grid Computing (CCGrid), pp. 586–595. IEEE (2015)

24. Mercier, M.: MPI+PRV+TIT-traces_nas-Benchmarks_2016-02-08-10-10-44, February 2016. http://academictorrents.com/details/53b46a4ff43a8ae91f674b26c65c5cc6187f4f8e

25. NASA: NAS Parallel Benchmarks, February 2016. https://www.nas.nasa.gov/publications/npb.html

26. Pascual, J.A., Miguel-Alonso, J., Lozano, J.A.: Locality-aware policies to improve job scheduling on 3D tori. J. Supercomput. **71**(3), 966–994 (2015)

27. Ridruejo Perez, F.J., Miguel-Alonso, J.: INSEE: an interconnection network simulation and evaluation environment. In: Cunha, J.C., Medeiros, P.D. (eds.) Euro-Par 2005. LNCS, vol. 3648, pp. 1014–1023. Springer, Heidelberg (2005). doi:10.1007/11549468_111

28. Phatanapherom, S., Uthayopas, P., Kachitvichyanukul, V.: Dynamic scheduling II: fast simulation model for grid scheduling using HyperSim. In: Proceedings of the 35th Conference on Winter Simulation: Driving Innovation, pp. 1494–1500. Winter Simulation Conference (2003)

29. Proebsting, T., Warren, A.M.: Repeatability and benefaction in computer systems research. Technical report, The university of Arizona (2015). http://reproducibility.cs.arizona.edu/v2/RepeatabilityTR.pdf

30. Ruiz, C., Harrache, S., Mercier, M., Richard, O.: Reconstructable software appliances with kameleon. SIGOPS Oper. Syst. Rev. **49**(1), 80–89 (2015)

31. Stanisic, L., Legrand, A.: Effective reproducible research with org-mode and Git. In: Lopes, L., et al. (eds.) Euro-Par 2014. LNCS, vol. 8805, pp. 475–486. Springer, Cham (2014). doi:10.1007/978-3-319-14325-5_41

32. Takefusa, A., Matsuoka, S., Nakada, H., Aida, K., Nagashima, U.: Overview of a performance evaluation system for global computing scheduling algorithms. In: Proceedings of the Eighth International Symposium on High Performance Distributed Computing, pp. 97–104. IEEE (1999)

33. tcbozzetti: tcbozzetti/trabalhoconclusao, February 2016. https://github.com/tcbozzetti/trabalhoconclusao

34. oar team: Batsim protocol description (2016), https://github.com/oar-team/batsim/blob/master/doc/proto_description.md

35. oar team: Kamelot (2016). https://github.com/oar-team/oar3/blob/master/oar/kao/kamelot.py

36. Xia, H., Dail, H., Casanova, H., Chien, A.: The microgrid: using emulation to predict application performance in diverse grid network environments. In: Proceedings of the Workshop on Challenges of Large Applications in Distributed Environments (2004)

37. Yu, J., Buyya, R.: A taxonomy of scientific workflow systems for grid computing. SIGMOD Rec. **34**(3), 44–49 (2005)

Planning and Metaheuristic Optimization
in Production Job Scheduler

Dalibor Klusáček$^{(\boxtimes)}$ and Václav Chlumský

CESNET a.l.e., Brno, Czech Republic
{klusacek,vchlumsky}@cesnet.cz

Abstract. In this work we present our positive experience with a unique advanced job scheduler which we have developed for the widely used TORQUE Resource Manager. Unlike common schedulers using queuing approach and simple heuristics, our solution uses planning (job schedule construction) and schedule optimization by a local search-inspired metaheuristic. Using both complex simulations and practical deployment in a real system, we show that this approach increases predictability, performance and fairness with respect to a common queue-based scheduler. Presented scheduler has been successfully used in the production infrastructure of the Czech Centre for Education, Research and Innovation in ICT (CERIT Scientific Cloud) since July 2014.

Keywords: Scheduling · Planning · Performance · Fairness · Simulation

1 Introduction

The pros and cons of queuing vs. planning have been discussed in the past thoroughly [5]. Classical queuing approaches such as the well known EASY backfilling algorithm provide limited predictability and thus employ additional mechanisms in order to avoid certain unwanted features such as potentially (huge) starvation of particular jobs, etc. Approaches based on full planning represent an opposite approach. Instead of using "ad hoc", aggressive scheduling, they build and manage an execution plan that represents job-to-machine mapping in time. For example, Conservative backfilling establishes reservation for every job that cannot execute immediately, i.e., a guaranteed upper bound of its completion time is always available [13]. This increases predictability but may degrade system performance and requires more computational power. At the same time, the accuracy of such predictions is typically quite low, as provided estimates concerning job execution are typically very imprecise and overestimated.

In theory, the planning-based approach has been often combined with some form of advanced scheduling approach using, e.g., a *metaheuristic* [20] to further optimize the constructed execution plan. These works were often theoretical or used a (simplified) model together with a simulator, while realistic implementations in actual resource managers were not available. Those promising results were then *rarely repeated in the practice* and most of the mainstream production

© Springer International Publishing AG 2017
N. Desai and W. Cirne (Eds.): JSSPP 2015/2016, LNCS 10353, pp. 198–216, 2017.
DOI: 10.1007/978-3-319-61756-5_11

systems like PBS Pro, SLURM or Moab/Maui have adopted the queuing approach [1,6], focusing on performance and scalability while limiting the (theoretical) benefits of increased predictability related to the planning systems. Neither metaheuristics nor other advanced optimization techniques are used in current mainstream systems.

In this paper we *bridge the gap between theory and practice* and demonstrate that planning supplied with a schedule-optimizing metaheuristic is a plausible scheduling approach that can improve the performance of an existing computing system. We describe and evaluate newly developed job scheduler (compatible with the production TORQUE Resource Manager) which supports planning and optimization. The presented scheduler has been *successfully used in practice* within a real computing infrastructure since July 2014. It constructs a preliminary job execution plan, such that an expected start time is known for every job prior its execution. This plan is further evaluated in order to identify possible inefficiencies using both *performance* as well as *fairness*-related criteria. A local search-inspired metaheuristic is used to optimize the schedule with respect to considered optimization criteria. The suitability and good performance of our solution is demonstrated in two ways. First, we present *real-life performance results* that are coming from the deployment of our scheduler in the CERIT Scientific Cloud, which is the largest partition of the Czech national grid and cloud infrastructure MetaCentrum, containing ~5,200 CPUs in 8 clusters. Second, we use several simulations to evaluate the solution against previously used queuing approach. Importantly, we have adopted the novel *workload adaptation* approach of Zakay and Feitelson [21] in order to overcome the shortcomings of "classical" simulations with static workloads.

This paper is a significantly extended and updated version of our short-paper presented at HPDC 2015 [8]. We have included more details concerning the design of the scheduler (Sect. 3) and significantly extended the evaluation (Sect. 4), adding more results from practical deployment as well as presenting a set of newly performed detailed simulations using the model of Zakay and Feitelson [21]. Theoretical background of this work has been described in our earlier work [10] which has presented new methods for efficient use of metaheuristic algorithms for multi-criteria job scheduling. However, instead of a real resource manager, this work only used a simulator with static historic workloads while considering simplified problem models [10].

This paper starts with the related work discussed in Sect. 2. Next, we describe the design and features of our new scheduler. Section 4 presents detailed evaluation of the scheduler's performance, while Sect. 5 concludes the paper.

2   Related Work

Nowadays, major production resource management systems such as PBS Pro [14], SLURM or Moab/Maui [6] use (priority) queues when scheduling jobs on available resources, applying some form of popular scheduling heuristics — typically FCFS and backfilling. On the other hand, during the past two decades many works have shown that the use of planning represents some advantages [9,13]. Unlike the traditional "aggressive" queuing approach where scheduling decisions are taken in an ad hoc fashion often disregarding previous and future scheduling decisions, a planning-based approach allows to make plans concerning job execution. The use of such a plan (job schedule) allows to make a partial prediction of job execution, providing information concerning expected start times of jobs to the users of the system, thus improving predictability [13]. Conservative backfilling [13] represents a typical baseline solution for planning systems.

As far as we know, fully planning-based schedulers using, e.g., the Conservative backfilling algorithm, are less popular in practice than "classical" queue-based solutions [12]. Typically, only few waiting jobs are usually planned ahead, while no predictions are made for the remaining jobs. For example, PBS Professional Administrator's Guide recommends that at most 100 jobs should be planned ahead (backfill_depth parameter in [14]). Notable exceptions represent fully planning-based systems such as Computing Center Software (CCS) [7] and its successor Open CCS[1], that use planning and are used in practice.

Within the CERIT system, a form of Conservative backfilling has been used prior our new scheduler has been adopted. The scheduler maintained several queues with different maximal walltime limits (1h, 2h, 1d, 2d, 4d, 1w, 2w and 2m). Job queues were periodically reordered by fair-sharing algorithm. To reflect aging, resource usage records (fair-share usage) were subject to decay [6] by the aging factor of 0.5 which was applied each 72 h, i.e., each 3 days the current user's fair-share usage was dived by 2. To avoid excessive job starvation, waiting jobs obtained a reservation when their waiting time reached a given threshold. However, by default this threshold was equal to 0 s implying that every waiting job obtained a reservation.

In many (theoretical) works, planning-based approach has been also used in conjunction with further optimization. Simply put, a prepared execution plan has been *evaluated* with respect to selected optimization criteria and further *optimized* using some form of a metaheuristic [11,15,18,20]. As far as we know, evaluation and/or metaheuristics are not applied in nowadays production systems. In the past, Global Optimising Resource Broker (GORBA) [17] represented an experimental planning-based system designed for scheduling sequential and parallel jobs as well as workflows. It was using Hybrid General Learning and Evolutionary Algorithm and Method (HyGLEAM) optimization procedure, combining local search with the GLEAM algorithm [16] which is based on the principles of evolutionary and genetic algorithms. Sadly, this system was a proprietary solution and it seems that it is no longer operational.

3   Planning and Optimizing Job Scheduler

This section describes the new planning-based job scheduler that uses a schedule-optimizing metaheuristic. The scheduler is compatible with the TORQUE

---

[1] https://www.openccs.eu/core/.

Resource Manager system, which is used in the Czech National Grid Infrastructure MetaCentrum. TORQUE is an advanced open-source product providing control over batch jobs and distributed computing resources [1]. It consists of three main entities — the server (**pbs_server**), the node daemons (**pbs_mom**) and the job scheduler (**pbs_sched**). The scheduler interacts with the server in order to allocate jobs onto available nodes. While the server and the node daemons are mostly unchanged, the default simple queue-based FCFS scheduler [1] has been replaced in this case. When using TORQUE, it is a common practice to use other than the default scheduler [1].

The new scheduler contains four major parts. The first part is the data structure that represents the *job schedule*. The schedule is *built and maintained* using schedule construction and maintenance routines that represent the default scheduling algorithm, working similarly to the well known *Conservative backfilling* [13]. Maintenance routines are used to adjust the schedule in time subject to dynamic events such as (early) job completions, machine failures, etc. Remaining parts perform the *evaluation* and the *schedule optimization*. We now closely describe these major parts in detail.

3.1   Data Representation of Job Schedule

The *schedule* is represented by a rather complex data structure that keeps all important information regarding planned job execution. In fact it consists of three separate structures. First, there is the linear list of jobs (*job_list*), where each job in the list stores information regarding its allocation, e.g., CPU/GPU IDs, the amount of RAM memory per node, amount of disk space, etc. Also the planned start time and completion time is stored for each job. Second structure (*gap_list*) stores "gaps", i.e., "unused" parts of the schedule. It is used to speed up the scheduling algorithm during the backfilling phase. Each gap is associated with its start time, duration and a list of available resources (CPUs, GPUs, RAM, HDD, etc.). Both jobs and gaps are ordered according to their expected start times. The third part of the schedule is called *limits_list* and is used to guard appropriate usage of resources. For example, it is used to guarantee per-user limits concerning maximum CPU usage. Similarly, it is used to check that a given class of jobs does not exceeds its maximum allowed allocation at any moment in the planned future (e.g., jobs running for more than a week cannot use more than 70% of all system resources).

All these structures and their parameters are kept up-to-date as the system runs using methods described in Sect. 3.2. For practical reasons, independent instances of *job_list*, *gap_list* and *limits_list* are created for every cluster in the system. First, such solution speeds up the computation of schedule as changes and updates are often localized to a given cluster while it also allows to simplify management of heterogeneous infrastructures, where different clusters may have different properties and usage constraints. Although the job schedule in fact consists of three major parts (*job_list*, *gap_list* and *limits_list*), for simplicity we will mostly use the term *schedule* in the following text when describing the pseudo codes of the scheduler.

3.2   Scheduling Algorithms

The job schedule is built, maintained and used according to the dynamically arriving events from the **pbs_server** using the core method called SCHEDULINGCYCLE which is shown in Algorithm 1. SCHEDULINGCYCLE invokes all necessary actions and auxiliary methods in order to update the schedule and perform scheduling decisions. At first, all jobs that have been completed since the previous check are removed from the *schedule* (Line 1). Next, the *schedule* is updated (Line 2) using the UPDATE function which is described in Algorithm 2.

During the update it is checked whether existing (planned) job start times are still relevant (see Lines 1–6 in Algorithm 2). If not, those are adjusted according to the current known status. There are several reasons why planned start times may change. Commonly, jobs are finishing earlier than expected as the schedule is built using processing time estimates which are typically overestimated. Also, in some situations jobs are shifted into later time slots, e.g., due to fairness-related constraints and/or via the optimization algorithm. In both cases, jobs are checked one by one and a start time of each job is adjusted (see Line 3), i.e., it is moved into the earliest possible time slot with respect to previously adjusted jobs while respecting existing usage limits. Next, *limits_list* and *gap_list* structures are updates accordingly (see Lines 4–5 in Algorithm 2). During the update process, the relative ordering of job start times is kept, i.e., a later job cannot start earlier than some previous job. This approach is a runtime-optimized version of the *schedule compression method* used in Conservative backfilling [13].

Once the schedule is updated, all newly arrived jobs are inserted into the existing schedule (Lines 3–7 in Algorithm 1) using the Conservative backfilling-like approach. It founds the *earliest gap* in the initial *schedule* which is suitable for the new *job*. This approach is identical with the method used in Conservative backfilling for establishing job reservations [13]. It significantly increases system utilization while respecting the start times of previously added jobs. In this case, the applied data representation represents major benefit as all gaps in the current schedule are stored in a separate list (*gap_list*) which speeds up the whole search procedure. When the suitable gap is found and the job is placed into it

---

Algorithm 1. SCHEDULINGCYCLE

1: remove finished jobs from *schedule*;
2: *schedule* := UPDATE(*schedule*);
3: **while** new jobs are available **do**
4:     *job* := get new job from **pbs_server**;
5:     *schedule* := backfill *job* into the earliest suitable gap in *schedule*;
6:     *schedule* := UPDATE(*schedule*);
7: **end while**
8: notify **pbs_server** to run ready jobs according to *schedule*;
9: **if** $(time_{current} - time_{previous}) \geq 60\,\mathrm{s}$ **then**
10:     *schedule* := SCHEDULEOPTIMIZATION(*schedule*);
11:     $time_{previous} := time_{current}$;
12: **end if**

Algorithm 2. UPDATE(*schedule*)

1: **for** $i := 1$ to number of jobs in *schedule* **do**
2:    $job := i$-th job from *schedule*;
3:    *schedule* := adjust *job*'s start time subject to *limits_list*;
4:    update *limits_list*;
5:    update *gap_list*;
6: **end for**
7: **return** *schedule*;

(Line 5 in Algorithm 1) the *schedule* is appropriately updated and another incoming job is processed.

Once all new jobs are placed into the *schedule*, the scheduler checks whether some jobs are prepared to start their execution. Those jobs are immediately scheduled for execution as depicted on Line 8 in Algorithm 1. Finally, the *schedule* is periodically optimized (see Line 10 in Algorithm 1) by a metaheuristic which we describe in the following section.

3.3 Evaluation and Metaheuristic

The real contribution of our scheduler is related to its ability to "control" itself and adjust its behavior in order to better meet optimization criteria. This is done by the periodically invoked metaheuristic optimization algorithm which is guided by the schedule evaluation. We use a simple local search-inspired metaheuristic called *Random Search (RS)* [10] and focus both on the performance- and the fairness-related criteria. We minimize the *avg. wait time* and the *avg. bounded slowdown* to improve the overall performance [4]. *User-to-user fairness* is optimized using the *Normalized User Wait Time (NUWT)* metric [10]. For a given user, NUWT is the total user wait time divided by the amount of previously consumed system resources by that user. Then, the user-to-user fairness is optimized by minimizing the mean and the standard deviation of all NUWT values. It follows the classical fair-share principles, i.e., a user with lower resource usage and/or higher total wait time gets higher priority over more active users and vice versa [6]. The calculation of NUWT reflects consumptions of multiple resources (CPU and RAM utilization), representing a solution suitable for systems having heterogeneous workloads and/or infrastructures [6].

The *Random Search (RS)* optimization algorithm is implemented in the SCHEDULEOPTIMIZATION function (see Algorithm 3) that uses one input — the schedule that will be optimized. In each iteration, one random job from the schedule is selected and it is removed from its current position (Lines 3–4). Next, this job is returned to the schedule on a randomly chosen position (Line 5) and the new schedule is immediately updated (Line 6). The modified schedule is evaluated with respect to applied optimization criteria. This multi-criteria evaluation is performed using a simple weight function[2] that has been successfully used

---

[2] Our system uses equal weights ($w = 1$) for wait time and bounded slowdown while the normalized user wait time (fairness) has ten times higher weight ($w = 10$).

Algorithm 3. SCHEDULEOPTIMIZATION($schedule$)

1: $schedule_{best}$:= $schedule$;
2: **while** not interrupted **do**
3:     job := select random job from $schedule$;
4:     remove job from $schedule$;
5:     move job into random position in $schedule$;
6:     $schedule$:= UPDATE($schedule$);
7:     **if** $schedule$ is better than $schedule_{best}$ **then**
8:         $schedule_{best}$:= $schedule$;
9:     **end if**
10:    $schedule$:= $schedule_{best}$;   (reset candidate)
11: **end while**
12: **return** $schedule_{best}$;

in our previous works [9,10]. If the new $schedule$ is better than the best so far found $schedule_{best}$ then the $schedule_{best}$ is updated with this new, better $schedule$. Otherwise, the $schedule_{best}$ remains unchanged (Lines 7–9). Then the $schedule$ is updated/reset with the $schedule_{best}$ (Line 10) and a new iteration starts. Once the loop ends, the newly found $schedule_{best}$ is returned (Line 12).

The metaheuristic is fully randomized and does not employ any "advanced" search strategy. In fact, during the design process we have observed that this simple randomized optimization is very robust and produces good results, often beating more advanced methods such as Simulated Annealing or Tabu Search. The beauty of RS is that it is simple (i.e., fast) and — unlike, e.g., Simulated Annealing — its performance does not rely on additional (hand-tuned) parameters.

Certainly, optimization is a potentially time consuming operation. Therefore, the optimization is only executed if the last optimization ended at least 60 s ago (see Lines 9–12 in Algorithm 1). This interval has been chosen experimentally in order to avoid frequent — thus time consuming — invocations of the SCHEDULEOPTIMIZATION function. Furthermore, several parameters are used when deciding whether to interrupt the main loop of the optimization procedure or not (Line 2 in Algorithm 3). We use the maximal number of iterations and the given time limit. Currently, the time limit is 20 s and the number of iterations is set to 300 in our system.

3.4 User Perspective: System Interfaces

From the user perspective, the newly developed scheduler does not introduce any major difference with respect to other standard schedulers. It uses the same syntax of the qsub command as a "normal" TORQUE-based system, so users can use the same commands as they are used to from different systems. The TORQUE's pbs_server have been slightly extended, such that it can read job-related data from the schedule and then provide them to the users. For this purpose, the pbs_server queries the schedule and then displays the information obtained, including currently planned start time and execution node(s).

We support both textual (`qstat` command) and graphical user interfaces using a complex web application called *PBSMon*[3] which monitors the whole infrastructure and workload.

4 Evaluation and Deployment

The developed scheduler and its optimization metaheuristic has been thoroughly tested using various methodologies. In this section we present the results of three different evaluation scenarios. First, Sect. 4.1 shows the comparison of system performance before and after the new scheduler has been deployed in practice. These results represent the actual behavior of the system, but include one major but unavoidable drawback — the comparison is not based on the same workload, since the results were obtained from a real system in two different consecutive time periods. This problem can be avoided by testing the new scheduler (and its predecessor) using a computer testbed, where the same set of jobs is submitted to both schedulers and their resulting performance is compared. Although this approach is quite realistic, such a comparison is very time consuming (see discussion in Sect. 4.2), limiting the "size" of the data sets that can be used. Therefore, we also include a third type of evaluation, where the major features of both the original and the newly proposed scheduler have been implemented within a job scheduling simulator and a large data set from the actual system has been used. This comparison is presented in Sect. 4.3.

In all cases, the proposed planning-based scheduler using Random Search metaheuristic (denoted as *Plan-RS*) has been evaluated against the backfilling-based algorithm (denoted as *Orig-BF*) that was originally applied in the system (see Sect. 2). Additional algorithms were not considered either because their implementations within TORQUE were not available or their performance was very poor (e.g., plain FCFS without backfilling). All experiments used the original inaccurate runtime estimates.

4.1 Real-Life Deployment

First, we present real-life data that were collected in the Czech Centre for Education, Research and Innovation in ICT (*CERIT Scientific Cloud*) [3], where our new scheduler has been operationally used since July 2014. *CERIT Scientific Cloud* provides computational and storage capacities for scientific purposes and shares them with the Czech National Grid and Cloud Infrastructure *MetaCentrum*. Both MetaCentrum and CERIT use the same version of TORQUE resource manager. Before July 2014, CERIT was using the same scheduler (Orig-BF) as MetaCentrum. CERIT consists of 8 computer clusters with ∼5,200 CPU cores that are managed by our new scheduler (Plan-RS) since July 2014.

Following comparative examples are based on the historic workload data that were collected when either the original Orig-BF scheduler or the new Plan-RS

---

[3] http://metavo.metacentrum.cz/pbsmon2/.

scheduler were used respectively. In the former case (Orig-BF), the data come from the January – June 2014 period. In the latter case the data are related to the new scheduler (Plan-RS) and cover the July – December 2014 period[4].

The first example in Fig. 1(left) focuses on the average system CPU utilization. It was observed that — on average — the new scheduler was able to use additional 10,000 CPU hours per day compared to the previous scheduler. This represents 418 fully used CPUs that would otherwise remain idle and causes that the avg. CPU utilization has increased by 9.3%.

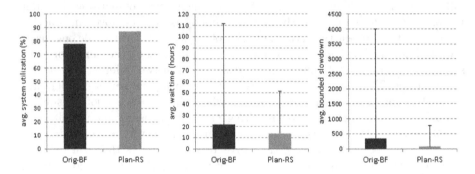

Fig. 1. Real-life comparisons showing (from the left to right) the avg. system utilization, the avg. wait time and the avg. bounded slowdown.

Although the increased utilization is beneficial, it may come at the cost of decreased performance for selected classes of jobs, which is a known feature [13]. As users tend to watch how the system is processing their jobs, improved utilization, i.e., higher throughput, may cause that users will send more jobs into the system. As the total available computing power is limited, these "additional jobs" may have to wait longer until resources become available. Moreover, reservations established by backfilling often represent a pessimistic scenario as jobs are typically completing earlier than their estimates suggest [19]. Even though existing reservations are shifted to those appearing free time slots (see the discussion on schedule compression in Sect. 3.2), short/narrow jobs would still have a higher chance to fill these gaps compared to long and/or highly parallel jobs. Therefore, we have performed further analysis of the data focusing on additional performance indicators.

First, we have compared the avg. wait time and the avg. bounded slowdown as well as their standard deviations for the two considered schedulers. The results are shown in Fig. 1 (2nd and 3rd chart from the left, respectively), where the "error bar" depicts the standard deviation of the metric. As we have observed, the original Orig-BF scheduler often produced very bad wait times and slowdowns for many jobs, causing high average values and large deviations. From

---

[4] Those two periods were chosen because the physical infrastructure was identical during that time. Since January 2015, the system became larger (4,512 CPUs vs 5,216 CPUs) which would skew any direct comparison of system performance.

this point of view, Plan-RS was much more efficient, significantly decreasing both the averages and the deviations. Given the increased utilization observed in Fig. 1(left) this is a good news.

Furthermore, we have also analyzed the average job wait time with respect to job parallelism (number of requested CPUs) as shown in Fig. 2(left). The results for Plan-RS are again promising as most job classes now have better average wait times compared to the former Orig-BF scheduler, i.e., Plan-RS is not causing significant delays for (highly) parallel jobs.

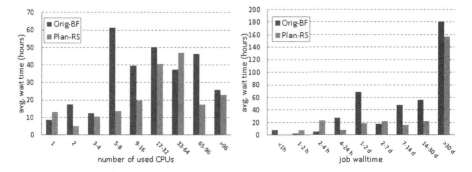

Fig. 2. Real-life comparison of job wait times with respect to job parallelism (left) and job walltime (right).

Also, job walltime (processing time estimate) is an important factor that has some influence on job's chances to obtain a good (early) reservation. Longer jobs are less likely to obtain early reservations, i.e., their wait times may be (very) large in some cases. Therefore we have compared average wait times of jobs with respect to their walltime estimates as were specified by users. As can be seen in Fig. 2 (right), there are no significant side effects associated with the use of Plan-RS. Importantly, with a single exception (2–7 days), the average wait time of jobs that have their runtime estimate larger than 4 h was always smaller compared to the former Orig-BF scheduler. Furthermore, such jobs represent nearly 83% of the whole workload, i.e., they are very frequent, yet they are not significantly delayed by the new scheduler which is very important. To sum up, our new Plan-RS scheduler has increased the utilization in CERIT system, without producing any significant undesirable side effect. In fact, also the avg. wait time and the avg. bounded slowdown have been significantly reduced compared to the original Orig-BF scheduler.

As discussed in Sect. 3.3, user-to-user fairness is maintained by minimizing the mean and the standard deviation of Normalized User Wait Times (NUWT). Figure 3 shows the fairness-related results for both schedulers. The mean and the standard deviation (shown by error bar) of NUWT values are very close for Orig-BF and Plan-RS (see Fig. 3(left)). More detailed results are shown in Fig. 3 (middle and right), showing the NUWT values per user and the corresponding

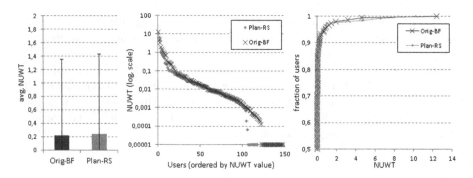

Fig. 3. Fairness-related results showing the avg. Normalized User Wait Time (NUWT) and its (per user) distribution as well as corresponding CDF.

cummulative distribution function (CDF) of NUWT values, respectively. The results for both schedulers are quite similar — most users (∼97%) have their NUWT below 1.0, meaning that they spent more time by computing than by waiting which is beneficial and indicate that both Plan-RS and Orig-BF are capable to maintain reasonable fairness level.

In order to demonstrate the capability of our metaheuristic to improve the quality of the schedule in time we have also recorded all successful optimization attempts during the October – December 2014 period. Then, we have plotted the corresponding relative improvements (and deteriorations) of those criteria with respect to the time. Figure 4 shows the results for wait time and fairness criteria respectively. Commonly, the main reason that an attempt was accepted is that the user-to-user fairness was improved. This is an expected behavior. In the CERIT system, user-to-user fairness is not directly guaranteed by the underlying Conservative backfilling-like algorithm, and it can only be improved through the optimization. Without optimization, the only way to assert fairness is to periodically re-compute the schedule from scratch, i.e., reinsert all waiting jobs into the schedule following a new job ordering computed according to updated user priorities. This is potentially very time consuming, thus non-preferred option. Therefore, it is very common for the optimization algorithm to find a schedule with improved fairness. Figure 4 also reveals that the majority of accepted optimization attempts represents rather decent improvements, where the relative improvement of a given criterion is less than 2% in most cases. Still, several large improvements can be seen for both criteria during the time (and few more are not shown since the y-axis is cropped for better visibility). These rarer attempts are very important as they help to reduce those few extremely inefficient assignments that can be seen in nearly every production workload. As the optimization is continuously evaluating the schedule, it is able to detect jobs having (very) high wait times, slowdowns, etc. Then, it can develop better schedules where these extremes are reduced. These results help to explain the large improvement of wait times and slowdowns observed in Fig. 1.

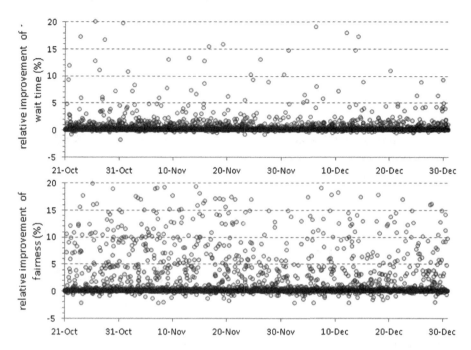

Fig. 4. Successful optimization attempts over the time.

We were also careful about the runtime requirements of our rather complex solution. Therefore, we have measured how the size of the schedule (number of jobs) affects the runtime of critical schedule-maintaining routines. For this analysis, the runtime of the *backfilling-like* policy was measured as well as the time needed to perform the subsequent *schedule-update* routine which updates the schedule-related data structures subject to modifications (see Sect. 3.2). Also the total runtime (backfilling + update) and the average runtime of one iteration of Random Search metaheuristic were recorded. The results are presented in Fig. 5, where the y-axis shows consumed runtime (in microseconds) and the x-axis depicts the number of jobs in the schedule.

The results show that there is no simple correlation between the overall size of the schedule and algorithm runtime. This is a natural behavior caused by several factors. First of all, jobs being added to the schedule have different requirements — some jobs are generally very flexible, i.e., they can be executed on several clusters while other jobs can only use a small subset of system's clusters. Then the algorithm runtime may vary significantly depending whether one, two, or more cluster schedules must be analyzed for a given job. Since we use backfilling, if a suitable gap is found in an early time slot (close to the beginning of the schedule), the runtime is lower as we do not have to traverse the whole schedule, and vice versa. Moreover, the physical system consists of 8 different clusters that have different types of nodes and amounts of system resources and each such cluster has its own *schedule* instance. Naturally, *schedule* for larger

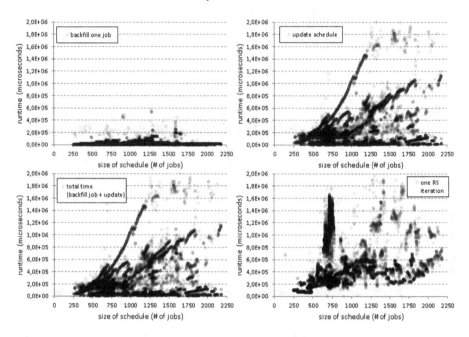

Fig. 5. Runtime requirements with respect to the number of jobs in the schedule.

cluster requires more runtime to be backfilled/updated. Still, some basic trends are visible in the figures, such as approximately linear upper bound of requested runtime. With the current typical backlog of CERIT system — where the number of jobs in the schedule is usually bellow 2,200 — 61% of jobs require less than 0.2 s to be placed in the schedule (backfill + update), most jobs (96%) then require less than 1 s while 99% of jobs fit within 2 s. Clearly, schedule construction does require nontrivial time, however we usually have <1,000 new job arrivals per day which is well within the current capacity of our implementation and we have not observed any delays/overheads so far.

The avg. runtime of one iteration of Random Search (RS) may be higher than of previous routines (see the bottom right part of Fig. 5), which is natural. First of all, the evaluation of the whole schedule requires some time. Second, when an iteration is not improving, the schedule must be reset to its previous state which requires an additional update. Therefore, the runtime of one RS iteration is often at least twice as high as the corresponding runtime of the update procedure. Finally, while the backfill + update part of the scheduler is only executed upon new job arrival, RS is executed periodically (∼60 s). If there is a "complicated schedule" at that time, the chart of RS runtime will show a large peak, as this runtime-demanding schedule is repeatedly updated. An example of such situation is visible in the chart, showing a rather large peak of runtime for schedules having ∼700 jobs. This particular peak was caused by a specific situation on one of the cluster's schedules where a set of similar jobs — all belonging to a single user — have remained for a couple of days. It was basically impossible to optimize the schedule for such jobs, and frequent time-demanding updates (schedule resets) were inevitable, producing a runtime peak clearly visible as a clump of dots in the chart.

4.2 Comparison Using Testbed

Another possible way how to properly compare the proposed solution is to test both the former Orig-BF and the new Plan-RS schedulers using a simulation testbed, feeding both schedulers with identical workloads. The problem is that such experiments are very time consuming. One cannot simply use a long, realistic workload "as is" because the experiment would last for several weeks/months depending on the original length of the workload. Instead, only several "promising" job intervals from a workload can be extracted. We have chosen those with a significant activity and contention (using the number of waiting jobs at the given time as a metric). Based on this information we have extracted those promising intervals that lasted for at least 5 days. Such intervals were more likely to show differences between the two schedulers. Furthermore, all job runtimes and all corresponding inter-arrival times between two consecutive jobs were divided by a factor of 7. The resulting workload was then proportional to the original one, exhibiting similar behavior but having 7-times shorter duration (makespan), making the simulation possible within a reasonable time frame. For example, if the original data covered one week then it took only 1 day to perform the whole simulation. Eight such sub-workloads were then used — four of them based on data from the CERIT's Zewura cluster, two from the HPC2N log and the two remaining came from the KTH-SP2 log. Detailed analysis and further description of this experiment have been already presented in [8], therefore we only briefly recapitulate that the proposed Plan-RS scheduler dominated over Orig-BF in all cases. Table 1 shows the relative decrease of the avg. wait time (WT) and the avg. bounded slowdown (SD) achieved by the Plan-RS scheduler with respect to the Orig-BF scheduler[5].

Table 1. Achieved relative decrease (in %) of the avg. wait time (WT) and the avg. bounded slowdown (SD) when using the new Plan-RS scheduler.

	Zewura				HPC2N		KTH-SP2	
	Set 1	Set 2	Set 3	Set 4	Set 1	Set 2	Set 1	Set 2
WT	−18.8%	−40.0%	−57.2%	−41.1%	−81.0%	−26.6%	−31.6%	−7.2%
SD	−32.6%	−49.7%	−84.7%	−39.3%	−89.6%	−42.0%	−64.0%	−45.7%

---

[5] The small size and short makespan of these experiments meant that there were few distinctive users in the workload — most of them with just few jobs — making the use of the fairness-related criterion rather impractical and inconclusive in this case.

4.3   Comparison Using Simulator

As explained in Sects. 4.1 and 4.2, evaluation based on practical deployment as well as testbed-based comparison are somehow problematic (different workloads and time-related constraints, respectively). Therefore, we have also used the *Alea* job scheduling simulator [2] where both Orig-BF and Plan-RS have been emulated. Moreover, instead of using the classical static approach where a given workload is "replayed" in the simulator, we have adopted the recently proposed dynamic approach of Zakay and Feitelson [21], where job submission times are not dictated by the workload but are the result of the (simulated) scheduler-to-user interaction. As explained in [21], job submission times in a real system depend on how users react to the performance of previous jobs. Moreover, usually there are some logical structures of dependencies between jobs. It is therefore not reasonable to use a workload "as is" with fixed (original) job submission timestamps, as the subsequent simulation may produce unrealistic scenarios with either too low or too high load of the system, skewing the final results significantly. Instead, dependency information and user behavior can be extracted from a workload trace, in terms of job batches, user sessions and think times between the completion of one batch and the submission of a subsequent batch. Then, each user's workload is divided into a sequence of dependent batches. During the simulation, these dependencies are preserved, and a new user's batch is submitted only when all its dependencies are satisfied (previous "parent" batches are completed). This creates the desired feedback effect, as users dynamically react to the actual performance of the system, while major characteristics of the workload including job properties or per-user job ordering are still preserved. More details can be found in [21,22] while the actual implementation of the model (using user agents instead of standard workload reader) is available within the Alea simulator [2].

We have used a workload trace from the CERIT system that covered 102,657 jobs computed during January – April 2015[6]. Again, we have compared the "historical" Orig-BF with the newly proposed Plan-RS scheduler. All experiments using Plan-RS have been repeated 20 times (and their results averaged) since RS is not deterministic and uses a randomized approach. The results for the avg. wait time and the avg. bounded slowdown are shown in Fig. 6, error bars in the left chart shows the standard deviation of the 20 runs of Plan-RS. As previously (see Sects. 4.1 and 4.2), Plan-RS decreases significantly the wait time and the bounded slowdown. The explanation is quite the same as was in Sect. 4.1 and can be nicely demonstrated on the CDF of job wait times which we show in Fig. 6(right). The mean wait time for Plan-RS is 1.6 h, while the CDFs for both scheduler show that 85% of jobs wait shorter than 1.6 h. This can only mean — and it is clearly visible in the CDF — that Plan-RS decreases some of those excessive wait times of the remaining 15% of jobs.

Concerning the fairness, the Plan-RS performed much better than Orig-BF as shown in Fig. 7. The mean and the corresponding standard deviation

---

[6] This workload is available at: http://www.fi.muni.cz/~xklusac/workload/.

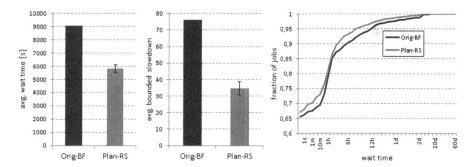

Fig. 6. Performance-related results showing (from left to right) the avg. wait time, the avg. bounded slowdown and the CDF of job wait times.

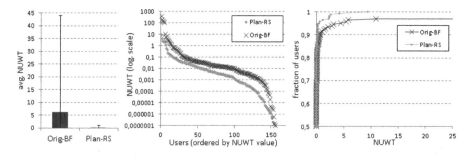

Fig. 7. Fairness-related results showing (from left to right) the mean Normalized User Wait Time (NUWT), NUWT histogram wrt. users and corresponding CDF.

of NUWT values were significantly lower compared to Orig-BF. When analyzed on a detailed per-user basis (see the middle and the right chart in Fig. 7), the results clearly show that Plan-RS decreases NUWT across the whole user base.

In the final experiment, we have developed a new *experimental model to measure user (dis)satisfaction* with the system performance. Here we were inspired by the future work discussed in the recent Zakay and Feitelson paper [22], which suggest that (in reality) users may leave if the performance is too poor. In our case a user agent does not leave the system, instead it "reports" that it is not satisfied with the current waiting time. Also, it measures "how large" this dissatisfaction is by calculating the actual to expected wait time ratio. In our simple model, a user agent expects that the system shall start its jobs in a time which is proportional to job's requirements. In other words, the longer a job is (higher walltime estimate) and the more CPUs it requires the higher is the tolerable wait time and vice versa. However, this dependence is not linear, since our experience shows that real users usually have some "upper bound" of their patience. For example, if a job requiring 1 CPU starts within an hour, then users are usually satisfied. However, that does not imply that a job requiring 64 CPUs can wait for 64 h. We have similar experience concerning walltime, i.e., user's patience is not linear with respect to job duration, instead it quickly

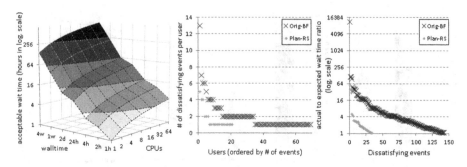

Fig. 8. Acceptable wait time with respect to CPU and walltime requirments (left), the number of dissatisfying events per user (middle) and all dissatisfying events ordered by their seriousness (right).

runs out. Therefore, we have developed a simple formula to calculate "acceptable wait time" for a given job which captures this nonlinearity[7]. Figure 8(left) shows the non-linear distribution of acceptable wait times with respect to job durations and their parallelism, as produced by the applied formula. Of course, this simple "hand tuned" formula is just a rough approximation used for demonstration purposes and it certainly does not represent a truly realistic model of user's expectations.

During a simulation, *job's acceptable wait time* is calculated upon each new job arrival. If more jobs of a single user are present in the system we sum up their acceptable wait times. Then, whenever a job is started, a corresponding user agent checks whether the actual wait time was within the calculated overall limit. If not, a user agent "reports dissatisfaction" and calculates the level of such dissatisfaction, which is the actual wait time divided by the acceptable wait time. Further details can be found in the `AgentDynamicWithSatisfactionModel` class of the simulator [2]. The results of such experiment are shown in Fig. 8(middle) and (left), showing the number of dissatisfying events per user and all dissatisfying events ordered by their seriousness, respectively. It shows superior performance of Plan-RS, which is able to significantly minimize the number of "complaining users", the number of excessively waiting jobs, as well as the "size", i.e., seriousness of such job delays.

5   Conclusion

In this paper we have provided a detailed analysis of the real production scheduler which uses *planning* and *metaheuristic-based schedule optimization*. Using

---

[7] The formula is: $acceptable\_wait = (\ln(req\_CPUs) + 1) \cdot (walltime/factor)$. req_CPUs denotes the number of requested CPUs and job's *walltime* is divided by an integer ($factor \geq 1$) which increases as the walltime increases, emulating the non-linear user's wait time expectations. Currently, we use five factors $1, 2, .., 5$, which apply for walltimes $<3h$, $3h..7h$, $7h..24h$, $1d..7d$, $\geq 1w$, respectively.

various types of evaluation we have demonstrated that both planning and some form of optimizing metaheuristic can be used in practice. In reality, the planning feature is useful for users as well as for system administrators. On several occasions, the constructed plan revealed problems long before someone else would normally notice (e.g., suboptimal job specification leading to very large planned start time). Also, system administrators often use prepared plan when reconsidering various system-wide setups, e.g., too strict limits concerning resource usage. Certainly, this approach is not suitable for every system. Not surprisingly, planning (in general) is more time-consuming approach compared to plain queuing. The time needed for construction and maintenance of job schedules grows with the size and complexity of the system and its workload (see Sect. 4.1). Surely, our current implementation can be further improved. For example, all schedule-related routines are currently sequential — running in a single thread — and can be relatively easily parallelized. So far, this is not an issue within CERIT system and no problems concerning scalability/speed were recorded so far. Our scheduler is freely available at: https://github.com/CESNET/TorquePlanSched.

Acknowledgments. We kindly acknowledge the support and computational resources provided by the MetaCentrum under the program LM2015042 and the CERIT Scientific Cloud under the program LM2015085, provided under the programme "Projects of Large Infrastructure for Research, Development, and Innovations". We also highly appreciate the access to CERIT Scientific Cloud workload traces. Last but not least, we thank Dror Feitelson for his kind help and explanation concerning the dynamic workload model presented in [21].

References

1. Adaptive Computing Enterprises, Inc., Torque 6.0.0 Administrator Guide, February 2016. http://docs.adaptivecomputing.com
2. Alea simulator, February 2016. https://github.com/aleasimulator
3. CERIT Scientific Cloud, February 2016. http://www.cerit-sc.cz
4. Feitelson, D.G., Rudolph, L., Schwiegelshohn, U., Sevcik, K.C., Wong, P.: Theory and practice in parallel job scheduling. In: Feitelson, D.G., Rudolph, L. (eds.) JSSPP 1997. LNCS, vol. 1291, pp. 1–34. Springer, Heidelberg (1997). doi:10.1007/3-540-63574-2_14
5. Hovestadt, M., Kao, O., Keller, A., Streit, A.: Scheduling in HPC resource management systems: queuing vs. planning. In: Feitelson, D., Rudolph, L., Schwiegelshohn, U. (eds.) JSSPP 2003. LNCS, vol. 2862, pp. 1–20. Springer, Heidelberg (2003). doi:10.1007/10968987_1
6. Jackson, D., Snell, Q., Clement, M.: Core algorithms of the maui scheduler. In: Feitelson, D.G., Rudolph, L. (eds.) JSSPP 2001. LNCS, vol. 2221, pp. 87–102. Springer, Heidelberg (2001). doi:10.1007/3-540-45540-X_6
7. Keller, A., Reinefeld, A.: Anatomy of a resource management system for HPC clusters. Annu. Rev. Scalable Comput. **3**, 1–31 (2001)
8. Klusáček, D., Chlumský, V., Rudová, H.: Planning and optimization in TORQUE resource manager. In: 24th ACM International Symposium on High Performance Distributed Computing (HPDC), pp. 203–206. ACM (2015)

9. Klusáček, D., Rudová, H.: Performance and fairness for users in parallel job scheduling. In: Cirne, W., Desai, N., Frachtenberg, E., Schwiegelshohn, U. (eds.) JSSPP 2012. LNCS, vol. 7698, pp. 235–252. Springer, Heidelberg (2013). doi:10.1007/978-3-642-35867-8_13

10. Klusáček, D., Rudová, H.: A metaheuristic for optimizing the performance and the fairness in job scheduling systems. In: Laalaoui, Y., Bouguila, N. (eds.) Artificial Intelligence Applications in Information and Communication Technologies. SCI, vol. 607, pp. 3–29. Springer, Cham (2015). doi:10.1007/978-3-319-19833-0_1

11. Koodziej, J., Xhafa, F.: Integration of task abortion and security requirements in GA-based meta-heuristics for independent batch grid scheduling. Comput. Math. Appl. 63(2), 350–364 (2012)

12. Li, B., Zhao, D.: Performance impact of advance reservations from the Grid on backfill algorithms. In: Sixth International Conference on Grid and Cooperative Computing (GCC 2007), pp. 456–461 (2007)

13. Mu'alem, A.W., Feitelson, D.G.: Utilization, predictability, workloads, and user runtime estimates in scheduling the IBM SP2 with backfilling. IEEE Trans. Parallel Distrib. Syst. 12(6), 529–543 (2001)

14. PBS Works. PBS Professional 13.0, Administrator's Guide, February 2016. http://www.pbsworks.com

15. Pooranian, Z., Shojafar, M., Abawajy, J., Abraham, A.: An efficient meta-heuristic algorithm for grid computing. J. Comb. Optim. 30(3), 413–434 (2015)

16. Stucky, K.-U., Jakob, W., Quinte, A., Süß, W.: Solving scheduling problems in grid resource management using an evolutionary algorithm. In: Meersman, R., Tari, Z. (eds.) OTM 2006. LNCS, vol. 4276, pp. 1252–1262. Springer, Heidelberg (2006). doi:10.1007/11914952_14

17. Süß, W., Jakob, W., Quinte, A., Stucky, K.-U.: GORBA: a global optimising resource broker embedded in a Grid resource management system. In: International Conference on Parallel and Distributed Computing Systems, PDCS 2005, pp. 19–24. IASTED/ACTA Press (2005)

18. Switalski, P., Seredynski, F.: Scheduling parallel batch jobs in grids with evolutionary metaheuristics. J. Sched. 18(4), 345–357 (2015)

19. Tsafrir, D., Etsion, Y., Feitelson, D.G.: Backfilling using system-generated predictions rather than user runtime estimates. IEEE Trans. Parallel Distrib. Syst. 18(6), 789–803 (2007)

20. Xhafa, F., Abraham, A.: Metaheuristics for Scheduling in Distributed Computing Environments. SCI, vol. 146. Springer, Heidelberg (2008)

21. Zakay, N., Feitelson, D.G.: Preserving user behavior characteristics in trace-based simulation of parallel job scheduling. In: 22nd Modeling, Analysis and Simulation of Computer and Telecommunication Systems (MASCOTS), pp. 51–60 (2014)

22. Zakay, N., Feitelson, D.G.: Semi-open trace based simulation for reliable evaluation of job throughput and user productivity. In: 7th IEEE International Conference on Cloud Computing Technology and Science (CloudCom 2015), pp. 413–421. IEEE (2015)

Topology-Aware Scheduling on Blue Waters with Proactive Queue Scanning and Migration-Based Job Placement

Kangkang Li[1(⊠)], Maciej Malawski[2], and Jarek Nabrzyski[1]

[1] Department of Computer Science and Engineering,
University of Notre Dame, Notre Dame, IN, USA
{kli3,naber}@nd.edu
[2] Department of Computer Science,
AGH University of Science and Technology, Krakow, Poland
malawski@agh.edu.pl

Abstract. Modern HPC systems, such as Blue Waters, have multidimensional torus topologies, which make it hard to achieve a high system utilization and a high scheduling efficiency. The low system utilization is majorly caused by system fragmentation, which includes both internal fragmentation due to convex prism shape requirement, and external fragmentation resulted from contiguous allocation strategy. The low scheduling efficiency comes from using a brute force search to find the free block with a matching shape for each job, which is highly time consuming. In this paper, we address the topology-aware scheduling problem on Blue Waters, with the objective of improving system utilization and scheduling efficiency. To improve scheduling efficiency, we propose an efficient free partition detection method. To improve system utilization, we propose a job scheduling strategy with proactive queue scanning and a migration-based job placement algorithm. Through extensive simulations of modeled trace data, we demonstrate that our approach improves the system utilization.

Keywords: Topology-aware scheduling · Proactive queue scanning · Free partition detection · Migration · Job placement

1 Introduction

Many high performance computing systems use various types of multidimensional torus topologies for their interconnects. Four of the top ten supercomputers in the Top500 list (June 2016) have torus networks (one 3D, two 5D, and one 6D). They are widely used in systems such as Blue Waters (3D) [6], IBM's Blue Gene/Q (5D) [15], and Fujitsu's K computer (6D) [2]. In the Blue Waters system for instance, the network consists of X, Y, Z 3D dimensions with toroidal interconnect. Each dimension has 24 Gemini routers, making the system 24*24*24 torus interconnect structure. Each coordinate on X, Y, Z dimensions

© Springer International Publishing AG 2017
N. Desai and W. Cirne (Eds.): JSSPP 2015/2016, LNCS 10353, pp. 217–231, 2017.
DOI: 10.1007/978-3-319-61756-5_12

is associated with a Gemini router. Each Gemini router is directly associated to two computing nodes, and is connected to its six neighbour routers along X, Y, Z dimensions (each dimension has two neighbour routers).

This torus topology influences the way jobs should be scheduled and placed in the system. For example, BlueGene allows allocating network links exclusively to the selected jobs to optimize their performance, but it can leave unused nodes within the system partitions, which leads to a lower utilization. On Blue Waters, a pre-defined Shape Table is adopted to accommodate each job's request. In order to allocate a job, the scheduler has to exhaustively search the entire system to find the free block with a matching shape, which leads to a high time complexity and a low scheduling efficiency.

In order to improve the application performance and runtime consistency, Blue Waters system adopts a contiguous allocation strategy [4,5] and a convex prsim shape is allocated to each job. This strategy degrades the system utilization. On the other hand, non-contiguous allocation strategy [3,12] can improve the system utilization, but it causes job performance to go down due to communication interference and increased latency. These reasons motivate us to investigate various topology-aware job scheduling strategies.

One key factor to low system utilization on Blue Waters is system fragmentation, which includes both internal and external fragmentation. The internal fragmentation results from the convex prism shape allocation, which allocates more nodes to a job than it needs. The external fragmentation, on the other hand, is caused by contiguous allocation strategy, which separates free system resources into smaller, non-contiguous blocks interspersed by allocated resources. This leads to the situation when sufficient number of free nodes cannot be contiguously allocated for a job. In this paper, we focus on developing efficient job scheduling strategies to reduce system fragmentation, hoping that it can improve system utilization.

Blue Waters system is using Adaptive Computing's Moab scheduler as system scheduler [6]. The scheduler is in charge of assigning each waiting job a priority and placing waiting jobs into the system. The ordered priority regulates the schedule order for waiting jobs in the queue and determines which jobs to select and when to allocate the selected jobs. In this paper, without loss of generality, we assume the queue is *never empty* and is already *ordered* by assigned priority. Each job is characterized by its own resource demand (number of nodes), and estimated walltime. The objective is to design an efficient job scheduling strategy to achieve a high system utilization and a high scheduling efficiency. Meanwhile, we must preserve the performance of jobs and avoid communication interference. Therefore, following the suggestions of system administrators of Blue Waters, we still need to maintain contiguous allocation strategy and allocate convex prism shape for input jobs.

The paper is organized as follows: In Sect. 2, we propose a scheduling strategy with proactive queue and system scanning. In Sect. 3, we present the free partition detection method and the multiple knapsack model for the job placement problem. In Sect. 4, we present our migration-based job placement algorithm for solving the multiple knapsack problem. In Sect. 5, we conduct simulations to validate the efficiency of our approach. The related work is discussed in Sect. 6 and we give our conclusions and future work in Sect. 7.

2   Scheduling with Proactive Queue and System Scanning

In this section, we present a scheduling strategy based on proactive queue and system scanning. In our approach, the scheduler allocates waiting jobs in the queue to the system in scheduling cycles. At each scheduling cycle, the scheduler maintains a scan window to proactively scan the queue. In the meantime, the scheduler also scans the system to detect a set of free partitions. The size of the scan window is the depth of the scanning from the head of the waiting queue, as shown in Fig. 1. This queue scanning generates a set of jobs in the scan window ordered by priority.

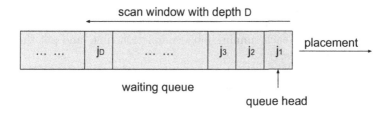

Fig. 1. Proactive queue and system scanning

The system scanning detects a set of free partitions in the system. This set of free partitions represents all available contiguous resource areas. These areas can be represented as a set of *bins*. Each bin is a 3D convex rectangular prism. Once the set of jobs in the scan window is obtained, we will group these jobs and try to place them together onto the set of free bins, all at once. This scheduling strategy has the potential to improve system utilization as multiple jobs are scheduled together, which leads to a better resource allocation. In the paper, we use the two terms (bins and partitions) interchangeably.

As described in Algorithm 1, at one scheduling cycle, starting from current queue head job, the scheduler scans the queue with depth D, and generates the set J of D waiting jobs ordered by priority. Meanwhile, the scheduler scans the system to obtain the set P of M free partitions. After that, the scheduler places each job in J (waiting job set) into P (free bin set) until all jobs in J are allocated or one job $j_i \in J$ is rejected. The detailed placement process will be discussed in Sect. 4. As each job's information (number of nodes, estimated walltime) in the scan window is known to us, this job placement process is in fact an off-line job placement.

If all jobs in J are allocated, we will wait until next scheduling cycle. Otherwise, if one job $j_i \in J$ is rejected, we will perform backfilling and place "backfilled" jobs into P. In order to implement backfilling, we need to first determine

---

Algorithm 1. Scheduling with Proactive System and Queue Scanning

---

1: **if** at one scheduling cycle **then**
2:      scan the queue and generate the set J of D waiting jobs: $J = \{j_1, ..., j_D\}$
3:      scan the system and generate the set P of M free partitions: $P = \{p_1, ..., p_M\}$
4:      Job Placement (J, P) ▷*Algorithm 5*
5:      **if** $j_i \in J$ is rejected **then**
6:          calculate the start time of j_i and reserve space for it
7:          perform backfilling
8:      **else**
9:          wait until next scheduling cycle

---

the start time of j_i and reserve space for it, which requires the following three steps:

1. Obtain the list of running jobs in the system, and sort them increasingly by their remaining completion time.
2. Starting from the time point of current scheduling cycle to the future, record the time point upon each running job's completion time, and put those time points in the timeline.
3. Go through the timeline and calculate the largest free partition in the system upon the time point of each running job's completion time. Once one sufficient largest free partition is found to accept j_i at time point t, we stop the search. Time point t is then recorded as the start time of job j_i, and the corresponding largest free partition is reserved for j_i.

With the start time t determined and space reserved, we will perform backfilling and allocate qualified backfilled jobs according to the ordered priority. The qualified backfilled jobs are those in the queue which can finish execution before the start time t of job j_i. Once P cannot accept "backfilled" jobs, we will terminate current scheduling cycle and wait until the start time of j_i. If the start time of j_i stretches multiple scheduling cycles, we will keep using "backfilled" jobs to fill in P at each scheduling cycle until the start time of j_i.

3   Free Partition Detection and Multiple Knapsack Model

As mentioned before, Blue Waters currently uses a pre-defined Shape Table to accommodate the request of each job. This Shape Table contains all topological shapes of sub-torus for job allocation. For instance, for a job with 8 node request, it corresponds to a shape of 2*2*2 in the Shape Table. In order to schedule such a job, the scheduler has to exhaustively search the entire system to find the free sub-torus block with a matching shape of 2*2*2, which is computational expensive. As an improvement, we propose an efficient free partition detection method to search the largest rectangular contiguous partition in the system.

The system is sliced into layers along the Y dimensions (X or Z dimension is also applicable), as illustrated in Fig. 2. Each dimension has side length of M

($M = 24$ in the case of Blue Waters). To obtain a maximum rectangular free block on one layer, it takes time of $O(M^2)$ through the method of construction. As for the entire 3D system, it takes another $O(M^2)$ to go through the combinations of all the layers. Therefore, it takes total $O(M^4)$ to obtain the largest free rectangular partition in the system. We can schedule multiple jobs into this partition all at once instead of just one job.

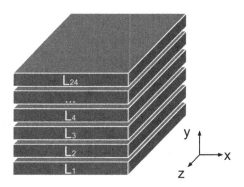

Fig. 2. Partitioning of the system into layers by Y axis

Given job shape, job placement into bins can be expressed as a 3D multiple knapsack problem. Each bin can be considered as a knapsack and input jobs are the items waiting to be put into the knapsacks. Let $J = \{j_1, j_2, ..., j_D\}$ be the set of all D waiting jobs ordered by priority in the scan window. Each job j_i has weight w_i, with profit p_i. Let $K = \{k_1, k_2, k_3, ..., k_M\}$ be the set of M knapsacks, which comes from the free bin set $P = \{p_1, p_2, p_3, ..., p_M\}$ obtained in Algorithm 1. Each knapsack k_j has capacity of C_j, which will be reduced as more jobs are placed into the knapsack. We want to find a placement for the D jobs together into the set P of free bins to maximize the total profit. The mathematical formulation is as below:

$$Max : \sum_{i=1}^{D} \sum_{j=1}^{M} x_{ij} p_i \tag{1}$$

$$Subject\ to : \sum_{j=1}^{M} x_{ij} \leq 1, \quad \forall i = 1, 2, ..., D \tag{2}$$

$$\sum_{i=1}^{D} x_{ij} w_i \leq C_j, \quad \forall j = 1, 2, ..., M \tag{3}$$

$$x_{ij} \in \{0, 1\}, \quad \forall i = 1, 2, ..., D, \ \forall j = 1, 2, ..., M \tag{4}$$

$$C_j \geq 0, \quad \forall j = 1, 2, ..., M \tag{5}$$

$x_{ij} = 1$ means job i is put into knapsack j, and $x_{ij} = 0$ means job i is not put into knapsack j. The physical meaning of both weight w_i and profit p_i is the

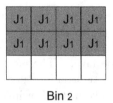

Fig. 3. Illustration of difference in internal fragmentation from job placement

job size, which is the number of requested nodes of job i. The capacity of each knapsack can never be negative, but it will be reduced as more jobs are put into this knapsack.

Based on this multiple knapsack model, maximizing the system utilization can be transformed into maximizing the objective of Eq. 1. As the sizes of input jobs and capacities of free bins are heterogeneous, this multiple knapsack problem is NP-hard and requires a heuristic algorithm, one example of which is presented in the next section.

4   Migration-Based Job Placement

In this section, we propose a migration-based job placement heuristic algorithm to solve the multiple knapsack problem. The intuition of this heuristic is to minimize the internal fragmentation brought in by the job placement process.

Once the set J of waiting jobs in the scan window and the set P of free partitions are obtained in one scheduling cycle, we will place each incoming job in J into one of the bins in P. However, the extent of internal fragmentation (the number of idle nodes due to using convex shape) is different if we place a job in different bins. Figure 3 gives a 2D example.

As shown in Fig. 3, there is an incoming job J_1 with 8 nodes request. If we place it in Bin 1, it will lead to one idle node (the grey area), as the topological layout of Bin 1 is 3*3. However, if we place it in Bin 2, it leads to no internal fragmentation, as the layout of Bin 2 is 3*4. Therefore, Bin 2 is a better choice and more preferable than Bin 1 in minimizing the internal fragmentation.

Thus, for each job, there are preference differences in placing it into different bins. Each bin is ranked by the extent of the internal fragmentation this bin can bring in. We are looking for the best bin that leads to the minimal internal fragmentation. However, if the resources in the best bin are not sufficient for an incoming job, we have two options.

1. **Direct Placement:** Among all the bins which have enough resources to accept the incoming job, we select the one with minimal internal fragmentation.
2. **Migration-based Placement:** We try to find one "victim" job on the best bin, and migrate it into another bin, as shown in Fig. 4. In that case, we can make some more room for accepting the incoming job.

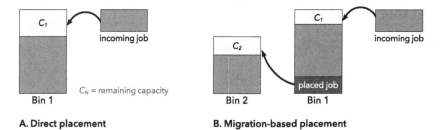

Fig. 4. An illustration of the job placement. When using direct placement, the incoming job is assigned to bin 1 with the enough remaining capacity C_1. When using migration, we can find an already placed job ("a victim") to be migrated to another available bin with enough capacity, such as bin 2 in the picture above

The first option is not optimal as it misses the opportunity to place the incoming job on the best bin, especially when the internal fragmentation on the best bin is much less than that on the other bins. Therefore, we want to take advantage of migration to do the placement. However, migration has constraint. For the migrated victim job, there might be an internal fragmentation increase due to the change of host bin. As our objective is to reduce the overall internal fragmentation from job placement, if the internal fragmentation increase of the migrated victim job is too large, migration will be meaningless. In that case, we would rather select direct placement without migration.

While implementing the migration, we need to find a qualified victim job for migration, which is not always possible. There are three conditions that a qualified victim job must meet:

1. it can make enough room to accept the incoming job.
2. it can find a new available bin with enough remaining capacity to accept the victim job itself.
3. the migration constraint must be satisfied, i.e., despite the internal fragmentation increase from the migrated victim job, the Migration-based Placement is better than Direct Placement in minimizing the internal fragmentation.

If such a qualified victim job is found in the best bin, we will choose to apply Migration-based Placement (Algorithm 2). If more than one qualified victim jobs exist in the best bin, we choose the victim job with the minimal internal fragmentation increase to migrate. However, if we cannot find a qualified victim job in the best bin, we will try to place the job in the next-best bin. If the incoming job still cannot be placed, we continue to try the next-next-best bin. This search goes on until the incoming job is placed or all the bins have been tried.

As shown in Algorithm 2, for the incoming job j_i, we first sort all the bins increasingly by the internal fragmentation of placing j_i in each bin p_j. The call for Direct Placement (Algorithm 3) returns $frag\_value$, which is the minimal value of the internal fragmentation among all the bins that are enough to accept

---

Algorithm 2. Migration-based Placement

1: **Input:** job j_i, the set P of M bins: $P = \{p_1, ..., p_M\}$
2: sort and rank each bin p_j increasingly by the extent of internal fragmentation of placing job j_i in p_j
3: $frag_value = $ Direct Placement(j_i, P)
4: **for** $j = 1$ to M **do**
5:    **if** C_j is enough for accepting j_i **then**
6:       place j_i in p_j
7:    **else if** Migration Test $(j_i, p_j, frag_value) == $ **true then**
8:       perform migration and place j_i on p_j
9:    **else**
10:      **continue**

Algorithm 3. Direct Placement

1: **Input:** job j_i, the set P of M bins: $P = \{p_1, ..., p_M\}$
2: sort and rank each bin p_j increasingly by the extent of internal fragmentation of placing job j_i in p_j
3: **for** $j = 1$ to M **do**
4:    **if** C_j is enough for accepting j_i **then**
5:       **return** internal fragmentation of placing j_i in p_j
6:    **else**
7:       **continue**

---

j_i. After that, starting from the first bin on the sorted list (the best bin), we try each p_j to place the job j_i in it. If p_j is enough for accepting j_i, we just directly place j_i in p_j. Otherwise, we use $frag\_value$ to test the migration constraint (in Algorithm 4). If migration constraint is satisfied and a qualified victim job is found, we then perform migration and place j_i in p_j.

In Algorithm 4, first, for each already placed job j_k on p_j that can make enough space for the incoming job j_i, we try to find j_k a new best available bin, which is the one that has enough resources for j_k and leads to the minimal internal fragmentation increase among all the bins (except p_j). After that, we test migration constraint. If migration constraint is satisfied, we then mark j_k as a qualified victim job. If more than one qualified victim jobs exist, we select the best victim job on bin p_j which has the minimal internal fragmentation increase. Notably, the migration here is one-hop migration, which means that we only consider the migration of the victim job caused by the incoming job. The re-placement of victim job will not trigger another migration.

With D jobs and M bins in one scheduling cycle, assuming the average number of already placed jobs on a bin is K, the time complexity of Algorithm 4 is $O(KM)$, which is no more than $O(D)$. With one loop, the time complexity of Algorithm 3 is $O(M)$. Therefore, the total complexity of Algorithm 2 is $O(MKM) + O(M)$, which is no more than $O(MD)$ and pretty efficient.

The overall job placement algorithm presents in Algorithm 5 above, which corresponds to line 4 of Algorithm 1. The input is the set J of D waiting jobs in

---

Algorithm 4. Migration Test

1: **Input:** job j_i, bin p_j, $frag\_value$
2: **for** each placed job j_k on bin p_j **do**
3:     **if** j_k's migration save enough space for j_i **then**
4:         **for** all the bins (except p_j) **do**
5:             find j_k a new best available bin (except p_j)
6:             calculate the internal fragmentation increase of migrating job j_k
7:             test migration constraint using $frag\_value$
8:             **if** migration constraint is satisfied **then**
9:                 mark job j_k as a qualified victim job
10: **if** one or more than one victim job exist on p_j **then**
11:     select the best victim job on bin p_j which has minimal internal fragmentation increase
12:     **return true**
13: **else**
14:     **return false**

Algorithm 5. Job Placement

1: **Input:** the set P of M bins: $P = \{p_1, ..., p_M\}$
            the set J of D waiting jobs: $J = \{j_1, ..., j_D\}$
2: **for** $i = 1$ to D **do**
3:     Migration-based Placement (j_i, P) ▷ Algorithm 2
4:     **if** j_i cannot be placed **then**
5:         reject j_i
6:         **break**

---

the scan window and the set P of free bins in one scheduling cycle. For each job $j_i \in J$, we apply Migration-based Placement algorithm (Algorithm 2) to place it into the set P of free partitions. When it comes to a job j_i that cannot be placed into P, we reject it and terminate this placement process.

As mentioned before, all jobs in the scan window are known to us, therefore, this job placement process is in fact an off-line job placement, where migration is an emulated process with no migration overhead. As time complexity of Algorithm 2 is $O(MD)$, the total time complexity of Algorithm 5 is $O(MD^2)$ with D input jobs, which is very efficient.

5   Performance Evaluation

In this section, we conduct simulations to evaluate our approach of improving system utilization. According to the information from administrators of Blue Waters, the current scheduling policy they use only achieves a system utilization of around 50% to 60%. We will show that our approach can significantly improve that utilization value.

The evaluation is performed using Blue Waters traces. For simplicity and without loss of generality, we have used Blue Waters trace model, preserving the

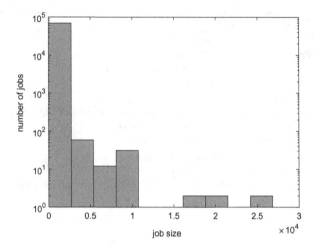

Fig. 5. Job size distribution

trace characteristics. Based on the study of trace data, we found that the largest job can almost occupy the entire system's capacity (only a few jobs like this). The minimal size job is single node job, which constitutes around 70% of the entire trace workload.

As convention, jobs with node request more than 3000 nodes are classified as extra-large jobs, and jobs with node request between 1000 to 3000 are large jobs. Jobs with node request between 100 to 1000 are medium jobs, and jobs with node request below 100 nodes are small jobs. The extra-large jobs can cause the system to drain for a long time until enough space is available to place such a large job. This drainage brings the system utilization down for a long time. To deal with these extra-large jobs, reducing system fragmentation is not enough as extra-large jobs can require half or more of system's capacity. Therefore, other approaches such as relaxing priority order are necessary to deal with extra-large jobs.

We focus on input workload that consists of small, medium and large jobs for our simulation, which constitutes 99.8% of the entire trace workload. Even if there are a few extra-large jobs, most jobs are below 3000 nodes, as shown in Fig. 5. Similarly, we also present the distribution of job walltime throughout the trace, as shown in Fig. 6. Although the dominant jobs are short, mid-length and long jobs are taken into account as well.

Using random initial input, we start with the system around half occupied. The simulation input workload has 2000 jobs, which is the approximate number of new job submissions in one day. The scheduling cycle is set as 15 min. That is, one iteration of scheduling repeats every 15 min. We allocate jobs and record system utilization at each scheduling cycle (every 15 min). As the total input workload has 2000 jobs, it requires many scheduling iterations to complete the allocation of all input jobs.

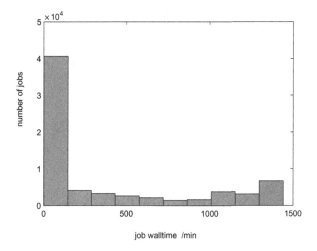

Fig. 6. Job walltime distribution

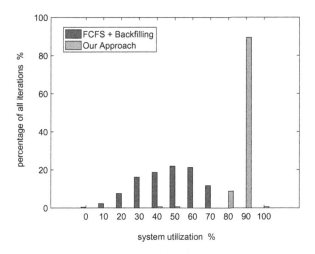

Fig. 7. Histogram of our approach with scan window size of 1000

Moreover, to prevent the scenario that the system is in low utilization because there are not enough "backfilled" jobs to be used for fully utilizing the system's capacity, we also have another set of "backfilled" jobs besides the input workload of 2000 jobs. This set of "backfilled" jobs are used for providing sufficient "backfilled" jobs to maintain system utilization. This setting is practical as the waiting queue usually has plenty of jobs for allocation.

We conduct three groups of simulations to find out the impact of scan window size on the performance of our approach, which includes a scheduling strategy using proactive queue scanning and a migration-based job placement algorithm.

In Figs. 7 and 8, the scan window size are 1000 and 500, respectively. We can see that, in most time of the scheduling iterations, our approach achieves

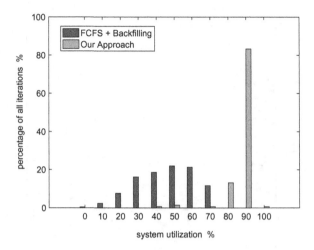

Fig. 8. Histogram of our approach with scan window size of 500

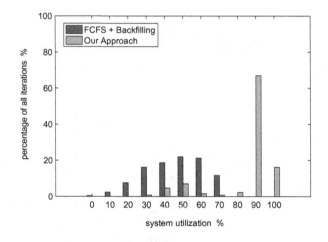

Fig. 9. Histogram of our approach with scan window size of 100

a system utilization on the level of around 90%. On the other hand, the FCFS + Backfilling strategy leads to the utilization on the level of around 40% to 70%. This shows that, our approach can improve the system utilization greatly, compared to both FCFS + Backfilling strategy and current strategy used on Blue Waters.

However, when the scan window size is 100, there are some scheduling iterations where the utilization is down to around 40% to 50%, as shown in Fig. 9. This is due to the fact that the window size is small and the free bins in the system are not fully filled. Based on this, we conclude that, large window size leads to a better system utilization. However, despite these short periods of low utilization, in most time of scheduling cycles, our approach still maintains a system utilization of around 90% when scan window size is 100, which outperforms FCFS + Backfilling strategy and current strategy used on Blue Waters. The source code of our approach is open to community [1].

6   Related Work

To improve the task placement of applications with 2D, 3D and 4D Cartesian topologies and nearest-neighbor communication, a Topaware tool can be used [7]. There are tools such as Caypat for profiling an MPI application and to detect Cartesian grid communication patterns. This information can be used to provide runtime mapping of processes to the computing nodes using MPICH node ordering. The Topaware method requires the user to specify the required number of nodes along each torus dimension and finds the ordering by allocating nodes on subsequent XZ planes, taking into account the gaps resulting from service nodes. For mapping the 2D virtual topology to the 3D torus, a folding method is used. Topaware was evaluated using the WRF, VPIC, S3D and MILC applications.

An overview process of mapping techniques and algorithms [13] for HPC systems is presented in [8]. It discusses algorithmic strategies for topology mapping, such as graph partitioning, mapping enforcement techniques (resource binding and rank reordering), as well as existing solutions and their implementations. This provides a formal definition of the mapping as an optimization problem, and discusses the metrics such as dilation or congestion.

One of the reasons for system fragmentation lies in the discrepancy in job length/execution time, which leads to a irregular hole/fragmentation between neighbouring jobs with different finish time. In order to tackle this type of fragmentation, a walltime-aware scheduling strategy is designed in [14], which packs jobs with similar length and places them near to each other. In particular, two algorithms are developed: similar-length allocation and paired job filling. The similar length allocation algorithm tries to match waiting jobs with running jobs that share similar completion time. The paired job filling algorithm selects two jobs with the same size and similar length from the queue and schedules both jobs together. Notably, paired job filling algorithm is similar to our scheduling strategy, where multiple waiting jobs in the queue are grouped and placed together to reduce potential fragmentation.

Migration is an efficient resource management tool, which has been discussed in [9–11]. In [9], the authors present the analysis and application of scheduling algorithms that augment a baseline first come first serve (FCFS) scheduler. The author presents simulation results for migration and backfilling techniques on BlueGene/L. These techniques are explored individually and jointly to determine their impact on the system. An efficient Projection Of Partitions (POP) algorithm for determining the size of the largest free rectangular partition in a toroidal system is developed. The results demonstrate that migration may be effective for a pure FCFS scheduler, but that backfilling produces even more benefits. It is also shown that migration may be combined with backfilling to produce more opportunities to better utilize a parallel machine.

7   Conclusions and Future Work

In this paper, we addressed the problem of improving system utilization and scheduling efficiency on Blue Waters system that uses a 3D torus topology. To improve the scheduling efficiency, we propose an efficient free partition detection method. To improve the system utilization, we first propose a job scheduling strategy based on proactive queue and system scanning. After that, we model the job placement problem into a multiple knapsack model and design a migration-based job placement algorithm to give a heuristic solution. The simulations of modeled trace data demonstrate that our approach works well in terms of improving system utilization. In our future work, we will extend our study on reducing system fragmentation and improving system utilization. In particular, we will focus on improving system's capability to directly accept the incoming large and extra-large jobs. We will investigate various strategies such as relaxing priority order and migration to avoid the system drainage caused by the incoming large and extra-large jobs and to maintain system utilization without the backfilling process.

References

1. https://github.com/kangkangkenli/2016-jsspp-tas
2. Ajima, Y., Takagi, Y., Inoue, T., Hiramoto, S., Shimizu, T.: The tofu interconnect. In: 2011 IEEE 19th Annual Symposium on High Performance Interconnects, pp. 87–94. IEEE, August 2011
3. Chang, C., Mohapatra, P.: Performance improvement of allocation schemes for mesh-connected computers. J. Parallel Distrib. Comput. **52**(1), 40–68 (1998)
4. Chiu, G.-M., Chen, S.-K.: An efficient submesh allocation scheme for two-dimensional meshes with little overhead. IEEE Trans. Parallel Distrib. Syst. **10**(5), 471–486 (1999)
5. Ding, J., Bhuyan, L.N.: An adaptive submesh allocation strategy for two-dimensional mesh connected systems. In: International Conference on Parallel Processing, ICPP 1993, vol. 2, pp. 193–200, August 1993
6. Enos, J., Bauer, G., Brunner, R., Islam, S.: Topology-aware job scheduling strategies for torus networks. In: Proceedings of the Cray User Group Meeting (2014)
7. Fiedler, R., Whalen, S.: Improving task placement for applications with 2D, 3D, and 4D virtual Cartesian topologies on 3D torus networks with service nodes. In: Proceedings of Cray User's Group (2013)
8. Hoefler, T., Jeannot, E., Mercier, G.: An overview of process mapping techniques and algorithms in high-performance computing. In: Jeannot, E., Zilinskas, J. (eds.) High Performance Computing on Complex Environments, pp. 75–94. Wiley, June 2014
9. Krevat, E.: Scheduling Algorithms to Improve Utilization in Toroidal Interconnected Systems. Ph.D. thesis (2003)
10. Li, K., Zheng, H., Wu, J.: Migration-based virtual machine placement in cloud systems. In: 2013 IEEE 2nd International Conference on Cloud Networking (CloudNet), pp. 83–90. IEEE (2013)
11. Li, K., Zheng, H., Jie, W., Xiaojiang, D.: Virtual machine placement in cloud systems through migration process. Int. J. Parallel Emergent Distrib. Syst. **30**(5), 393–410 (2015)

12. Lo, V., Windisch, K.J., Liu, W., Nitzberg, B.: Noncontiguous processor allocation algorithms for mesh-connected multicomputers. IEEE Trans. Parallel Distrib. Syst. **8**(7), 712–726 (1997)
13. Mansour, N., Ponnusamy, R., Choudhary, A., Fox, G.C.: Graph contraction for physical optimization methods: a quality-cost tradeoff for mapping data on parallel computers. In: Proceedings of the 7th International Conference on Supercomputing, ICS 1993, pp. 1–10. ACM, New York (1993)
14. Tang, W., Lan, Z., Desai, N., Buettner, D., Yu, Y.: Reducing fragmentation on torus-connected supercomputers. In: Proceedings of the 2011 IEEE International Parallel & Distributed Processing Symposium, IPDPS 2011, pp. 828–839. IEEE Computer Society, Washington, DC (2011)
15. Zhou, Z., Yang, X., Lan, Z., Rich, P., Tang, W., Morozov, V., Desai, N.: Improving batch scheduling on blue Gene/Q by relaxing 5D torus network allocation constraints. In: IPDPS 2015 (2015)

Analyzing the Performance of Allocation Strategies Based on Space-Filling Curves

Jose A. Pascual[1]($\boxtimes$), Jose A. Lozano[1,2], and Jose Miguel-Alonso[1]

[1] Intelligent Systems Group (ISG),
University of the Basque Country UPV/EHU, Donostia-San Sebastian, Spain
{joseantonio.pascual,ja.lozano,j.miguel}@ehu.eus
[2] Basque Center for Applied Mathematics (BCAM), Bilbao, Spain

Abstract. Future exascale supercomputers will be composed of thousands of nodes. In those massive systems, the search for physically close nodes will become essential to deliver an optimal environment to execute parallel applications. Schedulers manage those resources, shared by many users and jobs, searching for partitions in which jobs will run. Significant effort has been devoted to develop allocation strategies that maximize system utilization, while providing partitions that are adequate for the communication demands of applications. In this paper we evaluate a class of strategies based on space-filling curves (SFCs) that search for partitions in which nodes are physically close, compared to other alternatives that relax this requirement (e.g. non-contiguous), or make it even more strict (e.g. contiguous). Several metrics are used to assess the quality of an allocation strategy, some based on system utilization, some others measuring the quality of the resulting partitions. Contiguous allocators suffer from severe degradation in terms of system utilization, while non-contiguous allocators provide inadequate partitions. Somewhere in the middle, SFC allocators offer good system utilization while using quite compact partitions. The final metric to decide which allocator is the best depend on the severity of the slowdown suffered by applications when running in non-optimal partitions.

Keywords: Space-filling Curves · Scheduling · Allocation · Partitioning · Contiguity · Non-contiguity

1 Introduction

In the coming years, supercomputer vendors will deliver massive exascale systems with many thousands of nodes (millions of computing cores) to execute parallel jobs (applications). These jobs are composed of tasks that communicate among them using an underlying fabric: an interconnection network (IN) which determines the way compute nodes are connected.

J.A. Pascual is currently with the APT group in The University of Manchester.

© Springer International Publishing AG 2017
N. Desai and W. Cirne (Eds.): JSSPP 2015/2016, LNCS 10353, pp. 232–251, 2017.
DOI: 10.1007/978-3-319-61756-5_13

Most supercomputers are shared by many users, who request the execution of jobs through a submission queue. The *scheduler* is in charge of selecting the job or jobs to run, following a given policy. The most common scheduling policies are First Come First Serve (FCFS) [6] and Backfilling [6]. Often, several jobs can fit in the system simultaneously, as the size of a job is normally smaller than the size of the complete system (in terms of compute cores).

Once a job is selected, an *allocator* must find a set of free nodes (a partition) and perform the mapping of job tasks onto system nodes. An allocation strategy is used to carry out the search. We can differentiate two broad classes of strategies. *Contiguous* strategies look for convex sets of free nodes, normally with hyper-rectangular shapes. *Non-contiguous* strategies remove this shape restriction. Contiguous strategies try to reduce the execution time of jobs, as they allocate partitions with very low inter-node distance, and free of interference from other partitions in which other jobs run. However, they can cause *internal fragmentation*, as they normally reserve for a job a set of nodes larger than the number of job's tasks. *External fragmentation* is also common, when enough nodes are available to run a job, but they are not arranged with the required shape. Thus, the price of contiguity is a low level of system utilization. For this reason, non-contiguous strategies were developed [15,16,26]: jobs *may* run in sub-optimal conditions, as inter-node distances are longer and communications overlap (jobs are not isolated), but fragmentation is minimized (system utilization is greatly improved) and, at the end, the overall system performance in terms of throughput of jobs *should* be improved. Therefore, different allocation strategies search for different trade-offs between job performance vs. system utilization. Achieved job throughput depends on both factors. These issues, internal and external fragmentation, appear in the Blue Waters supercomputer as reported in [14].

An issue that should not be ignored is the impact, in terms of performance, of the way job tasks are mapped onto the nodes of the allocated partition [3,19,20]. The benefits of contiguous strategies are maximized only with good mappings that optimize the inter-application communications [18]. Mappings in which tasks are not physically close, and need to contend for channels with messages of other jobs, are the reason behind the reduced performance of non-contiguous allocation strategies.

We consider in this paper another class of allocation strategies that fit somewhere in the middle between contiguous and non-contiguous as defined above, and are based on Space-filling Curves (SFC) [13]. These SFC strategies "see" the supercomputer as a linear list of nodes, and perform contiguous allocation in this 1D space. Therefore, partitions are sub-lists of consecutive nodes [9,13]. Then 1D lists are mapped onto a higher-dimensional space, in a way that depends on the selected space-filling curve [1,11]. These mappings do not guarantee that the resulting partition in the nD space is consecutive and convex. However, they are designed to keep *locality* between nodes: they are physically close. Compared to pure contiguous mappings, SFC mappings are better in terms of utilization, as internal fragmentation does not occur (the allocator can always search for a

1D list with the required number of nodes) and external fragmentation is less severe. It remains to be verified if the locality guaranteed by SFC allocation is good enough to provide a good execution environment for parallel jobs, matching (or getting close to) that of contiguous allocation.

In summary, in this paper we evaluate how SFC-based allocations trade-off per-partition benefits (locality, isolation) with system-wide benefits (mainly, utilization), when used in supercomputers built around interconnection networks with nD-mesh shapes. To provide a context, we compare them with a convex, contiguous strategy and with a non-contiguous strategy. For this study we use a diverse collection of metrics. Some are indicators of the quality of the partitions, hinting how well applications would run on them. Others measure the performance of the system-wide scheduling process. The evaluation of all the strategies has been performed using simulation, fed with a large collection of workloads generated synthetically. Our experiments verify the intuitions outlined in this introduction, showing how non-contiguous and SFC based strategies perform very well in terms of system utilization but, for other metrics that consider fitness of partitions to applications, contiguous allocation is better. In order to provide an answer to the question "which strategy is the best in terms of job throughput?", we only provide a partial answer: it depends on the behavior of the applications that constitute the workload, when executed in differently shaped partitions.

The rest of the paper is organized as follows. Section 2 describes the metrics used to compare allocation strategies. In Sect. 3 we describe the SFC strategy. In Sect. 4 we describe more formally the scheduling, allocation and search strategies under evaluation. The workloads used in the experiments are described in Sect. 5, where we provide additional details about the experimentation set-up. In Sect. 6 we discuss system-wide results of the different strategies, and we continue in Sect. 7 with an analysis of the quality of the delivered partitions. Section 8 is devoted to the search of a trade-off between application slowdown (due to the use of non-optimal partitions) and system utilization. Section 9 closes the paper with some conclusions and future lines of research.

2   Performance Metrics

We measure allocation strategies using two groups of metrics, the first focused on system utilization, and the second focused on the quality of the partitions.

2.1   Scheduling-Focused Metrics

– **Utilization** indicates the average ratio of active nodes during a measuring time of interest. A node is active if it has been allocated to a running job. Using only utilization to assess system-wide performance can be deceptive, as a strategy with low utilization but that allows faster execution of applications can result in better job throughput [23]. However, it is an excellent indicator of the overhead that results from the use of strategies that search for contiguity or locality.

– **Makespan:** It represents the total time required to process a given input workload. If we do not take into account the effects of partition shape on execution speed, as we do in our experiments, this metric also indicates the cost of looking for contiguity or locality.

Note that these two metrics are related with others not included here, such as **fragmentation** (internal and external). Higher degrees of fragmentation result in lower utilization, and longer makespan.

2.2 Partition-Focused Metrics

The metrics described here depend strongly on the characteristics (topology) of the underlying interconnection network. For the purpose of this evaluation, we focus on nD meshes (they could be easily extended to tori). Given a partition P (with an arbitrary shape, convex or not) composed of $S = |P|$ compute nodes of coordinates $\mathbf{a} = (a^1, \cdots, a^n)$, being n the number of dimensions of the network, and being $d(\mathbf{a_i}, \mathbf{a_j})$ the Manhattan distance (number of hops) between nodes $\mathbf{a_i}$ and $\mathbf{a_j}$ of the partition, we define the following metrics:

1. **Average pairwise distance (APD):** Average distance between all pairs of nodes in P.
$$APD = 2 \times \frac{\sum_{i=1}^{S} \sum_{j=i+1}^{S} d(\mathbf{a_i}, \mathbf{a_j})}{(S+1) \times S} \tag{1}$$

2. **Number of affected nodes:** Size of the area covered by the partition, thus the number of nodes that may be participating in the communications. If the partition is not convex, the affected area may include nodes assigned to other running applications.

$$NA = \prod_{i=1}^{n} \left(\max_{\mathbf{a} \in P}\{a^k\} - \min_{\mathbf{a} \in P}\{a^k\} + 1 \right) \tag{2}$$

where $\max_{\mathbf{a} \in P}\{a^k\}$ and $\min_{\mathbf{a} \in P}\{a^k\}$ are the maximal and minimal coordinates in the k-th dimension of all nodes $\mathbf{a}$ in the partition.

In Fig. 1 we have represented three partitions and the nodes that will be affected by the communications. As we can see, in the fist contiguous partition (Fig. 1a) all communications remain internal, without affecting neighboring jobs. The second and third non-contiguous partitions (Figs. 1b and c) show how the affected area extends outside the partition. In Fig. 1d, which represents the three partitions put together, we can see how the affected areas of the three partitions are overlapping.

Low values of APD are expected to correlate with reduced execution times of applications running in the partition. However, as explained in [21], this correlation is direct only if the application use an all-to-all communications pattern. The extent of which jobs benefit from good distance-related metrics depends strongly on the characteristics of the application and *the applied mapping*. Also,

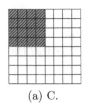

(a) C.

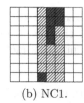

(b) NC1.

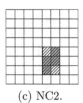

(c) NC2.

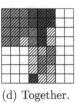

(d) Together.

Fig. 1. Nodes affected by the communications of three applications allocated contiguous and non-contiguously.

interference from other applications, that can be severe if all partitions have large numbers of affected nodes, have an important bearing on the performance of the communications [10]. The assessment of application run times falls outside the scope of this paper.

3   Space-Filling Curves

A space-filling curve (SFC) maps a one-dimensional list of points onto a nD hypervolume. The first of this kind of curves was discovered by Hilbert [7], but others have been developed such as the Z-order curve. The first version of the Hilbert curve performed only 1D to 2D mappings, but it was later extended to higher dimensions [2]. The Z-order curve was able to perform multi-dimensional mappings since the beginning.

The idea of using SFCs to map parallel jobs onto network nodes was first introduced in [15]. With this approach, network nodes are ordered using a *rank*. Allocation (search of partitions) is done in this 1D, rank-ordered list, instead of using, for example, the 2D coordinates. A 1D partition is afterwards mapped onto the actual nD space using the transformations defined by the chosen SFC. Two are the main advantages of these SFC allocation strategies: the search is simple, as it deals with 1D structures, and the resulting nD partitions are very compact, keeping high levels of locality. In Fig. 2 we have represented some examples of mappings from a 1D space to 2D and 3D spaces, using the two different SFCs. In the upper side of the figure, we show the consecutive sets of nodes (partitions) resulted from a 1D allocation. Below we see the same partitions when mapped to 2D and 3D, using the Z-order curve (left) and the Hilbert curve (right). Next we explain how these mappings are performed.

- The **Z-order curve** [17] is a function that maps multi-dimensional points by interleaving the binary representation of their coordinate values. For example, the point (2,4) in 2D would be mapped to the point (1D) with z value 010-100 (010100). The use of this curve preserves locality between points, but does not guarantee contiguity.
- The **Hilbert curve** is a function that traverses the polyhedron vertices of an n-dimensional hypercube in Gray code order [25]. For example, in 2D the sequence of gray codes (0,0), (0,1), (1,1), (1,0) corresponds to the 1D points: 0, 1, 3, 2. This curve preserves the contiguity and locality between the nodes.

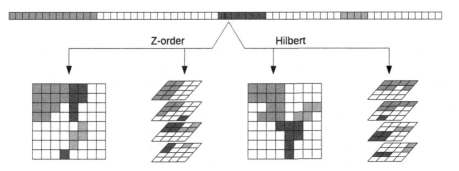

Fig. 2. Mappings of 1D consecutive partitions onto 2D and 3D spaces using Z-order and Hilbert space filling curves.

Table 1. Locality, expressed as APD, for five sets of partitions that are consecutive in 1D and then mapped to nD using the Z-order curve (Z) and the Hilbert curve (H). The higher the set identifier, the smaller the average size of the partitions within.

	1D	2D		3D		4D		5D		6D	
	-	Z	H	Z	H	Z	H	Z	H	Z	H
Set 1	337.24	27.58	22.08	12.35	10.40	8.69	7.64	7.42	6.45	6.55	6.00
Set 2	148.81	19.51	14.50	9.54	7.47	7.18	5.97	6.20	5.14	5.65	4.88
Set 3	81.02	13.97	10.73	7.89	6.26	6.15	5.04	5.42	4.62	5.04	4.34
Set 4	48.70	12.28	8.66	7.13	5.46	5.59	4.57	5.03	4.22	4.70	3.93
Set 5	21.88	7.01	5.55	4.73	3.92	3.98	3.42	3.70	3.20	3.54	3.07

The objective of SFC allocation strategies is to obtain nD partitions with good locality (to benefit inter-task communications in the interconnection network). This locality has been evaluated in [13,24] for 2D and 3D networks. Now we extend this study to higher dimensions. We have measured the locality achieved by both curves when mapping to 2D (64×64), 3D ($16 \times 16 \times 16$), 4D ($8 \times 8 \times 8 \times 8$), 5D ($4 \times 4 \times 4 \times 4 \times 4$) and 6D ($4 \times 4 \times 4 \times 4 \times 4 \times 4$) meshes. We generated five sets of 1D contiguous partitions, labeling each set as k=1..5. Each set k contains thirty partitions of different sizes, being the maximum size $\frac{4096}{2^k}$. This means that Set 1 contains much larger partitions than Set 5.

We first calculated the locality of these 1D sets in terms of APD. Next we did the same after the mapping to nD, using both Z-order and Hilbert curves. Results are summarized in Table 1. It is clear that locality in the mapped partitions increases with the number of dimensions in the IN. This is due to the increased degree of the network nodes. The results also indicate that the Hilbert curve preserves locality better than the Z-order curve, mapping the points to closer locations, for any number of dimensions. Note that these are static experiments, that neither consider the complete scheduling process nor the way locality affects job's run times. We will explore these issues later in this paper. We want to remark that Hilbert-based allocation is used in the SLURM scheduler [12].

4   Scheduling Policies and Allocation Algorithms

In this section we further explore the scheduling process, with focus on allocations algorithms. Scheduling consists of determining which queued job (submitted by a user) will be selected for execution. This is carried out following a established policy [6] such as FCFS, backfilling, Shortest Job First (SJF), etc. The most used policy is backfilling, which tries to avoid a "head-of-line blocking" problem of FCFS. While FCFS selects the jobs in strictly order of arrival, backfilling allows to advance jobs when the job at the head of the queue cannot be executed because the necessary resources are not available. However, a job is allowed to be advanced only when its execution is not expected to delay the starting time of the job at the head of the queue. A requisite to implement backfilling is, thus, an estimation of the run time for the jobs. Normally, users are expected to provide this estimation. Backfilling improves system utilization while respecting submission order.

Once a job has been selected, the allocator is in charge of reserving the set of nodes onto which the tasks of the job will be mapped. In this work we consider contiguous strategies, non-contiguous strategies, and SFC-based strategies.

4.1   Contiguous Allocation with Hyper-rectangular Partitions

These kind of strategies look for convex partitions with shapes $a \times b$, $a \times b \times c$, $a \times b \times c \times d$, etc. depending on the dimensionality of the underlying IN. These partitions result in optimal values of distance-related metrics. Furthermore, they provide a very desirable property: isolation. This means that partitions do not overlap, and inter-task communications in a job are implemented in the IN without requiring the intervention of nodes in other partitions. In other words, communications in different partitions do not interfere. Both properties together make this kind of partitions the optimal place to execute communication-intensive parallel applications – the ones expected to run in a supercomputer [20,23]. However, looking for contiguous partitions is not cheap (due to external fragmentation), and the overall system utilization is drastically reduced (when compared with other alternatives).

Searching for a partition of a particular shape requires traversing the system (a data structure representing it) in a particular order. The First-Fit (FF) policy stops the search as soon as the suitable partition has been found – or when the search ends unsuccessfully. In this work we use a search algorithm that implements this policy, called Improved First Fit (IFF) [22]. It searches for hyper-rectangles in multi-dimensional cube networks.

4.2   Allocation Strategies Based on Space-Filling Curves

These strategies are contiguous and consecutive in the 1D representation of the system, but result in non-convex shapes when mapped to higher dimensions. However, as shown in the previous section, they result in partitions with high levels of locality: good values in terms of distance-related metrics. These values are not as good as those provided by the contiguous strategy, and resulting partitions (communications) do overlap. The achieved benefit of SFC allocation comes in terms of high levels of system utilization.

The search of partitions can be done using First Fit (FF), Best Fit (BF) or other strategy. We consider in this work:

- Strategies based on Z-order curves, searching with FF (ZORD-FF) and BF (ZORD-BF). Note that these strategies take into account locality, but may result in non-contiguous, non-convex partitions.
- Strategies based on Hilbert curves, searching with FF (HILB-FF) and BF (HILB-BF). The resulting partitions are contiguous, but convexity is not guaranteed.

4.3   Non-contiguous Strategy

We have also evaluated a simple, non-contiguous allocation strategy with FF search (NC-FF). It looks for free nodes using the node identifier, without any special consideration. We will see that it results in excellent results in terms of utilization, but bad per-partition, distance-related metrics.

4.4   Mapping Tasks onto Partitions

We insist in this point: once the scheduler has a job (collection of tasks) and a partition (collection of nodes), it is necessary to map tasks onto nodes. This stage has a huge impact on the performance of applications [3,20], but evaluating this effect would be very costly and is beyond the scope of this paper. We leave this as future work, and we use here a simple, consecutive mapping strategy: tasks are assigned to nodes consecutively using their identifiers.

5   Experimental Set-Up and Workloads

In this section we describe the simulation-based evaluation environment used in this work. A fundamental part of experiments with simulators is the collection of workloads used to feed them. Thus, we start describing the workloads.

5.1   Workloads

We have used several, synthetically-generated, *workloads*. A workload is defined as a sequence of (parallel) jobs submitted to the system, and includes the following per-job pieces of information:

1. **Size:** The number of nodes requested to run the job.
2. **Shape:** If the scheduler uses a contiguous allocation strategy, then the shape of the requested hyper-rectangle must be supplied. If not specified, the scheduler use the job size and generate a valid hyper-rectangle. Note that if size and shape do not match in terms of number of nodes, there will be internal fragmentation.

3. **Duration:** This value must be provided as part of the workload because we are simulating only the scheduling mechanisms – but it should be the result of the execution of the job in the assigned partition. Thus, for the experiments reported in this work, it simply matches the estimated run time, and does not reflect any effect of the partitioning (and mapping) strategies on execution time.
4. **Estimated run time:** Required when using a scheduler implementing backfilling. In this evaluation, we assume that this time is the real execution time (duration).

As we can seen, we do not include in the workload the arrival time of jobs. We consider a situation of maximum input load in which all jobs arrive simultaneously *but ordered* to the waiting queue, thus emulating a production system in which there are always several jobs awaiting. This is to avoid situations of low system utilization due to an empty queue. It also provides a meaning to the makespan metric: the time to consume the full workload.

We use beta distributions with different parameters to generate sizes and/or shapes. The generation of hyper-rectangles is not trivial because, for a given job size, several shapes can be valid to contain it. For example, 16 nodes can be arranged as a 4×4 or 8×2 [23]. Moreover, some sizes such as 7 can only be arranged contiguously as a 7×1 partition if internal fragmentation is not allowed. Considering this fact, we have defined two different types of workloads (Fig. 3):

- **Unshaped workloads:** The workload includes job sizes, but does not specify shapes. The contiguous scheduler generates a valid shape automatically, as the smallest nD cube (shaped $a \times a \times ... \times a$) able to host the job, where n matches the dimensionality of the IN. Using this criterion, partitions are symmetrical and compact, but internal fragmentation may be severe.
- **Shaped workloads:** The workload includes a per-job shape specification, and the job size is just the number of nodes in this shape. Thus, there is not internal fragmentation. This is assumed to be the best way of running applications, as the user has selected a shape that, supposedly, optimizes inter-task communications.

For each type of workload we have generated three sets of 150 jobs, using in each of them a different average job size: small (S), medium (M) and large (L). This has been carried out limiting the maximum size that a partition can have. The resulting size distributions are represented in Figs. 3a and b respectively. Finally the duration of the jobs must be generated. In this case we generate 10 different durations for a job. Considering all together, we have managed 2 types $\times 3$ average sizes $\times 10$ durations $= 60$ workloads of 150 jobs each.

5.2   Experimental Set-Up

We have analyzed the different schedulers using an in-house developed scheduling simulator that takes as input parameters a workload, a scheduling policy (such as

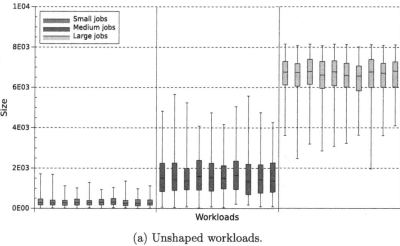

(a) Unshaped workloads.

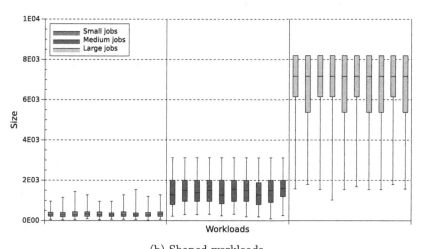

(b) Shaped workloads.

Fig. 3. Boxplot of the two types of workloads used to evaluate allocation strategies. Each type is composed of three sets (large, medium and small) of 10 workloads each. The figure shows the minimum, the maximum, the median and the fist and third quartile.

FCFS or backfilling), an allocation strategy (contiguous, non-contiguous, SFC-based, etc.) and, if required by the experiment, a slow-down factor to be applied to the duration of the jobs specified in the input workload. We will see later the usefulness of this parameter. The simulator's output reports in a set of metrics, including those explained in Sect. 2.

In all the experiments we use an implementation of backfilling called "conservative" [6]. Then we consider six different allocation strategies and the 60 workloads defined above. Reported results are averages of the metrics obtained for the 10 sets of job durations.

As underlying INs we consider a 3D ($32 \times 32 \times 32$) and 5D ($8 \times 8 \times 8 \times 8 \times 8$) mesh, both with 32768 nodes. These dimensions have been chosen because they are used by supercomputers currently operational i.e. Blue Gene P (3D) [8], Blue Gene/Q [4] from IBM, Cray systems with the 3D Gemini interconnect [5], etc. We evaluated both meshes and tori but, as the main results are not significantly different, and for the sake of brevity, we only report results with meshes.

6   Analyzing System-Wide Results

Experiments were designed to understand to what extent the search of contiguity or locality has a bearing on system utilization and makespan. In Fig. 4 we have represented the results (utilization and makespan) obtained for the different simulation configurations and workloads. Note that ZORD-FF and HILB-FF are represented together as SFC-FF, because they yield identical results (the same applies to ZORD-BF and HILB-BF, summarized as SFC-BF). This is a direct consequence of the use of the same search strategy over the same 1D space, and the topology of the IN is irrelevant – differences will appear when evaluating the resulting nD partitions. Results labeled as NC-FF correspond to the non-contiguous strategy and, again, do not depend on the IN topology. CONT3D and CONT5D correspond to the contiguous strategy in the 3D and the 5D mesh respectively.

Let us start focusing on unshaped workloads: those in which the user specifies only a job size. The contiguous scheduler tries to find a nD rectangular partition for it. This process is expected to hurt performance severely, particularly for high values of n, due to the effects of internal fragmentation. Results, summarized in Fig. 4 show this effect very clearly. Utilization with hyper-rectangular partitions is, in general, very poor, being negatively affected by the dimensionality of the IN and the average job size. The first factor determines the internal fragmentation, and the second has a bearing on external fragmentation. Makespan values confirm these findings. They are longer for workloads with larger average job size, because each job requires more resources and, thus, fewer jobs can run simultaneously.

At the other end of the spectrum, NC-FF yields excellent results, independently of the underlying topology. When we relax all kinds of shape or locality expectations in the partitions, the probability of finding a free set of nodes fitting a job request is drastically increased. This is especially noticeable when dealing with medium to large jobs.

Locality aware, SFC-based strategies show excellent results, close to those of NC-FF for small jobs, although slightly worse for larger jobs. The search strategy does not play a significant role, with FF and BF search performing similarly. Thus, the increased cost of the exhaustive search done by BF does not provide any benefit.

Finding specific shapes is more costly than finding arbitrary node sets, and result in higher levels of external fragmentation. We have not measured this

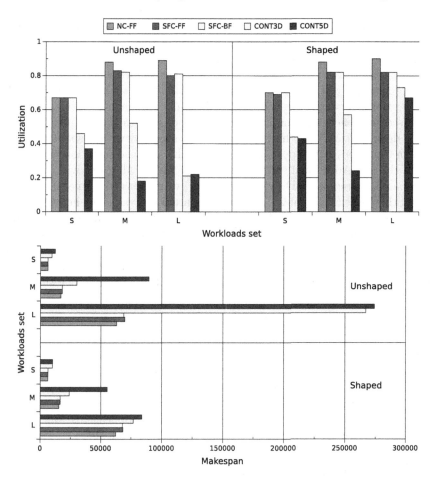

Fig. 4. Representation of the utilization and makespan obtained by the allocation strategies using both unshaped and shaped workloads and both 3D and 5D networks.

Table 2. Number of allocation failures due to external fragmentation: enough free nodes are available, but not in the required arrangement.

	CONT3D			CONT5D			SFC-FF			SFC-BF		
Workloads	S	M	L	S	M	L	S	M	L	S	M	L
Shaped	4649.80	10356.10	11870.20	7085.60	10791.00	11852.50	94.20	580.8	257.30	79.90	432.80	198.70
Unshaped	4575.50	9835.80	2956.50	5026.00	10656.20	3706.00	126.20	1071.70	194.90	102.10	885.70	161.70

effect (fragmentation), but have characterized this cost by measuring how often the scheduler tries to find a partition for a job, and fails. Results are summarized in Table 2. Remember that a workload has 150 jobs. Clearly, the CONT3D and CONT5D schedulers work much harder than the others and fail too often. Not because the required nodes are not there, but because they are not arranged as requested. SFC alternatives have an easier job, as shape restrictions are limited to consecutiveness in a 1D space. The NC-FF strategy fails only when free consecutive nodes are not enough to match the size of the selected job.

The user submitting the job may know the best partition shape to run an application, and we try to reflect this fact with the shaped workloads. The contiguous scheduler will honor the request, searching for the specified shape. In contrast, the non-contiguous scheduler will ignore this request totally, and the SFC-based schedulers will simply look for a set of physically close nodes matching the desired size. Note that, when jobs are specified with a shape, internal fragmentation does not appear, as the size of the assigned partition will be the same of the job. Additionally, note that the contiguous allocator will not necessarily search for regular, nD hyper-rectangles (where n is the dimensionality of the IN): they user may request a 2D, planar partition, even if the network is 5D.

Results with these workloads are also summarized in Fig. 4. Note that, without the effect of internal fragmentation, the main factor affecting utilization is external fragmentation (not finding the requested shape). The relative performance of NC-FF against SFC-based schedulers remain, as both ignore the requested shapes. However, contiguous strategies offer much better results.

7   Analysis of the Quality of the Partitions

Utilization metrics tell us only partial information about the performance of a supercomputer - scheduler combination. Utilization may be low but, if applications run faster, at the end of the day the supercomputer is more productive. With the experiments carried out we cannot verify if SFC based strategies are adequate to run communication-intensive parallel applications. But we can obtain some metrics that can be used as indicators of that adequacy, see Sect. 2.2.

7.1   Average Pairwise Distance

A low value of APD for a partition indicates how compact that partition is. Communications will use short paths, thus (presumably) benefiting communication-intensive applications. We have summarized in Table 3 averages of these metrics for the partitions used by the different schedulers, for both 3D and 5D (mesh-shaped) INs. In all cases, partitions have better (lower) APD in 5D meshes than in 3D meshes. This is due to the topological characteristics of the IN, with higher degree for 5D, that results in shorter distances. Thus, this fact does not require further discussion.

When job requests are unshaped, the cubic partitions used by the contiguous scheduler are very compact, being this allocation strategy the absolute winner. Partitions used by SFC-based allocators are very good, with Hilbert generating partitions almost as compact as the cubes. Non-contiguous partitions exhibit very poor distance-based metrics.

Results for the workload with shaped job requests may be misleading. In general, the distance-based metrics obtained for all strategies except the contiguous are the same seen for unshaped workloads, see again Table 3, as those strategies

Table 3. Average pairwise distance of the partitions found by the allocation algorithms. These results were obtained using two sets of workloads (see Sect. 5) simulated into two cube-shaped network topologies (3D and 5D).

	Unshaped workloads						Shaped workloads					
	3D			5D			3D			5D		
	S	M	L	S	M	L	S	M	L	S	M	L
CONT	**6.56**	**11.34**	**18.80**	**4.77**	**6.88**	**9.54**	9.42	14.37	21.96	**4.80**	**6.76**	**9.94**
HILB-FF	7.10	12.35	20.30	5.02	7.21	10.26	**7.33**	**12.16**	**20.04**	5.15	7.10	10.15
ZORD-FF	9.08	14.88	23.64	5.92	8.29	11.07	9.34	14.79	22.68	6.07	8.27	10.80
HILB-BF	7.09	12.37	20.32	5.01	7.21	10.26	**7.32**	**12.11**	**20.05**	5.15	7.09	10.15
ZORD-BF	9.03	15.05	23.76	5.89	8.36	11.09	9.34	14.71	22.72	6.07	8.23	10.81
NC-FF	21.91	24.86	26.56	9.79	11.04	11.71	22.46	25.19	27.06	9.94	11.2	11.82

ignore the shape request. This is not the case when the partitions are contiguous. In fact, in the 3D mesh, the Hilbert-based SFC allocator provides "better" partitions than those used by the contiguous allocator. In the description of the workloads provided in Sect. 5, we clearly stated that it is assumed that the user submitting a job will choose the *best* partition shape for it. It may happen that the requested shape is not the same of the underlying IN. For example, a job of size 1024 may request specifically a planar 32×32 partition, that fit perfectly in a plane of the 3D network. If the scheduler does not honor the shape request, it could be assigned to a partition with a 3D shape of size $11 \times 11 \times 11$ (exactly or approximately) with excellent distance metrics but that may not allow optimal inter-task communications. This happens when the *virtual topology* of the application differs from the *physical topology* of the partition [20]. As the Hilbert-based allocator ignores shape requests, prioritizing compactness, this strategy is the best performer in terms of distance-based metrics for 3D networks. For 5D networks, the high degree of the topology shortens the distance-related metrics for all strategies, making this effect less visible.

After seeing these results, we wonder if APD can be considered as a real indicator of performance. As explained in [21], the answer is a clear "no", because a partition is good only if, after the mapping, it matches the communication demands of the application, and APD does reflect this fact. Furthermore, we should not ignore a side-effect of sharing a supercomputer: the possible interference between applications running simultaneously. However, in general, SFC based strategies will provide compact partitions to execute parallel jobs.

7.2   Nodes Affected Metric

The nodes affected metric tries to reflect the degree of isolation of the partitions. Low values (identical or close to the size of the partition) are indicators of very isolated partitions that share few or none network resources (routers, links) with other partitions. Larger values evidence partitions that require the use of resources "belonging" to neighboring partitions. It is well known that isolation is highly beneficial for parallel jobs [10, 18, 20, 23].

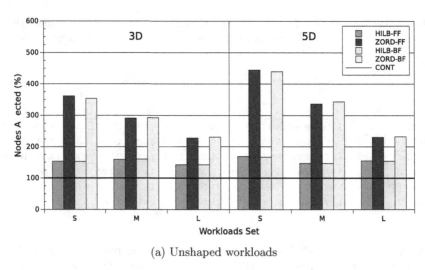

(a) Unshaped workloads

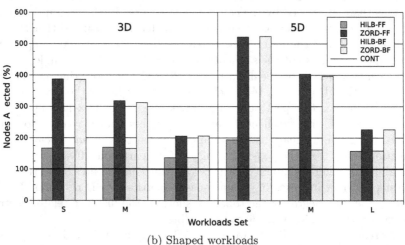

(b) Shaped workloads

Fig. 5. % of nodes affected by the partitions obtained by the allocation strategies. Results are normalized, being 100% the result achieved by the CONT strategy.

In Fig. 5 we have summarized the results of this metric for the partitions used by the different allocators. They are normalized, being the 100% the results achieved by the contiguous allocator (that guarantees isolation). The NC-FF strategy uses partitions that cover almost the whole IN and, thus, the corresponding numbers would distort the figure. For this reason, they have not been included.

When job requests do not specify shape, SFC-based partitions result in larger numbers of affected nodes, compared to the minimum provided by the cubic partitions (see Fig. 5a). In particular, the Hilbert mappings have on average

50% more nodes. As an example, this means that a job of size 7000 (a typical size in the large workload) may be interfering with around 3500 nodes belonging to other applications. The Z-curve mapping is considerably worse, with affected areas 125–350% larger than those corresponding to cubic partitions. Noticeably, this excess area is smaller for larger jobs, and larger for 5D networks than for 3D networks. When dealing with specified shapes, results show a similar pattern, but are slightly worse for SFC-based allocators, see Fig. 5b.

In summary, Hilbert-based allocators do a decent job guaranteeing compact and relatively isolated partitions, in addition to provide network utilization values close to those achieved with the non-contiguous allocator. The latter is the winner in terms of utilization, but the cost to pay is the use of scattered partitions with large distances between nodes and intense interference. At the other end, the contiguous allocator provide the best execution environment for applications, but result in severe fragmentation.

8 Trading Off Costs and Benefits of Allocation Strategies

Without a detailed study of the applications executed by the jobs, and the strategies used to map tasks to nodes, it is simply not possible to make a definite statement about which allocator is the best one. We need to know if applications running in nicely isolated, contiguous partitions do actually execute faster than in scattered partitions. We have evidence that, in fact, they do [18,20,23], but the degree of improvement depends greatly on the particular application – actually, application set – that conform the workloads. We can take for granted, given the measurements included in the previous sections, that SFC-based allocators based on the Hilbert curve should be preferred to NC-FF, as it yields similar utilization levels while providing much more compact partitions.

It is not clear, though, under which circumstances the contiguous allocator *could* be the one of choice. Here we explore this issue. Let t be the average job duration in the contiguous and isolated partitions provided by CONT. Let s be the average slowdown experienced by the same jobs when running in SFC-based partitions that do not guarantee those properties. Thus, the average job duration with HILB-FF would be $t \times s$. Note that we are assuming that $s > 1$.

Similarly, let U_H be the utilization of the system with HILB-FF, and U_C the utilization with CONT. Now, we are assuming that $U_H > U_C$.

As our workload has w jobs of size n, its total computational demand (use of resources) is $D_C = (w \times n \times t)$ for CONT, and $D_H = (w \times n \times (t \times s))$ for HILB-FF. The makespan for the workload can be computed as its computational demand divided by the achieved system utilization (actually, utilization U is computed as (D/M)). Thus $M_C = (D_C/U_C)$ and $M_H = (D_H/U_H)$.

Now we are ready to state that HILB-FF is *the preferred choice* over CONT if its makespan for the applied workload is shorter, that is, when $M_H < M_C$. This can be expanded as:

$$\frac{w \times n \times t \times s}{U_H} < \frac{w \times n \times t}{U_C} \qquad (3)$$

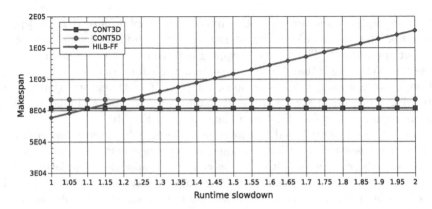

Fig. 6. Makespan of CONT3D, CONT5D and HILB-FF for different slowdown factors.

The inequality can be simplified, expressing it as:

$$\frac{s}{U_H} < \frac{1}{U_C} \tag{4}$$

Therefore, to make a good choice of allocator we need to know its utilization result (that depends mainly on the allocation strategy and the characteristics of the network and, thus, is application-agnostic) and the average slowdown experienced by applications (which can vary drastically with the specifics of the applications forming the workload).

Equations 3 and 4 can be transformed to obtain answers to this question: which values of slowdown are acceptable for an allocator (compared to CONT) that compensate an increase in per-job run time with a higher utilization and, therefore, a shorter makespan? We have represented this in Fig. 6. The horizontal lines represents the baseline makespans for CONT, which are different for 3D and 5D. The raising line corresponds to the makespans achievable by HILB-FF for different values of slowdown s. These values correspond to the shaped, large workload described before, but the trend is exactly the same for other workloads.

The crossing point is at $s = 1.1$ for 3D meshes. This means that when applications need on average less than 10% extra time to end when running on HILB-FF generated partitions, then HILB-FF is a good choice of allocator. However, for higher degrees of slowdown, the CONT allocator is the best choice, consuming the workload faster even without fully utilizing all the resources available. For 5D meshes the crossing point is higher, at $s = 1.2$, or 20% allowed slowdown for HILB-FF. This is because of the large penalty to pay in terms of fragmentation when using networks of high dimensionality. An exhaustive exploration of the actual values of s for different, realistic workloads is left as future work. Some preliminary work carried out in [18,23] shows that for some applications we can expect values of s exceeding 3.

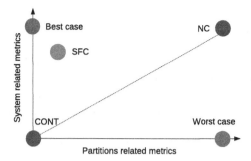

Fig. 7. Visual representation of the relative advantages of different allocation strategies, based on system-level and partition-related metrics.

9   Conclusions and Future Work

In this work we have evaluated the quality of SFC based allocation strategies for schedulers of supercomputers. This evaluation has been carried out using synthetic workloads with different characteristics (size, duration, shape), submitted to systems with a 3D and 5D mesh topology. These strategies have been compared with a contiguous (CONT) and a non-contiguous (NC-FF) strategy.

CONT prioritizes the utilization of contiguous and isolated partitions, optimal for the execution of applications. The prize to pay is a large overhead due to fragmentation, that results in low levels of system utilization. On the contrary, NC-FF prioritizes utilization, assigning nodes to partitions independently of their positions in the network. The prize to pay is a collection of sparse and overlapping partitions.

Allocators based on space filling curves have demonstrated excellent properties, in particular when Hilbert is the curve of choice. They perform allocation in a linear (1D) space, which results in utilization levels close to those of non contiguous approaches as represented in Fig. 7. The obtained 1D partitions are then mapped to the nD topology of the actual system, resulting in very compact sets of nodes (see again Fig. 7). The partitions achieved this way offer distance metrics similar to those of CONT strategies, although they do not guarantee isolation. However, SFC allocators have characteristics that are close to those of a theoretical, optimum allocator.

The relative merit of the different allocators depends on factors such as the search strategy (FF, BF), the topology of the IN (number of dimensions, related to node degree) and the properties of the workloads submitted to the system. We have studied "shaped" and "unshaped" workloads. The former assume that the user knows and requests the most appropriate shape to run an application, and the CONT scheduler honors this request – at a cost: in busy systems, it is difficult to find a partition of a specific shape. None of the remaining strategies take this request into consideration, using only the number of nodes in the request to search for a partition.

Finally we have seen that the benefits that SFC-based strategies obtain in terms of utilization, may disappear if we consider the (relative) slowdown that applications would suffer when running in non-optimal, overlapping partitions. If the penalty is over 10% for 3D meshes (20% for 5D meshes), then the CONT strategy is the best, even if utilization figures tell a different story. Otherwise, for lower penalties, SFC based strategies should be the chosen.

As future lines of work, we plan to make a deeper analysis of the impact of non contiguous partitions on applications' slowdown. As we have focused on nD meshes, we plan to extend this work to other kinds of IN, for example based on trees. Finally, we want to propose and assess a *hybrid* allocation strategy, able to provide contiguous and isolated partitions for those applications requiring them, and other SFC based partitions for less demanding applications, with the objective of achieving high system utilization without penalizing applications.

Acknowledgments. This work has been partially supported by the Research Groups 2013–2018 (IT-609-13) program (Basque Government), TIN2013-41272P (Ministry of Science and Technology). Jose A. Lozano is also supported by BERC program 2014–2017 (Basque government) and Severo Ochoa Program SEV-2013-0323 (Spanish Ministry of Economy and Competitiveness). Jose Miguel-Alonso is member of the HiPEAC European Network.

References

1. Alber, J., Niedermeier, R.: On multi-dimensional hilbert indexings. Theory Comput. Syst. **33**, 195–392 (2000)
2. Alber, J., Niedermeier, R.: On multidimensional curves with hilbert property. Theory Comput. Syst. **33**(4), 295–312 (2000)
3. Balzuweit, E., Bunde, D.P., Leung, V.J., Finley, A., Lee, A.C.S.: Local search to improve coordinate-based task mapping. Parallel Comput. **51**, 67–78 (2016)
4. Chen, D., Eisley, N.A., Heidelberger, P., Senger, R.M., Sugawara, Y., Kumar, S., Salapura, V., Satterfield, D.L., Steinmacher-Burow, B., Parker, J.J.: The IBM Blue Gene/Q interconnection network and message unit. In: Proceedings of 2011 International Conference for High Performance Computing, Networking, Storage and Analysis, pp. 1–10. ACM, New York (2011)
5. Cray Inc. http://www.cray.com/assets/pdf/products/xe/idc_948.pdf
6. Feitelson, D.G., Rudolph, L., Schwiegelshohn, U.: Parallel job scheduling — a status report. In: Feitelson, D.G., Rudolph, L., Schwiegelshohn, U. (eds.) JSSPP 2004. LNCS, vol. 3277, pp. 1–16. Springer, Heidelberg (2005). doi:10.1007/11407522_1
7. Hilbert, D.: Über die stetige abbildung einer linie auf ein flächenstück. Ann. Math. **38**, 459–460 (1891)
8. IBM Journal of Research, Development staff. Overview of the IBM Blue Gene/P project. IBM Journal of Research and Development 52(1/2), 199–220
9. Johnson, C.R., Bunde, D.P., Leung, V.J.: A tie-breaking strategy for processor allocation in meshes. In: 39th International Conference on Parallel Processing, ICPP. Workshops 2010, San Diego, California, USA, pp. 331–338. IEEE Computer Society, 13–16 September 2010
10. Jokanovic, A., Sancho, J., Rodriguez, G., Lucero, A., Minkenberg, C., Labarta, J.: Quiet neighborhoods: key to protect job performance predictability. In: Parallel and Distributed Processing Symposium (IPDPS), pp. 449–459, May 2015

11. Lawder, J.K., King, P.J.H.: Using space-filling curves for multi-dimensional indexing. In: Lings, B., Jeffery, K. (eds.) BNCOD 2000. LNCS, vol. 1832, pp. 20–35. Springer, Heidelberg (2000). doi:10.1007/3-540-45033-5_3

12. Lawrence Livermore National Laboratory. Simple linux utility for resource management. https://computing.llnl.gov/linux/slurm/

13. Leung, V., Arkin, E., Bender, M., Bunde, D., Johnston, J., Lal, A., Mitchell, J., Phillips, C., Seiden, S.: Processor allocation on cplant: achieving general processor locality using one-dimensional allocation strategies. pp. 296–304 (2002)

14. Li, K., Malawski, M., Nabrzyski, J.: Topology-aware scheduling on blue waters with proactive queue scanning and migration-based job placement. In: 20th Workshop on Job Scheduling Strategies for Parallel Processing (JSSPP) (2016)

15. Liu, W., Lo, V., Windisch, K., Nitzberg, B.: Non-contiguous processor allocation algorithms for distributed memory multicomputers. In: Proceedings of ACM/IEEE Conference on Supercomputing, pp. 227–236. IEEE Computer (1994)

16. Lo, V., Windisch, K., Liu, W., Nitzberg, B.: Noncontiguous processor allocation algorithms for mesh-connected multicomputers. IEEE Trans. Parallel Distrib. Syst. **8**, 712–726 (1997)

17. Morton. A computer oriented geodetic data base and a new technique in file sequencing. Technical report, Ottawa, Ontario, Canada (1966)

18. Navaridas, J., Pascual, J.A., Miguel-Alonso, J.: Effects of job and task placement on the performance of parallel scientific applications. In: Proceedings 17th Euromicro International Conference on Parallel, Distributed, and Network-Based Processing, pp. 55–61. IEEE Computer Society, February 2009

19. Pascual, J.A., Miguel-Alonso, J., Lozano, J.A.: Strategies to map parallel applications onto meshes. In: de Leon, F., et al. (eds.) Distributed Computing and Artificial Intelligence. AISC, vol. 79, pp. 197–204. Springer, Heidelberg (2010). doi:10.1007/978-3-642-14883-5_26

20. Pascual, J.A., Miguel-Alonso, J., Lozano, J.A.: Optimization-based mapping framework for parallel applications. J. Parallel Distrib. Comput. **71**(10), 1377–1387 (2011)

21. Pascual, J.A., Miguel-Alonso, J., Lozano, J.A.: Application-aware metrics for partition selection in cube-shaped topologies. Parallel Comput. **40**(5–6), 129–139 (2014)

22. Pascual, J.A., Miguel-Alonso, J., Lozano, J.A.: A fast implementation of the first fit contiguous partitioning strategy for cubic topologies. Concurrency Comput. Pract. Experience **26**(17), 2792–2810 (2014)

23. Pascual, J.A., Miguel-Alonso, J., Lozano, J.A.: Locality-aware policies to improve job scheduling on 3D tori. J. Supercomputing **71**(3), 966–994 (2015)

24. Walker, P., Bunde, D.P., Leung, V.J.: Faster high-quality processor allocation. In: Proceedings of the 11th LCI International Conference on High-Performance Cluster Computing (2010)

25. Weisstein, E.W.: Hilbert Curve. http://mathworld.wolfram.com/HilbertCurve.html

26. Windisch, K., Lo, V., Bose, B.: Contiguous and non-contiguous processor allocation algorithms for k-ary n-cubes. IEEE Trans. Parallel Distrib. Syst. **8**, 712–726 (1995)

Choosing Optimal Maintenance Time
for Stateless Data-Processing Clusters
A Case Study of Hadoop Cluster

Zhenyun Zhuang[(✉)], Min Shen, Haricharan Ramachandra,
and Suja Viswesan

LinkedIn Corporation, 2029 Stierlin Court, Mountain View, CA 94043, USA
{zzhuang,mshen,hramachandra,sviswesan}@linkedin.com

Abstract. Stateless clusters such as Hadoop clusters are widely deployed to drive the business data analysis. When a cluster needs to be restarted for cluster-wide maintenance, it is desired for the administrators to choose a maintenance window that results in: (1) least disturbance to the cluster operation; and (2) maximized job processing throughput. A straightforward but naive approach is to choose maintenance time that has the least number of running jobs, but such an approach is suboptimal.

In this work, we use Hadoop as an use case and propose to determine the optimal cluster maintenance time based on the *accumulated job progress*, as opposed the *number of running jobs*. The approach can maximize the job throughput of a stateless cluster by minimizing the amount of lost works due to maintenance. Compared to the straightforward approach, the proposed approach can save up to 50% of wasted cluster resources caused by maintenance according to production cluster traces.

1 Introduction

With the rapidly growing scale of data volume, data processing is increasingly being handled by clusters that consist of multiple machines. A data processing job may take certain time to finish, hence the intermediate state (e.g., what input data are processed, what are the partial output) of the job may change over the course of the processing. The intermediate states can be persisted as the job processing runs, and the persisted intermediate state can serve useful purposes such as progress tracking. However, persisting such states also incur additional design complexity and storage overhead. Depending on whether the intermediate state can be persisted or not, data processing clusters can be characterised into two categories: *stateful* and *stateless*. Stateful clusters are able to persist intermediate state of varying granularity (e.g., percentages of processed input data), while stateless clusters do not persist such state. Examples of stateless clusters are web server clusters and Hadoop clusters.

The distinction between stateful clusters and stateless clusters goes beyond progress tracking and design complexity. One particular aspect is the impact

© Springer International Publishing AG 2017
N. Desai and W. Cirne (Eds.): JSSPP 2015/2016, LNCS 10353, pp. 252–273, 2017.
DOI: 10.1007/978-3-319-61756-5_14

on cluster maintenance. When cluster-level maintenance is needed, the cluster temporarily goes offline to perform hardware/software upgrade or change. After maintenance is done, the cluster goes online again and begins to serve data-processing jobs. An interesting question is what happens to disrupted jobs due to maintenance, that is, can these jobs be resumed seamlessly? Being able to resume disrupted jobs has the advantage of avoiding repeated data processing and hence saving cost. For stateful clusters, job resuming is possible, and the degree of the saving depends on the granularity of the saved state. On the other hand, stateless clusters are unable to resume disrupted jobs. These jobs have to be started from scratch after cluster maintenance.

For stateless clusters, since cluster maintenance has to disrupt ongoing jobs and the partially finished jobs have to redo their work after the maintenance, choosing appropriate cluster maintenance time is critical for the purpose of saving computing resources. Choosing the most appropriate maintenance time is not as straightforward as people typically think. Instead, we found that the naive and straightforward approach is far from being optimal in terms of resource saving. In this work, we address this problem of choosing optimal cluster maintenance time for stateless clusters. For easy grasping the design, we use Hadoop as the use case to present our design.

Hadoop [1] clusters, being part of the data pipeline that drives many of today's business, are commonly used to carry out various types of data processing. A Hadoop cluster typically consists of one or two NameNodes, one Resource Manager[1] and up to thousands of DataNodes. The NameNode maintains the name space of the entire underlying HDFS [2], and serves as the central point of control for client interactions. Depending on Hadoop versions and configurations, the NameNodes can be configured as primary/secondary, active/standby or high availability (HA). Nevertheless, the NameNode is the single point of failure of the Hadoop cluster for non-HA setup. The Resource Manager keeps the state of Hadoop cluster resource usage (e.g., Memory and CPU) and schedules the running of submitted Hadoop jobs. Each MapReduce-based Hadoop job typically consists of a set of mapper tasks and another set of reducer tasks[2]. The mapper tasks will be scheduled first; and towards completing, the reducer tasks will be invoked to take over the data output from mappers and continue the data processing.

Hadoop cluster may occasionally need maintenance for various reasons including software upgrade (e.g., NameNode or Resource Manager upgrade), hardware failures, configuration change, and problem debugging. In this work, the notion of "Hadoop cluster maintenance" is defined as the entire cluster is not being able to run Hadoop jobs during maintenance; and we do not differentiate the causes of cluster maintenance, be it NameNode or Resource Manager. Whenever such cluster-wide maintenance is performed, all the running Hadoop jobs are destroyed and outstanding works are forfeited. Due to current limitations

---

[1] The previous version of Hadoop 1 does not have Resource Manager.

[2] There are other frameworks such as Spark based, but they are not gaining significant popularity at this time.

of Hadoop implementation, the job state is not persisted and hence the jobs cannot be resumed from last state. Once the cluster maintenance is completed, unfinished jobs require resubmission after the NameNode is started again. As a result, all unfinished jobs before maintenance will have to lose the partially done work, and the corresponding Hadoop resources (e.g., CPU, Networking) are wasted. Note that for a unfinished job, both completed and uncompleted map/reduce tasks will have to rerun.

Though it is invariably true that an unfinished Hadoop job requires a resubmission regardless of the maintenance time chosen before it is completed, the *amount of forfeited work* varies with different maintenance time. The more forfeited work due to maintenance, the less Hadoop throughput will be expected since the lost work will be redone. The amount of forfeited work is directly affected by the *number* of mapper/reducer tasks the job has invoked and their *running time* between the job startup time and the maintenance starting time. In this work, we aim at improving Hadoop cluster throughput by minimizing the forfeited work caused by cluster maintenance.

Assuming the maintenance window length is fixed (e.g., 1 h), the key question is *when* the maintenance should start. We further assume the maintenance is not urgent enough for an immediate maintenance, hence any maintenance window suffices as long as it is before some deadline (e.g., 1 day). This assumption in general holds for typical software-upgrade caused maintenance. Though a straightforward approach of determining the maintenance time is to look at the number of running jobs (or tasks) and choose the time when *minimum* number of jobs/tasks are *running* before the allowed deadline, as we will demonstrate later, this approach is rather naive and hence not optimal.

To improve Hadoop cluster throughput, we propose to determine cluster maintenance time based on the accumulated job progress instead of the number of running jobs. The main objective is to minimize the forfeited work while improving Hadoop throughput. We take into account the maintenance urgency and observe the amount of accumulated work in order to choose the moment to make the maintenance. Hadoop throughput is the critical performance metric analyzed. By using historical traces of a busy Hadoop cluster, we evaluate the proposal and present the significant improvements when comparing the proposal with the one where the maintenance time is chosen when the least number of jobs are running (CL-based). Based on the data, the improvement can be up to 42% in saving the wastage of Hadoop resource usage.

To summarize our work, we make the following contributions with this writing:

1. We consider the problem of determining optimal maintenance time for a stateless cluster such as Hadoop cluster. We have explained that the naive approach of "number of running jobs" is sub-optimal;
2. We propose to use *accumulated job progress* as the maintenance criteria for determining cluster maintenance time;

3. We perform experimentation and instrumentation to validate the proposal;
4. We provide analysis of key Hadoop job statistics based on one of our busiest Hadoop clusters.

For the remainder of the paper, after providing some necessary technical background in Sect. 2, we then motivate the problem being addressed in this paper using an example scenario in Sect. 3. We propose the design and solution in Sect. 4 and perform performance evaluation and show the results in Sect. 5. We discuss several issues/scenarios relevant to cluster maintenance in Sect. 6 and present related works in Sect. 7. And finally Sect. 8 concludes the work.

2   Background and Scope

We begin by providing background information regarding Hadoop architecture and Hadoop job workflow.

2.1   Hadoop Architecture and Hadoop EcoSystem

Inspired by Google File System [3], BigTable [4] and MapReduce [5], Hadoop is designed to provide distributed data storage (via HDFS [2]) and distributed data processing (via MapReduce [5]) at a massive scale. Hadoop has evolved from the core components of HDFS [2] and MapReduce to a plethora of products and tools including [6,7]. In addition to MapReduce framework, other frameworks such as Spark [8] are also being used. Our work considers how to determine the Hadoop cluster maintenance time. Though with a focus on MapReduce framework, the problem and proposed solution also apply to other frameworks.

Hadoop has two versions as of today. In the latest version of V2, a Hadoop cluster consists of one or two NameNode, one Resource Manager Node and up to thousands of DataNodes. The NameNode manages the HDFS namespace, while Resource Manager does the job scheduling. Resource Manager works with application masters and node managers running on each DataNode to schedule and run Hadoop jobs.

2.2   Hadoop Job Workflow

Hadoop jobs are submitted by Hadoop clients. Once a job is submitted, Resource Managers will initiate an Application Master on a DataNode and collaborate with node managers of DataNodes to invoke a set of containers as required by the Hadoop job. Each container can run a single mapper or reducer. Mappers are firstly scheduled to run, and towards the completion, the reducers will be invoked to fetch the data output from mappers and perform reducing tasks. The data exchange between mappers and reducers are typically referred to as "shuffling".

Each container requests certain amount of memory (e.g., heap size) from the node manager. Since the memory size of the entire Hadoop cluster is typically fixed and quite limited for commodity hardware based Data Nodes, the number of concurrently running containers is also limited.[3]

The submitted Hadoop jobs will leave a state in Hadoop Job History server for later retrieval. There is typically a limit on the number of job states kept by Job History server.

3   Problem Definition and Motivation Scenarios

We provide a motivating scenario to illustrate the problem and the impact of choosing different maintenance time on Hadoop performance.

3.1   Hadoop Throughput Is the Critical Performance Metric

Current Hadoop implementations do not persist the job state during cluster maintenance[4]. When the Hadoop cluster is restarted from maintenance, all unfinished jobs will need to be re-submitted and start over.

In Fig. 1 we plot 21 days memory usage of a busy Hadoop cluster. This cluster has two NameNodes being configured with primary/secondary setup, and it consists of about 2000 data nodes and totally 40 TB of available memory for running Hadoop jobs. Each Hadoop container running in this cluster on average takes about 2 GB of memory. We can see that most of the time the cluster is saturated with memory usage, hence the throughput is one of the critical performance metric we want to optimize. We also see that cluster maintenance is occasionally performed, which can be seen from the close-to-zero memory usage period.

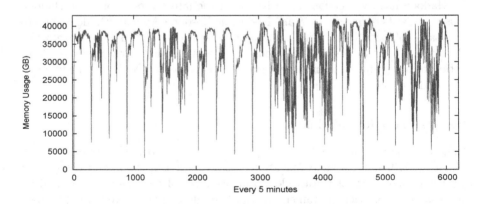

Fig. 1. Memory usage of a Hadoop cluster.

---

[3] Due to performance concerns, the total JVM heap size allocated to all containers on a Data Node should not exceed the physical RAM size of the node.

[4] Efforts are going on to allow job state persistence [9], however facing the challenges of implementation complexity, usability and adoption cost.

Hadoop clusters are typically deployed for batch data processing and used by multiple clients. Thanks to the exploding size of today's data and the increasing demand for data processing driven by various business requirements, the throughput of Hadoop clusters (i.e., number of jobs completed in an unit of time) is the primary performance metric we should optimize.

3.2 Problem We Are Addressing in This Work

Without careful considerations of the impact of different cluster maintenance time, a poorly selected maintenance window will result in suboptimal Hadoop performance in the forms of low job throughput and wasted computing resources. We have seen cases that the Hadoop cluster maintenance window is chosen by Hadoop administrators in a rather ad hoc fashion. Though urgent remedies of the cluster require immediate maintenance, most of the maintenance requests including minor software upgrade are non-urgent, hence we can afford a delayed maintenance up to certain deadline.

In this work we assume the cluster maintenance duration (i.e., the amount of time when the cluster is down for maintenance) is fixed (e.g., 1 h), which is typically true for most software updates[5]. So the question that needs to be answered is *when* the maintenance should start. Maintenance time determination answers this question. The goal of determining optimal maintenance time is maximizing the throughput (i.e., the number of completed jobs) of the Hadoop cluster.

A straightforward but naive approach we can easily come up with is choosing the maintenance starting time with the minimum number of running jobs (or tasks). However, as we elaborate later, such an approach is not optimal.

3.3 Illustrative Example

We use the following scenario to elaborate why the straightforward approach of determining cluster maintenance time based on number of running tasks or jobs is not optimal. For easy presentation, we denote such approach as Current-Load (CL) based approach. Consider the a scenario where totally four Hadoop jobs are scheduled at different time, as shown in Fig. 2(a). For simplicity, we assume each job has only 1 mapper task and 1 reducer task.

In the figure we highlighted a few time points that are possible starting time for cluster maintenance. The Current-Load based approach would choose the time of T_2 to start NameNode maintenance, since there is only 1 running Hadoop job at T_2, while at T_1 and T_3 there are 2 running jobs. However, starting maintenance at T_2 would mean all the accumulated works of job J_2 will be lost, and the corresponding consumed Hadoop processing resources (i.e., CPU, networking, IO) would be wasted. As shown in Fig. 2(b), the amount of wastage is non-negligible.

---

[5] The problem considered won't change even with non-fixed maintenance duration; but having this assumption simplifies the presentation.

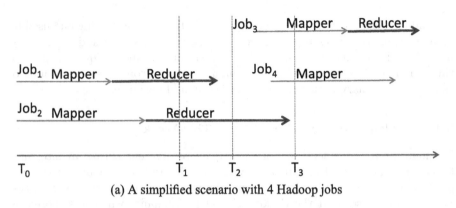

(a) A simplified scenario with 4 Hadoop jobs

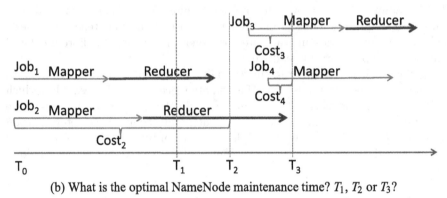

(b) What is the optimal NameNode maintenance time? T_1, T_2 or T_3?

Fig. 2. An illustrative example showing why the straightforward approach is not optimal.

On the other hand, if the maintenance time starts at T_3, though the number of running jobs is 2, the aggregated amount of wasted work ($Cost_3 + Cost_4$) is much less than the wasted work ($Cost_2$) if maintenance starts at T_1. Since after maintenance all the broke Hadoop jobs will need to be re-submitted, the forfeited work (i.e., mapping and reducing) will in turn needs to be re-done, which is a waste of Hadoop processing resources and reduced Hadoop job completion rate. Having less wasted work essentially mean the Hadoop cluster can run more jobs in given amount of time, hence higher job throughput.

3.4   Characteristics of Hadoop Jobs

We also obtained the characteristics of the Hadoop jobs running on one experimental Hadoop cluster. The job set includes totally 135, 808 Hadoop mapreduce jobs which are retrieved from the job history server. For each of the jobs, we measure the following metrics: (1) number of tasks (i.e., mappers and reducers) in a job; (2) total execution time; and (3) aggregated resource usage (i.e., cost).

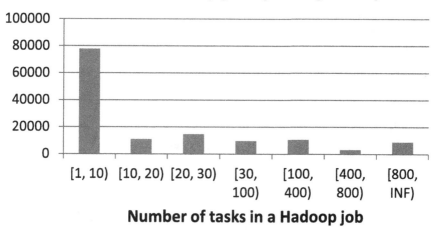

Fig. 3. Characteristics of profiled 135 K Hadoop jobs (X-axis is the different buckets (number of tasks in a job); Y-axis is the number of Hadoop jobs in each bucket).

Since Hadoop mapreduce jobs consist of both mappers and reducers, and they need to run in separate containers, the number of tasks for a Hadoop job is defined as the summation of the mappers and reducers. The execution time of a Hadoop jobs is defined as the summation of average *mapping time* and the average *reducing time*[6]. For the resource usage, we consider a custom metric of "container * (execution time)", which is the product of how many containers and how long on average a container (i.e., mapper and reducer) runs. Based on our experiences with running the experimental cluster, the top performance bottleneck of the Hadoop cluster is the limited number of concurrent running containers, hence it makes a lot of sense to use the "container * time" as the cost metric.

Figures 3, 4 and 5 display the characterizing results. For each of the metrics we considered, we show the distributions of Hadoop jobs under different buckets. The average number of tasks a Hadoop job has is 211, the average execution time is 186 s, and the average cost of each Hadoop job is 37775 container * second, or about 10 container * hours. If cluster maintenance is performed during the runs of these jobs, on average, half of the cost (i.e., 5 container * hours) incurred by each job will be lost.

3.5 Summary

We have thus far described that a straightforward Current-Load based approach fails to consider the nature of Hadoop resource usage, and hence not optimal.

---

[6] The shuffling and reducing phases may overlap, so for simplification, we define the *reducing time* as the maximum of reducing time and shuffling time reported by job history server.

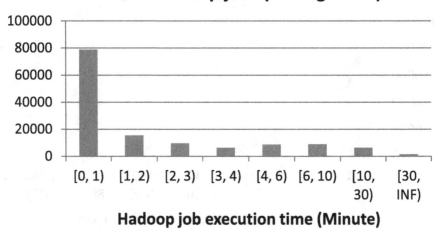

Fig. 4. Characteristics of profiled 135 K Hadoop jobs (X-axis is the different buckets (Execution time in minute); Y-axis is the number of Hadoop jobs in each bucket).

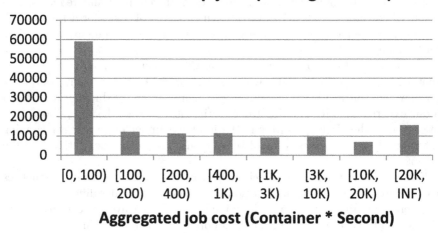

Fig. 5. Characteristics of profiled 135 K Hadoop jobs (X-axis is the different buckets (Aggregated job cost of container * Second); Y-axis is the number of Hadoop jobs in each bucket).

Depending on scenarios, the forfeited Hadoop work due to cluster maintenance can be significant.

By considering the resource used by running Hadoop jobs, a new approach which is based on accumulated works can achieve better resource usage efficiency and higher job throughput thanks to the minimum wasted resource usage.

We denote the approach of determining cluster maintenance time based on the amount of accumulated completion of tasks as Accumulated-Work (AW) based approach.

4 Solution

We now present the design and detailed algorithm of the proposed Accumulated-Work (AW) based solution.

4.1 Overview

Our proposal depends on forecasting of future workload. Given the irregularities of Hadoop jobs (i.e., starting/finishing time, number of tasks, run time), we devise a simple, but effective, predictor by assuming the distribution of those quantities will be similar over some periods (e.g., on a day-to-day basis or week-by-week basis). For simplicity, in this work we use the day-to-day model[7]. Then the way to determine appropriate maintenance time is by selecting the right threshold to trigger the maintenance.

The high level flow of the algorithm is illustrated in Fig. 6. The algorithm consists of a Hadoop workload profiling component that analyzes the load of the cluster, the job properties, etc. Then the algorithm forecasts the future workload (e.g., next 1 day) using the forecasting component. Based on the forecasting result and urgency level of incoming cluster maintenance request, a threshold value is chosen. The threshold value will be used to determine the starting time of the next cluster maintenance. Whenever the monitored cluster workload (e.g., number of running jobs as in CL-based approach, amount of accumulated work as in AW-based approach) falls below the threshold, maintenance can start.

The maintenance request may come with different urgency level in the form of deadlines (e.g., within next 24 h). Such urgency level is fed into the threshold determination component with a function of $Th = f(level)$. Many forms of the f function can be defined, and the higher urgency, the larger threshold value (so that the maintenance can be early kicked off). In this work, we choose a percentile-based approach which will be elaborated in Sect. 4.4.

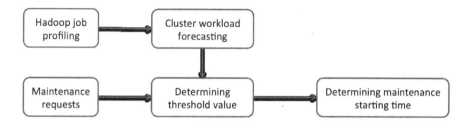

Fig. 6. Flow chart of AW-based maintenance determination algorithm.

---

[7] Our particularly studied Hadoop cluster shows consistency of both day-to-day and week-to-week pattern.

4.2   Cost Metric and Objective Function

The proposed AW-based solution chooses the cluster maintenance time based on the amount of accumulated works of the running Hadoop jobs. These works include both mapper and reducer tasks. Each of these tasks runs for certain amount of time. There are three types of tasks at a particular timestamp (i.e., time point): completed tasks (denoted by $Task_{completed}$), running tasks ($Task_{running}$) and tasks that are waiting to be scheduled ($Task_{waiting}$). The accumulated work is the aggregated works of all completed and running mapper and reducer tasks. For $Task_{completed}$, the accumulated work is determined by the running time of the particular task, that is, the difference between "finish time" and "start time". For $Task_{running}$, the considered run time is the difference between current timestamp and the job's "starting time".

The cost metric of AW-based solution is the aggregated accumulated work from all Hadoop jobs at any time point. Using AW_{T_i} to denote the cost at time T_i, and AW_{T_i,Job_j} to denote the accumulated work of job Job_j at T_i. So we have $AW_{T_i} = \sum AW_{T_i,Job_j}$, and AW_{T_i,Job_j} consists of the accumulated work of all $Task_{completed}$ and $Task_{running}$.

The objective function of AW-based approach is to choose a time point T_k that the minimum AW_{T_i} is achieved. By comparison, the objective function of the baseline CL-based approach is to achieve minimum number of concurrently running jobs.

4.3   Workload Profiling and Forecasting

In order for both CL-based and AW-based approaches to work, it is important to profile and forecast the workload of the Hadoop cluster. Profiling can be done by periodically querying the state of the Hadoop cluster, such as retrieving information from Job History server. The profiling results can come in different forms such as probability density functions; in this work, we consider a simplified form of percentiles for easier presentation, as shown in Fig. 7.

For workload forecasting, it can be achieved by applying various forecasting models such as time series based ones like ARIMA [10]. Time series forecasting

---

Algorithm (a): Workload profiling and forecasting
Variables:
1    $T_{profile}$: Cycle of profiling the Hadoop workload

1   For every $T_{profile}$ of time:
2   Start a new cycle of workload profiling;
3   Obtain workload profiles (e.g., percentiles);

Fig. 7. Main algorithm (A).

model breaks the data values into three parts: seasonal, trending and noises. Depending on specific scenarios, the workload may have different strengths on different parts. For instance, for a Hadoop cluster that mostly serves regularly scheduled jobs such as weekly aggregation of data or daily updates based on streaming data, the seasonal part will be very strong. On the other hand, if a Hadoop cluster mainly run ad-hoc experimental jobs, the noise part will dominate.

4.4   Determining Threshold for Cluster Maintenance

Once the forecasting model is established, then the Hadoop administrators can predict the workload in the future. When a new cluster maintenance is needed within certain time period (e.g., 1 day), the administrators can choose a threshold value for cluster maintenance based on the forecasted workloads.

In cases of non-perfect forecasting model which could be caused by irregularities of the Hadoop workloads, the administrators could adjust the threshold value for determining the maintenance time a bit to accommodate. For instance, if the forecasting model predicts the workload will vary between 100 and 1 K in the coming day. To ensure a maintenance time is indeed chosen, the administrator could choose a threshold value of 200 (as opposed to 100). Whenever the workload value drops below the threshold, the maintenance can start. The threshold value should not be arbitrarily large either (e.g., 900), as otherwise the opportunity cost associated with not finding an below-threshold time will be more substantial and defeats the benefits.

Based on our experiences with multiple Hadoop clusters, non-trivial clusters[8] typically exhibit irregular workloads and hence it is very difficult to characterize with reasonable forecasting models. For instance, on the particular cluster we used for this study, the running Hadoop jobs come from a mix of regularly scheduled ones and ad-hoc ones. Moreover, the users and jobs of the cluster are undergoing a major shift. The trending part, however, is not much.

To accommodate the generic cases where Hadoop clusters run irregular workloads, we choose a percentile-based method to determine the threshold. Specifically, we profile the previous days' workload, and calculate the percentile values of the past periods. Then we choose a particular percentile P (e.g., 5%) of the workload and base the maintenance time determination on the corresponding workload value.

Note the percentile value is determined by the maintenance urgency. For more urgent maintenance, a larger percentile value is chosen in hope of kicking off the maintenance early. On the other hand, if the maintenance is not urgent, smaller percentile value is desired. One approach is to rate the maintenance urgency on a scale of 1 to 100, where 1 indicates the most urgent level, and then choosing the corresponding percentile value as the threshold, as shown in Fig. 8. With

---

[8] Those clusters that have sufficiently large of number of data nodes and run heterogenous workload.

such a scaling of 1 to 100, the threshold value can be easily obtained by treating the emergency level as the percentile values, that is, $AW_{thre} = P_{Level_{urg}}$. For instance, for a low-emergency maintenance request rated at level-1, a P_1 value will be chosen, where P_1 means a value where 1% of all values are below it.

For CL-based approach, the forecasted workload indicates how many jobs are concurrently running at any time in the forecasting period. The threshold value is based on the profiled workload and maintenance urgency. The time stamps in the future that have forecasted workload intensity falls below the threshold are the possible cluster maintenance starting time.

For AW-based approach, the forecasted workload deducts the amount of accumulated workload at any future time. Once the corresponding threshold value is chosen, a process similar to that of CL-based approach, maintenance time can be similarly determined.

4.5   Determining Cluster Maintenance Time

Once the cluster maintenance threshold is determined, the maintenance time can be determined by comparing to the real-time workloads to the threshold value. This step performs periodical querying of the Hadoop Job History server, as elaborated in Fig. 9. Every time of T_{jh}, it obtains the snapshot of the job history information and extracts all jobs. For every running job J_i, it gathers all finished or running tasks T_{mr}. Then it iterate all the tasks and aggregates consumed computing resource to AW_{aggr}. Finally, it compares the aggregated AW_{aggr} to the threshold value AW_{thre} determined in Fig. 8. If AW_{aggr} is less than AW_{thre}, the maintenance can start. Meanwhile, if the maintenance deadline (e.g., 1 day) has expired, the maintenance can start.

Algorithm (b): determining maintenance threshold
  Variables:
1   AW_{thre}: The threshold of the accumulated work for deciding maintenance time
2    $Level_{urg}$: The urgency level of maintenance

1   For every maintenance request issued;
2   Obtain forecasted workloads based on recent workload profiles;
3   Determine the maintenance urgency level $Level_{urg}$;
4   Determine AW_{thre} based on forecasted workloads and $Level_{urg}$;

Fig. 8. Main algorithm (B).

Algorithm (c): determining maintenance time
Variables:
1   T_{jh}: Cycle of fetching from Hadoop Job History server
2   AW_{aggr}: Currently aggregated computing resources used by all running jobs
3   AW_{thre}: The threshold of the accumulated work for deciding maintenance time
4   J_i: A Hadoop job started but unfinished
5   T_{mr} A finished or running Hadoop mapper/reducer task

1   Every T_{jh} of time:
2   Obtain the snapshot of the job history information;
3   For every running job J_i:
4   Get all finished or running tasks T_{mr};
5   Aggregate consumed resource to AW_{aggr};
6   If $AW_{aggr} > AW_{thre}$ or deadline expires:
7   Maintenance starts;

Fig. 9. Main algorithm (C).

5   Evaluation

In this section, we will use the actual traces from our Hadoop cluster to illustrate how to apply the proposed AW-based approach that is based on accumulated work on running jobs. For comparison, we also consider the baseline of CL-based approach, which is based on the number of running jobs.

5.1   Methodology

We use the historical job information kept on Hadoop Job History server. For each Hadoop job completed, the Job History server maintains the meta data of the job and its mapper/reducer tasks. The meta data includes submission time, starting and finishing time, user account, number of mappers and reducers, etc.

The considered Hadoop cluster is able to run 20 K containers concurrently, and the average job run time is only about 10 h, hence there are up 48 K mapper/reducer tasks are completed in a single day. The Job History server, however, is only able to keep most recent 20 K jobs for our setup.

We have continuously collected 3-week of job history. We have to query the job history server multiple times due to configuration limits. There are two limits in history server for how many jobs are kept, both are configurable. The first is the log retention period, which determines how long to keep the job logs on HDFS. This is by default set to 1 week. The second is the 20 K limits, which is the maximum number of jobs that history server will load into memory and serve from the web page. For our busy cluster, 20 K jobs only correspond to less than one-day of job history.

Even though we retrieve from Job History server frequently, due to the large number of jobs and frequent cluster maintenances, we believe some jobs are still missed in certain time periods. So we cleaned our data by eliminating some dirty periods. For easier presentation, we use a 2-day period with clean data to elaborate the evaluation results. The first day is used as the profiling period.[9] The second day is the period to evaluate the approaches.

5.2 Profiling Statistics of First Day

For the first day, we obtain the meta data of each job, hence we know the running time period (i.e., the start and finish time) and the number of mappers and reducers running during this time period. Then we can deduct the number of running jobs and the accumulated works of any time during the 24 h. We plot the percentile values of concurrent jobs and accumulated works in Fig. 10(a) and (b), respectively.

For the Hadoop cluster maintenance, we consider three scenarios based on the maintenance urgency: low-urgency, medium-urgency and high-urgency. For low-urgency maintenance request, we choose a threshold of 1%, essentially means about 1% of the entire time, the maintenance is able to kick off. If the checking interval is every minute, then on average, the expected starting maintenance time is 100 min (i.e., $\frac{1}{1\%}$). Similarly, for medium-urgency maintenance request, we consider two possible thresholds of 2% and 5%, which respectively have maintenance waiting time of 50 min and 20 min. For high-urgency maintenance request, we choose two possible thresholds of 10% and 20%, with expected maintenance waiting time of 10 and 5 min, respectively.

For both CL-based and AW-based approaches, the possible time points of maintenance (i.e., the time when the respective metrics fall below the corresponding particular percentile values.) are determined. The opportunity *cost* of each maintenance time point is obtained based on the amount of forfeited work. The cost unit of the accumulated works is "container * second", intuitively indicting the resource used by some containers concurrently running for some time.

5.3 Cost Results of Second Day

For the second day, we obtain the number of concurrent Hadoop jobs and the accumulated Hadoop work for each timestamp, shown in Fig. 11. These values will be used to determine possible cluster maintenance kickoff time based on threshold values for both CL-based and AW-based approaches.

The assumption of our design is the relatively stable distribution of accumulated works across days. To understand how well the assumption holds, we plot

---

[9] In production, the profiling efforts are running continuously.

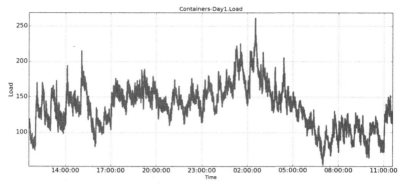

(a) Concurrent running jobs

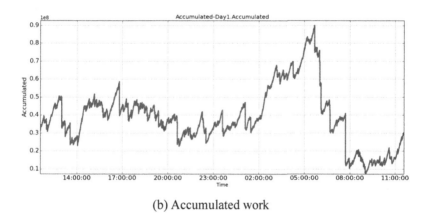

(b) Accumulated work

Fig. 10. Statistics of the first day.

the CDFs (Cumulative Distribution Function) of these two days in Fig. 12. From the figure, we see very similar CDF curves.

We also compare the cost of both CL-based and AW-based approaches. For each approach, the threshold values corresponding to different urgency levels of cluster maintenance requests are listed in Table 1. Based on the threshold values, the timestamps of all possible maintenance kicking off are recorded. Then the opportunity costs (i.e., the amount of forfeited Hadoop works) are obtained for each timestamp. Finally the average values of all the possible opportunity costs are calculated for both approaches.

The results of all 5 maintenance urgency levels are displayed in Fig. 13. As shown in the figure, AW-based approach consistently results in much lower opportunity compared to CL-based approach. For some urgency levels (e.g., *Low* and $Medium_1$), the AW-based cost is only **half** of that of CL-based. For other urgency levels, the saving is about 40%.

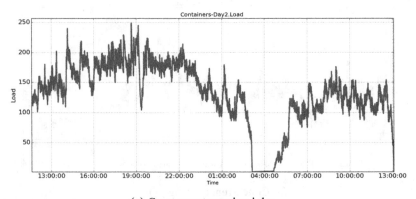

(a) Concurrent running jobs

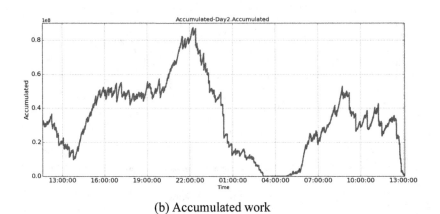

(b) Accumulated work

Fig. 11. Statistics of the second day

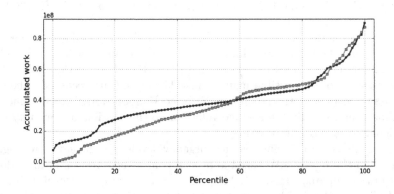

Fig. 12. Comparing the CDF (Cumulative Distribution Function) of two days.

Table 1. Threshold values for kicking off cluster maintenance.

Maintenance urgency	Percentile	CL-based	AW-based
Low	1	7493	8745211
$Medium_1$	2	7924	10.7M
$Medium_2$	5	8884	12.9M
$High_1$	10	9913	14.7M
$High_2$	20	11652	24.3M

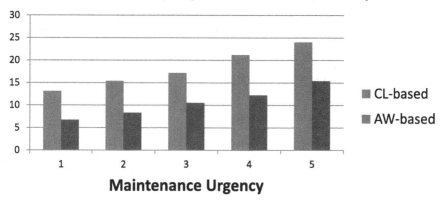

Fig. 13. Comparing the amount of forfeited work by CL-based and AW-based approach under different maintenance urgency levels.

Specifically, at urgency level of $High_1$, for CL-based approach, the average opportunity cost is about 21,157,000 container * second, or about 5877 container * hour. The average cost of AW-based approach is about 12,240,000 container * second, or about 3,400 container * hours. Compared to CL-based approach of 5, 877 container * hours, the difference is 2,477 container * hours for every cluster maintenance is done. In other words, AW-based approach can save 42% of the wasted resources as resulted from CL-based approach.

6   Discussions

In this section, we discuss several issues/clarifications related to the considered problem and proposed approach.

6.1   HDFS Federation

HDFS federation is aimed at solving the single-NameNode inefficiency by splitting the entire HDFS namespace to multiple ones. Since different NameNodes correspond to different namespaces, NameNode maintenance will still lose unfinished jobs which access the particularly maintained namespace. In addition, even with HDFS federation, people usually perform maintenance on all namespace at once.

6.2 HA (High Availability) Setup

HA is an advanced setup for Hadoop NameNode that can alleviate the single-node failure problem. When configured with HA, two NameNodes work together to allow seamless NameNode maintenance. One of the NameNode will be active at any time, while the other be passive. When the active NameNode is down for any reason, the passive NameNode will take over the responsibility. During NameNode-caused cluster maintenance, NameNode will not lose unfinished jobs. However, the tasks might fail during rolling upgrade, hence will need to be rescheduled. Moreover, for cluster maintenances caused by other reasons (e.g., Resource Manager), Hadoop jobs are still lost.

6.3 Resource Manager Maintenance

Though most of the cluster maintenances are caused by NameNode updates, Resource Manager (RM) can also trigger cluster maintenance. RM node maintenance also loses jobs. Thereare features in YARN [11] that adds HA (High Availability) to RM. For now, this HA feature only allows automatically resubmission of previously unfinished jobs. New features are being added which preserve workloads.

6.4 Maintenance Announcement

The scenario we consider in this work is to automatically decide the cluster maintenance time and execute the maintenance without the Hadoop users' awareness and actions. A slightly different approach is to keep users informed beforehand by announcing the forthcoming maintenance time so that users do not submit jobs that will not complete before the maintenance starts. Such an approach does not really help maximizing the key performance metric of Hadoop job throughput, since the cluster resources are anyway wasted as users stop submitting jobs. In our experiences, we have seen such under-utilization of the cluster before announced maintenance window.

Moreover, though users may be aware of the maintenance window from the announcement and stop submitting ad hoc jobs (e.g., the one-time running jobs), most non-ad-hoc jobs (e.g., hourly running jobs) can rarely take advantage of the announcement. Those jobs are scheduled to run periodically and are very inconvenient for the users to pause and resume.

In addition, the AW-based approach can be used in tandem with the announcement-based approach, as the algorithm and its associated observations can be used to determine the optimal maintenance time window to announce to users. In other words, if AW-based profiling has identified the pattern of accumulated workloads, then a maintenance window with smallest accumulated workloads can be chosen and be announced to users.

7 Related Work

7.1 Hadoop Performance Optimization

Various optimizations have been proposed to improve Hadoop throughput and response time [12–15]. In particular, [13] proposes to improve on the job execution mechanism. [14] studies the impact of adopting SSD for storage. [15] proposes a new MapReduce Scheduler for special environments. Our work is orthogonal with these works.

7.2 Workload Forecasting

To forecast various types of computing workload (e.g., networking traffic, incoming traffic), many models such as [10,16] have been proposed. Work [17] proposes time series based model to forecast when to add more network bandwidth. In another recent work [18], a time series based forecasting model is used to predict LinkedIn's Espresso [19]/Databus [20] traffic. Work [21] proposes a real-time rolling grey forecasting method to achieve increase in forecast accuracy. Work [22] uses a novel self-adaptive approach that selects suitable forecasting methods for a given context, and the user only has to provide a general forecasting objectives.

7.3 Determining Maintenance Time

We searched thoroughly for related works in the areas of determining optimal cluster maintenance time. Though there are some works [23,24] dealing with maintenance scheduling for different systems, to our best knowledge, we haven't seen any similar work that attempts to optimize the maintenance time for Hadoop clusters. Moreover, due to the unique characteristics of Hadoop mapreduce jobs during cluster maintenance (i.e., combinations of mappers and reducers, lost intermediate job states during cluster-wide maintenance), the impact of Hadoop cluster maintenance considerably differs from other types of maintenance. For this reason, we believe our study exhibits uniqueness with regard to these aspects.

8 Conclusion

This work presents an optimization technique to maximize overall throughput of a "stateless system" such as Hadoop cluster system. We propose to use *accumulated job progress* as the cluster maintenance criteria as opposed *number of running jobs*. Such a design can significantly save the forfeited computing resources caused by cluster maintenance.

References

1. Apache Hadoop. https://hadoop.apache.org/
2. HDFS Architecture Guide. https://hadoop.apache.org/docs/r1.2.1/hdfs_design. html
3. Ghemawat, S., Gobioff, H., Leung, S.-T.: The Google file system. In: Proceedings of the Nineteenth ACM Symposium on Operating Systems Principles (SOSP 2003), Bolton Landing, pp. 29–43 (2003)
4. Chang, F., Dean, J., Ghemawat, S., Hsieh, W.C., Wallach, D.A., Burrows, M., Chandra, T., Fikes, A., Gruber, R.E.: Bigtable: a distributed storage system for structured data. ACM Trans. Comput. Syst. **26**(2), 4:1–4:26 (2008)
5. Dean, J., Ghemawat, S.: MapReduce: simplified data processing on large clusters. In: Proceedings of the 6th Conference on Symposium on Opearating Systems Design & Implementation (OSDI 2004), San Francisco, vol. 6, p. 10 (2004)
6. Apache HBase. http://hbase.apache.org/
7. Vavilapalli, V.K., Murthy, A.C., Douglas, C., Agarwal, S., Konar, M., Evans, R., Graves, T., Lowe, J., Shah, H., Seth, S., Saha, B., Curino, C., O'Malley, O., Radia, S., Reed, B., Baldeschwieler, E.: Apache Hadoop YARN: yet another resource negotiator. In: Proceedings of the 4th Annual Symposium on Cloud Computing (SOCC 2013) 2013
8. Apache Spark. http://spark.apache.org/
9. Provide ability to persist running jobs. https://issues.apache.org/jira/browse/ HADOOP-3245
10. Box, G.E.P., Jenkins, G.M.: Time Series Analysis: Forecasting and Control, 3rd edn. Prentice Hall PTR, Upper Saddle River (1994)
11. Vavilapalli, V.K., Murthy, A.C., Douglas, C., Agarwal, S., Konar, M., Evans, R., Graves, T., Lowe, J., Shah, H., Seth, S., Saha, B., Curino, C., O'Malley, O., Radia, S., Reed, B., Baldeschwieler, E.: Apache Hadoop YARN: yet another resource negotiator. In: Proceedings of the 4th Annual Symposium on Cloud Computing (SOCC 2013), Santa Clara (2013)
12. Joshi, S.B.: Apache Hadoop performance-tuning methodologies and best practices. In: Proceedings of the 3rd ACM/SPEC International Conference on Performance Engineering (ICPE 2012), Boston (2012)
13. Gu, R., Yang, X., Yan, J., Sun, Y., Wang, B., Yuan, C., Huang, Y.: SHadoop: improving MapReduce performance by optimizing job execution mechanism in Hadoop clusters. J. Parallel Distrib. Comput. **74**(3), 2166–2179 (2014)
14. Wu, D., Luo, W., Xie, W., Ji, X., He, J., Wu, D.: Understanding the impacts of solid-state storage on the Hadoop performance. In: Proceedings of the 2013 International Conference on Advanced Cloud and Big Data (CBD 2013), Washington, DC (2013)
15. Sharma, B., Wood, T., Das, C.R.: HybridMR: a hierarchical MapReduce scheduler for hybrid data centers. In: Proceedings of the 2013 IEEE 33rd International Conference on Distributed Computing Systems (ICDCS 2013), Washington, DC, pp. 102–111 (2013)
16. Durbin, J., Koopman, S.J.: Time Series Analysis by State Space Methods. Oxford University Press, Oxford (2001)
17. Papagiannaki, K., Taft, N., Zhang, Z.-L., Diot, C.: Long-term forecasting of internet backbone traffic. Trans. Neural Netw. **16**(5), 1110–1124 (2005)

18. Zhuang, Z., Ramachandra, H., Tran, C., Subramaniam, S., Botev, C., Xiong, C., Sridharan, B.: Capacity planning and headroom analysis for taming database replication latency: experiences with Linkedin internet traffic. In: Proceedings of the 6th ACM/SPEC International Conference on Performance Engineering (ICPE 2015), Austin, pp. 39–50 (2015)
19. Qiao, L., Surlaker, K., Das, S., et al.: On brewing fresh espresso: Linkedin's distributed data serving platform. In: Proceedings of the 2013 ACM SIGMOD International Conference on Management of Data (SIGMOD 2013), pp. 1135–1146 (2013)
20. Das, S., Botev, C., et al.: All aboard the databus! Linkedin's scalable consistent change data capture platform (SoCC 2012), New York (2012)
21. Xia, T., Jin, X., Xi, L., Zhang, Y., Ni, J.: Operating load based real-time rolling grey forecasting for machine health prognosis in dynamic maintenance schedule. J. Intell. Manuf. **26**(2), 269–280 (2015)
22. Herbst, N.R., Huber, N., Kounev, S., Amrehn, E.: Self-adaptive workload classification and forecasting for proactive resource provisioning. In: Proceedings of the 4th ACM/SPEC International Conference on Performance Engineering (ICPE 2013), pp. 187–198. ACM, New York (2013). http://doi.acm.org/10.1145/2479871.2479899
23. Moghaddam, K.S., Usher, J.S.: Preventive maintenance and replacement scheduling for repairable and maintainable systems using dynamic programming. Comput. Ind. Eng. **60**(4), 654–665 (2011)
24. Carr, M., Wagner, C.: A study of reasoning processes in software maintenance management. Inf. Technol. Manag. **3**(1–2), 181–203 (2002)

Open Issues in Cloud Resource Management

Narayan Desai and Walfredo Cirne[✉]

Google Inc., Mountain View, CA, USA
nld@google.com, walfredo@google.com

Abstract. Cloud computing seeks to provide a global computing utility service to a broad base of users. Resource management and scheduling are prime challenges in building such a service. In this paper, we first provide an overview of clouds from a resource management and scheduling perspective. We then discuss key challenges in these areas, describing prime opportunities for new research.

1 Cloud Computing Overview

Cloud platforms provide a broad community with sufficient computing resources to run arbitrary computational workloads [10]. Clouds are typically built from many discrete warehouse-scale computing platforms. These platforms are distributed around the world in order to limit the size of fault domains and provide close proximity to customers.

Clouds pose interesting challenges in resource management and scheduling [12]. The closest prior art is large parallel supercomputers, which have been in production for over 20 years. However, while much can learned from such systems, they have generally catered to batch workloads. That is, a job is submitted to a queue, where it is deferred until sufficient free resources are available to run it. The primary goal of these systems is to maintain good utilization while maintaining reasonable response times for individual jobs [7]. These systems often have fixed configurations for years [6].

By contrast, the first use case for clouds was supporting interactive workloads, where requests must be processed in a real-time fashion. Also, these systems are driven by external demand, whether it be serving web pages or API endpoints. These workloads are often business critical, so matching instantaneous demand is critical. Over time, cloud use cases have broadened to include large-scale batch computing as well. These two classes of workload have different requirements. By contrast, batch workloads are broadly latency insensitive, though they may have time-to-solution requirements on a larger timescale (e.g. hours or days). For this reason, these workloads demand different properties from the system [4].

Most importantly, clouds seek to maintain the illusion of infinite capacity, because such illusion simplifies user interactions with the platform, allowing them to focus on their applications and dynamically scale them as needed, instead of building detailed capacity plans. Cloud providers implement this capability using several mechanisms. First, they combine discrete user workloads into an

© Springer International Publishing AG 2017
N. Desai and W. Cirne (Eds.): JSSPP 2015/2016, LNCS 10353, pp. 274–278, 2017.
DOI: 10.1007/978-3-319-61756-5_15

aggregated, smoothed demand curve with lower capacity variations than individual workloads. Second, they build a predictive model of future demand [5]. This predictive model is in turn used to build new capacity ahead of demand, hence providing the illusion of infinite capacity. This dynamic aspect of cloud provisioning is a major departure from the system acquisition approach used by traditional HPC centers, where fixed systems are procured for long time scales with few changes over time.

2 Resource Management for Clouds

Effective cloud resource management requires solutions to three major challenges. The first is product definition for resources, with associated service level objectives (SLOs). The second is capacity planning with enough notice to provision capacity before it is needed. The third is scheduling, where the workload is matched to physical resources. We discuss each in turn.

A cloud *product definition* specifies what a customer can request. For example, each virtual machine instance type in Google Cloud Platform has a fixed resource configuration for the amount of RAM, CPU, network, and storage [13]. These configurations are often defined by cloud providers in order to enable efficient allocation and packings of customer requests onto the physical cloud platform hardware, while providing a rich set of choices for the cloud users.

The product definitions also include SLOs establishing expected behaviors, such as the expected mean time between failure of VM instances, or whether a workload can be evicted from its resources, once they have been assigned. The key challenge here is to devise offerings that are compelling to the customers while leaving room for cloud engineers to optimize providing the necessary resources.

Predictive demand models allow cloud providers to *procure capacity in advance of demand*. The goal of these models is to ensure that user requests can be satisfied, while minimizing the number of platform resources left idle. These models typically include inputs from several sources. Organic growth describes the observed growth rate over time of a given service or class of loads. Inorganic growth characterizes events that significantly change consumption patterns (e.g., the "Black Friday" shopping day in the USA). Slack is the margin included in a capacity plan to ensure that requests can be satisfied, even when there is variance in the actual workload, or prediction errors.

The final major component of cloud resource management is the actual *scheduling of resources* to serve the user workload. The process has many goals, including traditional scheduling goals like ensuring good utilization and satisfying resource requests "quickly enough", as well as minimizing system fragmentation and inter-workload interference. This aspect of the system is broadly similar to more traditional cluster scheduling problems, although cloud systems are dominated by interactive requests for resources, so batch optimization heuristics can't be used, and the arrival rate of new requests is often quite large [4].

3   Research Opportunities in Clouds

The appeal of the cloud model is predicated upon on the tacit promise that the cloud will have resources available when the user needs them. Methods that keeps this promise while increasing utilization or reducing costs are valuable, as are ways to make this promise easier to keep.

Defining and managing SLOs is a key challenge. SLOs [9] are promises made by the cloud provider. These promises might govern the availability of an API or the performance it provides (e.g., the latency to satisfy a resource request). These SLOs are usually measured statistically over a time interval. Well-chosen SLOs can increase the utility of a platform to users in several ways. By making stronger promises, SLOs can make a platform useful for applications with a wider range of requirements. By making weaker promises, SLOs can decrease costs and provide more opportunities for resource optimizations [2]. In all of these cases, SLOs cast a long shadow on the design, costs and usage experience of cloud platforms.

Much work remains to be done in defining meaningful SLOs for parallel workloads. So far, the primary focus in cloud has been on singleton allocations like a task or VM. But often parallel workloads need guarantees for an ensemble. Such guarantees can cover instantaneous capacity availability (e.g., keep 95% of the VMs running at any time) and performance (including connectivity among VMs). Furthermore, the guarantee on availability needs to be augmented with performance and sustained throughput guarantees.

A key challenge in SLO research is *defining the interface between users and providers*, as to provide guarantees (SLOs) that users need, while preserving the flexibility for providers to innovate "under the hood". Part of the benefit of a richer cloud interface should be *increased efficiency*. For example, not all load submitted to the cloud is composed of interactive servers; much is batch in nature, so the batch load potentially can "fill the trough" of the serving load, as long as users have adequate throughput or deadline SLOs. Likewise, different kinds of product SLOs can enable providers to judiciously reallocate unused resources without "overselling" to the user. In fact, this already happens with Google's preemptible VMs [11] and Amazon's spot market [1].

Large users provide another difficult set of challenges. When users' requests are large (i.e., a sizable fraction of the cloud capacity) or very bursty, smooth projections of demand don't result in accurate capacity plans. The net result is that, like on supercomputers, large workloads are costlier to support than aggregates of smaller workloads with a similar total volume. Interfaces to communicate better about the needs of this class of user activity, methods to share risk of future demand spikes (e.g., options), and approaches that can efficiently accommodate load spikes all hold promise.

Similarly, *resource heterogeneity* poses challenges for cloud providers. Clouds have long been comprised of homogeneous, CPU-centric resources. However, recent advances in GPUs and other accelerators have demonstrated their value to a wide range of workloads. Similarly, while clouds started with simple networks, some of them have since exceeded supercomputer networks in complexity.

Both of these trends have resulted in systems that are heterogeneous — which poses new challenges in resource management [11]. That means that the platform's resources can no longer be treated as a single resource pool, resulting in lower utilization, resource stranding, or even inability to satisfy user requests even when enough capacity is available in aggregate. As accelerators and more specialized networks continue to develop and are deployed, we expect this trend will only worsen.

Another promising research area is to build *synergistic offerings*. With the range of SLOs and pricing offered by different products and providers, can we build hybrid offerings that offer a price, predictability, availability or benefit to users or providers? Cycle computing [3] has provided a compelling example of this, where ensembles are annotated with a deadline, and then cheap resources (AWS Spot, or GCE Preemptible) are used as much as possible, with more expensive guaranteed resources used to ensure that the deadline is met. Similar approaches can be used to attack problems that users and providers have [8].

4 Conclusions

There has never been a better time to work in resource management. Cloud computing has increased the relevance and importance of resource management to a first class concern. While massive systems have already been constructed and operated in production, much work remains in order to provide enough compute to satisfy the world's demand, with the performance and costs required, as well as supporting use cases not currently addressed. JSSPP remains a prime venue to showcase and discuss advances on many aspects of this problem, as it has been for the parallel scheduling community for 20 years.

Acknowledgments. We would like to acknowledge the comments and suggestions of John Wilkes and Dalibor Klusáček.

References

1. Ben-Yehuda, O.A., Ben-Yehuda, M., Schuster, A., Tsafrir, D.: Deconstructing Amazon EC2 spot instance pricing. ACM Trans. Econ. Comput. **1**(3), 1–20 (2013)
2. Carvalho, M., Cirne, W., Brasileiro, F.V., Wilkes, J.: Long-term SLOs for reclaimed cloud computing resources. In: Lazowska, E., Terry, D., Arpaci-Dusseau, R.H., Gehrke, J. (eds.) Proceedings of the ACM Symposium on Cloud Computing, pp. 20:1–20:13. ACM (2014). https://research.google.com/pubs/pub43017.html
3. Cycle Computing LLC, February 2017. https://cyclecomputing.com/
4. Di, S., Kondo, D., Cirne, W.: Characterization and comparison of cloud versus grid workloads. In: IEEE International Conference on Cluster Computing, CLUSTER 2012, pp. 230–238 (2012)
5. Di, S., Kondo, D., Cirne, W.: Google hostload prediction based on Bayesian model with optimized feature combination. J. Parallel Distrib. Comput. **74**(1), 1820–1832 (2014)

6. Feitelson, G.D.: Workload Modeling for Computer Systems Performance Evaluation, 1st edn. Cambridge University Press, New York (2015)

7. Feitelson, D.G., Rudolph, L.: Metrics and benchmarking for parallel job scheduling. In: Feitelson, D.G., Rudolph, L. (eds.) JSSPP 1998. LNCS, vol. 1459, pp. 1–24. Springer, Heidelberg (1998). doi:10.1007/BFb0053978

8. Huang, H., Wang, L., Tak, B.C., Wang, L., Tang, C.: CAP3: a cloud auto-provisioning framework for parallel processing using on-demand and spot instances. In: Proceedings of the 2013 IEEE Sixth International Conference on Cloud Computing, CLOUD 2013, Washington, DC, pp. 228–235. IEEE Computer Society (2013)

9. Jones, C., Wilkes, J., Murphy, N., Smith, C., Beyer, B.: Service level objectives. In: Beyer, B., Jones, C., Petoff, J., Murphy, N. (eds.) Site Reliability Engineering: How Google Runs Production Systems. O'Reilly Media (2016). https://landing.google.com/sre/book.html

10. Mell, P., Grance, T.: The NIST definition of cloud computing. Technical report 800-145, National Institute of Standards and Technology, Gaithersburg, MD, USA (2011)

11. Google cloud platform: Preemptible VM instances. https://cloud.google.com/compute/docs/instances/preemptible

12. Tian, W., Zhao, Y.: Optimized Cloud Resource Management and Scheduling. Theory and Practice, 1st edn. Morgan Kaufmann (2014)

13. Google Cloud Platform: Machine types, February 2017. https://cloud.google.com/compute/docs/machine-types

Author Index

Printed in the United States
By Bookmasters